THE CONSTITUTION IN 2020

The Constitution in 2020

Edited by

Jack M. Balkin
Reva B. Siegel

OXFORD

UNIVERSITY PRESS

2009

OXFORD
UNIVERSITY PRESS

Oxford University Press, Inc., publishes works that further
Oxford University's objective of excellence
in research, scholarship, and education.

Oxford   New York

Auckland   Cape Town   Dar es Salaam   Hong Kong   Karachi
Kuala Lumpur   Madrid   Melbourne   Mexico City   Nairobi
New Delhi   Shanghai   Taipei   Toronto

With offices in

Argentina   Austria   Brazil   Chile   Czech Republic   France   Greece
Guatemala   Hungary   Italy   Japan   Poland   Portugal   Singapore
South Korea   Switzerland   Thailand   Turkey   Ukraine   Vietnam

Copyright © 2009 by Jack M. Balkin and Reva B. Siegel

Published by Oxford University Press, Inc.
198 Madison Avenue, New York, New York 10016

www.oup.com

Oxford is a registered trademark of Oxford University Press

Library of Congress Cataloging-in-Publication Data
The Constitution in 2020 / Jack M. Balkin and Reva B. Siegel, eds.
p.   cm.
Includes bibliographical references and index.
ISBN 978-0-19-538797-1; 978-0-19-538796-4 (pbk.)
1. Constitutional law—United States. 2. Law reform—United States.
3. Constitutional history—United States.
I. Balkin, J. M. II. Siegel, Reva B., 1956–
KF4550.C576 2009
342.7302'9–dc22   2008045169

1 3 5 7 9 8 6 4 2
Printed in the United States of America
on acid-free paper

FOR OUR FAMILIES, AND FOR OUR STUDENTS

Contents

THE CONSTITUTION IN 2020

❧ 1 ❧

Introduction

The Constitution in 2020

JACK M. BALKIN AND REVA B. SIEGEL

T HE ESSAYS COLLECTED in this book are the result of a conversation that began in 2005, when a group of constitutional scholars met at Yale Law School to discuss what the law of the U.S.
Constitution should look like in the year 2020. Why 2020? To clarify our
constitutional vision, we chose a time close enough that it is within practical reach, yet remote enough that we could imagine ourselves free to interpret the Constitution differently than the Supreme Court now does.

Since the mid-1970s, conservative social and political movements
have dominated American politics. They have tried to re-create the
Constitution in their own image. Conservative presidents have appointed
the overwhelming majority of federal judges, stocking the bench with
movement jurists who will adopt positions favored by conservatives
on key questions of constitutional law. Through these appointments
and in electoral politics, conservatives have sought to reinterpret the
great achievements of twentieth-century constitutionalism, blunting
some, rolling back others, and twisting still others to promote their
favored policies. At this moment, at the beginning of the twenty-first
century, it is crucial for us to rethink our commitments and ask what the
Constitution means for us today.

This book contests the conservative belief that we should cleanse constitutional law of contemporary understandings and restore the Constitution to an imagined past, a time when we obeyed the founders. We think this goal is inadequate; it simply disguises the values of a contemporary political movement as the framers' intentions. Intellectual honesty and constitutional fidelity demand more. Instead of pretending that we can return the Constitution to an imagined past, we must assume responsibility for integrating past and present and redeem the promises of that great document in our own time.

What is the difference between the conservative movement's position and our own? We believe that our obligation to the Constitution involves more than blind deference to the past. Living in faith with the past requires judgment and synthesis, in order to integrate past understandings with present conditions and with the best traditions of our people. This is a responsibility we are proud to acknowledge. The conservative narrative that presents constitutional restoration as a dogmatic obedience to the founders' expectations disguises normative judgment and denies accountability. It would infantilize the living and deny their ethical responsibility for vindicating the Constitution's commitments.

When we accept responsibility for vindicating the Constitution's commitments, sometimes we must work to restore past understandings, and sometimes we must try to redeem constitutional guarantees that have not yet been met. We think that the past several decades of conservative judging have often departed from the best understandings of the Constitution, as the contributors to this book explain in detail. But the goal of constitutional interpretation is not only restorative—it is also redemptive. Our Constitution is not only a bond with the past; it is a bond with the future, expressing commitments that the American people have yet fully to achieve.

The people of the United States, through their Constitution, are engaged in a long-term project, one that spans many generations. It is the project of creating a "more perfect union," striving, as the Constitution's Preamble tells us, to "establish justice, insure domestic tranquility, provide for the common defense, promote the general welfare, and secure the blessings of liberty to ourselves and our posterity." This task was not completed in 1789, when the document was ratified; it is not completed today. It belongs to each generation to do its part.

The basic premise of redemptive constitutionalism is that our Constitution is always a work in progress. Redemptive constitutionalism is a great American tradition, responsible for many features of our constitutional system that Americans now take for granted: the protection of basic rights and liberties, including the right of free speech and free exercise of religion; federal power to regulate the economy and provide basic social services like Social Security and Medicare; and guarantees of equality for all Americans. When many were complacent about Jim Crow or sex discrimination, or actively sought to defend them, there were Americans who argued that the Constitution guaranteed equal citizenship. Had it not been for their vision, and their determination to vindicate the Constitution's fundamental commitments, our nation would be far less just, less equal, and less free today.

To say that we have imperfectly realized the Constitution's commitments is not to deny the nation's achievements. To the contrary: this understanding of our Constitution is the source of the nation's greatness. Each generation builds on the best of the past and strives, as the Preamble instructs us, to create a better future for our posterity.

For proof of this idea, we need only look to history: The Constitution once protected slavery. It does no longer. It once sanctioned Jim Crow. It does no longer. The Constitution once permitted a wide variety of forms of political and artistic censorship; it once treated women as men's servants, and gays and lesbians as criminals. It does no longer. All these changes came about because people believed in their Constitution and in the importance of continually examining our practices in the light of our principles.

Because each generation must honor the Constitution's commitments in its own time, the Constitution as it is applied in practice will inevitably change, responding to altered circumstances and conditions. This is not a defect; it is a feature of our constitutional tradition. It is how each generation makes the Constitution its own.

Americans honor their constitutional heritage, but they do not worship it uncritically. The Constitution of today draws on a rich history of past accomplishments, starting with the Declaration, the Revolution, the founding, the second founding of Reconstruction, the New Deal, and the civil rights revolution. In these great epochs, those who forged the constitutional understandings that we today take as foundational did *not* treat the past as sacrosanct—it was their opponents who did.

There have been long periods in which unjust policies and defective interpretations of the Constitution reigned supreme. We often hear people talk as if the greatness of our nation and the justice of our Constitution were fixed and guaranteed at the founding; if we only would bind ourselves to the wisdom of the framers, all would be well. But those who fetishize the founders do not keep faith with them; those who framed the Constitution forged a framework for nation building, a framework for developing a political community committed to justice. As we strive to realize this commitment, we are more faithful to the constitutional project than those who supported slavery, segregation, sex discrimination, and religious intolerance in the name of the fathers. In every generation, people have defended injustice in the name of an imagined past. And in every generation, people have countered this complacency by invoking a different conception of our origins and traditions, remembering our history as a people in quest of justice.

Constitutional argument appears backward-looking, to consist in little more than appeals to text, history, and precedent. But this obscures its true genius. Americans appeal to history to make claims on one another about our deepest commitments as a nation. We appeal to history as we debate with one another how to face the future.

The Constitution, Justice Oliver Wendell Holmes once said, is made for people of fundamentally different views. We live in a world of heterogeneous beliefs and sustained conflicts about values. And we live in a democracy: a system of government in which we must live together and rule together despite deep normative disagreements. We turn to the past not because the past contains within it all of the answers to our questions, but because it is the repository of our common struggles and common commitments; it offers us invaluable resources as we debate the most important questions of political life, which cannot fully and finally be settled. In this process, we draw on the text, history, and traditions of the U.S. Constitution to make the founders' Constitution our own. Over and over again, we have looked to our collective past to imagine our collective future.

These understandings suggest how we should think about the role of courts in a democratic society. In the closing decades of the twentieth century, conservatives argued that we should restrict and conform constitutional law to the expectations of the framers. They claimed that decisions that deviated from the framers' understandings lawlessly imposed personal or political predilections. Fidelity to the past was a source of truth and safety—the only means of restraining a dangerous and unelected judiciary.

Conservatives urged the nation to be deeply suspicious of courts. They described the federal judiciary as a force for evil in America and as a source of decay in our culture and institutions. They continued to do so even as they appointed most of the judges in the federal system. They have denounced the judiciary as an elite institution conspiring against ordinary Americans, even though conservative judges appointed by conservative politicians have generally followed the views of conservative elites. They have summed up their judicial philosophy in a series of slogans: conservatives are for "strict construction" and "interpreting law rather than making it"; they are against "legislating from the bench" and "judicial activism." Each of these claims has proven to be intellectually vacuous, in practice meaning little more than that judges should decide cases in ways that conservatives like.

At the same time, conservatives have offered a different portrait of the judiciary: Judges who reach decisions they like are apolitical and dispassionate purveyors of a timeless law of the fathers, with no political will and exercising a minimum of personal judgment. Chief Justice Roberts well captured this idea when he asserted that he was nothing more than an umpire, blandly calling balls and strikes but taking no position on the great issues of the day; Justice Scalia and Justice Thomas portray themselves as if they were simply obedient servants of the Constitution's original meaning when in fact they speak to a mobilized conservative movement through their decisions.

The conservative vision of the judiciary has been schizophrenic. In cases where decisions deviate from the substantive results conservatives prefer, conservatives denounce judges as arrogant villains. In cases that announce decisions conservatives favor, conservatives depict judges as impersonal arbiters of a law of the distant past in which they exercise no judgment and no responsibility.

This view makes little sense, and it does not illuminate how the judiciary actually interacts with the national political process. Judges exercise independent judgment, but they still reason as members of a political community. Their decisions draw on contemporary values and respond to complex currents in public opinion. That is why popular mobilizations have played so central a role in our Constitution's history. The constitutional revolution of the New Deal followed a groundswell of popular sentiment for change, to which an older Court had been unresponsive. The Warren Court worked hand in hand with the representative branches of the national government, promoting civil rights measures and bringing local majorities in line with national values.

Our constitutional history demonstrates that an engaged citizenry is essential to the health of a constitutional order. If Americans seek to influence the development of constitutional doctrine in the twenty-first century, they must do as past generations have done before: They must win the battle of ideas and convince their fellow citizens that their values and their vision are most true to America's great constitutional traditions. If they can do this, the work of the courts will eventually follow.

In a democratic society, courts best perform their institutional role as partners in a larger dialogue: They respond to popular visions of the Constitution's values and help to translate these values into law. Constitutional ideas usually emerge from the bottom, not the top. Constitutional values come from successful political mobilizations, from political and cultural struggles over long periods of time. Courts do not lead these mobilizations, though they can give them new and distinctive articulation.

Just as judicial doctrines often follow political mobilizations, courts are not always the most important players in developing and enforcing constitutional norms. In many areas of social life, the minimum protections of equal citizenship cannot be secured by courts alone. Decisions made by legislatures and executive officials about our rights are just as important, if not more important, than the development of rights by the judiciary. Many of the chapters in this book address this central truth, as they emphasize the centrality of legislative and popular constitutionalism. Because ours is a democratic Constitution, the responsibility for articulating constitutional values often falls to the institutions of democracy and civil society.

The tradition of redemptive constitutionalism to which this book contributes has been the source of some of our nation's greatest achievements. It produced the New Deal and the civil rights revolution, two features so central to our self-understanding that both liberals and conservatives accept them as part of our constitutional heritage, even when they disagree about what they mean. At one point in history, conservatives doubted the legitimacy of *Brown v. Board of Education;* now, they proclaim that they are its most ardent defenders. That is proof enough of the centrality of redemptive constitutionalism in our tradition.

But the key to the future is not a return to the battles of the past. Seeing ourselves merely as defenders of the achievements of the New Deal and civil rights era bespeaks a narrative of loss and decline. The country has changed, and its needs are different. Americans today need not seek a restoration of the glory days of the Warren Court. Clinging to a simple story of restoration would be particularly ironic, for the work of the Warren Court was itself redemptive. Our successes will come from new mobilizations that emphasize a new constitutional vision that better articulates enduring constitutional values. Describing what might be part of that new vision is the task of this book.

The goal of these chapters is to start a conversation, not to end it. We do not offer a finished blueprint for the future, but the considered views of two dozen leading law professors on the constitutional issues they regard as most important. The contributors discuss a wide range of topics, including not only the traditional concerns of civil liberties and religious freedom, but also issues of economic and social justice and America's place in a changing world.

The authors in this volume do not always agree with each other in their prescriptions. But if they diverge in questions of interpretive method, the place of religion, or the centrality of citizenship, they share a belief: that our understanding of our constitutional commitments evolves in history, that the nation has yet fully to meet many of these commitments, and that the aspiration to do so helps make this nation great.

Consider the most important achievements of twentieth-century constitutionalism: a federal government with the power to regulate the economy, protect the environment, protect the rights of consumers and workers, and prohibit discrimination in employment; universal suffrage; a robust conception of freedom of speech; a legal process that is procedurally fair; guarantees of reproductive freedom and racial, gender, and religious equality. Each of these aims was once regarded as radical and impractical. Yet they are now foundational: rights and responsibilities of government that Americans have come to expect.

In the following chapters, the contributors help us imagine what could be; to see past the current doctrines of courts, the current preoccupations of legislatures and presidents, and the current limitations of contemporary politics. They imagine a future that Americans will someday consider just and reasonable.

PART I

Interpreting Our Constitution

✌ 2 ✌

Fidelity to Text and Principle

JACK M. BALKIN

Is OUR CONSTITUTION a living document that adapts to changing circumstances, or must we interpret it according to its original meaning? For years now, people have debated constitutional interpretation in these terms. But the choice is a false one. Constitutional interpretation requires fidelity to the original meaning of the Constitution and to the principles stated by the text or that underlie the text. Constitutional interpretation also requires *construction*—deciding how best to implement and apply the constitutional text and principles in current circumstances. This is the method of *text and principle*. It is faithful to the original meaning of the constitutional text and its underlying purposes. It is also consistent with a basic law whose reach and application evolve over time, a basic law that leaves to each generation the task of how to make sense of the Constitution's words and principles. In each generation the American people are charged with the obligation to flesh out and implement the Constitution's guarantees in their own time. They do this through building political institutions, through passing legislation, and through creating precedents, both judicial and nonjudicial. That is the best way to understand the interpretive practices of our constitutional tradition and the work of the many political and social movements that have transformed our understandings of the Constitution's guarantees.

Original Meaning versus Original Expected Application

Constitutional interpretations are not limited to applications specifically intended or expected by the framers and adopters of the constitutional text. For example, the Eighth Amendment's prohibitions on "cruel and unusual punishments" bans punishments that are cruel and unusual as judged by contemporary application of these concepts (and underlying principles), not by how people living in 1791 would have applied those concepts and principles.

The Constitution's text contains determinate rules (the president must be thirty-five, there are two houses of Congress), standards (no "unreasonable searches and seizures," a right to a "speedy" trial), and principles ("freedom of speech," "equal protection"). If the text states a determinate rule, we must apply the rule because that is what the text offers us. If it states a standard, we must apply the standard. And if it states a general principle, we must apply the principle. Interpretation requires that we pay attention to the reasons why constitutional designers choose particular language. Adopters use fixed rules because they want to limit discretion; they use standards or principles because they want to channel politics through certain key concepts but delegate the details to future generations. When the Constitution uses abstract principles like freedom of speech or equal protection, we must apply them to our own circumstances in our own time. When adopters use language that delegates constitutional construction to future generations, fidelity to the Constitution requires future generations to engage in constitutional construction.

This marks the major difference between my approach and the one popularized by one of originalism's most prominent champions, Justice Antonin Scalia.[1] Justice Scalia agrees that we should interpret the Constitution according to "the original meaning of the text, not what the original draftsmen intended."[2] He also agrees that the original meaning of the text should be read in light of its underlying principles. But he insists that the concepts and principles underlying those words must be *applied* in the same way that they would have been applied when they were adopted. As he puts it, the principle underlying the Eighth Amendment

> is not a moral principle of "cruelty" that philosophers can play with in the future, but rather the existing society's assessment of what is cruel. It means not… "whatever may be considered cruel from one generation to the next," but "what we consider cruel today [i.e., in 1791]"; otherwise it

would be no protection against the moral perceptions of a future, more brutal generation. It is, in other words, rooted in the moral perceptions *of the time*.[3]

Scalia's version of original meaning is not original meaning in my sense, but actually a more limited interpretive principle, *original expected application*. Original expected application asks how people living at the time the text was adopted would have expected it would be applied using language in its ordinary sense (along with any legal terms of art). Justice Scalia can accommodate new phenomena and new technologies—like television or radio—by analogical extension with phenomena and technologies that existed at the time of adoption. But this does not mean, Scalia insists, that "the *very acts* that were perfectly constitutional in 1791 (political patronage in government contracting and employment, for example) may be *un*constitutional today."[4]

Mistakes and Achievements

Scalia realizes that his approach would allow many politically unacceptable results, including punishments that would clearly shock the conscience today. So he frequently allows deviations from his interpretive principles, making him what he calls a "faint-hearted originalist."[5] For example, Scalia accepts the New Deal settlement that gave the federal government vast powers to regulate the economy that most people in 1787 would never have dreamed of and would probably have strongly rejected.[6]

Scalia's originalism must be fainthearted precisely because he has chosen an unrealistic and impractical principle of constitutional construction, which he must repeatedly leaven with respect for precedent and other prudential considerations. The basic problem with looking to original expected application for guidance is that it is inconsistent with so much of our existing constitutional traditions. Many federal laws securing the environment, protecting workers and consumers— even central aspects of Social Security—go beyond original expectations about federal power. So too do independent federal agencies like the Federal Reserve Board and the Federal Communications Commission and federal civil rights laws that protect women and the disabled from private discrimination. Even the federal government's power to make paper money legal tender probably violates the expectations of the founding generation.[7] The original expected application is also inconsistent with constitutional guarantees of sex equality for married women,[8] with constitutional protection of interracial marriage,[9] with the constitutional right to use contraceptives,[10] and with the modern scope of free speech rights under the First Amendment.[11]

The standard response to this difficulty is that courts should retain nonoriginalist precedents (i.e., those inconsistent with original expectations) if those precedents are well established, if they promote stability, and if people have justifiably come to rely on them. Interpretive mistakes, even though constitutionally illegitimate when first made, can become acceptable because we respect precedent. As Scalia explains, "The whole function of the doctrine" of stare decisis "is to make us say that what is false under proper analysis must nonetheless be held true, all in the interests of stability."[12]

There are four major problems with this solution. First, it undercuts the claim that legitimacy comes from adhering to the original meaning of the text adopted by the framers and that decisions inconsistent with the original expected application are illegitimate. It suggests that legitimacy can come from public acceptance of the Supreme Court's decisions or from considerations of stability or economic cost.

Second, under this approach, not all of the "incorrect" precedents receive equal deference. Judges will inevitably pick and choose which decisions they will retain and which they will discard based on pragmatic judgments about when reliance is real, substantial, justified, or otherwise appropriate. These characterizations run together considerations of stability and potential economic expense with considerations of political acceptability—which decisions would be too embarrassing now to discard—and political preference—which decisions particularly rankle the jurist's sensibilities. Thus, one might argue that it is too late to deny Congress's power under the Commerce Clause to pass the Civil Rights Act of 1964 but express doubts about the constitutionality of the Endangered Species Act. One might accept that states may not engage in sex discrimination but vigorously oppose the constitutional right to abortion or the unconstitutionality of antisodomy statutes. This play in the joints allows expectations-based originalism to track particular political agendas and allows judges to impose their political ideology on the law—the very thing that the methodology purports to avoid.

Third, allowing deviations from original expected application out of respect for precedent does not explain why we should not read these mistakes as narrowly as possible to avoid compounding the error, with the idea of gradually weakening and overturning them so as to return to more legitimate decision making. If the sex equality decisions of the

1970s were mistakes, courts should try to distinguish them in every subsequent case with the goal of eventually ridding us of the blunder of recognizing equal constitutional rights for women.

This brings us to the final and most basic problem: Our political tradition does not regard decisions that have secured equal rights for women, greater freedom of speech, federal power to protect the environment, and federal power to pass civil rights laws as mistakes that we must unhappily retain. It regards them as genuine achievements of American constitutionalism and sources of pride. These decisions are part of why we understand ourselves to be a nation that has grown freer and more democratic over time. No interpretive theory that regards equal constitutional rights for women as an unfortunate blunder that we are now simply stuck with because of respect for precedent can be adequate to our history as a people. It confuses achievements with mistakes, and it maintains them out of a grudging acceptance. Indeed, those who argue for limiting constitutional interpretation to the original expected application are in some ways fortunate that previous judges rejected their theory of interpretation; this allows them to accept as a starting point nonoriginalist precedents that would now be far too embarrassing for them to disavow.

An originalism that focuses on original expected applications cannot account for how social movements and post-enactment history shape our constitutional traditions. It holds that social movements and political mobilizations can change constitutional law through the amendment process of Article V. They can also pass new legislation, as long as that legislation does not violate original expected application—as much federal post–New Deal legislation might. But no matter how significant social movements like the civil rights movement and the women's movement have been in our nation's history, no matter how much they may have changed Americans' notion of what civil rights and civil liberties belong to them, they cannot legitimately alter the correct interpretation of the Constitution beyond the original expected application.

The model of text and principle views the work of social movements and post-enactment history quite differently. The constitutional text does not change without Article V amendment. But members of each generation of Americans can seek to persuade each other about how the text and its underlying principles should apply to their circumstances, their problems, and their grievances. And because conditions are always changing, new problems are always arising, and new forms of social conflict and grievance are always emerging, the process of argument and persuasion about what the Constitution's principles mean is never ending.

When people try to persuade each other about how the Constitution applies to their circumstances, they naturally identify with the generation that framed the constitutional text and they claim that they are being true to its principles. They can and do draw analogies between the problems, grievances, and injustices the adopters feared or faced and the problems, grievances, and injustices of their own day. They also can and do draw on the experiences and interpretive glosses of previous generations—like the generation that produced the New Deal or the civil rights movement—and argue that they are also following in their footsteps.

Most successful political and social movements in America's history have claimed authority for change in just this way: either as a call to return to the enduring principles of the Constitution or as a call for fulfillment of those principles. Thus, the key tropes of constitutional interpretation by social movements and political parties are restoration, on the one hand, and redemption, on the other. Constitutional meaning changes by arguing about what we already believe, what we are already committed to, what we have promised ourselves as a people, what we must return to, and what commitments remain to be fulfilled.

When political and social movements succeed in persuading other citizens that their interpretation is the right one, they replace an older set of implementing constructions and doctrines with a new one. These constructions and implementations may not be just or correct judged from the standpoint of later generations, and they can be challenged later on. But that is precisely the point. In each generation, We the People of the United States make the Constitution our own by calling upon its text and its principles and arguing about what they mean in our own time. That is how each generation connects its values to the commitments of the past and carries forward the constitutional project of the American people into the future.

From the standpoint of text and principle, it matters greatly that there was a women's movement in the 1960s and 1970s that convinced Americans that both married and single women were entitled to equal rights and that the best way to make sense of the Fourteenth Amendment's principle of equal citizenship was to apply it to women as well as men, despite the original expected application of the adopters. The equal protection decisions of the 1970s that protected women's equal citizenship are not mistakes that we must grudgingly live with. They are constructions and applications of text and principle that have become part of our constitutional tradition. They might be good or bad constructions; they might be incorrect or incomplete. That is for later generations to judge. But when people accept them, as Americans accept the notion of equality for women today, they do not do so simply on the basis of reliance interests—i.e., that we gave women equal rights mistakenly in the 1970s, and now it's just too late to turn back. They do so in the belief that this is what the Constitution *actually means*, that this is the best, most faithful interpretation of constitutional text and principles.

Originalism based on original expected application fails because it cannot comprehend this feature of constitutional development except as a series of errors that it would now be too embarrassing to correct. Justice Scalia properly notes that his reliance on nonoriginalist precedents is not consistent with originalism, but rather a "pragmatic exception."[13] And that is precisely the problem with his view: The work of social movements in our country's history is not a "pragmatic exception" to fidelity to the Constitution. It is the lifeblood of fidelity to our Constitution—it is part of an ongoing project of vindicating constitutional text and principles in history.

None of this means that the original expected application is irrelevant or unimportant. It helps us to understand the original meaning of the text and the general principles that animated the text. But it is important not as binding law but rather as an aid to interpretation, one among many others. It does not control how we should apply the Constitution's guarantees today, especially as our world becomes increasingly distant from the expectations and assumptions of the adopters' era.

Original Meaning and Constitutional Construction

The idea of "original meaning" can be confusing because we use "meaning" to refer to at least five different things: (1) semantic content ("what is the meaning of X in English?"); (2) practical applications ("what does this mean in practice?"); (3) purposes or functions ("the meaning of life"); (4) specific intentions ("I didn't mean to hurt you") or (5) associations ("what does America mean to me?").

In constitutional interpretation, fidelity to "original meaning" refers only to the first of these. We follow the original meaning of words in order to preserve the Constitution's legal meaning over time, as required by the rule of law. Otherwise, if the dictionary definitions of words changed over time, their legal effect would also change, not because of any conscious act of lawmaking, but merely because of changes in language. So, for example, when Article IV says that the United States must protect the states from "domestic violence," we should employ the original meaning, "riots" or "insurrections," not the contemporary meaning, "spousal assaults." By contrast, the words "equal protection of the laws" mean today what they did in 1868; we must apply these same concepts in modern circumstances. Sometimes, the text refers to terms of art or uses figurative or nonliteral language; in that case, we must look to history to figure out what principles underlie that term of art or figurative or nonliteral language. For example, the Copyright Clause in Article I, section 8, refers to "writings," which is a nonliteral use. It refers to more than written marks on a page but also includes printing and (probably) sculpture, motion pictures, and other media of artistic and scientific communication.[14]

When the text provides an unambiguous, concrete and specific rule, the principles or purposes behind the text cannot override the textual command. For example, the underlying goal of promoting maturity in a president does not mean that we can dispense with the thirty-five-year age requirement. But where the text is ambiguous, or where it offers a general or abstract standard or principle, we must look to the principles and purposes behind the text to help us understand how to apply it in current circumstances. We can and should use history to articulate these constitutional principles, but the principles we derive from history should be at roughly the same level of abstraction as the text itself. The fact that adopters chose text that features general and abstract concepts is normally the best evidence that they sought to embody general and abstract principles of constitutional law, whose scope and application must be worked out by later generations.

In some cases, the constitutional text states a principle like "freedom of speech" or "equal protection." Other principles we infer from the constitutional structure as a whole. For example, there is no single separation of powers clause in the Constitution; rather, we must derive the principle of separation of powers from how the various institutions and structures outlined in the constitutional text relate to each other. The principle of democracy—which includes the subprinciple that courts should generally defer to majoritarian decision making— is nowhere specifically mentioned in the constitutional text, and yet it may be the most frequently articulated principle in constitutional argument. It is, ironically, the principle that people most often use to object to courts inferring constitutional principles not specifically mentioned in the text. Although the principle of democracy does not directly appear in the text, we infer it from various textual features that presume democracy and from the basic character of our government as a representative and democratic republic. It also informs our construction of other principles found in the text like freedom of speech and equal protection of the laws.

Finally, many other materials gloss text and principles and help apply them to concrete circumstances. These include not only original expected application but also post-enactment history, including the work of social movements that have changed our constitutional common sense, and judicial and nonjudicial precedents. These materials offer a wide range of theories and interpretations about how to understand and apply the Constitution. They are entitled to considerable weight. However, because glosses and precedents accumulate and change over time, and because they often point in contrasting directions, they are not always dispositive of constitutional meaning.

Constitutional doctrines created by courts and institutions and practices created by the political branches flesh out and implement the constitutional text and underlying principles. But they are not supposed to replace them. Doctrines, institutions, and practices can implement the Constitution well or poorly depending on the circumstances, and some implementations that seem perfectly adequate at one point may come to seem quite inadequate or even perverse later on. Because the Constitution, and not interpretations of the Constitution, is the supreme law of the land, later generations may assert—and try to convince others—that the best interpretation of text and principle differs from previous implementing glosses, and that we should return to a better interpretation of text and principle, creating new implementing rules, practices, and doctrines to serve this end. The tradition of continuous arguments about how best to implement constitutional meaning generates changes in constitutional doctrines, practices, and law. That is why, ultimately, there is no conflict between fidelity to text and principle and practices of constitutionalism that evolve over time.

Fidelity and Institutional Constraints

Original expectations originalists may object that the text-and-principle approach is indeterminate when the text refers to abstract standards like "equal protection" rather than to concrete rules. Therefore, it does not sufficiently constrain judges. That might be so if text and principle were all that judges consulted when they interpreted the Constitution. But, in practice, judges (and other constitutional interpreters) draw on a rich tradition of sources that guide and constrain interpretation, including pre- and post-enactment history, original expected application, previous constitutional constructions, structural and intertextual arguments, and judicial and nonjudicial precedents. In practice, judges who look to text and principle face constraints much like those faced by judges who purport to rely on original expected application. As we have seen, the latter cannot and do not use original expected applications for a very large part of their work, because a very large part of modern doctrine is not consistent with the original expected application. So even judges who claim to follow the original understanding are, in most cases, guided and constrained by essentially the same sources and modalities of argument as judges employing the method of text and principle.

I think there is a deeper problem with the objection that the method of text and principle does not sufficiently constrain judges. Many theories of constitutional interpretation conflate two different questions. The first is the question of what the Constitution means and how to be faithful to it. The second asks how a person in a particular institutional setting—like an unelected judge with life tenure—should interpret the Constitution and implement it through doctrinal constructions and applications. The first is the question of *fidelity*; the second is the question of *institutional responsibility*.

Theories about constitutional interpretation that conflate these two questions tend to view constitutional interpretation from the perspective of judges and the judicial role; they view constitutional interpretation as primarily a task of judges and they assess theories of interpretation largely in terms of how well they guide and limit judges. For example, one of the standard arguments for original expectations originalism is that it will help constrain judges in a democracy. From the perspective of these theories, nonjudicial interpreters are marginal or exceptional cases that we explain in terms of the standard case of judicial interpretation.

I reject this approach. Theories of constitutional interpretation should start with interpretation by citizens as the standard case; they should view interpretation by judges as a special case with special considerations created by the judicial role. In like fashion, constitutional interpretations by executive officials and members of legislatures are special cases that are structured by their particular institutional roles. The political branches must do more than simply not violate the Constitution; they have affirmative obligations to construct institutions and laws that will carry out the Constitution's purposes. Much of the most important constitutional work does not come from courts. It comes from acts of constitutional construction by executive officials and legislatures, at both national and local levels, building institutions, programs, and practices that flesh out and implement constitutional text and principles in ways that courts cannot.

Why emphasize the citizen's perspective? The people of each generation must figure out what the Constitution's promises mean for themselves. Many of the most significant changes in constitutional understandings (e.g., the New Deal, the civil rights movement, the second wave of American feminism) occurred through mobilizations and countermobilizations by social and political movements that offered competing interpretations of what the Constitution really means. Social and political movements argue that the way the Constitution has been interpreted and implemented by judges and other political actors is wrong and that we need to return to the Constitution's correct meaning and redeem the Constitution's promises in our own day.

Often, people do not make these claims in lawyerly ways, and usually they are not constrained by existing understandings and existing doctrines in the way that we want judges to be constrained. In fact, when social movements initially offer their constitutional claims, many people regard them as quite radical or off the wall. There was a time, for example, when the notion that the Constitution prohibited what we now call sex discrimination seemed quite absurd. Yet it is from these protestant interpretations of the Constitution that later constitutional doctrines emerge. Many of the proudest achievements of our constitutional tradition have come from constitutional interpretations that were at one point regarded as crackpot and off the wall.

I hasten to add that most of these arguments go nowhere. Only a few have significantly changed how Americans look at the Constitution. Successful social and political movements must persuade other citizens that their views are correct, or, at the very least, they must convince people to compromise and modify their views. If movements are successful, they change the minds of the general public, politicians, and courts. This influence eventually gets reflected in new laws, new constitutional doctrines, and new constitutional constructions by the judiciary and the political branches. Successful social and political mobilization changes political culture, which changes constitutional culture, which, in turn, changes constitutional practices outside of the courts and constitutional doctrine within them.

The causal influences, of course, do not run in only one direction. Judicial interpretations like those in *Brown v. Board of Education*[15] or *Miranda v. Arizona*[16] can become important parts of our constitutional culture; they can be absorbed into ordinary citizens' understandings of what the Constitution means, and they can act as focal points for citizens' reactions. Nevertheless, we cannot understand how constitutional understandings change over time unless we recognize how social movements and political parties articulate new constitutional claims, create new constitutional regimes, and influence judicial and political constructions.

To understand how these changes could be faithful to the Constitution, we must have a theory that makes the citizen's perspective primary. I do not claim that all social mobilizations that produce new constitutional constructions are equally faithful or equally admirable. But some are both faithful and admirable, and a theory of constitutional interpretation—which is also a theory of constitutional fidelity—must account for them. Original expectations originalism is virtually useless for this purpose, because it views many of the most laudatory changes in our understandings of the Constitution as not faithful to the Constitution and therefore illegitimate.

For similar reasons, original expectations originalism cannot really constrain judges because too many present-day doctrines are simply inconsistent with it; as a result, judges must pick and choose based on pragmatic justifications that are exceptions to the theory. Indeed, the exceptions threaten to swallow the theory in many areas of the law. Because original expectations originalism conflates the question of constitutional fidelity with the question of judicial constraint, it offers the wrong answer to both questions.

Constraining judges in a democracy is important. But in practice most of that constraint does not come from theories of constitutional interpretation. It comes from institutional features of the political and legal system. Some of these are internal to law and legal culture, like the various sources and modalities of legal argument described above. Others are external to legal reasoning but nevertheless strongly influence what judges produce as a group.

First, judges are subject to the same cultural influences as everyone else; they are socialized both as members of the public and as members of particular legal elites. Second, the president's ability to pick jurists with views roughly similar to his own and the Senate's countervailing advise and consent power determine and limit who gets to serve as a judge, helping to ensure that most successful judicial candidates come from within the political and legal mainstream. Third, lower federal courts are bound to apply Supreme Court precedents. Fourth, the Supreme Court is a multimember body whose decisions in contested cases are usually decided by the median, or "swing," justice. Over time, this keeps the Court's work near the center of public opinion. If the Court strays too far from the views of the national political coalition for too long, new judicial appointments act as a corrective by changing the Court's composition and the identity of the median Justice.

This combination of internal and external features constrains judicial interpretation in practice far more effectively than any single theory of interpretation ever could; it helps to frame which constitutional interpretations are reasonable and available to judges and which are off the wall. Equally important, it keeps judicial decisions in touch with popular understandings of our Constitution's basic commitments, continually translating, shaping, and refining constitutional politics into constitutional law.

Fidelity to the Constitution means applying its text and its principles to our present circumstances and making use of the entire tradition of opinions and precedents that have sought to vindicate and implement the Constitution. Reasonable people may disagree on what those principles mean and how they should apply. But the larger point about constitutional interpretation remains. We decide these questions by reference to text and principle, applying them to our own time and our own situation and, in this way, making the Constitution our own. The conversation between past commitments and present generations is at the heart of constitutional interpretation. That is why we do not face a choice between living constitutionalism and fidelity to the original meaning of the text. They are two sides of the same coin.

This chapter is adapted from a longer work, *Abortion and Original Meaning*, 24 Const. Comm. 291 (2007).

Notes

1. See Antonin Scalia, *Originalism: The Lesser Evil*, 57 U. Cin. L. Rev. 849, 862–64 (1989); Antonin Scalia, *Common Law Courts in a Civil-Law System: The Role of the United States Courts in Interpreting the Constitution and Laws*, in *A Matter of Interpretation: Federal Courts and the Law* 3, 17 (Amy Guttman, ed., 1997).

2. Scalia, *Common Law Courts in a Civil-Law System*, at 38.

3. Scalia, *Response*, in *A Matter of Interpretation: Federal Courts and the Law* 129, 145 (emphasis in original).

4. *Id.* at 140–41 (emphasis in original).

5. Scalia, *Originalism: The Lesser Evil*, at 861–64.

6. See, e.g., *Gonzales v. Raich*, 545 U.S. 1, 17 (2005) (Scalia, J., concurring).

7. See Kenneth Dam, *The Legal Tender Cases*, 1981 Sup. Ct. Rev. 367, 389 ("difficult to escape the conclusion that the Framers intended to prohibit" use of paper money as legal tender); Hearings before Senate Comm. on the Judiciary, 100th Cong., 1st sess., Nomination of Robert H. Bork to Be Associate Justice of the Supreme Court of the United States: Part 1, at 84–85 (1987).

8. See *Frontiero v. Richardson*, 411 U.S. 677 (1973).

9. *Loving v. Virginia*, 388 U.S. 1 (1967).

10. *Griswold v. Connecticut*, 381 U.S. 479 (1965); *Eisenstadt v. Baird*, 405 U.S. 438 (1971).

11. E.g., *Cohen v. California*, 403 U.S. 15 (1971) (protecting public expressions of profanity); *Brandenburg v. Ohio*, 395 U.S. 444 (1969) (protecting advocacy of sedition and law violation); *New York Times v. Sullivan*, 376 U.S. 254 (1964) (holding unconstitutional aspects of common law of defamation); Scalia, *Response*, at 138 (contemporary First Amendment protections are "irreversible" "whether or not they were constitutionally required as an original matter").

12. Scalia, *Response*, at 139.

13. Scalia, *Response*, at 140.

14. See Scalia, *Common Law Courts in a Civil-Law System*, at 37–38 (the text of the First Amendment must be construed as a synecdoche in which "speech" and "press" stand for a whole range of different forms of expression, including handwritten letters).

15. 347 U.S. 483 (1954).

16. 384 U.S. 486 (1966).

3

Democratic Constitutionalism

ROBERT C. POST AND REVA B. SIEGEL

PROGRESSIVES USED TO conceptualize the Constitution as "living law,"[1] as a "living charter"[2] "capable of growth."[3] Believing that the Constitution was responsive to evolving social needs and to ideals of fundamental justice, they acted in the 1960s and 1970s to end school segregation, to secure fundamental fairness in the criminal justice system, to enforce the separation of church and state, and to recognize gender equality in work and family. By the 1980s, conservatives had united Americans estranged by these changes into a political movement that sought to roll back the rulings of the Warren and Burger Courts. Conservatives accused Congress of overreaching and the Court of legislating from the bench in ways that betrayed the founders' Constitution.

For decades now, progressives have sought to defend their constitutional understandings against this conservative mobilization. Even so, many on the left are intimidated by the charge that a living Constitution expresses political preferences instead of law. They avoid discussing constitutional law as responsive or as a warrant for significant social change, and they instead seek ways of demonstrating their fidelity to a Constitution that was created in the distant past. Some have set out to justify progressive commitments through forms of originalism advocated by the conservative movement, while others would insulate the remains of Warren and Burger Court case law through theories of "superprecedents" or minimalism.

It is time to reconsider these defensive modes of reasoning. The American people have now elected a president with a mandate for change. In this chapter we ask what progressives might learn from the recent conservative insurgency without internalizing its modes of reasoning or its deep hostility to the achievements of the Warren and Burger Courts.

To explore this question, we draw on the theory of democratic constitutionalism that we have elsewhere elaborated at some length.[4] Our analysis is positive, not normative. The object of these brief reflections is to situate questions about interpretive method that have dominated constitutional theory in the last several decades in a dynamic understanding of our constitutional order. We begin in the first section by observing that important aspects of American constitutional law evolve in response to substantive constitutional visions that the American people have mobilized to realize. We argue that these responsive features of the law help sustain the Constitution's authority in history. We demonstrate in the second section that claims of originalism asserted in the late twentieth century expressed such a substantive and mobilizing constitutional vision, although the official ideology of originalism seeks to deny this historical fact.

Examining how originalism established its authority through the lens of democratic constitutionalism, we conclude in the third section that an essential prerequisite for a constitutional mobilization is the development of a motivating constitutional vision, as well as the confidence to act on it, which in part depends upon the capacity to express that constitutional vision as law. A theory of constitutional interpretation matters, but it is no substitute for a substantive constitutional vision. Progressives are not likely to act with the authority of the recent conservative mobilization until they have the vision and confidence to break from its premises.

The Theory of Democratic Constitutionalism

The Constitution serves many functions. Many of its provisions, like those that specify the minimum ages for representatives and senators, establish basic "rules of the game" for the government of the United States. The meaning of these rules is relatively specific and clear, and on the whole they tend not to be controversial. Other constitutional provisions, by contrast, express general norms and standards. The enforcement of these provisions can generate intense political dispute. Constitutional provisions like the Due Process Clause, the First Amendment, and the Equal Protection Clause express national ideals; they establish a "realm of meaning"[5] that Robert Cover has memorably called "nomos."[6] Law embodying nomos matters because it expresses a national "identity."[7] Law embodying nomos is, however, controversial because the American people are heterogeneous in their understanding of national identity.

It is for this reason that ongoing struggles about constitutional meaning have shaped the content of our constitutional law.[8] Although these struggles might seem to threaten the Constitution's legitimacy, conflict can actually help to sustain the Constitution's authority when conducted in accordance with the understandings of American constitutional order. If courts were to impose the Constitution's meaning in matters about which citizens care deeply, the American people would soon become alienated and estranged. We would no longer be able to recognize the Constitution as "ours," as the expression of "We, the People." The legitimacy of the Constitution depends on this relation of recognition.

How, then, can our Constitution continue to inspire loyalty and commitment despite persistent disagreement about its content? Why do Americans remain faithful to their Constitution even when their constitutional views do not prevail? We suggest that this is because Americans believe in the possibility of persuading others—and therefore ultimately the Court—to embrace their views about constitutional meaning.

Trust in the responsiveness of the constitutional order plays a crucial role in preserving the Constitution's authority. When this trust exists, citizens can defer to authoritative judgments about the Constitution's meaning that diverge from their own. The maintenance of this trust depends upon citizens having meaningful opportunities to persuade each other to adopt alternative constitutional understandings. Paradoxically, the possibility of disagreement about the Constitution's meaning preserves constitutional authority, because it enables persons of very different convictions to view the Constitution as expressing their most fundamental commitments and to regard the Constitution as foundational law.

We have elsewhere used the term "democratic constitutionalism" to express the paradox that constitutional authority depends on *both* its democratic responsiveness *and* its legitimacy as law.[9] Americans want their Constitution to have the authority of law, and they understand law to be distinct from politics. They understand that the rule of law is rooted in professional practices that are distinct from popular politics and that will often require divergences between the Court's judgments about the Constitution and their own. Because Americans view the Court's interpretation of the Constitution as law, they will defer to judicial claims about the national nomos with which they disagree so long as they have some outlet for objection and the possibility of one day influencing the shape of the law. But if the Court's interpretation of the Constitution seems wholly unresponsive, the American people will in time come to regard it as illegitimate and oppressive, and they will act to repudiate it as they did during the New Deal.

How can the Constitution function as our fundamental law, as the limit and foundation of politics, and yet remain democratically responsive? The most familiar and uncontroversial mechanism for translating political values into constitutional law is the procedure for amending the Constitution contained in Article V. Article V amendments, however, are so very rare that they cannot provide an effective avenue for connecting constitutional law to popular commitments. Other mechanisms are needed to maintain trust in the responsiveness of constitutional law, especially in situations of aggravated dispute.

One such mechanism, well recognized by historians and political scientists, is the appointment of Supreme Court justices. Those opposed to Warren Court precedents, for example, were attracted to President Ronald Reagan's pledge to halt the slide toward "the radical egalitarianism and expansive civil libertarianism of the Warren Court."[10] They threw their support behind Reagan because he pledged to nominate justices who would adopt a "philosophy of judicial restraint."[11] It is well documented that the Reagan Justice Department self-consciously and successfully used judicial appointments to alter existing practices of constitutional interpretation and so to change constitutional meaning to bring it more into line with the beliefs of the supporters of the Reagan revolution.[12]

Presidential politics and Supreme Court nominations, however, are blunt and infrequent methods of affecting the content of constitutional law. A more broad-based and continuous pathway of change is the practice of norm contestation, which seeks to transform the values that underlie judicial interpretations of the Constitution. The Reagan administration, for example, used litigation and presidential rhetoric to challenge and discredit the basic values that had generated Warren Court precedents.[13]

Second-wave feminism offers a rich example of successful norm contestation. As late as 1970, it was thought that distinctions based upon sex were natural and that government could reasonably enforce traditional sex roles. The Equal Protection Clause was accordingly interpreted to tolerate sex discrimination. But as movements joined in struggle over the legitimacy of these traditional understandings, common sense began to evolve. Discrimination based on sex came to seem unreasonable. Because judges interpret constitutional text to express their implicit understanding of the world, the Court began to read the Fourteenth Amendment to require elevated scrutiny for classifications based on sex. The Court altered its understanding of the Equal Protection Clause even though the Equal Rights Amendment, which proposed to use the procedures of Article V to amend the Constitution to prohibit discrimination based on sex, was never ratified.[14]

Originalism from the Standpoint of Democratic Constitutionalism

There are many ways in which constitutional meaning is rendered responsive to changing social values. Social values shape constitutional interpretation, even the interpretation of those who profess to read the Constitution in ways that claim to separate law from politics. The conservative originalism associated with Justices Antonin Scalia and Clarence Thomas is a good example.[15]

This form of originalism was first systematically articulated as a constitutional theory in the 1970s by prominent academics like Raoul Berger. Berger argued that the *only* legitimate way to interpret the Constitution was to remain faithful to its text and original understanding. The conservative movement employed this claim of methodological exclusivity to attack the liberal decisions and precedents of the Warren Court era. Because Reagan era conservatives could not reason from precedent as Southerners challenging *Brown* had done a generation earlier, they instead sought to discredit liberal precedents by arguing that text and original meaning were the sole legitimate pathways of constitutional interpretation. They insisted that the primary purpose of the Constitution was to *bind* judicial decision making to meanings created in discrete and limited moments of constitutional lawmaking, like the 1789 founding or the 1868 ratification of the Fourteenth Amendment.

The New Right claimed that the Supreme Court had enforced its own liberal preferences rather than the Constitution and that it was necessary to appoint judges who would reverse Warren and Burger Court decisions in order to extricate constitutional law from the contamination of politics. Conservatives sought to justify constitutional change as fidelity to the rule of law. Yet liberal critics have repeatedly shown that originalism was inconsistently applied in practice and so provided a thinly disguised method of infusing constitutional law with conservative political values. For example, Justices Scalia and Thomas are each fervently committed to a color-blind Constitution, even though historians agree that the text and original understanding of the Fourteenth Amendment permitted government to offer race-based assistance to newly freed slaves.[16] Neither Thomas nor Scalia would permit the federal government to segregate schools in the District of Columbia, even though the only applicable constitutional provision is the Due Process Clause of the Fifth Amendment, which was ratified at a time when the Constitution contemplated slavery.[17] Selective, inconsistent, and issue-specific applications of originalism are easy to identify and have been repeatedly emphasized by originalism's liberal critics.[18]

If the strength of originalism actually lay in its objective separation of law from politics, one would expect such reiterated and withering criticism to have had some effect. But it has not. Democratic constitutionalism suggests that the power of originalism in fact lies elsewhere, in the way it aligns constitutional vision and constitutional law. If one examines how the theory of originalism has been deployed outside the academy to mobilize support among the political constituencies responsible for electing conservative presidents like Reagan, George H. W. Bush, and George W. Bush, it becomes clear that originalism's appeal grows out of the conservative constitutional ideals it expresses.

Reagan conservatives denounced Warren and Burger Court precedents as threatening traditional American ways of life, and they used the theory of originalism to signify their intention to appoint a Court that would be faithful to the founders' Constitution and "restore" traditional understandings of religion, family, private property, and race to American constitutional law. What made originalism so compelling was the way its claims about interpretive method conveyed a motivating constitutional vision and the authority to assert that vision as law. The association of the originalist interpretive method with a particular substantive vision was not an accidental but an essential feature of its popular appeal.[19]

Originalism was not successful because of its objectivity or its certainty, but because, as we have demonstrated in detail elsewhere, it served as a "living constitutionalism" for the right.[20] That is why it has been useless for liberals to attack the inconsistencies of originalism. What has powered originalism all along has been the attraction of its substantive constitutional vision, its nomos. The constitutional vision conservatives embrace as "original" expresses fundamental ideals that conservatives believe should define America. Conservative originalists do not merely believe that the Constitution is law; they believe it is *good* law. The genius of originalism is that it gave conservatives confidence to claim that their ideals were law that entitled them to overthrow Warren and Burger Court precedents and to impose conservative constitutional values on Americans who disagreed with them.

Implications for Progressive Constitutionalism

The saga of originalism offers important lessons for progressives. First, Americans mobilize because they care about constitutional ideals. It is exactly backward to argue that the most important need of progressives is for a method of constitutional interpretation. Academic theories of legal justification do not mobilize public opinion; they do not inspire popular political campaigns to "take back the Court." Academic arguments may ultimately help transmute practical aspirations and grievances into legal form, but constitutional mobilization begins far outside the domain of jurisprudence. Just as the New Right advanced a constitutional nomos rooted in images of family, religion, and social control, so progressives need to articulate a convincing vision that will express their own distinctive commitments.

Second, progressives must be able to express these commitments in the language of law. The capacity to assert constitutional vision as constitutional law creates the uniquely American kind of authority that empowers citizens to challenge the judgments of government officials and to insist that others in the community accept or accommodate their constitutional views. It is striking how stories about the founding gave conservatives confidence to assert that their ideals represented the law of the Constitution, which conservatives were prepared to impose on the entire nation.

Third, progressives can make claims on the founding without elevating the founding over other forms of constitutional authority in the ways that conservatives have. They can instead select from among the traditional modalities of interpretation those which are the best suited to give authoritative legal expression to their constitutional understandings—just as conservatives have. Throughout our history Americans have made claims about the Constitution's meaning in diverse ways. They have appealed to legal precedent, historical experience, constitutional structure, normative traditions, constitutional purposes, and fundamental legal and ethical principles. Constitutional debate frequently involves struggle for control over the collective recollection of crucial and traumatic events like the Civil War or the New Deal. In debates over the reach of Congress's Commerce Clause power, for example, progressives and conservatives argue about the meaning of the Great Depression, not the founding.

It would be a great and ironic mistake for progressives to credit originalism's claim to methodological exclusivity, for even the foremost exponents of originalism on the Court appeal to many modalities of constitutional argument; they invoke the post-ratification history of the Constitution with as much confidence as they appeal to its ratification history. In *Parents Involved in Community Schools v. Seattle School District #1*,[21] for example, liberals and conservatives on the Court divided on the question of whether school districts could engage in voluntary school integration. Neither liberal nor conservative justices bothered to discuss the original understanding of the Fourteenth Amendment; debate instead centered on the meaning and legacy of *Brown*.[22] Contrast *Parents Involved* to the Court's decision last term in *District of Columbia v. Heller*,[23] where the Court split along nearly identical lines in a case concerning the right to carry firearms. In *Heller* both liberal and conservative justices debated the original meaning of the text of the Second Amendment. Reading *Heller* alongside of *Parents Involved* demonstrates that sometimes constitutional law is minted in the coin of original meaning, but sometimes it plainly is not. Even those justices who insist that originalism is the only appropriate way to interpret the Constitution will instead appeal to post-ratification history if that history better conveys their constitutional vision. The question for progressives is how their distinctive constitutional vision may best be transmuted into claims of constitutional law. This in turn depends on the substance of that vision. It is not a question that can be answered in the abstract.

Fourth, it would also be a mistake for progressives to embrace minimalism, a theory that invites judges to construe the Constitution in narrow and shallow ways. Minimalism is aimed at judicial interpreters and counsels against change. It seems unlikely to mobilize progressives to "take back the Court" or to orient the judiciary to break with the conservative constitutional premises that have been incorporated into doctrine in the last several decades. Minimalism cannot endow current generations of Americans with the confidence or role authority to assert their own understanding of the Constitution's meaning. Minimalism may offer *stare decisis* justifications for preserving achievements of the

Warren and Burger Courts, but it could never produce decisions like those challenging race and sex discrimination in *Brown* and *Frontiero*.[24] Had citizens and judges heeded minimalism's counsel in the past, there would have been no *Brown* or *Frontiero*. To adopt minimalist premises now is to foreswear such decisions in the coming decades—a problematic constraint for those who believe the nation has not yet fully honored its constitutional commitments.

Embrace of a general interpretive method cannot substitute for a substantive constitutional vision, and in some circumstances might even encumber its expression. The recent conservative mobilization teaches that authority flows to those who can relate the Constitution's fundamental commitments to the beliefs and concerns that animate the American people and who can identify the modes of argument that give this vision its most powerful legal form.

Notes

1. Louis D. Brandeis, *The Living Law*, 10 Ill. L. Rev. 461 (1916).

2. *Michael H. v. Gerald D.*, 491 U.S. 110, 141 (1989) (Brennan, J., dissenting).

3. Brandeis Papers (Harvard University) (draft of Brandeis's dissent in *United States v. Moreland*, 258 U.S. 433 (1922)).

4. Robert Post & Reva Siegel, Roe *Rage: Democratic Constitutionalism and Backlash*, 42 Harv. Civil-Rights Civil-Lib. L. Rev. 373 (2007).

5. Robert M. Cover, *Foreword: Nomos and Narrative*, 97 Harv. L. Rev. 4, 28 (1983).

6. *Id*. at 4 (emphasis omitted).

7. *Id*. at 28.

8. Any historian or political scientist knows that our "[c]onstitutional law is historically conditioned and politically shaped." H. Jefferson Powell, *A Community Built on Words: The Constitution in History and Politics* 6 (2002).

9. Post & Siegel, *supra* note.

10. Edwin Meese III, *The Supreme Court of the United States: Bulwark of a Limited Constitution*, 27 S. Tex. L. Rev. 455, 464 (1986).

11. Ronald Reagan, *Statement on Senate Confirmation of Sandra Day O'Connor as an Associate Justice of the Supreme Court of the United States*, 1981 Pub. Papers 819 (Sept. 21, 1981), available at http://www.presidency.ucsb.edu/ws/index.php?pid=44281.

12. *See* Dawn E. Johnsen, *Ronald Reagan and the Rehnquist Court on Congressional Power: Presidential Influences on Constitutional Change*, 78 Ind. L.J. 363 (2003).

13. *See* Office of Legal Pol'y, U.S. Dep't of Justice, Guidelines on Constitutional Litigation 3 (Feb. 19, 1988), available at http://islandia.law.yale.edu/acs/conference/meese-memos/guidelines.pdf; Edwin Meese III, *A Return to the Founders*, Nat'l L.J., June 28, 2004, at 22.

14. *See* Reva B. Siegel, 2005–06 Brennan Center Symposium Lecture, *Constitutional Culture, Social Movement Conflict and Constitutional Change: The Case of the de facto ERA*, 94 Cal. L. Rev. 1323 (2006).

15. The argument of this section is elaborated in greater depth in Robert Post & Reva B. Siegel, *Originalism as a Political Practice: The Right's Living Constitutionalism*, 75 Fordham L. Rev. 545 (2006); Reva B. Siegel, *Dead or Alive: Originalism as Popular Constitutionalism in* Heller, 122 Harv. L. Rev. 191 (2008).

16. Eric Schnapper, *Affirmative Action and the Legislative History of the Fourteenth Amendment*, 71 Va. L. Rev. 753, 754 (1985); Jed Rubenfeld, *Affirmative Action*, 107 Yale L.J. 427, 428–30 (1997).

17. To get some idea of how distant originalism is from any actual historical understanding of the Constitution, one need only contemplate Justice Thomas's remarkable affirmation, "I take my stand firmly with Frederick Douglass, who defied Americans to find a single pro-slavery clause" in the Constitution. Clarence Thomas, *The Higher Law Background of the Privileges or Immunities Clause of the Fourteenth Amendment*, 12 Harv. J.L. & Pub. Pol'y 63, 64 (1989).

18. Mark Graber, *Clarence Thomas and the Perils of Amateur History*, in *Rehnquist Justice: Understanding the Court Dynamic* 70–71 (Earl M. Maltz, ed., 2003).

19. For a political and social history of originalism in the late twentieth century, see Siegel, *supra* note 15 (tracing the spread of originalist claims about the Second Amendment).

20. Post & Siegel, *supra* note 15.

21. *Parents Involved in Community Schools v. Seattle School District #1*, 127 S.Ct. 2738 (2007).

22. *Brown v. Board of Education*, 347 U.S. 483 (1954).

23. *District of Columbia v. Heller*, 128 S.Ct. 2783 (2008).

24. *Frontiero v. Richardson*, 411 U.S. 677 (1973).

PART II

Social Rights and Legislative Constitutionalism

✺ 4 ✺

The Minimalist Constitution

CASS R. SUNSTEIN

THERE SHOULD BE a large difference between our hopes for the Constitution of 2020 and our hopes for the United States in 2020. A program for constitutional law ought not to be the same as a program for political change. Too much of the time, both liberals and conservatives have lost sight of this point.

I believe that by 2020, the nation should adopt a broad understanding of what "security" requires, including not only protection against bullets and bombs, but also protection against desperate conditions, including those produced by an absence of decent education or minimal health care. This understanding should take the form of a new set of national commitments, some of them quite ambitious. But these commitments should not come from the federal judiciary; they should be endorsed by an engaged and reflective citizenry.

For 2020, we should aim for a minimalist approach to the Constitution. Minimalists want to avoid broad, ambitious judicial rulings. They reject efforts to read the Constitution to fit with the views of any party platform. They do not see *Brown v. Board of Education* nor *Roe v. Wade* as setting the right path for the future. They do not have a heroic picture of the federal judiciary; they do not believe that the Court should seek to be in the forefront of social movements. They reject the view, prominent among progressives in the 1960s and

1970s, that we should hope for two, or ten, or a hundred decisions like *Brown*.

To be sure, minimalists endorse *Brown* itself, seeing it as the culmination of a long line of cases and as reflecting a minimal understanding of the notion of racial equality under law. But they believe that, with its breadth and ambition, *Roe* was a large mistake. A more narrow ruling, based on principles of sex equality and focused on the particular measures at issue in *Roe*, would have been much better than the wholesale rejection of the "pro-life" position in the Court's far-reaching opinion. At least as a presumption, far-reaching opinions should be resisted.

Minimalists do insist on firm protection of a core of constitutional rights, including freedom of political speech and the right not to be deprived of one's freedom without a fair hearing (not least when national security is threatened). Freedom of speech is central to democratic self-government, and minimalists do not want to unsettle the idea that political dissenters may not be silenced.[1] Minimal guarantees of equality on the basis of race and sex, forbidding laws that threaten to create second-class citizenship, do not raise minimalist hackles.[2] In a free society, courts also protect the rule of law, which includes the right to test the question of whether one has been lawfully detained. But minimalists reject the liberal activism of the Warren Court, and they are fearful that conservative activism of the most extreme sort may be the wave of the future. They do not want judges to seize on ambiguous constitutional provisions to issue broad rulings that limit democratic prerogatives.

Minimalists are entirely aware that in the last two decades, a new form of judicial activism has emerged from private organizations, law schools, and even the nation's courtrooms. Purporting to revere history, the new activists claim that they are returning to the original Constitution. The reformers include a number of federal judges. Usually appointed by Ronald Reagan, George H. W. Bush, or George W. Bush, some of these judges do not hesitate to depart radically from entrenched understandings of constitutional meaning. They would like to interpret the Constitution to strike down limits on presidential power, affirmative action programs, gun control legislation, and restrictions on commercial advertising; they seek to impose severe restrictions on Congress's authority; they want to invalidate campaign finance regulation, environmental regulations, and much else.

Minimalists know that this ambitious program is the culmination of a large-scale shift in conservative thought. In the 1960s and 1970s, many principled conservatives were committed to a restrained and cautious federal judiciary. Some of them squarely embraced minimalism—holding out Justice Felix Frankfurter, the great conservative on the Warren Court, as their jurisprudential hero. In some of their best moments, minimalist conservatives attacked *Roe v. Wade*, which protected the right to abortion, and *Miranda v. Arizona*, which protected accused criminals; principled conservatives saw these rulings as unsupportable judicial interference with political choices. Democracy was their watchword; they wanted courts to back off. They asked judges to respect the decisions of Congress, the president, and state legislatures; they spoke of the people's right to rule themselves. They wanted courts to proceed cautiously and incrementally.

This is far less true today. Minimalism has lost much of its popularity in conservative circles. Increasingly, conservatives have been drawn to "movement judges"—judges with no interest in judicial restraint, with a willingness to rule broadly and a demonstrated willingness to strike down the acts of Congress and state governments. Movement judges have an agenda, which, as it happens, overlaps a great deal with the extreme wing of the Republican Party.

In many areas, the new activists have enjoyed important victories, and to a greater or lesser extent, their program may turn out to be the wave of the future. Consider the fact that the Rehnquist Court overturned more than three dozen federal enactments between 1995 and 2004—a record of aggressiveness against the national legislature that is unequaled in the nation's history. In terms of sheer numbers of invalidations of acts of Congress, the Rehnquist Court seems to qualify as the all-time champion. A few illustrations:

- The Rehnquist Court threw most affirmative action programs into extremely serious doubt, suggesting that public employers will rarely be able to operate such programs and that affirmative action will be acceptable only in narrow circumstances.
- The Rehnquist Court used the First Amendment to invalidate many forms of campaign finance legislation—with Justices Scalia and Thomas suggesting that they would strike down almost any legislation limiting campaign contributions and expenditures.
- For the first time since the New Deal, the Rehnquist Court struck down congressional enactments under the Commerce Clause. As a result of the Court's invalidation of the Violence against Women Act, a large number of federal laws have been thrown into constitutional doubt. Several environmental statutes, including the Endangered Species Act, are in constitutional trouble.

- Departing from its own precedents, the Rehnquist Court sharply limited congressional authority to enforce the Fourteenth Amendment. In the process, the Court struck down key provisions of the Americans with Disabilities Act, the Religious Freedom Restoration Act, and the Violence against Women Act—all of which had received overwhelming bipartisan support in Congress.
- The Rehnquist Court used the idea of states' sovereign immunity to strike down a number of congressional enactments, including parts of the Age Discrimination in Employment Act and the Americans with Disabilities Act.
- For the first time in the nation's history, the Rehnquist Court ruled that Congress lacks the power to give citizens and taxpayers the right to sue to ensure the enforcement of environmental laws.

Of course, the Rehnquist Court was not a radical court. The Court did not overrule *Roe v. Wade*. It rejected President George W. Bush's boldest claims of authority to detain suspected terrorists. It struck down laws that criminalize same-sex relationships. It did not entirely eliminate affirmative action programs. In especially controversial decisions, it invalidated the death penalty for mentally retarded people and for juveniles. But let us not lose sight of the forest for the trees. Even if those who seek to reorient the Supreme Court have not received all that they want, they succeeded in producing a body of constitutional law that is fundamentally different from what it was in the 1980s. By 2020, much more might happen.

Notably, many of the more cautious decisions were issued by a bare majority of 5–4 or a close vote of 6–3; with small changes in the Court's composition, the moderate decisions would not be moderate at all. We can easily foresee a situation—by 2020 or well before—in which federal judges take many more steps in the directions in which they have been heading. They might dramatically increase the power of the president, especially in a world that is likely to be pervaded by the risk of terrorism. They might not only invalidate all affirmative action programs, but also elevate commercial advertising to the same status as political speech, thus preventing controls on commercials by tobacco companies (among others); strike down almost all campaign finance reform; reduce the power of Congress and the states to enact gun control legislation; and significantly extend the reach of the Takings Clause, thus limiting environmental and other regulatory legislation.

For 2020, what should be asserted instead is a form of judicial minimalism, one that generally gives the democratic process wide room to maneuver. Unlike their programmatic counterparts on the Left and the Right, minimalist judges usually hope to do little more than is necessary to resolve cases. As a matter of principle, minimalists favor shallow rulings over deep ones, in the sense that they seek to avoid taking stands on the largest and most contested questions of constitutional law. They prefer outcomes and opinions that can attract support from people holding many different theoretical positions. Minimalist judges try to avoid the deepest questions about the meaning of the free speech guarantee, the extent of the Constitution's protection of "liberty," what it means to respect the "free exercise" of religion, and the scope of the president's authority as commander in chief of the armed forces.

Above all, minimalists attempt to reach *incompletely theorized agreements*, in which the most fundamental questions are left undecided. They believe that such agreements are a practical necessity in a diverse society. They also believe that such agreements allow people to show one another a large measure of mutual respect. Minimalists have no desire to revolutionize the law by reference to first principles. They know that such principles are contested and that it is hard for diverse people, and diverse judges, to agree on them. They think that law, and even social peace, are possible only because people usually set aside their deepest disagreements and are able to decide what to do without agreeing on exactly why to do it.

Minimalists believe that a free society makes it *possible for people to agree when agreement is necessary and unnecessary for people to agree when agreement is impossible*. For minimalists, constitutional law consists in large part of a series of incompletely theorized agreements, in which judges accept a certain approach to free speech, or equality, or religious freedom without necessarily agreeing on the deepest foundations of that approach.

Minimalists celebrate the system of precedent in exactly this spirit. Judges may not agree with how previous judges have ruled, but they can agree to respect those rulings—partly because respect promotes stability and partly because respect makes it unnecessary for judges to fight over the most fundamental questions whenever a new problem arises. For example, some liberal judges believe that affirmative action programs should almost always be upheld, and some conservative judges believe that such programs should almost always be struck down. (I think that liberal judges are close to correct here and that, outside of the extreme cases, the question of affirmative action should be settled democratically, not by federal judges.) But if judges respect precedent, they will not simply follow their own judgments; they will pay heed to what others have said before them. Members of constitutional movements will not much hesitate to reject precedents that they believe to be wrong; minimalists are far more cautious about undoing the fabric of existing law.

Minimalists also favor narrow rulings over wide ones. They like to decide cases one at a time. They prefer decisions that resolve the problem at hand without also resolving a series of other problems that might have relevant differences. Minimalist judges may say, for instance, that it is permissible to adopt some kinds of affirmative action plans but not others; everything depends on context. Minimalists might conclude that the president is not permitted to try suspected terrorists using military commissions, without offering broad pronouncements about the nature of the president's authority as commander in chief. In general, minimalists refuse to venture broader judgments that might turn out, on reflection, to be unwarranted.

Of course, minimalists know that narrow rulings can create big problems for lower courts, other branches of government, and ordinary citizens who want to know what the law is. When predictability is important, minimalism might not be worthwhile. But in the most controversial areas, minimalists are willing to pay uncertainty's price, believing that it is even worse to set out law that might turn out to be badly wrong.

By itself, minimalism is a method and a constraint; it is not a program, and it does not dictate particular results. We can easily find liberal minimalists and conservative minimalists. Justice Ruth Bader Ginsburg's approach to the law is complex, but in many domains, it is fair to describe her as a liberal minimalist. She likes to decide cases, rather than set out general principles; and she is reluctant to embrace large-scale generalities about the foundations of the law. Conservative minimalism is nicely captured in the opinions of Justice Sandra Day O'Connor. On the Supreme Court, O'Connor was no ideologue; she wasn't a part of any movement. But much of the time, her votes were in a conservative direction. She contributed a great deal to decisions cabining affirmative action and increasing government's power to protect fetal life, but she refused to vote to forbid affirmative action in all circumstances or to overrule *Roe v. Wade*. Minimalists are cautious by nature, and the minimalist camp is large and diverse. The point is that they greatly prefer nudges over earthquakes.

I have emphasized that minimalists insist on certain core principles, and we should hope that those principles will be reaffirmed in 2020. Of course, insistence on such principles provides indispensable protection to those who benefit from them, but it also performs an important educative and cultural function. Most important, minimalists believe that the government may not punish political dissenters in any way; minimalists are committed to democratic self-government, and they see protection of dissent as a central part of that commitment. If the war on terror or some unanticipated developments threaten the right to dissent, minimalists are more than willing to combat the threat.

Minimalists also protect the right not to be deprived of freedom without a fair hearing—a right that, in their view, separates a free society from a despotic one more than any other. Even in the face of danger to national security, minimalists believe that it is appropriate to vindicate the right to maintain one's liberty. They do not take any general stand against presidential authority—especially when the nation faces serious threats from its enemies. But the right to a fair hearing stands on the firmest ground. As I have suggested, minimalists believe that the Constitution does not tolerate second-class citizenship, and hence minimalists are willing to strike down laws that threaten to make members of certain racial groups or women into second-class citizens.

It is reasonable to wonder: Is minimalism progressive? Or is it actually conservative? There is no simple answer. Minimalists are literally conservative; they seek to conserve existing constitutional understandings. Insofar as existing constitutional doctrines have a progressive character, minimalists are progressive. Insofar as progressives distrust judicial power and seek to cabin it, minimalists can claim to fall in the progressive camp. Certainly, minimalists welcome the idea that serious national commitments, progressive in character, might emerge through political processes. But insofar as progressives seek to use the federal judiciary to wield certain ideals of equality or liberty against state and federal governments, minimalists cannot be characterized as progressive. Indeed, minimalism can be endorsed by people with many disparate views about progressive politics. Minimalists include those who support progressive goals and those who abhor such goals.

For political change, it is possible to imagine any number of programs for 2020. Perhaps the nation should take the old ideal of citizenship more seriously than it now does. Perhaps it should mount a much more ambitious attack on crime; certainly, it should take new steps to ensure equality for African Americans, other ethnic and racial minorities, gays and lesbians, and women. In my view, a general goal should be to see the idea of "security" in quite general terms. Franklin Delano Roosevelt did exactly that when the nation's security was last threatened. In 1944, Roosevelt proposed a Second Bill of Rights, which included a right to a decent education; a right to adequate medical care; a right to earn enough to provide adequate food, clothing, and recreation—and more.[3] Roosevelt believed that the nation must attempt to provide genuine opportunities and decent security to all. Indeed, Roosevelt believed that the Second Bill of Rights should take its place among the nation's "constitutive commitments"—those that help to define, or constitute, the nation's self-understanding.

I believe that Roosevelt was entirely right to do so—and that the Second Bill of Rights should be recovered in its nation of origin. A broad initiative to protect health care, for example, could claim clear foundations in Roosevelt's Second Bill of Rights.

What I am emphasizing here is that this program should not be confused with a constitutional one, purporting to construe the founding document and operating through the federal judiciary. Liberals, no less than conservatives, have often forgotten this point. Minimalists insist on it.

Notes

1. The question of campaign finance regulation raises separate issues, and many minimalists are sympathetic to such regulation on democratic grounds. See Stephen Breyer, *Active Liberty* (New York: Knopf, 2005). Certainly, minimalists reject the ambitious claim that campaign finance regulation is impermissible by its very nature.

2. See the discussion of minimalism's substance in Cass R. Sunstein, *One Case at a Time* (Cambridge, Mass.: Harvard University Press, 1999).

3. See Cass R. Sunstein, *The Second Bill of Rights: FDR's Unfinished Revolution and Why We Need It More than Ever* (New York: Basic, 2004).

Economic Power and the Constitution

FRANK MICHELMAN

Economic power is command over money and what money can buy. Exertions of economic power by one person obviously can impinge on the prospects and conditions of life of other people, sometimes modestly and indirectly (a $1,000 gift to your local public library) and sometimes quite drastically and directly ("you're fired!"). That is what makes regulation of the economy a legitimate social concern. No less obviously, the play of economic power is a part of the free society Americans want. Americans expect their Constitution and law-making under it to accommodate, support, and broadly shape the play of economic power—say, by setting important background conditions for economic power's formation and distribution. Think of competition policy, education policy, jobs creation policy.

In the matter of economic power, how might the Constitution and constitutional law be made to serve the country better in the future than they have in the past?

Before tackling that key question, it will help to lay alongside the idea of constitutional law that of the "constitutive commitments" of American society, as Cass Sunstein has called them.[1] Constitutive commitments are highest-priority, popular, canonical expectations for the conduct of the U.S. government. They are the stuff of public political sensibilities and debates, not of lawyers' constitutional law. Sunstein gives as examples the claims, in the United States today, to be free to join a union without risking your job, to be secure against racial discrimination by private employers, and to social security. The public's expectations of government's recognition of these claims have arisen, and could subside, without amendment of the Constitution; they exist alongside constitutional law, not inside it. By shortchanging the claims or reneging on the commitment to fashion laws and policies with a view to honoring them, Congress would not violate any law. Yet such governmental conduct would, Sunstein suggests, be widely received as an equally grave violation of the public trust, unless and until there had taken place in our country a mutation in public judgments on a scale for which a constitutional amendment would be a suitable form of expression.

Sunstein's examples of effective American constitutive commitments are all concerned with economic power. Whether the commitments are, in fact, exactly what he says is not our concern here. Rather, in aid of our coming inquiry about how best to work on constitutional law, it makes good sense to ask: What constitutive commitments regarding economic power would prevail in the United States, if *we* could have our way (and I'll come shortly to who "we" are)? What would be some constitutive commitments regarding economic power that *we* would wish to have in force (so to speak) in American society? A rough, preliminary account of their general shape—which is all that can be offered here—can help to guide some thoughts about objectives for the legal Constitution of 2020.

To ask about American constitutive commitments we might like to see in place is not to solicit any statement of a grand philosophical theory of social justice. Much more modestly, we seek the makings of a center-left practical consensus on ideals regarding economic power, those that are worth working for and supporting. Center-left, because we want a consensus broad enough to have some hope of being politically efficacious in a generation's time. Nonphilosophical, because to put that together we can't be fussy about consensus members' differing speculative reasons for convergence on the commitments.

It follows that the illustrative package I'll propose is bound to feel tepid to some readers. It won't contain all the commitments that every left-leaning view would find worth pursuing, because it can't contain any that would repel too many views. Similar considerations dictate that the commitments in the package will be very roughly stated, in terms left open to interpretation. The test will be whether the package is robust enough to imply some worthwhile directions—and some worthwhile reservations—regarding work on constitutional law that has some chance to be effective between now and 2020. That will be your call, reader. If you answer yes, that makes you a part of the "we" who can then go on to ask about the indicated aims for the Constitution and constitutional law of 2020.

Here, then, is a proposal for some, maybe not all, of the constitutive commitments regarding economic power that the center-left would like to see prevailing in the United States:

Basic needs, including work. No one should ever lack the means of access to levels of subsistence, housing, health care, and safety that meet a basic American standard; nor to education for which he or she is qualified; nor to the means of providing the same for his or her children and other dependents; nor to work, including conditions of work that are safe, civil, and consistent with dignity. Work, when available on such conditions and sufficiently remunerated, is considered (or is preferred as) a means of access that satisfies this commitment. (Of course, I have just let loose a mouthful of ill-defined notions, but, for reasons already stated, no finer definition is needed or is advisable. The same holds for the other items in the list.)

Equal opportunity. A person's prospects for the accrual and enjoyment of, or participation in, economic power should not be hindered by factors of race, sex, or any other conditions of birth, family, or heritage. Relative prospects should not correlate with such factors.

Political influence and access. Economic power should not be convertible into political power. Ability to spend should not affect political access or influence nor control of public policy.

Safeguards for basic personal rights (or fundamental interests). Basic rights of dignity, liberty, and safety should not stand at unacceptable risk from the play of economic power in society.

Open and diverse media. Undue concentrations of power to decide the contents and directions of public discourse and cultural exchange should be prevented.

Competitive markets. Undue concentrations of power to control or constrain the alternatives open to consumers should be prevented.

I have not sweated exact phrasing, nor need I defend omission of more radical-leaning formulations. This list is exact and radical enough to support reflection—to which we now proceed—on the ways, means, and limits of working on constitutional law in the pursuit of left-leaning social goals respecting economic power.

What is constitutional law? From the typical lawyer's standpoint, it consists of rules and standards drawn from the Constitution and prior interpretations thereof, by which judges test the lawfulness of acts and omissions by organs of American government, when parties come to court seeking relief from such acts and omissions and correction of them. (Robin West offers an important contrasting view,[2] but let us stick for now with the more common one.) What would people who subscribe to our list of favored constitutive commitments see as objectives for the constitutional law of 2020? I would say the following (disregarding, for the moment, feasibility, and with explanation to follow):

Conduciveness. We would want a body of constitutional law that does not invite judicial obstruction of creditable legislative and other governmental efforts to carry out the commitments and that does treat pursuit of the commitments as justification for proportionally minor infringements of adjacent constitutional guarantees.

A gadfly judiciary. We would want a body of constitutional law that provides the judicial branch with a suitable platform for prodding both government action and public opinion in the direction of affirmation and performance of the commitments.

Private relationships. We might want a body of constitutional law that has application to the legal norms governing the conduct and relationships of nongovernmental actors.

Global consciousness. We would want a body of constitutional law that is receptive to influence by the norms and practices of a broader community of constitutional-democratic jurisdictions and tribunals.

We turn now to explanations of this list of aims for American constitutional law and also of some limitations and omissions.

Many doubt whether working on constitutional law is at all the right choice for anyone seeking to improve the performance of U.S. society regarding economic power. Such doubts are easily understandable. Effective pursuit of the constitutive commitments on our list plainly requires complexly designed and coordinated governmental action in the forms of taxes, transfers, subsidies, and policy instruments affecting markets, industries, families, education, health, internal and external trade, and the monetary system. The choices needing to be made are endless, subtle, technical, interactive, uncertain, subject to experience, and guaranteed to raise honest disagreements every step of the way. It is far from clear how courts of law can inject themselves into such matters with much credibility, authority, or legitimacy.

And yet the courts are always with us, and the courts can get in the way. Experience on this point is clear. Judges honoring claims to constitutional protection for freedoms of speech and association can stymie efforts to fashion a set of media policies aimed against undue concentrations of power to control public discourse, or a set of electoral practices designed to minimize conversions of economic into political power. Judges honoring claims to private liberty, property, and freedom from racial classifying may block employment legislation directed toward equal opportunity or decent conditions of work, or housing legislation aimed at giving everyone a chance for adequate housing. Judges honoring claims to states' rights may block such actions when they emanate from the central government.

The exact form of a well-conceived response is not so easy to lay down, because it really is true that governmental efforts on behalf of commitments on our wish list can bump up against commitments we also share to expressive and associational liberties, to privacy and self-determination, and to ensuring that individuals are recognized as themselves and not reduced to a race or a sex. To wish courts and constitutional law completely out of the way whenever a governmental action is ostensibly addressed to a commitment on our list is to suppose that total judicial quiescence gives us our best chance of achieving results that reflect a focused and prudent weighing of *all* the constitutionally sensitive concerns in view. It is to place our trust in governments untethered to courts. For those who hesitate to do so, the preferred course will be to work on the forms and attitudes of judicial involvement, not to seek its disappearance; more on this below.

Let us now turn our minds to ways in which we might hope to make constitutional law a part of the solution and not just a part of the problem.

Courts plainly can do *something* with constitutional law to help advance the ball in a positive way. Using defensible interpretations of the law of the Constitution, courts have abolished poll taxes, weeded out punitive welfare and education policies (like long waiting periods for new arrivals in a state), reduced cavalier and abusive administration of social programs, even prohibited the use by states of school-financing methods that seem outrageously geared to giving costlier public schooling to the children of the wealthy than to those of the poor.

Judicial efforts along these and similar lines have met with varying and sometimes limited success. The reason, simply stated, is that even when constitutional law appears favorably disposed, sometimes the background politics are not and a backlash ensues. A master strategist would try to select occasions for such efforts where success in court could be a flashpoint for evoking latent, favorable sympathies in the background politics, rather than for arousing massive resistance. But even when the sorts of judicial actions we've just described go well, they mostly nibble around the edges of the commitments on our wish list. No imaginable improvement of either constitutional law or background politics will equip courts to engineer the sorts of measures apparently required to get to the cores of these commitments. Envisioning such endeavors, we find ourselves confronting familiar concerns about limited judicial competence and authority in the midst of social and economic complexity.

But hold on. Two of our listed commitments, "equal opportunity" and "safeguards for basic rights," seem at least partially to evade these concerns. Americans largely recoil from thinking that a person should have to be white, provide sexual services, join the company union, or submit to being locked inside a store overnight in order to get or keep a job. It should be no more awkward for a court, on constitutional grounds, to block private economic power from imposing such conditions than to block a government from doing so, and indeed constitutions in some other countries are read as commissioning courts to do just that. Not, however, in the United States. Here, a judge-made, so-called state action rule—along with a related view of the Constitution as only restricting, but never mandating, government action—currently stops courts from applying constitutional standards to relations and transactions between private parties or from requiring lawmakers to enact protective legislation.[3]

One might, accordingly, think that a clear objective for 2020 is to wean our courts away from such a constricted view of the reach of constitutional rights. But again, the case is at least a little clouded. Typically, in a private dispute where the party on "our" side can claim a constitutionally sensitive interest at stake, the other party can claim a countering protection for property, privacy, or freedom—of religion or conscience, or from compelled expression, or simply to do business on terms acceptable to that party. Such claims can sometimes be invoked quite plausibly against demands for unhindered access to privately provided work, education, or housing, or to the shopping mall or TV station for politicking purposes. To move wholesale in the direction of "constitutionalizing" the law of private relations means inviting upper-echelon judges to reweigh the orderings of constitutionally resonant interests that have sometimes prompted the general, background law to weigh in on "our" side of the question. Is that what we want just now? To make presidentially selected judges the keepers of our hopes?

To complicate matters further, it is wrong to suppose that all these choices have easy or obvious answers even from "our" point of view. Should mall owners be stripped of all control over politicking on the premises? Should parents be disallowed from conditioning inheritance on marriage within their faith? Should churches be disallowed from reserving jobs or the occupancy of residences they own for co-religionists? Should employers and employees never be allowed to opt for employment that either side can terminate freely at any time, without having to give reasons? Don't we see constitutionally resonant concerns on both sides? And don't we then have to ask ourselves which we trust more these days and in the coming years to work out resolutions reflecting "our" mix of values and concerns: elected governments acting alone, or governments acting under limits imposed by judges applying constitutional norms to the best of their understandings?

Maybe, then, we do want judges reviewing legislation aimed at fulfilling our wish list, but with minds generously open to the possibility that such aims can sometimes justify a resultant impingement on other constitutionally sensitive interests—as election laws aimed at preventing the conversion of economic to political power can impinge on First Amendment interests, or rent laws aimed at making sure that people's basic needs are met can impinge on property and free-contract interests, or a constitutional requirement for states to reduce reliance on local tax revenues to fund public schooling can impinge on an interest in local popular control of educational policies and programs. Speaking more generally, we would want our reviewing courts to be staffed by judges for whom black and white are not the only shades, who know the law but retain a sense of proportion, who are good at striking balances, and who feel comfortable doing so. We would want judges capable of grasping the idea that a constitutional guarantee like freedom of expression points not only at securing an individual's freedom to speak his or her mind without state interference, but also at achievement of a social state of affairs in which access to public communicative exchange is freely and fully open to everyone.

The means of obtaining a judiciary animated by such dispositions are mainly political and beyond the reach of this chapter. But might there be ways internal to the professional practice of constitutional law to help move both reviewing courts and U.S. political society in the desired directions?

One of them might be: Encourage judicial globalization. As Vicki Jackson explains,[4] U.S. judges from all over the ideological spectrum are feeling the attractions (although not, of course, without heated opposition) of a transnational, judicial conversation on democratic constitutionalism, which is issuing a loose set of common judicial approaches to domestic constitutional interpretation and adjudication. The attraction is one that we have every reason to encourage, in our roles as citizens and our work as lawyers. First, because the transnational discourse is substantively capacious, it is sensitive to the social reformist aspiration of constitutional guarantees while still fully regardful of the needs of individuals for protection against the state. Second, the transnational discourse correspondingly leans toward the balance-prone mode of legal analysis we have reason to want; and in fact the discourse provides, through its leading doctrine of proportionality, persuasive models and methods for the disciplined conduct of analysis in that mode.

Now, let us shift direction. Let us (as some economists like to say) suppose a can opener. Suppose our Constitution contained an amendment tracking the "basic needs" item on our list: "Everyone has the right to subsistence, work, [etc.,] that meet a basic American standard, and governments at all levels shall take reasonable legislative and other measures, in view of available resources, to achieve the realization of this right."

South Africa's current constitution contains provisions very similar to that. South African judges do not read them as conferring on any individual a legally enforceable claim to the actual, present fulfillment of needs, nor yet as authorizing courts to dictate to the government regarding the strategies and policies for getting those needs met over time. Rather, the socioeconomic guarantees in South African constitutional law are read as can openers—as giving rise to what have been called "weak" judicial remedies.

Weak remedies are a creative device for keeping independent judiciaries in the constitutional game even where they work under obvious institutional limitations, as with the furtherance of a constitution's socioeconomic guarantees. Experience in South Africa and some other countries suggests that such provisions can, in favorable conditions, supply the judicial branch with a useful basis on which to engage governments in a kind of public cross-examination of their relevant laws and policies. The constitution's social-rights guarantee can provide a platform from which a respected court can make a positive difference by issuing reasoned critiques of challenged governmental choices and courses of conduct—sometimes finding them deviant from the legal standard of an all-things-considered reasonable effort; maybe, or maybe not, issuing an order roughly in the vein of "don't just stand there, do something."

But then, what are these requisite "favorable conditions"? Mainly, they comprise an attitude of the background culture: Fidelity to the constitution must count heavily in people's ideas of what to expect and demand of their government. This condition is evidently met in South Africa. The government there makes no secret of its wish for the courts to shut up in the socioeconomic realm—a strong indication that judicial monitoring is believed to matter politically in that country. In South Africa, the platform clauses in the constitution (the can openers) plainly have the backing of constitutive commitments that are real, current, and manifest in the culture.

So what is the lesson for the American center-left seeking a constitutional-legal strategy regarding economic power? Well, the weak remedies approach presupposes the can opener, so the indicated strategy seemingly would be to work at producing constitutional amendments on basic needs, media policy, and so on.

Now, let's face it: Constitutional amendment is next to impossible under U.S. rules. In this instance, the effort would have to overcome ferocious partisan resistance on the substance. It also would have to overcome a long-standing, widespread, entrenched American understanding that the business of a court of law is to rule a given act or course of conduct lawful or unlawful; it most certainly is not to kibitz the government.

The prospects for an amendment do not appear bright, and it seems the political energy would be better spent on the ordinary politics of elections and legislation, in pursuit of both a "legislated constitution" à la West[5] and a correspondingly crystallized set of popular constitutive commitments. If constitutive commitments come first, there is some chance that constitutional law will follow.

Notes

1. See Cass R. Sunstein, *The Second Bill of Rights: FDR's Unfinished Revolution and Why We Need It More than Ever* 62–63 (New York: Basic, 2004).

2. Robin West, "The Missing Jurisprudence of the Legislated Constitution," this volume.

3. Mark Tushnet, "State Action in 2020," this volume, unpacks the deep tie-in of state action with a view of the Constitution as restrictive but not mandatory.

4. Vicki C. Jackson, "Progressive Constitutionalism and Transnational Legal Discourse," this volume.

5. Robin West, "The Missing Jurisprudence of the Legislated Constitution."

✺ 6 ✺

Social and Economic Rights in the American Grain

Reclaiming Constitutional Political Economy

WILLIAM E. FORBATH

W ORK AND LIVELIHOODS; poverty and dependency; economic security and insecurity: For most of our history, their constitutional importance was self-evident. The framers of 1789 had no doubt that personal liberty and political equality demanded a measure of economic independence and material security. They proclaimed that the new national Constitution, plus "equality of rights and liberty" at the state level, would ensure just that measure for all hardworking white men and their families. The main prompting for the Fourteenth Amendment was to give African American men the same rights of contract and property that were thought to ensure white men the opportunity to pursue a calling and earn a decent livelihood. In the wake of industrialization and urbanization, generations of reformers declared that the United States needed a "new economic constitutional order" and a "Second Bill of Rights," securing the old promises of individual freedom, opportunity, and well-being via new government duties and new social and economic rights. Laissez-faire, unchecked corporate power, and the deprivations and inequalities they breed weren't just bad public policy; they were constitutional infirmities.

Today, however, with the important exception of employment discrimination, work, livelihoods, social provision, and the material bases of citizenship have vanished from the constitutional landscape. That is a scandal, for the United States is no different from other nations: Constitutional democracy is really impossible here, just as it is elsewhere, without some limits on social and economic deprivation. Mounting poverty and poverty wages; growing job insecurity; a renaissance of sweat shops; a lack of decent education, health care, housing, and other basic social goods: Millions of Americans thus afflicted lack more than money. They are at constant risk of physical and social debilitation. They can't make effective use of their basic civil and political rights. They can't participate on anything like a roughly equal footing in the world of work and opportunity or in the polity, where the terms of social and economic cooperation and competition are meant to be open to democratic scrutiny and revision. "Equal liberty" and the "consent of the governed"—the basic precepts of constitutional democracy—are a hoax in a system that allows such savage inequalities as does the United States.

Yet, "welfare rights," as most Americans understand them, have been tried and rejected. And "redistribution" is more likely to seem constitutionally suspect than constitutionally commanded. What is to be done? How, if at all, should the Constitution be interpreted to safeguard social rights or a social minimum in the twenty-first century?

To understand where we're going, it's good to know where we've been. So, the first part of this chapter is historical. We're all familiar with the anti-redistributive, laissez-faire, or *Lochner* tradition in American constitutional law and politics. Many important judges and scholars are bent on reviving it. *Lochner* revivalists are also originalists; for them, history obliges us to return to the constitutional political economy embodied in *Lochner*. They are wrong to claim that history can bind us to one particular account of our past constitutional commitments. In political economy, as elsewhere, our constitutional past is full of contending commitments and understandings; it offers less determinate and more choice-laden meanings for the present. The right-wing originalists are correct, however, in their practical understanding of constitutional change. Movements for change need an account of past constitutional contests and commitments that add up to a vision of the nation that the Constitution promises to promote and redeem; and the right-wing revivalists have succeeded in constructing such an account, which has aroused citizens, lawmakers, and judges to act boldly on its behalf.

Lately, we progressives have not had any good constitutional narratives to counter the laissez-faire, *Lochner*ian account of an America fundamentally committed to rugged individualism, personal responsibility, and private property safe from state interference and redistribution. The most frequent counters have been these:

1. The New Deal interred *Lochner*; it settled that the Constitution does not speak substantively to economic regulation and redistribution, leaving them to the give and take of the political process. True, some liberal and progressive lawyers and scholars in the 1960s and '70s tried to establish a constitutional right to welfare, but they failed. Now, we admit that social rights or positive rights or affirmative governmental duties are simply foreign to our constitutional traditions.

2. The liberal and progressive champions of constitutional welfare rights were correct. The Supreme Court was on the verge of recognizing a right to welfare when Richard Nixon won a razor-thin victory over Hubert Humphrey and named new, conservative justices who halted that train of doctrinal development. A Humphrey Court would have completed the task; and the liberal and progressive champions still hold fast to the arguments fashioned in the '60s and '70s.

3. The New Deal did more than inter *Lochner*. It gave rise to a new set of constitutive commitments embodied in the "greatest speech of the twentieth century,"[1] Roosevelt's 1944 State of the Union, proposing a Second Bill of (social and economic) Rights. FDR's speech is all but forgotten today. Still, the Second Bill of Rights remains constitutive of our national identity, and we should honor it, at least to the extent of protecting all Americans from desperate want.[2]

None of these counterstories fits the bill. The first two cede the constitutional past to conservatives' right-wing political economy. That is bad history. And while I'm no strategist, I think it's also bad politics. The third counternarrative reaches deeper into the past, but it isn't credible. If FDR's Second Bill of Rights should be read as a defining statement of modern America's constitutive commitments, why has it been forgotten, and why do social rights seem foreign in today's United States?

By contrast, the history on offer here gives shape and depth to social and economic rights in the American grain; it is at least as resonant today as its laissez-faire rival, and it shows how the tangled knot of race and class thwarted efforts to enact FDR's Second Bill of Rights and why

FDR's language of social rights is forgotten. Instead of enacting the Second Bill of Rights, the New Deal ended up creating a divided system of social insurance, which rested on generous *private* social provision for a broad and fortunate swath of Americans and a miserly, racialized system of public welfare assistance for the poor. Finally, the history and analysis on offer here illuminate the present as a critical moment, when this divided New Deal system is in crisis, and the opportunity beckons for renewing and reinventing social citizenship for all Americans.

Social rights are coming back. For the first time in a generation, we saw the leading 2008 Democratic presidential contenders championing "universal rights" to health care and to decent education. Their rhetoric often sounded in the key of social citizenship:[3] Certain basic social goods must be available to every member of the national community; the market must not govern who enjoys them; no one can justly be excluded. Every American is *entitled* to a decent education. Every American has a *right* to health care.

It is a good time, then, to recall the provenance of social rights. I'll outline this deeper constitutional-historical narrative, and then I'll sketch a couple of the plans for new social provision that have the most traction today. I'll note these plans' promises and their pitfalls and suggest some ideas and sources of political energy for making them more inclusive and bringing the racialized poor into the fold of twenty-first-century U.S. social citizenship.

Social and Economic Rights: A Whirlwind Historical Tour

We need to reacquaint ourselves with the rich, reform-minded, *distributive* tradition of constitutional law and politics. And we also need to examine how it arrived at its present infirm state. Elsewhere, I have reconstructed this story in some detail.[4] Here, a condensed account will do. The core of the U.S. social citizenship tradition always has been a commitment to enabling every American to participate in the common world of citizenship, work, and opportunity. Its roots lie in the same eighteenth-century sources as the *Lochner*ian outlook, and it never conceded to conservatives the classic liberal language of individual liberty, risk taking, and personal responsibility. Rather than redistribution of income after the fact, U.S. social citizenship traditions have emphasized redistributing opportunities and life chances, incentives and rewards to effort, and "predistributing" the initial endowments and security (like education and health and old-age insurance) necessary to take risks and fulfill personal responsibilities and citizenly duties. This puts the moral basis of a progressive program on the bedrock promises of liberal capitalism: work for the willing, a decent income for those who work, and opportunity to rise above the minimum by making full use of one's talents and abilities. For much of U.S. history, this was the economic heart of the constitutional promise of "equal rights." Until the 1970s, it had a deeply gendered aspect. It also remains hard ground on which to plant social rights claims that aren't rooted in work, opportunity, and responsibility, but simply in our common vulnerability and interdependence. We'll return to these challenges.

As far back as the mid-nineteenth century, Abraham Lincoln and the other founders of the Republican Party held that equal rights demanded not only equal legal rights to contract and own property but a fair distribution of initial endowments, and therefore free homesteads and federally funded public state universities alongside free elementary and secondary education.

FDR's Second Bill of Rights, with its emphasis on education, employment, and earnings, expressed this outlook. At the same time, New Deal constitutionalism reflected the modern (late nineteenth- to early twentieth-century) progressive insight that industrial America's political economy was not a natural but a "manmade" order, constructed in ways that made poverty, unemployment, and vulnerability in illness and old age inevitable hazards of modern marketplace life. Made vivid by the Great Depression, this insight combined with the specter of rising fascism in Depression era Europe to link social security and freedom in New Deal thought. "A necessitous man is not a free man."[5] "Every man has a right to life," Roosevelt proclaimed, and a "right to make a comfortable living." The government "owes to everyone an avenue to possess himself of a portion of [the nation's wealth] sufficient for his needs, through his own work."[6] By the same token, "economic or social insecurity due to old age[,]...infirmity, illness or injury...[or] unemployment" was an injury to liberty itself, and government must enable "all Americans" jointly and severally to insure themselves against those injuries.[7] Thus, alongside education, "training and retraining,"[8] decent work, and decent pay, FDR's Second Bill of Rights set out rights to decent housing and social insurance, including health care.

Old understandings of constitutional rights, Roosevelt explained, were inadequate in industrial America. The terms of our basic rights "are as old as the Republic," but new conditions demand new readings. The old constitutional economic guarantees, like equality in the enjoyment of the "old and sacred possessive [common-law] rights" of property and labor had rich significance for the "welfare and happiness" of ordinary Americans in the preindustrial United States. Now, only recognition of new governmental responsibilities would enable "a return to values lost in the course of...economic development" and "a recovery" of the old rights' once robust social meaning. "'To Promote the General Welfare,' it is our plain duty to provide for that security upon which welfare depends...the security of the home, the security of livelihood, and the security of social insurance."[9]

Why then have we forgotten FDR's Second Bill of Rights? And how did constitutional welfare rights for the very poor become the paradigmatic social right for progressive lawyers and constitutional scholars in the 1960s? FDR's Second Bill of Rights emerged from deep and widely shared constitutional aspirations. But another fundamental feature of the political and constitutional order of FDR's day was white supremacy. Mass disenfranchisement in the South (not only blacks but the majority of poor and working-class white southerners lost the vote by dint of devices like the poll tax) meant that an astonishingly small proportion of the region's adult population was entitled to vote. The solid South was ruled by a planter and new industrialist oligarchy. That oligarchy chose the bulk of the South's congressional delegation, and they, in turn, formed a reactionary core to counter the heart of Roosevelt's liberal coalition. They insisted that New Deal social and labor standards rest on decentralized state administration, and they demanded that key bills exclude the main categories of southern labor. More encompassing and inclusive bills, those with national, rather than local, standards and administration, enjoyed solid support from northern Democrats (and broad but bootless support from disenfranchised southern blacks and poor whites), but the southern Junkers exacted their price. By the late '30s, southern Democrats openly joined ranks with conservative members of the minority party Republicans. This conservative coalition thwarted FDR's and congressional New Dealers' efforts to enact national health insurance, to remedy the many gaps and exclusions in the Social Security Act, and to create a federal commitment to full employment.

Social citizenship aspirations didn't vanish, however. Instead, they flowed into private channels. By the 1940s, the new industrial unions had emerged as the only powerful, organized constituency for social and economic rights. Blocked at every legislative crossroads, the unions during the 1940s–1960s fashioned a robust *private* welfare state by bargaining for private entitlements to job security, pensions, and health insurance for their members. Beyond the unionized sectors of the economy, industrial prosperity, liberal tax incentives, and the hope of thwarting unionization prompted large firms to adopt the main features of this generous, publicly subsidized, private welfare system.

So social rights talk fell into disuse after the 1940s, until it was reborn in the 1960s with a new shape and constituency. The private welfare state and the segmented and caste-ridden system of public social insurance bequeathed by the New Deal excluded most African Americans, whose anger exploded in many of the large cities of the North, where millions of southern blacks had moved over the preceding decades to escape Jim Crow and rural unemployment. For them, public assistance stood as the sole federal protection against poverty. Public assistance meant federal Aid to Families with Dependent Children (AFDC), and it was this separate, decentralized, and deeply gendered and racialized benefits program, stamped with many of the centuries-old degradations of poor relief, that the welfare rights movement sought to transform into a dignifying national right to a guaranteed income.

Many African American leaders tried to craft a broader social rights agenda—invoking FDR's Second Bill and its rights to decent work and livelihoods—but the mass constituencies and organizations for such an agenda weren't there. What Congress and Lyndon Johnson's administration's War on Poverty supplied were community action programs, thousands of attorneys, and tens of thousands of social workers and community resident-activists, often veterans of civil rights activism. They set about getting poor people to apply for welfare and attacking the social and legal barriers to their getting it.

Never before had poor African American women formed the rank and file of a nationally organized social movement. Like earlier movements for social and economic justice, they claimed decent income as a right; unlike the earlier movements, they did not tie this right to waged work. Most strands of social-citizenship thought constructed their programs and ideals in a gendered fashion, around the working man–citizen; a decent income and social provision were rights of (presumptively white male) waged workers and their dependents. By the 1960s, poor black women had had enough experience in urban labor markets to know that decent jobs were hard to find and enough experience with workfare to think it coercive and demeaning. A guaranteed adequate income also was a way to fulfill what, in the 1960s, remained a dominant norm: full-time mothering at home. The National Welfare Rights Organization (NWRO) demanded it as an unconditional right, essential to equal respect and an appropriate touchstone of equality in an affluent America.

The links and continuities with the civil rights struggle were not lost on the federal courts, as they decided cases undoing the exclusion of black women from welfare rolls. Hundreds of cases brought by Legal Services attorneys dramatically broadened eligibility standards; federal judges went a long way toward transforming a grant-in-aid to the states to be administered as meanly as local officialdom saw fit, into a no-strings and no-stigmas national right to welfare. The whole push of these developments was reflected in the Supreme Court's repeated insistence that public assistance for impoverished citizens was a basic commitment—not charity or largesse, but a right. The Court evoked the social and constitutional outlook of FDR and the New Deal: "From its founding the Nation's basic commitment has been to foster the dignity and well-being of all persons within its borders. We have come to recognize that forces not within the control of the poor contribute to their poverty."[10] And like FDR, the Court rang out the changes on the Preamble to the Constitution, only now on behalf of those conspicuously excluded from New Deal social citizenship: "Welfare...can help bring within the reach of the poor the same opportunities that are available to others to participate meaningfully in the life of the community." Public assistance, then, is a means to "promote the general Welfare, and secure the Blessings of Liberty to ourselves and our Posterity."[11]

Gaining welfare as a matter of right promised to relieve unjustifiable suffering and indignities. It was a social rights claim that highlighted the coercive and gendered aspects of older employment-based models of economic justice. But it would not do enough to help poor African Americans make their way into a shared social destiny of work and opportunity.

In any case, welfare rights were in trouble. Not only the racialized cast of welfare and the changing cast of the Supreme Court, but also the massive entry of white working- and middle-class women into the full-time paid labor force left AFDC vulnerable and exposed. Assailed for years, in 1996, a Republican Congress and a Democratic president (Bill Clinton) repealed poor Americans' federal right to welfare assistance, ending "welfare as we [knew] it."

Social and Economic Rights in the Twenty-First Century

To recall the historical heft of these century-long efforts to make good on the constitutional justice of livelihoods and social and economic rights is to see that these ideas are not strangers in the province of U.S.

constitutional experience. If the nation had remained true to the commitments made during Reconstruction and had southern blacks and poor whites enjoyed the vote during the New Deal, then the votes probably would have been there in Congress for more of the Second Bill of Rights legislation, and a divided, caste-ridden system of welfare and social provision might have been averted. But what can we draw today from this imperfect past?

First, as a practical matter, bear in mind: The divided system is collapsing. The end of welfare has made the "undeserving poor" into the "working poor." At the same time, the nation's once ample supply of stable, secure, decently paid unskilled or semi-skilled jobs has dwindled, and the generous private welfare state has been dismantled. Across the political spectrum, commentators liken the economic order of today to the harsh, laissez-faire capitalism of the Gilded Age, a century ago.

Long-term job security and job ladders are disappearing; temporary and contingent work is growing. Yet, unemployment insurance has been cut back. Since the 1980s, business leaders and lawmakers have been chipping away at the public and private social benefits forged during the New Deal and expansive postwar decades. We have seen a crusade against corporate and governmental responsibility for individual welfare, sweeping like a grim reaper through pension plans, health insurance, and labor standards; cutting the bonds of social solidarity; and shifting the burdens of and responsibilities for economic risk from government and corporations to workers and their families. From the progressive perspective, this marks a constitutional-political-economic crisis and an opportunity. With the end of the divided system of welfare for the poor and generous, publicly subsidized, private social provision for the working and middle classes has come the possibility of proposing new social rights for all working Americans and their families.

Next, as a matter of constitutional history and tradition, don't forget that legislation is an integral part of the constitutional framework, and many of our most important constitutional battles are fought outside the courts in movement building, public debate, and legislative and policymaking arenas. Quite simply, the progressive constitutional narrative I've sketched tells us that the United States that the Constitution promises to promote and redeem is one fundamentally committed to all Americans enjoying a chance to work and earn the decencies as well as the necessities of life and being insured for when they cannot work; having a chance to engage in the affairs of their communities and the larger society; and enjoying a chance to do something that has value in their own eyes. As the 2008 Democratic contenders showed, it is a narrative that remains resonant. What kinds of new framework statutes and insti-tutional innovations are best suited to bringing these old commitments back to the nation? And how should we address the perils of exclusion which any new effort at social citizenship brings in its wake?

The politics of promoting a twenty-first-century progressive consti-tutional political economy seems likely to begin with rights to decent and continuing education and health care. But these seem likely, in turn, to open onto other preventable forms of severe vulnerability and insecurity. With the dismantling of the old systems of social support and the balance of responsibility swinging wildly and unjustly toward the unaided individual and her family, a reformed Social Security sys-tem could become a centerpiece of a progressive constitutional political economy. This could create a shared system of social rights and social support for working families across classes and generations. In addition to providing pensions for the elderly and meeting the unmet needs of Americans in between jobs, a progressive Social Security system would underwrite periods of training and retraining, as well as periods of part-time work or time off for working parents with small children. Because Social Security is the nation's most popular "universal" program, the social policy mavens around Barack Obama have been right to promote bringing that program into the twenty-first century in just this fashion.

The risk is that such a reform will shortchange those millions of marginalized Americans likely to be excluded from a revamped Social Security system because they don't meet minimum contribution require-ments. Suppose, for example, that a revamped system were to begin providing income for periods of full- or part-time child or elder care in working people's lives. How might a rekindled poor people's movement overcome the concatenation of ethnic, racial, gender, and class mistrust and scorn that would greet efforts to extend such support to poor inner-city African Americans, Hispanics, and others lacking the requisite peri-ods of paycheck contributions?

Part of the answer might lie in this. The welfare rights movement of the '60s found no allies or common ground with the labor move-ment. But the wide gulf that used to separate organized labor from poor people of color has narrowed. Some of the most innovative and fast-growing provinces of the labor movement today are those populated by low-wage, service-sector black and Hispanic women workers. There, one finds local and statewide unions successfully prodding employers into partnerships that are turning demeaning jobs into decent ones in sectors that are largely immune from outsourcing but known for low-wage, dead-end work. Aware of the straits that lead constituents to cling to low-wage jobs *and* why they often can't hold onto them, these unions would have many good reasons to champion federal support for "care" work among the inner-city poor. Not least, such support for work outside the labor market would strengthen the bargaining power of individual poor workers and their unions inside the labor market. Union leaders and activists in a coalition laying claim to this kind of social right would assail the moral division of poor Americans into the deserving and undeserving based on who is doing full-time waged work; they'd speak for the dignity and deserts of poor people doing different kinds and combinations of waged and unwaged work at different moments in their lives and in the vicissitudes of cities' and regions' labor markets. Such a coalition for poor Americans could build on one of the most striking progressive developments since the 1990s: organized labor's reversal of a century-old anti-immigrant politics and its increasingly firm embrace of racial inclusion.

Imagine a President Obama forced, like FDR, to make good on his promise to help organized labor with pro-union legislation, reducing the extraordinary costs and risks of union organizing today. As it did in the 1930s, such a climate-changing development might release the great pent-up demand for unions among low-wage workers. And an upsurge in militancy and mobilization in those quarters could enable a pro-poor progressive coalition to push President Obama some distance away from some of his neoliberal inclinations in the direction of more robust and inclusive redistributive reforms, much as FDR was pushed beyond some of his classic liberal instincts by the unbidden support of the Congress of Industrial Organizations (CIO).

Fortunately, while unions are invaluable, they are not the only way that reformers are fashioning good jobs out of bad ones. There are other novel schemes afoot for restructuring the low-wage labor market and blueprints for imagining framework statutes aimed at securing this most dauntingly difficult social right. Consider a statute that progressives love to hate: the 1996 Personal Responsibility and Work Opportunity Reconciliation Act, which ended welfare as we knew it. The act took millions of welfare recipients off the rolls, forced them into dead-end jobs, and did not enable most of them to raise themselves and their families out of poverty. It disbursed billions of dollars to the states to administer as they pleased. True, the statute demanded that states meet certain federal requirements, but these addressed time limits on welfare and numbers of welfare recipients taken off the rolls. The statute set no goals along the axis of "making work pay." It allowed but it did not require the states to use the grants to assist former welfare recipients heading off to the world of work. Some states squander the money by contracting workfare to private temp agencies that channel clients to the worst kind of unstable, dead-end jobs; others have diverted the money into general state funds; but others have used the grants in fruitful ways, supporting a great variety of public and private, for-profit and nonprofit agencies aimed at getting welfare clients not only off the rolls but out of poverty. So, more than a dozen years later, we have some experience with federally funded but locally fashioned workforce institutions that succeed in improving the job prospects and long-term career trajectories of poor Americans. Some of these new model workforce intermediaries serve particular cities, others particular industries. Some have brought community colleges together with employers to incorporate career ladders into welfare-to-work programs. Others focus on training and organizing as ways to secure self-sufficiency and strong floors under wages.

Imagine a revised PRWORA. It still would devolve authority over block grant resources to states and localities. But instead of targeting simple workforce participation rates or welfare roll reductions, it would set goals and incentives aimed at decent livelihoods and opportunities to advance. It would require states to monitor the performance of local agencies, benchmark their progress, and encourage the local agencies to share best practices, and it would provide for judicial remedies if the state administrators or the state legislatures were not meeting their obligations to monitor the performance of local workforce intermediaries and to respond in case poorly performing ones fail to improve. Courts would not have the authority to specify the goals and strategies for local workforce intermediaries, nor to monitor local agencies themselves: Those tasks are beyond courts. But courts could compel the state agencies to perform their functions or face the transfer of federal resources into simple living allowances and training, child care, and transportation vouchers for workfare clients, unless and until the state got its act together.

Conclusion

Those are quick sketches of some of the terrain on which movements and initiatives for social rights might reemerge in the reform climate produced by an Obama presidency. The welfare rights movement appeared at a moment when the private economy seemed to be producing decent jobs and a decent mix of public-private social provision for working-class Americans. Today is different.

An Obama presidency, we can hope, may bring substantial new job creation and new means for working families to draw decent incomes from Social Security during periods of unemployment, job training, and child or elder care. Against this backdrop, pro-poor advocates could make a different case, demanding the simple justice of extending to poor Americans the social rights enjoyed by everyone else. And they could build a coalition with the most dynamic sector of the labor movement, transformed since the 1960s. The blueprints are there. What is lacking is political will. Here, as elsewhere, creating that political will may be aided by the stories we tell and the constitutional past we remember and commit ourselves to redeeming.

Notes

1. Cass R. Sunstein, *The Second Bill of Rights: FDR's Unfinished Revolution and Why We Need It More Than Ever* 9 (Basic Books, 2004).

2. *Id.*

3. See William E. Forbath, *Caste, Class, and Equal Citizenship*, 98 Mich. L. Rev. 1 (1999).

4. See *id.*; William E. Forbath, *The New Deal Constitution in Exile*, 51 Duke L.J. 165 (2001); Forbath, *Constitutional Welfare Rights: A History, Critique and Reconstruction*, 69 Fordham L. Rev. 1821 (2001).

5. Franklin D. Roosevelt, Acceptance of the Renomination for the Presidency, Philadelphia, Pennsylvania, June 27, 1936, 5 Public Papers and Addresses of Franklin D. Roosevelt 234 (Samuel I. Rosenman, ed., 1938).

6. Franklin D. Roosevelt, *New Conditions Impose New Requirements upon Government and Those Who Conduct Government*, Campaign Address at the Commonwealth Club, San Francisco, Cal. (Sept. 23, 1932), in 1 Franklin D. Roosevelt, The Public Papers and Addresses of Franklin D. Roosevelt 742, 754.

7. 80 Cong. Rec. 9223 (1936) (statement of Sen. Henry Ashurst).

8. U.S. Nat'l Resources Planning Bd., Security, Work, and Relief Policies 508 (1942).

9. Franklin D. Roosevelt, Message to the Congress Reviewing the Broad Objectives and Accomplishments of the Administration (June 8, 1934), in 3 The Public Papers and Addresses of Franklin D. Roosevelt 291–92.

10. *Goldberg v. Kelly*, 397 U.S. 254, 264–65 (1970).

11. *Id.*

❧ 7 ❧

State Action in 2020

MARK TUSHNET

I N JANUARY 1969, "two determined ladies," as a federal judge later referred to them, went through the door of McSorley's Old Ale House in New York City's Greenwich Village, sat down at the bar, and asked to be served. The bartender refused, because McSorley's served only men. The women sued, claiming that opening the bar only to men violated their constitutional rights. They had a problem, though: The Constitution says that "no state shall deny" equal protection to anyone, but McSorley's was an ordinary bar, owned and operated by a corporation. How was the "state" denying the women equal protection? No problem, the judge said. The government's liquor authorities regulated bars so extensively that McSorley's decision to keep the women out amounted to "state action."[1]

The McSorley's case arose when the women's movement was pressing hard for bans on sex discrimination. The state-action issue has almost disappeared because no similar social movement has much interest—for the moment—in pressing corporations to conform to the Constitution's requirements. That may change, though, and the state-action issue may reappear on the constitutional radar screen. And when it does, how should we think about it? Basically, by replacing it with an inquiry into what the doctrine is actually about: What duties do governments have to us?

Suppose New York provides "vouchers" for children in nonpublic schools. The state imposes lots of requirements for schools to be eligible to receive vouchers: They have to pay their support staff the minimum wage, they have to recycle the waste they produce, they have to teach a specified number of core courses, they have to test their students regularly, and much more. Now, imagine a school affiliated with an evangelical church that qualifies for the program and has an explicit policy of refusing to employ mothers with preschool-age children as teachers, because of its belief, rooted in religion, that such women should spend their time with *their* children. The question is: Is the school's policy *unconstitutional?*[2]

A lawyer today, in the early twenty-first century, would address that question by asking first whether the school was a so-called state actor, because today the only entities that have to comply with the Constitution are such actors. Under today's doctrine, the answer is almost certainly, no, the school isn't a state actor. Knowing that, though, tells us close to nothing about how to think about what we should do about the school's policy. The state-action doctrine is profoundly misleading, distracting us from paying attention to what truly matters. It should be abandoned—as it almost had been by the late 1960s.

Consider an example that sometimes crops up in discussions of abortion. Suppose that children and adults have a constitutional right to life. The government would certainly violate that right if it adopted a policy of arbitrarily seizing people walking down the street and shooting them. But suppose the government has a policy of providing no police services whatever to some neighborhood. The predictable effect is obvious: The neighborhood becomes a free fire zone for (private) criminals. And innocent people lose their lives as a result of the policy. It's not hard to argue that the government's policy violates the assumed constitutional right to life—and that's true even though no government official actually shoots anyone. The assumed constitutional right to life imposes a duty on government to protect people from private depredation. More generally, take any situation you worry about, and you'll see that the government either has done something to cause the problem, or hasn't done something that would alleviate the problem. In one case, there's obvious state action; in the other, there's apparently no state action—but maybe there's a violation by the government of its constitutional duty to do something to address the problem.

The example shows that the state-action doctrine is not really about what the state does, but what it has a *duty* to do. The Constitution's language generates the state-action requirement, but the Constitution's substance tells us when the state has in fact acted unconstitutionally—and, in particular, when the state's failure to act is unconstitutional.

What should we pay attention to when we try to answer the right question? Let us return to the problem with which we began, the voucher-accepting school that won't hire mothers with young children, and we can see what matters:

1. Maybe the school has a right based on the Free Exercise Clause to accept vouchers *and* to enforce its religious views about what mothers should do. The school would, in effect, be claiming a right to operate within a zone of religious autonomy into which the government's regulatory authority couldn't enter. To figure out whether the school's free exercise claim is a good one, we'd have to think about—obviously—the Free Exercise Clause. Whether the school is a state actor or not would play no role in our thinking.[3]

2. Maybe the school's policy violates the rights of mothers with preschool-age children. Here, the first thing to notice is that such women have *statutory* as well as constitutional rights. New York certainly has an antidiscrimination law. It's just another of the regulatory requirements with which the school—here, like every other employer—has to comply. Suppose New York's antidiscrimination law treats the school's policy as an impermissible form of gender-based discrimination. The affected women's statutory rights are violated, and we shouldn't care much about whether their constitutional rights are violated as well.

(There are some lawyers' worries to note: The remedies available under state law for violating the antidiscrimination law might not be as good as the remedies available under federal law for violating constitutional rights, and it's hard to enforce violations of state antidiscrimination laws in federal courts, which may be more competent than state courts. But even if these lawyers' concerns have some substance, they clearly shouldn't have a large effect on our deliberations about what to do about the school's policy.)

The problem gets a little trickier if New York's antidiscrimination law simply doesn't address the question of whether the school's policy is impermissible discrimination based on gender. From the affected women's point of view, the question becomes: Does New York have a constitutional *duty* to treat the policy as gender-based discrimination? The question of constitutional duty can arise in a slightly different form. Remember that New York imposes lots of conditions—duties—on schools if they are to be eligible to receive vouchers. Even in the absence of a state antidiscrimination law, maybe New York has a constitutional duty to include a nondiscrimination provision among the conditions of eligibility.

We can see how the state-action doctrine is really about constitutional duties by looking at one important Warren Court decision. The case involved a coffee shop located in a parking structure owned by the city of Wilmington, Delaware. The city rented out the space for the coffee shop, which refused to serve African Americans (the case was decided in 1961, before the national Civil Rights Act of 1964 prohibited racial discrimination in places like the coffee shop). When it was sued for discriminating, the city's parking authority said that *it* wasn't discriminating, the coffee shop was. So, the city said, the state-action doctrine meant that it couldn't be held liable for the discriminatory acts of the coffee shop. The Supreme Court disagreed. The best way to understand the decision is that the city had a duty under the Constitution to include an antidiscrimination provision in the lease it gave to the coffee shop.

The usual form taken by litigation in which the state-action issue arises obscures the connection between the state-action doctrine and the idea of constitutional duty. The women sued McSorley's, not the state liquor authorities, but the form of the litigation didn't matter. As the judge understood, the case presented the question of the state's duty to require that those it regulates must serve everyone without regard to gender. If we're careful, the accidents of litigation form won't distract us from understanding that the state-action doctrine is about government's duties.

Our constitutional tradition recognizes relatively few constitutional duties: The government has a duty to provide lawyers for poor people it prosecutes for crimes; it has to provide fair procedures when it takes away a person's liberty or property; and maybe a few more. Mostly, we leave people alone to try to work out their problems within the framework of our law of contracts and property. Or, when we think that contracts or property law might not work well—because one side has too much more power than the other, for example, or because the people making the contracts might disregard the interests of others their decisions would affect—we let legislatures regulate what people do. The examples here are the minimum wage and environmental protection laws with which the voucher-accepting school has to comply. Beyond that, we aren't too comfortable with the idea of *constitutional* duties, that is, things governments have to do even if they don't want to. Still, the point here is that we know how to think about the question of whether there's a constitutional duty to treat the school's policy as gender-based discrimination. The question is an ordinary, everyday question of *substantive* constitutional law. Starting off by saying "Well, the school isn't a state actor" doesn't tell us anything about how to think about the substantive question of constitutional duty.

3. Things get even trickier if New York's legislature has made a deliberate decision to *exclude* policies like the school's from its antidiscrimination law, or if it has made a deliberate policy decision against requiring nondiscrimination as a condition of eligibility. Maybe we want to say, "Some states should be allowed to impose nondiscrimination requirements, while others can be free not to. That way, we'll capture one of the benefits of federalism—the knowledge we'll gain from observation about what sort of voucher programs and nondiscrimination laws work best."

This is what the state-action doctrine actually did when it was first applied. It protected a realm of discretionary policymaking at the state level from displacement by the national government. The *Civil Rights Cases* (1883) held the national Civil Rights Act of 1875 unconstitutional because it required hotels and theaters—private actors—to refrain from discriminating on the basis of race. The Court's fundamental problem with the statute was that it foreclosed states from adopting varying policies with respect to discrimination. At its origin, the state-action doctrine was a federalism doctrine.

Times have changed. We know that the national government does indeed have the power to require that hotels and theaters refrain from racial discrimination—at least when it acts through national *legislation*. So, today, the state-action doctrine doesn't preserve a domain within which state legislatures are free to experiment. Instead, the state-action doctrine has become a tool for judicial restraint. It tells the courts that—sometimes—they should not interpret the Constitution to impose duties on states. The reason for this caution has to be fairly complicated. The basic idea has to be that imposing duties truncates the process of learning from experience that is one of federalism's benefits. But, because Congress can truncate that learning process, the state-action doctrine has to rest on some idea that Congress is better than the courts in figuring out when we've learned enough to know that it's a good idea to impose a specific statutory duty on places like schools getting vouchers.

The important point here is that saying that the school is not a state actor tells us nothing about whether the policy area with which we're concerned—here, antidiscrimination law and its application to schools that get vouchers—is one that would benefit from continued experimentation. Or, put another way, saying that the school is not a state actor should be the *conclusion* of the inquiry, not its starting point—a label we apply once we've decided that this is an area where experimentation remains valuable until Congress decides otherwise.

The state-action doctrine thus contributes nothing but obfuscation to constitutional analysis. It substitutes an inquiry into the status of some legal entity for an examination of that entity's substantive constitutional rights, or for an examination of whether a state legislature or the Congress has a constitutional duty to protect somebody's interests, or for an examination of the benefits (and costs) of giving legislatures discretion to adopt or refrain from adopting particular policies in specific policy areas. Every state-action decision can be translated into these substantive terms, and doing so clarifies precisely what is at stake.

Why, then, does the state-action doctrine persist? Today's state-action doctrine is largely the reinvention of the Burger and Rehnquist courts of a doctrine initiated by the reactionary post-Reconstruction Supreme Court. As Charles Black observed in 1967, at that time—a few years before Warren Burger became chief justice—the state-action doctrine was something of a bogeyman, a rhetorical device invoked (unsuccessfully) to scare people from using the federal courts to protect the interests of African Americans.[4]

Why would anyone think that the state-action doctrine might scare people away from enforcing constitutional rights or imposing constitutional duties? Again, the place to begin is the Constitution's language. When a criminal thug beats you up, everybody knows that the thug "acted" against you. It's harder to see what the government "did" to hurt you. Consider again the problem of litigation form. The thug's behind bars, and you sue the city council and police chief. They say, "Wait a minute. *We* didn't beat you over the head with a pipe; the criminal, who we've put in jail, did that. What's your problem?" That response to your lawsuit has a certain superficial appeal—but only until you make it clear that you're not suing them for beating you up but for failing to satisfy the constitutional duty you say they have to provide you with adequate protection against thugs.

The state-action doctrine might work as a bogeyman because it appeals to a vaguely libertarian sense that Americans have about the proper relation between them and their government. By saying that the Constitution applies only to governments, and not to private businesses or ordinary Americans, the doctrine seems to send the message that there's a domain of freedom into which the Constitution doesn't reach. Of course, freedoms can be exercised in morally distasteful ways, but— according to this view of the state-action doctrine—that's simply one of the costs of preserving freedom, which is itself one of the most fundamental goals of our constitutional system.

Unfortunately, the libertarian sense associated with the state-action doctrine is completely illusory because, as we have seen, state legislatures and the Congress can invade the domain of freedom purportedly carved out by the state-action doctrine. We might well want to preserve a domain of freedom, but the state-action doctrine doesn't do it. What does preserve our (competing) domains of freedom are the substantive constitutional rights we have, like the Free Exercise Clause the school might be able to invoke successfully. Switching our rhetoric from the state-action doctrine to substantive constitutional law would actually improve our understanding of the domains of freedom the Constitution protects.

The state-action doctrine serves another rhetorical function, and this one may be more important than the faux libertarian one. The Constitution in the early twenty-first century doesn't impose many duties on government, which is why plaintiffs lose state-action cases. Some ordinary people might be surprised and dismayed to learn that the government actually doesn't have a constitutional duty to protect them. Saying that a lawsuit actually seeking to enforce a constitutional duty failed not because there was no such duty but because there was no state action might provide cover for the disquiet we might feel if we were told that there was indeed no constitutional duty.

Consider here the famous case of Joshua DeShaney. Joshua was a young boy whose parents divorced. The divorce decree gave custody to Joshua's father, who turned out to be a violent, physically abusive parent. The father's abusive acts came to the attention of the state's child protective services agency, which conducted a superficial investigation and decided against intervening to protect Joshua. After a particularly savage beating left Joshua with enormous and permanent physical impairments, his guardian sued the protective services agency, claiming that *it* had violated Joshua's constitutional rights. The Supreme Court ordered that the suit be dismissed, invoking the state-action doctrine.

What was at stake in the DeShaney case? Obviously, no one was contending that Joshua's right not to be beaten by government officials was violated. Rather, the claim was that the government had failed to comply with a constitutional duty to protect Joshua from his father. A lot of Americans probably think that the very point of having a government is to ensure that someone—the police—will be available to help them when someone else threatens their physical security. That is, lots of people probably think that there's a constitutional duty to provide protection against physical violence inflicted by criminal thugs.

Maybe the Constitution shouldn't "require the State to protect the life, liberty, and property of its citizens against invasion by private actors," as the Court said in the DeShaney case. A more recent case shows why. This case involved another of the all-too-common incidents of violence against children in connection with divorce. Jessica Gonzales got a restraining order against her estranged husband, Simon, which directed that he stay away from their three daughters, except at prearranged times. Early one evening and without prearrangement, Simon picked the girls up as they were playing outside their house. A couple of hours later, Jessica called the police, showed them the restraining order, and demanded that the officers find the children and return them to her. The officers did nothing, even though the restraining order contained a notice to law enforcement officers saying, in capital letters, "You shall use every reasonable means to enforce this restraining order. You shall arrest...the restrained person when you have information amounting to probable cause that the restrained person has violated or attempted to violate any provision of this order." Jessica called the police again three hours later and was told to wait until midnight. When midnight arrived, Jessica again called, and then, an hour later, she went to the police station to file a formal complaint. At 3 a.m., Simon showed up at the police station with a semiautomatic handgun he had bought after he picked the girls up. He fired at the police; they fired back and killed him. When they went to his pickup truck, the police discovered the bodies of the three girls, whom Simon had killed.

Jessica sued the city for violating what she said was its constitutional duty to protect her and her children, a duty created by the restraining order's statement that the police "shall" arrest her husband if he violated it. The U.S. Supreme Court disagreed. The restraining order didn't give Jessica or the children any rights beyond the ones Joshua DeShaney had. But, at the end of the Court's opinion, Justice Antonin Scalia observed that Jessica and the children might have rights under *state* law that had been violated by the inaction of the police officers to whom Jessica complained.

That observation signals the complexity of the question of constitutional duty, and why sometimes we ought to leave the question of duty up to state legislatures to figure out. Impose a duty on the child protective services agency in the DeShaney case or on the police in the Gonzales case, and they may intervene too frequently, disrupting difficult but not physically threatening relations between parents and their children. Indeed, sometimes, the intervention might actually violate an independent constitutional right to family privacy—akin to the voucher-accepting school's claim that requiring it to hire mothers of young children violates its free exercise rights. So, this may be an area where legislatures are better at working out the policy implications of enforcing a statutory duty to intervene than the courts would be in imposing a constitutional duty.

And here another rhetorical function of the state-action doctrine comes in. It allows courts to pretend that they are enforcing rights rather than balancing competing constitutional interests. Indeed, figuring out whether there is or should be a constitutional duty of a particular sort *should* be a quite difficult task, and it's not clear why courts should do it all the time. Sometimes, the answer will be clear, as it was to the courts that decided the McSorley's and coffee shop cases. Sometimes, the answer may be less clear, as it was to the Rehnquist Court with respect to government duties to intervene against domestic violence. The crucial point, though, is that we ought to be trying to figure out what the government's constitutional duties are. The state-action doctrine distracts us by directing that we look at the status of particular entities, to find out whether they are "state actors" or "private actors." We would be well rid of it.

Notes

1. A similar restriction has been read into constitutional provisions dealing with the national government. So, the state-action doctrine probably should be called the "government action" doctrine, but the existing terminology is well established.

2. Let's assume that allowing church-related schools to accept vouchers doesn't violate the Constitution.

3. As we'll see immediately, the school's free exercise rights would have to be balanced against whatever rights mothers have. Saying that the school is not a state actor does not eliminate the need to engage in that balancing.

4. Charles L. Black, Jr., *Foreword: "State Action," Equal Protection, and California's Proposition 14*, 81 Harv. L. Rev. 69 (1967).

❧ 8 ❧

The Missing Jurisprudence
of the Legislated Constitution

ROBIN WEST

D OES THE FOURTEENTH Amendment and its Equal Protection Clause—the promise that "no state shall deny equal protection of the laws"—have any relevance to the progressive
project of reducing economic inequality in various spheres of life or, more
modestly, of ameliorating the multiple vulnerabilities of this country's
poor people? The short answer, I believe, is, it depends. It will depend,
in 2020, just as it depends now, on what we mean by the Constitution we
are expounding: the Constitution as read and interpreted by courts—
the adjudicated Constitution—or what I propose to call the legislated
Constitution, the Constitution looked to by the conscientious legislator
as he or she seeks to fulfill her political obligations. My claim in this
chapter is that the legislated, rather than the adjudicated, Constitution
can more plausibly be read as guaranteeing an equality that is supportive
of progressive goals rather than in tension with them. Programmatically,
I will suggest that progressive lawyers should take this opportunity of
their respite from judicial power and attend to the development of that
Constitution, so that we might at some point in the future urge fidelity
to it on the part of our representatives, rather than continue to attend,
with the same intense devotion that still characterizes our current legal
zeitgeist, to the adjudicated Constitution.

The very coherence of a "legislated Constitution," however, depends upon an accompanying jurisprudence (or, awkwardly, legisprudence), and that is a jurisprudence that is currently entirely missing from even the most utopian constitutional theorizing. I will conclude by suggesting what that jurisprudence might look like and what its creation, or rediscovery, will require.

Equality and the Adjudicated Constitution

The question before us in this chapter is whether the Fourteenth Amendment's guarantee of equality implies the existence of social or economic welfare rights, and consequently mandates some level of congressional or state legislative intervention, so as to give those rights substance. Now, as a matter of doctrine, this question is almost absurd. Doctrinally, it is as clear as these things can ever possibly be that the Equal Protection Clause, as expounded by courts, carries no such meaning.[1] What the "equal protection" promised by the Fourteenth Amendment requires, according to the Supreme Court's interpretive gloss, is a limited right to be free of the legislator's casual or malign discriminatory instincts toward specified groups, as expressed in laws that unequally discriminate for irrational reasons against those groups' members. The vague phrase "equal protection" is thereby given a specific, and narrow, content: The point of the clause is not a broad guarantee of protection (equal or otherwise) against various unstated evils or harms—such as private violence, or natural catastrophe, or war, or poverty, or economic subordination, or any other interference with welfare—but rather, a guarantee of protection against pernicious laws and lawmakers that irrationally discriminate against some group of citizens, when and if such affirmative government services are offered. The modifier "equal," on this reading, is reduced to a limited guarantee of legislative rationality. The point of the clause is not to render various groups equal, but to render them, if various conditions are met, equal beneficiaries of some governmental actions, and then only if the inequality is a function of irrational discriminatory animus. All of this has been much criticized by the Court's critics.

What's gone relatively unnoticed, however, or at least unremarked upon, in the course of the development of this judicial interpretation is the fate of the two-letter preposition in the phrase "equal protection of the laws." The "of" in the phrase "of the laws," again in the Court's reading of the amendment, is replaced by the preposition "against." We are not, under the judicial construction of the phrase, entitled to equal protection *of* the law, or *of* the state, or *of* the lawmaker, in virtually any sense. We are, rather, somewhat entitled to equal protection *against* law—or at least, some of us are sometimes protected against one kind of bad law, and that is a law that is bad because it irrationally discriminates on the basis of a short list of specified characteristics, such as race, ethnicity, sex, or religious affiliation. That transformation of the clause's meaning—from "equal protection *of* law" to "equal protection *against* law"—has been hugely consequential. The Fourteenth Amendment, intended, perhaps, as a guarantor of the benefits of law to those who had previously not enjoyed its protections, has become, instead, a guarantor against legalistic malfeasance. Law itself, on this formal understanding, rather than being construed as a blessing to be bestowed equally on all citizens, is construed as an evil, against which the Constitution stands guard.

What has this formal rather than substantive understanding of equality meant, in practice, for the country's poor? To be sure, it is not nothing—poor people are sometimes irrationally discriminated against by legislators.[2] But as a weapon for combating poverty itself, the promise of formal equality is baldly illusory. It is not, after all, *poverty* that is targeted by an antidiscrimination principle, even if such a principle can be read capaciously so as to prohibit discrimination against the poor. It is, rather, the irrational failure to grant poor individuals goods or privileges where that grant would be forthcoming but for the individual's impoverishment, and is being denied for no good reason. It is the failure, in effect, to spot the diamond in the rough, and to give the diamond his due; it is not the nickel-and-dimed living conditions of those persons—whether they are diamonds or not—who actually live in the rough, which is targeted by formal, rather than substantive, equality. For the occasional diamond so uncovered, this might be substantial protection indeed. For poor people in general, however, this is nothing—no protection at all.

An argument can surely be made that the Court's displacement of the "of" with "against," in the phrase "equal protection of law," as well as the formal understanding of equality that follows from it, is more than a little in tension with the Fourteenth Amendment's plain meaning, language, logic, and noncontroversial history. The amendment doesn't say that all citizens are granted a right to equal protection *from* law or *against* law; it says that all citizens are granted a right to the equal protection *of* law. Laws, and the states and legislators that produce them, are constructed by the most natural meaning of the amendment as being on the whole rather good things that states ought to bestow equally, so as to protect people from some evil or harm from which they might suffer in the absence of law's protection. It doesn't posit law itself as the evil against which individuals need protection. Rather, the *absence* of law is constructed by the most natural meaning of that sentence, as being the bad thing from which citizens must be protected. By the amendment's language, it is the absence of law, not the discriminatory law, which is conducive to the conditions against which states have a duty to protect us. Furthermore, states, by the plain language of the amendment, must affirmatively do something; thus, it seems to be state *in*action, not state action, which is unconstitutional. One thing states must do is protect people, and they must do it, furthermore, through affirmative acts of lawmaking.

Why, then, has the Supreme Court so steadfastly abided by its formal understanding of equality, which is so seemingly belied by the history and language itself?[3] Why, indeed, has it failed to even *acknowledge* these claims?[4] It seems to me that there are three possibilities. One possibility, suggested by a number of scholars, is institutional. The Court wants to require only what it can confidently enforce, and while it can mandate that irrational and discriminatory laws be struck—that action is relatively costless—it simply can't enforce a broad antisubordinationist or welfare-based understanding of equality upon unwilling state actors.[5] A second possibility—and this is more in line with the foundational assumption of the American Constitutional Society (ACS)—is that the Court has chosen this particular doctrinal path, as well as a number of others over the last half century, for essentially political and ideological reasons. I am dubious: I don't think this is a plausible account of the last half century of judicial practice.

Let me suggest a somewhat different explanation for the Court's attraction to formal equality and its hostility to substantive understandings of equality. At least a part of the story regarding the Court's insistence on a formal rather than substantive understanding of equality might be jurisprudential, rather than either political or institutional. Look at one striking feature of the formal meaning of equality embraced by the Court, which has gone relatively unexamined in scholarly literature: the degree to which the formal understanding of the constitutional equality guarantee—that legislators must treat likes alike, differences differently, and must more or less rationally ascertain those differences—echoes, in fact, perfectly mirrors, judicial understanding of the requirements of stare decisis, of the meaning of precedent, of the meaning of legal justice, of the rule of law, and so forth. Judges, when deciding virtually all cases, *must* treat likes alike and rationally discern differences, and they must do so, furthermore, toward the end of doing justice. Perhaps unsurprisingly, given this understanding of the meaning of justice, given our history of irrational racism emanating from legislatures, and given an incredibly wide degree of interpretive latitude, the twentieth-century Supreme Court wound up reading the equality provision of the Fourteenth Amendment as imposing the same legalistic requirement on legislators that it imposes on itself. Legislators, if subject to a mandate of equal treatment, no less than judges, and subject to the mandate of the rule of law, must treat like groups alike, just as judges must treat like litigants alike. Legislators should only differentiate between groups for good reasons and not bad, just as judges should only differentiate between litigants and cases for good reasons and not bad. Both branches should do so, furthermore, toward the end of maintaining as much continuity as possible, not creating disruption between the past and the present. The meaning of the "equality" to be required of legislators, but interpreted by judges, is thus overlaid with the judges' own understanding of the equality they require of themselves. Equal protection of the law in the judicial context clearly requires like treatment of likes; this is, again, the shared judicial understanding of what equality under law means. "Equal protection of law" in the legislative context, but as interpreted by judges, requires no less, but also no more.

My claim is that it is this overlay of the demands of adjudicative rationality (or nondiscrimination) on the mandate of equality that the Constitution imposes on legislatures that has perversely limited the substantive scope of the mandate. Constitutional equality, on the Court's reading, requires that legislators behave rationally, just as stare decisis, precedent, and the rule of law require that judges do likewise, and it does so toward the end of conserving and preserving the institutions of the past with as little disruption as possible. Equality, so says the Court, requires no more. It does not require that legislators undertake legislation to reduce the substantive economic inequality between persons or groups of persons. It does not require that legislators use law to protect anyone from anything. It does not require that law be the means by which social or economic equality is guaranteed, or comes to pass, or at least becomes more likely than not. It requires only that when legislators legislate, they do so rationally. It targets law itself as the evil that frustrates equality, rather than inequality as the evil against which we might sensibly seek out law's protection. It does so not because the language requires this reading or the history suggests it. If anything, the language and history both require something considerably more capacious. It does so because of judicial, jurisprudential habit. Legal equality, from a judicial point of view, means the rational differentiation of cases toward the end of like treatment. Constitutional equality, then, from a judicial point of view, imposes that adjudicative understanding of the equal protection they are constitutionally obligated to deliver—and notably, *only* that adjudicative understanding of the equal protection they are constitutionally required to deliver—on legislators.

It seems to me that this overlay—of a judicial understanding of what equality requires of judges onto a constitutional understanding of what the constitutional guarantee of equality requires of legislators—is not a lousy coincidence or an unfortunate verbal pun. Nor is it, in my view, a correctable doctrinal mistake. Formal equality is the jurisprudential ideal at the heart of the meaning of adjudicative law.[6] Treating likes alike is what judges do when they are doing their jobs morally and doing them well. Put that judicial ideal together with an undeniable social fact, to wit, that courts, as well as the larger legal culture, have rendered the Constitution, and constitutional law, a child of adjudicative law. The conclusion for the constitutional meaning of equality is overdetermined: It is a perfectly natural inference that the equality guaranteed by that body of adjudicative law, in the eyes of judges, is the equality guaranteed by adjudicative law quite generally. Formal equality is, therefore, from the pens and minds of judges, the limit of the equality required of legislators when they are enacting law.

The consequence of all of this is strikingly hostile to the very idea of affirmative welfare rights (in any of its various incarnations). Legislative irrationality, not worldly inequality, becomes the target of the guarantee of equality when equality is rendered formal. Law becomes the evil addressed through the constitutional guarantee, rather than the means by which the guarantee is made real. To provide equal protection, the legislator must behave rationally, meaning, in line with the directives suggested by current social reality, just as the judge, if she is to decide cases in accordance with the rule of law, must do so in a way that is rational and consistent with, rather than at odds with, the past. By insisting that the Equal Protection Clause means, basically, a promise of rationality in legislation, the Court has judicialized the legislator, at least with respect to equality: It has made him a mini-judge. The only ideals to which we hold him are the ideals and the constraints of judging: rationality in categorization and fidelity to the past. We limit to the vanishing point his understanding of his very purpose being that of transformation, or change, through law; limit to the vanishing point his understanding that the substantive equality that might be delivered through law might be part of his constitutional project, rather than law being the poison that frustrates equality. The Equal Protection Clause, read formally, emasculates the legislator from being an agent of effective change. The Equal Protection Clause, read formally, as a mandate that legislators as well as judges must rationally align their actions with the contours of social reality, has become an obstacle, not a vehicle, of progressive, egalitarian politics.

What does this portend for the future? Well, if the attraction to a formal rather than substantive understanding of equality is indeed a function of jurisprudential self-understanding, rather than institutional necessity or doctrinal mistake, then it is going to be next to impossible to dislodge. Quite generally, in law, if not in life, the past is indeed prologue. In all of adjudicatory law, but particularly in constitutional law, the past is read so as to better define and delimit the future. In fact, that's its point. That is just what judge-made law aims to do—to nail down the future, so to speak, to preordain it, to render it a known fact, rather than an unknown variable, an inchoate possibility. Perhaps for good-enough reasons, perhaps not, courts honor the past: Integrity and consistency have real moral weight. The past has substantial authority. That's the point of the entire enterprise; it is central to judicial identity. In the constitutional context, furthermore, the moral weight of the past is magnified: The courts will be even less willing to overturn or depart from an understanding of equality that is as central to a judicialized understanding of the ideal of law itself as is their interpretation of formal equality. They might tinker at the margins, but they are not going to ever depart from its core content. Partly for this reason, I believe, progressives should not look to the courts, even to idealized counterfactual courts staffed with judges appointed by the Obama-Biden administration of 2008, for either programmatic solutions to problems of economic and social injustice or even for more limited declarations of principle on which other institutional actors might act.

None of this, however, closes the door on the questions posed at the outset of this chapter regarding the true meaning of constitutionalism and the future of constitutional development. Obviously, the Equal Protection Clause may require minimal social justice, even though the Court has never held as much. I'm not suggesting for a moment that we turn our backs on the Constitution as a source of moral authority for a future War on Poverty or, more generally, as a cultural mandate to achieve a more egalitarian society in the twenty-first century. It does mean, though, that the American Constitution Society should at least entertain the possibility that courts might be jurisprudentially incapable of seeing in the Constitution a range of meanings that are quite self-evidently there, including a mandate of economic justice. What follows is that we need to ask whether the Constitution, or the constitutions, that might be developed outside the walls of courts might be fruitfully aligned with progressive activism against poverty, even if the adjudicated Constitution is not promising.

Equality and the Legislated Constitution

So, let me turn to what I call the legislated Constitution—by which I mean simply the Constitution that legislators are duty-bound to uphold. Instead of imagining a liberal judge in 2020, let's go whole hog and imagine an enlightened, or at least conscientious, idealized legislator. That legislator, state or federal, wants to do her moral, political, and constitutional duty by the citizenry. That legislator reads the Constitution and sees there a mandate that "no state shall deny equal protection of the law." For that legislator, the Constitution carries a direct, linguistically untortured command: The state must provide something, and what it must provide is equal protection of law.

How is this to be interpreted? It seems to me that there is a more natural fit between the well-understood political ideals of conscientious legislators, going back to the time of the ancient Greeks, and a foundational, constitutional commitment that the sovereign act in such a way as to equally protect the well-being of all and that it do so, in part, through the recognition of positive rights. The conscientious legislator is or ought to be accustomed to the idea that she acts so as to effect a change in social reality. Her ideal for moral action—what it means for her to legislate—is for that reason alone more consistent with a Constitution that requires, in the name of equal protection of all, substantial intervention into extant social reality, so as to address social and economic inequality. Just this bare minimum fit between commonly understood ideals of the art of legislation and the idea of positive rights contrasts pretty sharply with the position of even the conscientious judge of 2020 with the best moral and political values imaginable. There is just no such easy fit, and in fact it is an awkward fit at best and maybe no fit at all between the understood purpose of adjudication, particularly in the constitutional context, and a foundational commitment to act in such a way as to employ law so as to protect all and to protect equally. The judge acts on the basis of principle toward the articulation of a body of law the purposes of which—read generously—are to build continuity with the past, hold legislation and legislators at bay, and enforce individual rights to be free of overreaching or irrational law. He does not act on the basis of a concern for the well-being of all nor toward the end of protecting the well-being of all against unspecified evils, whether equally or otherwise.

The legislator, unlike the judge, does not and should not view her act as an attempt to secure an uninterrupted fidelity to the past, nor to avoid disruption, nor to maximize individual freedom by holding the legislator at bay, nor to uncover and articulate otherwise opaque legal rules through the analogical method of uncovering the rational like treatment of likes and then papering it with a carefully verbalized generality. The legislator, rather, *un*like the judge, presumably acts—legislates—in order to change a status quo; she does not act—adjudicate—in order to further cement and further rationalize extant social relations. The legislator, unlike the judge, ought to realize that the work of legislating must be directed toward the protection of the interests of all citizens against various evils or harms—and that her constitutional obligation, therefore, is to legislate in such a way so that protection is bestowed equally, rather than view her work as that of thwarting legislation toward the end of securing individualized rights. The conscientious legislator, at least, might be legitimately convinced that the duty to legislate in such a way as to protect the interests of all includes not only a duty to protect against the threat of foreign invasion and not only a duty to protect legal entitlements bestowed by the common law, but also, given our particular history, constitutional and otherwise, a duty to protect against exploitation and the subordination that can follow it. Likewise, given our economic and constitutional history, such a legislator might be persuaded that the evils to be protected against, by law, bestowed equally, include the evils that are the side-product of unbridled capitalism, as evidenced by the twentieth century's legislative interventions: the labor legislation of the New Deal, the civil rights codes of the 1960s, the environmental legislation of the '70s, the anti-age and disability discrimination acts of the '80s, and so on. Indeed, if we reverse our habitual identification of the core of constitutional law as consisting of a collection of judicial decisions, and look instead at legislative decisions made either pursuant to constitutional mandate or in part inspired by constitutional ideals as the core of constitutional law, then it becomes quite clear that the conscientious legislator has, at more than a few moments in the history of twentieth-century constitutional law, viewed her moral obligation and the constitutional mandate under which she works in just this way.

So, a substantive understanding of the Fourteenth Amendment's grand phrases is more consistent with the goals of legislation than goals of adjudication. At least, there is not the glaring inconsistency between the most natural reading of those clauses and the ideals and practical constraints of the legislature as there is with respect to adjudication. The lawmaker must act in such a way as to provide equal protection *of the law* to all. He must legislate in such a manner that all are equally protected against the harms that can be deterred or prevented through law. The constitutional mandate, understood as a directive to the lawmaker, rather than the adjudicator, concerns the ways in which law should or could be used in order to promote the equal protection of all. Understood this way, the Equal Protection Clause is not about protecting people from the product of legislation. It is about how to use legislation to protect people from other evils. Understood this way, at least this part of the Constitution constructs law, in other words, as a rather good thing, all things considered. Law is the means by which the constitutional entitlement is secured, rather than the evil against which the constitutional entitlement guards us. The lawmaker is the agent of the constitutional protection, rather than an irrational, whimsical, overly emotional or impassioned, frenzied, possibly corrupt, undoubtedly racist, homophobic, misogynist, vengeful, interest-obsessed, swashbuckling boozer, from whom the lonely and noble individual, in his rights-bearing glory, quite sensibly seeks protection.

Let me finish by suggesting what would be required, jurisprudentially, to make the promise of the equality guaranteed by the legislated Constitution coherent. We don't currently have a constitutional jurisprudence that supports even the existence, much less the coherence, of the legislated Constitution. We have, instead, a jurisprudence overwhelmingly committed to three definitional and foundational propositions, which, when taken together, virtually foreclose any possibility of developing a legislated Constitution. The first proposition: Law is, definitionally, some combination of that to which courts turn, when making law, and that which courts make when deciding cases, but either way, it is a part of the adjudicative, not the legislative, process. Second: The Constitution is law. Combining these two yields the third: The Constitution, as law, is to be interpreted by courts, and apparently exclusively so.

To develop a legislated Constitution, we would have to upset that conventional apple cart—which should not be all that hard to do. None of these definitional equivalencies are required by our constitutional history. Yes, the Supremacy Clause identifies the Constitution as law, but it does not define law as being "whatever courts say"—that came a hundred years later. When Chief Justice John Marshall declared in

Marbury v. Madison that it is the Court's role to say what "the law" is, he was, at least according to a growing number of historians, referring to the Court's duty to state the content of ordinary law. This duty to state the content of ordinary law does indeed require an inquiry into the constitutionality of legislative or common-law pronouncements. It doesn't follow, however, from either the Supremacy Clause or Marshall's utterance that the Court is the only, the ultimate, or the primary interpreter of constitutional meaning. The Constitution, in other words, is a part of the judicial inquiry into what ordinary legislated or common law *is*, and it is the Court's duty to state what that ordinary law is. The Constitution, however, might also be part of the legislative inquiry into what the ordinary law *should be*. If so, then it is the legislature's duty to act accordingly. In short, neither the Supremacy Clause nor Marshall's dictum, nor the two taken jointly, preclude the constitutional possibility, or the constitutional necessity, of a legislated Constitution—a developed body of statutory law that, with accompanying secondary literature, articulates the meaning of constitutional guarantees as understood and implemented by legislating bodies.

So where does this leave us? The historical work that needs to be done to sustain the case for the legislated Constitution is well under way. But, with respect to the jurisprudence needed to sustain the legislated Constitution, the work is not yet happening. Such a constitutional legisprudence would consist of four largely forgotten, though certainly not novel claims. First, it would require the development (or recapture) of an ancient understanding of the idea of "law" or, more specifically, of "natural law," as consisting of a set of moral imperatives that can and ought to guide the art of legislation, rather than as a set of moral imperatives that, at most, constrain legislation. Second, it would require an understanding of "constitutional law" as part of that law. We lost that at the mid-twentieth-century mark, when we began to understand Justice Marshall's ambiguous declaration in *Marbury* that the Court's duty is to say "what the law is" as an unambiguous declaration that it is the Court's duty to say what constitutional law requires of law. Third, it would require an understanding of the state as under a moral duty, a legal duty, and a constitutional duty to act in the interest of all, and not just a prohibition against acting in certain discriminatory ways. We lost that understanding, I believe, dating from the mid-twentieth-century's civil rights successes—with that period's profound distrust of state actors and its correlative sense that legalist ideals can only be achieved through constraining, rather than guiding, the legislator's hand. Fourth, it would require an understanding of law's point or purpose as being the protection of people from the oppressions of each other, and not just protection of the individual from the state. We lost that dating from the commencement of our "civil libertarian" tradition, which has been given a boost by reproductive and sexual freedom cases since the 1970s.

I hope that the American Constitutional Society, in its deliberations between now and 2020, will attend to the need to develop a jurisprudence that might support the legislated Constitution. Without it—without an understanding of what the Constitution requires the legislator to do, instead of only an understanding of what the Constitution forbids; without an understanding of the positive value of law, instead of only an understanding of its dangers; without an understanding of what, morally, a conscientious legislator must do in order to fulfill his or her distinctly political obligations when acting as a free and moral agent—the very basic claim of this society that constitutionalism supports the progressive hope of creating a more equal and less treacherous world hovers between the radically counterfactual and the flatly oxymoronic. The Constitution, interpreted by courts as ordinary law, will yield precious little by way of progress albeit quite a bit by way of law.

With such jurisprudence in place, we could at least begin to make sense of the specific claim that the Equal Protection Clause might actually require a congressional, legislated response to substantive inequality. More largely, we might begin to make sense of the very grand claim of the ACS that progressive politics is somehow supported by, or required by, or at least not antithetical to, constitutional mandates, properly understood. With such a jurisprudence in place, the platform of the American Constitutional Society might become a matter of common sense.

Notes

1. *United States v. Morrison*, 529 U.S. 598 (2000) (holding that the Equal Protection Clause does not require protection against violence); *Washington v. Davis*, 426 U.S. 229 (1976) (stating that the Equal Protection Clause does not require substantive racial equality); *San Antonio Indep. Sch. Dist. v. Rodriguez*, 411 U.S. 1 (1973) (holding that the Equal Protection Clause does not require a public education).

2. See, e.g., *Shapiro v. Thompson*, 394 U.S. 618 (1969) (stating that the burdens of differential welfare requirements regarding residency are an unconstitutional infringement on the right to travel); *Harper v. Virginia Bd. of Elections*, 383 U.S. 663 (1966) (deeming the poll tax on voting unconstitutional).

3. The historical argument that the Equal Protection Clause was intended to target state inaction rather than state action, and accordingly constructs positive rights to protection rather than negative rights against irrational legislation, was first made in the legal literature in Jacobus TenBroek, *Equal Protection under Law* (rev. ed., 1965). I've elaborated on the argument in the text regarding welfare rights in particular in Robin

West, *Progressive Constitutionalism: Reconstructing the Fourteenth Amendment* (1994); West, *Is Progressive Constitutionalism Possible?* 4 Widener L.J. (1999); and West, *Rights, Capabilities, and the Good Society*, 69 Fordham L. Rev. 1901 (2001).

4. The Court has also rejected other arguments for the protection of poor people through the Equal Protection Clause. See Peter Edelman, *The Next Century of Our Constitution: Rethinking Our Duty to the Poor*, 39 Hastings L.J. 1 (1987); Frank Michelman, *Foreword: On Protecting the Poor through the Fourteenth Amendment*, 83 Harv. L. Rev. 7 (1969); Michelman, *In Pursuit of Constitutional Welfare Rights: One View of Rawls' Theory of Justice*, 121 U. Pa. L. Rev. 962 (1973).

5. See Lawrence Sager, *Fair Measure: The Legal Status of Underenforced Constitutional Norms*, 91 Harv. L. Rev. 1212 (1978).

6. For an example of a full-blown political and legal philosophy built on this claim, see Ronald Dworkin's work, particularly *Law's Empire* (1986); *A Matter of Principle* (1985); and *Taking Rights Seriously* (1978). For a narrower explication of the role of analogical reasoning in judicial decision making, see Cass Sunstein, *On Analogical Reasoning* 106 Harv. L. Rev. 741 (1993). For a somewhat sympathetic and somewhat critical reading, see Judith Shklar, *Legalism: Law, Morals, and Political Trials* (1964).

Remembering How to Do Equality

JACK M. BALKIN AND REVA B. SIEGEL

D ECADES AGO, EQUAL protection law helped to bring about great transformations in the status of African Americans, women, and other subordinated groups. Today, constitutional equality doctrine is too often employed by a conservative judiciary to preserve the status quo. To restore a progressive constitutional vision, we need to understand how equality law was hijacked in the first place. And we need to remember the doctrinal tools that courts *and* legislatures employed to vindicate equality norms in the civil rights era. Refreshing our collective memory will help us imagine the shape of the next reconstruction.

Redemptive Constitutionalism

The Reconstruction era amendments were aptly named; they were truly reconstructive. Their framers sought to make equal citizens of newly freed slaves. The great purpose of the Fourteenth Amendment was trans-formative: "to put the citizens of the several States on an equality with each other as to all fundamental rights" and to "abolish...all class leg-islation in the States and do...away with the injustice of subjecting one caste of persons to a code not applicable to another."[1] The amendment's framers believed that all members of the political community were entitled to equal freedom, that law should not be used to create or maintain social caste, and that law should not single out groups for special burdens or benefits unrelated to important public purposes—the prohibition on so-called class legislation. Congress viewed itself as the first line of defense for these constitutional values. In section 5, Congress gave itself not only the power but also the responsibility to protect and enforce the Fourteenth Amendment's guarantees of equal citizenship.

The Fourteenth Amendment grew out of generations of abolitionist criticism of the founders' Constitution for its failure fully to guarantee basic rights and equality for all members of the political community. The amendment was an act of redemptive constitutionalism; it claimed to fulfill the greater purposes of the Constitution and the Declaration of Independence. The same constitutional text that made former slaves full citizens still demands equal freedom for all, announcing its commitments in a language of general applicability that each inheriting generation must decide how to honor.

When Americans make new claims on the Fourteenth Amendment, they reenact its origins. They invoke the amendment's text—as well as the Declaration—to dramatize the gap between our ideals and our practices. Sometimes, courts respond to these claims and help vindicate the amendment's transformative commitments, while at other times courts resist. Each generation builds on previous interpretations, preserving some and challenging others, with the goal of realizing equal freedom in its own time.

The post-ratification history of the Fourteenth Amendment is rich with examples of redemptive constitutionalism. Women in the abolitionist movement who worked for ratification of the Thirteenth Amendment in turn claimed equal rights under the Fourteenth Amendment. When the U.S. Supreme Court rejected their claims, women sought and ultimately gained the right to vote through the Nineteenth Amendment, ratified in 1920 and, fifty years later, secured guarantees of equal citizenship through new interpretations of the Fourteenth Amendment. Popular mobilizations of workers and others who needed government's help led the New Deal Court to reject the vision of liberty expressed in *Lochner v. New York*.[2] A long struggle for black civil rights led the Court in *Brown v. Board of Education*[3] to reject its previous apology for racial inequality in *Plessy v. Ferguson*.[4] In our own day, *Lawrence v. Texas*[5] overturned the Court's pinched vision of human freedom in *Bowers v. Hardwick*.[6] Over time, certain interpretations of the Fourteenth

Amendment have come to symbolize great wrongs that the American public has decisively rejected. *Plessy* and cases like it function as negative precedents. Their repudiation expresses our contemporary ideals of justice. They symbolize the country's continuing project of constitutional redemption.

As it was in the past, so it is in the present. After years of political retrenchment, the Court's equality doctrines now betray the Fourteenth Amendment's great promises. Increasingly, equality doctrine does not guarantee Americans equal liberty but instead protects the liberty of the privileged. Increasingly, equality doctrine does not challenge state action that preserves social caste but instead prevents government efforts to dismantle caste.

What Went Wrong?

Less than fifteen years after *Brown*, Americans began electing presidents who campaigned against the Warren Court and the civil rights revolution. These presidents appointed justices who changed the direction of equal protection law, claiming to condemn discrimination but defining it in increasingly narrow terms.

In the 1970s, a newly constituted Court began to define discrimination as a problem of forbidden classifications in law—not social subordination by law. This body of doctrine divided the world into laws with forbidden classifications, which courts would closely scrutinize, and laws without forbidden classifications, which courts presumed were wholly within the prerogative of the legislature. Reasoning in this fashion, the Court ruled that "equal protection" barred state action that expressly classified on the basis of race, yet permitted facially neutral laws that foreseeably burdened minorities.[7] The Court held that facially neutral laws were unconstitutional if enacted with a purpose to discriminate, but it defined discriminatory purpose extremely narrowly, requiring evidence of state action akin to malice.[8] At the same time that the Court limited judicial scrutiny of facially neutral laws with a disparate impact on minorities, the Court expanded judicial scrutiny of laws designed to help minorities.[9] It held that express classifications designed to help subordinated groups were as constitutionally suspect as those designed to keep subordinated groups down.[10]

In the early twenty-first century, then, equal protection doctrine focuses on *deliberate classification by the state* as the main cause of inequality in American society and *strict scrutiny by judges* as the main remedy. This framework entrenches inequality in at least four important ways.

First, the law defines inequality *underinclusively*, either as group classification or thinly concealed malice. But not all state action that subordinates employs group-based classifications, and not all inequality is produced by evil minds. Social stratification by gender and race has been sustained by many different kinds of public and private action. Bias in decision making often plays a role but so, too, do institutional arrangements and rules that entrench unequal resources and opportunities. Today's equal protection law tends not to reach these forms of bias. Instead, constitutional doctrine prohibits the kinds of openly invidious laws that legislatures no longer enact—while allowing laws whose hidden, unconscious, or structural bias is not openly expressed. In this way, equality law legitimates and immunizes laws that entrench structural inequalities that accumulated over the generations in which the United States openly enforced race and gender hierarchies.

Second, equal protection doctrine's focus on group classifications defines inequality *overinclusively*, because not all group classifications subordinate. The Court now treats race-based classifications that try to remedy inequalities and break down social stratification with the same degree of scrutiny—and judicial hostility—as classifications that deliberately advantaged dominant groups in the past. As Justice John Paul Stevens put it, the law professes not to know the difference between a welcome mat and a No Trespassing sign.[11]

Third, because doctrines of heightened scrutiny deny judges discretion in evaluating group-based classifications, judges are extraordinarily resistant to extending heightened scrutiny to new groups, even groups widely acknowledged to have suffered invidious treatment. In fact, the Supreme Court has not conferred suspect status on any group since the 1970s.

Fourth, current doctrine is based on a *bifurcated framework of review* that splits authority between legislatures and courts and discourages dialogue between them. Either, legislation is presumptively unconstitutional and the Court decides what constitutional equality requires; or legislation bears an almost irrebuttable presumption of democratic legitimacy, and neither the Court nor the political branches has the authority or the obligation to promote the Fourteenth Amendment's guarantees.

This all-or-nothing vision is false to the original vision of the Fourteenth Amendment, which grants Congress the power to enforce the amendment's provisions by appropriate legislation. These days,

Congress is no longer the first defender of equality; sometimes, it seems to have no obligations at all. And when Congress does use its section 5 powers, the Court treats these acts of legislative constitutionalism as presumptively unconstitutional encroachments on the Court's own interpretive authority—all the more so if Congress tries to prohibit forms of discrimination the Court itself has not deemed suspect. There is little in current doctrine that encourages dialogue between courts and the political branches about the meaning of the Fourteenth Amendment; nor is there much recognition that different branches of government could bring their distinctive authority and competence to the great task of vindicating the Constitution's guarantee of equality.

The Lost Tools of the Second Reconstruction

By 2007, in the *Parents Involved* decision,[12] the Court had come full circle—wielding the power it once used to strike down laws enforcing segregation to strike down laws promoting integration. Five justices read *Brown v. Board of Education* as a case demanding strict scrutiny for all racial classifications, even those designed to further integration. Only Justice Anthony Kennedy's concurrence kept the Court from rendering a wide variety of integration-promoting practices illegal. In *Parents Involved*, the plurality led by Chief Justice John Roberts misremembers *Brown*. It misstates the law of that case and misunderstands its spirit. *Brown* did not use the language of strict scrutiny; it held that racial separation caused stigmatic and emotional harm to minority schoolchildren. The Court did not embrace a general principle of strict scrutiny until it was finally ready to strike down laws against interracial marriage in the 1960s. Even then, strict scrutiny applied only to race-conscious policies that enforced segregation and white supremacy. Only after a new group of conservative justices joined the Court did strict scrutiny begin a new life in the 1970s and 1980s as a device to hold affirmative action programs unconstitutional.[13]

Although courts now identify strict scrutiny with the goals and purposes of the civil rights revolution, other pathways for protecting equality during the opening decades of the Second Reconstruction were far more important. They included:

1. *Legislative and executive constitutionalism*. The model of strict scrutiny assumes that legislatures and executive officials lack the desire, the obligation, and the authority to promote equality values. Their only

responsibility is to refrain from using suspect classifications. Yet the political branches took the lead during the Second Reconstruction, just as the original Reconstruction Congress had intended. Congress prohibited discrimination through superstatutes like the Civil Rights Act of 1964, the Voting Rights Act of 1965, and the Fair Housing Act of 1968. At the same time, Congress promoted equality for the poor through the Elementary and Secondary Education Act of 1965 and other War on Poverty and Great Society programs like Head Start. In 1972, Congress applied the 1964 Civil Rights Act to government employers and sent an Equal Rights Amendment to the states, emphasizing Congress' commitment to abolish sex discrimination as well as race discrimination. In the executive branch, administrative agencies implemented the new laws with regulations that promoted equality, including guidelines for school desegregation, rules to combat sex discrimination in the workplace, and antipoverty programs that promoted local participation by the poor. The Court worked with Congress; it read the new civil rights statutes broadly to promote egalitarian goals; and it looked to the president and Congress to secure enforcement of its rulings.

2. *Promoting equality through protecting civil liberties.* Dominant groups rarely give up their status willingly. Laws dismantling status hierarchies cannot redistribute opportunities to subordinate groups too transparently; they risk generating backlash, aggravating the very social dynamics they seek to abate. Indirection is often a friend of change. During the Second Reconstruction, the Court and Congress often promoted the equality of subordinated groups through doctrines that provided fair procedures and individual liberty for all. The Warren Court's revolution in criminal procedure protected racial minorities from police abuse, secured basic rights of legal representation, and limited prosecution tactics that played on racial prejudice. Through its free speech doctrines, the Court protected the right of the National Association for the Advancement of Colored People (NAACP) to organize and student groups to protest Jim Crow. In *Griswold v. Connecticut*,[14] *Eisenstadt v. Baird*,[15] and *Roe v. Wade*[16] the Court struck down criminal laws that helped enforce traditional gender roles in sex and reproduction. These decisions not only protected women's autonomy but also their equality in civil society, in ways that particularly benefited poor women. Through these different branches of constitutional law, the Warren and Burger Courts protected the politically weak through doctrines that protected the liberties of all.

3. *Fundamental interests and protection of the poor.* Finally, the Supreme Court recognized a set of fundamental interests protected by the Equal

Protection Clause that gave poor Americans access to key institutions of civil society. These decisions removed user fees and other resource-related restrictions on core forms of civic participation and limited some of the harsher expressions of class (and race and sex) inequality. They improved access to the criminal process,[17] lifted welfare-related burdens on the right to travel,[18] and guaranteed the right to vote without having to pay poll taxes.[19]

The executive, legislative, and judicial branches of government worked together during the civil rights era. Drawing on their distinctive forms of authority and competence, the different branches of government promoted equality in different ways. The Court interpreted the Constitution to prohibit unfair treatment on the basis of race and sex. But the Court also promoted equal rights for Americans by promoting their individual liberty and their practical freedom, constraining the use of general laws and discretionary law enforcement practices that bore harshly on the most vulnerable members of society.

In short, the Second Reconstruction promoted equality by promoting *equal liberty*. Equal liberty should not be confused with either formal liberty or formal equality. The practical reality of freedom matters as much as its formal possibility. When the Court protected liberty during the Second Reconstruction, it paid attention to the inequalities of resources and roles that shaped ordinary people's daily lives and their encounters with the law.

Prospects and Possibilities

How can we restore constitutional equality in the twenty-first century? Here are a few suggestions:

1. *Use liberty to promote equality*. The framers of the Fourteenth Amendment understood that liberty and equality are deeply intertwined. They originally hoped to secure equality for freed slaves not only through an Equal Protection Clause but also by guaranteeing the privileges and immunities of national citizenship. A guarantee of freedom can secure equality, just as a guarantee of equality can secure freedom. Sometimes, protecting liberties for all is an effective way of protecting minorities and unpopular groups from special impositions and affirming their equal citizenship. Gay rights is the most obvious example. *Lawrence v. Texas* protects the freedom of gays to enter into sexual relationships, yet equality values suffuse the opinion's talk of liberty and dignity: *Lawrence*

reasons that same-sex intimacy should be treated with the same respect that the law offers to cross-sex relations.

A liberty framework has proved particularly attractive for gay rights because it doesn't require that courts define a protected class. Sexual minorities do not have to understand themselves as part of a single group with a single identity in order to secure the right to equal treatment and equal respect. Using liberty to help minorities also avoids the problem—most obvious in affirmative action cases—of appearing to favor one group over another.

Protecting women's choices about sex and reproduction helps secure their equality with men, as the Supreme Court has increasingly come to recognize. Under prevailing social arrangements, rights to contraception and abortion promote both liberty and equality. Giving women control over the number and timing of their children helps women negotiate social and economic arrangements that presuppose the traditional division of family labor; it allows women to bear children with less harm to their employment prospects and their family's well-being. Once again, liberty and equality reinforce each other: Equality doctrines protect women's choices in their life pursuits, while liberty doctrines promote women's equality in making those choices.

The Warren Court also pioneered the idea of protecting fundamental rights and fundamental interests—rights that, once granted, must be granted equally. These rights and interests promote equality along class lines without using suspect classifications based on poverty or race.

Finally, criminal procedure guarantees and restrictions on state detention and surveillance also demonstrate how protecting liberty also protects equality. It is no accident that the Warren Court revolutionized criminal procedure while it promoted civil rights for minorities; it knew that the mistreatment of minorities in the criminal justice system entrenched their subordinate social status. In a post–9/11 world, where majorities seem only too happy to surrender other people's rights, we need civil liberties to limit the harassment of Muslims and immigrants and to prevent abusive racial profiling schemes.

2. *Decalcify doctrine.* Although the Equal Protection Clause is not the only vehicle for securing equality, it is still a crucial one. It cannot serve its purposes until we undo some of the problems that current doctrine has created.

Courts must give up their preoccupation with formal classification, which is neither a necessary nor sufficient marker of laws that threaten equal citizenship. We need new ways to decide which laws burdening women and minorities deserve closer scrutiny. One way to do this, borrowed from the law of employment, juries, and voting rights, is to make more use of rebuttable presumptions when policies have significant disparate impact, perpetuate traditional forms of inequality, or significantly contribute to social stratification. Courts need not invalidate these arrangements, but they can make the political branches accountable for them by requiring legislatures to explain why they chose policies that entrench historic forms of inequality or have strongly inegalitarian effects.

Courts should also give the political process more latitude in deciding when race or sex-conscious laws are needed to dismantle caste and secure equal opportunity. Even the most determined advocates of color blindness are usually willing to accept benign race-conscious motivations for facially race-neutral methods like Texas's "10 percent plan"—which guarantees college admission to the top students at all of the state's public high schools—or class-based affirmative action. That would make little sense if they thought that there were really no difference between benign and invidious motivation. The real issue isn't color blindness; it is how the burdens of these programs are distributed on ordinary people and whether the programs are structured in ways that provoke resentment. Courts should give institutional actors more latitude to create race-conscious policies that are designed to remedy past discrimination or to promote integration so long as the programs make efforts to diffuse the burdens on members of dispreferred groups.

Finally, courts should replace the bifurcated model of responsibility for protecting equality. That means adopting a suggestion made long ago by Justice Thurgood Marshall—a sliding scale approach to judicial scrutiny.[20] In addition, courts can use a variety of doctrinal moves to disturb existing structures and spur legislatures to act to promote constitutional values of equality, as described below.

3. *Share responsibility for guaranteeing equality.* Instead of treating policies that increase social stratification as presumptively legitimate, courts could adopt solutions that make legislatures accept responsibility for their decisions and give them a stake in promoting and enforcing constitutional equality. Courts can be catalysts, shaking up existing political coalitions and social practices and requiring legislatures to give reasons and make hard choices when their policies exacerbate inequality and place disproportionate burdens on minorities or the poor. Among other things:

(a) Courts can *name inequalities* produced by existing policies and require the political branches to justify policies that exacerbate inequality. Courts can employ *discourse-forcing* methods that require the political branches to explain how their policies respond to specific constitutional values.

(b) Courts can *interpret statutes and regulations* to avoid entrenching inequality and require legislatures either to accept the interpretations or publicly renounce them.

(c) Courts can introduce *rebuttable presumptions*—already used in jury, voting, and employment discrimination law—under which disparate impact triggers a duty to explain and justify policies. For example, courts could order "equality impact statements" that would require state actors to focus on and report on the effects of their policies on social stratification by race, gender, class, or other criteria. Without absolving or condemning legislatures, courts could force the political branches to take the political heat for what they are doing.

(d) Courts can declare existing policies unconstitutional, explain the constitutional principles at stake, and *let the political branches craft a remedy* that honors those principles. Courts can give the outward boundaries of a constitutional remedy, state the parameters they will use in reviewing the remedy, or explain what kinds of reasons and justifications the legislatures must provide. For example, in *Baker v. State*, the Vermont Supreme Court declared that the state's marriage laws discriminated against gays but instead of creating a judicial right to gay marriage, it asked the legislature to craft a solution.[21] The legislature responded with the country's first civil unions bill. State supreme courts protecting the right to education have also put the burden on state legislatures to craft workable guarantees of rights to education.

(e) Courts can *create safe harbors* that give incentives for political branches to reform their current practices in order to avoid liability. For example, in sexual harassment law, courts have given employers safe harbors for vicarious liability if they produce mechanisms for preventing harassment and resolving disputes. Safe harbors change the balance of incentives, giving the political branches reasons to be proactive in promoting equality values.

These strategies share responsibility and make the practice of equality a more dialogic enterprise between the courts and the political branches. Consider how this might work in the area of criminal law. Doctrines of strict scrutiny are ill suited to remedying the inequalities of race and poverty in the U.S. criminal justice system. Courts can't oversee the entire criminal justice system, yet the system's unequal impact on the poor and racial minorities is everywhere. Indeed, the system actually uses racial classifications in suspect descriptions and racial profiling, while facially neutral rules of criminal law have unmistakable racial impact. The proper response is not to insist, as the Supreme Court repeatedly has, that there are no constitutional issues of equality at all. That gives law enforcement officials carte blanche and lets the political branches completely off the hook. Instead, courts should try to make the political branches take political responsibility for the decisions they make, expressing constitutional concerns so that lawmakers and law enforcement officials feel pressure to take equality issues into account.

Or take welfare policy. In *Dandridge v. Williams*,[22] the Court upheld a draconian cap on welfare benefits that penalized beneficiaries for increases in family size. Justice Potter Stewart, hemmed in by the bifurcated framework of equality law, threw up his hands. He did not want to treat poverty as a suspect classification subject to strict scrutiny. But he believed that the alternative, asking whether there was any rational basis for the challenged legislation, foreclosed courts from doing anything at all. He noted that laws regulating "the most basic economic needs of impoverished human beings" raised very different issues from the "state regulation of business or industry" upheld during the New Deal: "We recognize the dramatically real factual difference...but we can find no basis for applying a different constitutional standard."[23] Stewart was disabled by an unworkable doctrinal structure. Yet this is not a case of either-or. Without making poverty a suspect classification, courts could use statutory interpretation or rebuttable presumptions to send the problem back to legislatures. They could require legislatures to demonstrate why their policies do more good than harm.

4. *Take advantage of jurisdictional redundancy.* America's federal system and the constitutional separation of powers give many different actors an opportunity to declare what the Constitution means. Equality law can benefit from having courts, legislatures, and executive officials all take responsibility for promoting equality. For similar reasons, we should not forget the role that federalism can play. Although the standard story of the civil rights revolution is that it fought against states' rights, it's worth remembering that much of the early progress in civil rights for African Americans came from enlightened state laws and judicial decisions and later spread nationally. Long before the 1964 Civil Rights Act, many states already had passed public accommodation laws, and by the time of *Brown*, the majority of states had banned de jure segregation either through statute or judicial decision. Many of the equality issues of the future will be worked out in state and local governments first. Similarly, decisions of state constitutional courts often pave the way for later interpretations of the federal Constitution.

Many of the most important tools for protecting equality in the twenty-first century will be dialogic—involving a back and forth between courts, the public, and the political branches. We are hardly alone in this conclusion. Many other countries already achieve similar effects through their different constitutional structures, including, most prominently, Canada's notwithstanding provision and the United Kingdom's use of declarations of incompatibility with the European Convention on Human Rights. Indeed, American constitutionalism has used these dialogic practices for generations without fully acknowledging them. We tend to associate equal protection with strict scrutiny of suspect classifications, but in fact many other practices have played a crucial role in promoting equality for historically subordinated groups. With a richer account of our own past practice, we might recognize commonalities between other constitutional traditions and our own.

Several of the chapters in this volume emphasize how legislative and executive constitutionalism can safeguard social and economic rights like housing, education, and health care. Often courts cannot mandate specific institutional reforms in these areas, but they can spur them on by creating incentives for the political branches to take constitutional values into account. Courts can also work constructively with government officials who try to put constitutional norms into practice. For example, in *Nev. Dep't of Human Res. v. Hibbs,*[24] the Court upheld the Family and Medical Leave Act; it recognized that Congress had the institutional capacity to enforce constitutional guarantees of sex equality in ways that courts could not. The path to greater equality in the twenty-first century will require the cooperation of all the branches of government. And it will bring us back to a vision of egalitarian liberty that redeems the promises of the Fourteenth Amendment.

Notes

1. Cong. Globe, 39th Cong., 1st sess., at 2766 (May 23, 1866) (remarks of Senator Jacob Howard).

2. 198 U.S. 45 (1905).

3. 347 U.S. 483 (1954).

4. 163 U.S. 537 (1896).

5. 539 U.S. 558 (2003).

6. 478 U.S. 186 (1986).

7. See *Washington v. Davis,* 426 U.S. 229 (1976).

8. See *Pers. Admin. of Mass. v. Feeney,* 442 U.S. 256 (1979).

9. See *Regents of Univ. of Cal. v. Bakke,* 438 U.S. 265 (1978).

10. See *Adarand Constructors v. Pena,* 515 U.S. 200, 245 (1995); *Richmond v. J.A. Croson Co.,* 488 U.S. 469 (1988).

11. See *Adarand* at 245 (Stevens, J., dissenting).

12. *Parents Involved in Community Schools v. Seattle School District No. 1,* 127 S. Ct. 2738 (2007).

13. See Reva B. Siegel, *Equality Talk: Antisubordination and Anticlassification Values in Constitutional Struggles over* Brown, 117 Harv. L. Rev. 1470 (2004).

14. 381 U.S. 479 (1965).

15. 405 U.S. 438 (1972).

16. 410 U.S. 113 (1973).

17. See *Gideon v. Wainwright*, 372 U.S. 335 (1963); *Griffin v. Illinois*, 351 U.S. 12 (1956).

18. See *Shapiro v. Thompson*, 394 U.S. 618 (1969).

19. See *Harper v. Va. Board of Elections*, 383 U.S. 663 (1966).

20. *San Antonio Metro. Sch. Dist. v. Rodriguez*, 411 U.S. 1, 70, 98–110 (1973) (Marshall, J., dissenting).

21. 170 Vt. 194 (1999).

22. 397 U.S. 471 (1970).

23. *Id.* at 485.

24. 538 U.S. 721 (2003).

PART III

Citizenship and Community

❧ 10 ❧

The Citizenship Agenda

BRUCE ACKERMAN

W HEN IT CAME to citizenship, the founders were full of paradox. Washington, Madison, and the rest were prepared to
die for their vision of the union, but when it came to writing
their commitment to American citizenship into the Constitution, they
fell silent. They knew that most of their countrymen would not join
them in giving federal citizenship priority over more local attachments,
and so the original Constitution failed to mention, let alone define, one
of its key premises: The founders speak in the name of We the People,
but never tell us who "we" are.

The question returned after four bloody years of the Civil War. And
the Fourteenth Amendment answered it squarely: It explicitly established the primacy of national citizenship in the new constitutional
order. Henceforth, state citizenship was derivative: Americans gained it
by choosing to reside in whatever state they liked, and the amendment
forbade the states from "abridg[ing] the privileges or immunities of citizens of the United States." But then it fell silent, leaving the courts, and
the rest of us, to figure out the precise contours of these privileges and
immunities.

The open-ended character of this great guarantee was immediately
recognized. It was the Citizenship Clauses, not Due Process or Equal
Protection, that originally provoked a great debate over the rights

guaranteed by the new nation emerging out of the bloody sacrifices of millions.

But then, another historical paradox. Precisely because the Citizenship Clauses were understood as most important, they were the centerpiece of the first great Supreme Court decision construing the Reconstruction amendments: the *Slaughterhouse Cases* of 1873. And precisely because the language of national citizenship was so new, the Supreme Court had trouble giving it legal meaning. By a 5–4 vote, the justices refused to believe that the American people had now put national citizenship at the core of their Constitution. They trivialized citizenship's "privileges," suggesting that they included little more than the right to move from state to state, to obtain a passport, and to claim diplomatic protection abroad. Anything more robust, the majority feared, would endanger familiar principles of federalism.

Over the next century, the Supreme Court reversed course, recognizing the Fourteenth Amendment as a source of a broad panoply of fundamental rights and requiring the states to comply with its commands. But it accomplished its nationalizing mission by promoting other clauses, most notably Due Process and Equal Protection, to central place. The Citizenship Clauses remain more or less a dead letter: Robert Bork was only exaggerating a bit when he said that they had as little legal meaning as an "inkblot." Despite his professed fidelity to the original understanding, Bork made this pronouncement[1] with supreme self-satisfaction as he cast this central Reconstruction text into the wilderness. But for the rest of us, the century-long silence should provoke a certain wonder.

We are in a curious situation. The Constitution assures us that "We the People of the United States" have created and reconstructed our supreme law over the generations. And yet the Court has refused to contribute to a robust constitutional discourse about the very citizenry that the Constitution celebrates.

The Court's silence contrasts with the eloquent efforts by twentieth-century Americans to expand and deepen the privileges of national citizenship. Women's suffrage during the Progressive Era, Social Security during the New Deal, the antidiscrimination laws of the civil rights era—all provide notable examples. All were initiated by political movements seeking to end second-class citizenship; but when they were received into our constitutional tradition, judges and lawyers dressed them up with other legal doctrines that belied their originating impulse. To this day, American politics revolves around efforts by one or another group to end second-class citizenship—but this phrase loses its resonance in our courts of law. This disjunction between law and politics is not inevitable. Despite centuries of silence, America's lawyers may yet reclaim the lost promise of national citizenship for the twenty-first century.

They won't be able to do it alone. The citizenship agenda will only become alive if Americans can once again affirm that their country isn't merely a vast free market zone, where individuals go their separate ways within a safe haven guarded by a mighty military. Lawyers have much to contribute to such a civic revival—but they won't get anywhere by trying to convince the current Supreme Court to restore the Citizenship Clauses to their central place. Despite professions of originalism, our right-wing judiciary will be in no rush to vindicate the privileges of citizenship against the economic forces threatening their effective exercise. In the run-up to 2020, the greatest legal contribution lies outside the courts. We must use our legal talents in a larger effort to reconstruct the institutional foundations of modern citizenship.

Many of our inherited civic institutions are dead or dying. Vietnam killed the citizen army. Television killed the political party as a popular institution. The citizen jury is on the fringe of everyday life. The only significant institution that still involves ordinary people is the public school, and it too is under attack.

Progressives have been fighting a rearguard battle in defense of the civic achievements of the twentieth century, including public education and progressive taxation, Social Security and Medicare, civil rights and environmental protection, union rights and workplace safety.

Many of these old progressive ideas deserve a central place in twenty-first-century life. But if the past is any guide, it won't be good enough to defend them against right-wing attack. From the American founding to the civil rights revolution, we have built our democracy through acts of bold institutional innovation—some more successful than others, but all pushing forward the movement to greater political inclusion, individual freedom, and social justice. If we are to move further down this path, there is an imperative need for large acts of institutional imagination.

This is the pressing task for the next generation of American lawyers. We should proceed in the distinctive spirit of realistic idealism. As realists, we should try to design institutional initiatives that will *actually work* in the real world, using all the tools of modern policy analysis for a hardheaded exploration of real-world options. Good intentions aren't enough. And yet we should also be unembarrassed idealists: We should not content ourselves with narrow variations on the status quo, but aim for practical frameworks that would enable ordinary Americans to take charge of their political and economic lives. We should seek to establish that the meaningful exercise of American citizenship is no pipe dream, but a practical project well worth a tough political struggle.

This has been the spirit of three collaborations with friends of mine that aim to kick off a new round of debate over the shape of the citizenship agenda: *Voting with Dollars*, with Ian Ayres; *Deliberation Day*, with Jim Fishkin; and *The Stakeholder Society*, with Anne Alstott (all Yale University Press paperbacks). In setting out three planks for a new citizenship agenda, we tried to rediscover the art of talking about big ideas in ordinary English, staying clear of Beltway techno-babble. This is the only way to convince millions of Americans that meaningful citizenship is a real-world possibility—if they only will take the future into their own hands.

I won't mind if you find our proposals wrongheaded or counterproductive; nobody can please everybody, and you may be provoked to come up with better ideas than we have offered. But I will have utterly failed if you find my proposals obscure or pedantic.

Let's begin with the problem of big money in politics. Only one-third of 1 percent of American registered voters gave $200 or more to presidential candidates in the 2004 election cycle, but more than 65 percent of all contributors donated more than $200. Traditional forms of campaign reform won't change this reality. The 2002 McCain-Feingold law increased contribution limits from $1,000 to $2,000, making it likely that the balance of financial power will become more top-heavy in the future. To democratize the system, we need something new: Give all voters a special credit card account containing $50 that they can spend only on federal election campaigns. Armed with their cards, voters could go to local ATM machines whenever they liked and send their "patriot dollars" to favored candidates and political organizations. A little over 120 million Americans went to the polls in 2004. If they also had a chance to go to their ATMs, they would have injected more than 6.1 billion federally funded patriot dollars into the campaign—greatly diluting the power of the private $4 billion spent by all candidates for federal office in the 2004 electoral cycle.

Patriot dollars would invigorate the politics of ordinary citizenship. When each American voter has 50 patriot dollars in his or her pocket, candidates will have a powerful incentive to reach out and grab that money. Fund-raising will become a community affair; a box lunch for 100 could gross $5,000! These outreach efforts will provoke millions of conversations: Who should get the money? Who is a charlatan and who is really concerned about the country?

Patriot dollars have many merits, but one great limitation. Once citizens go to their ATMs to beam their patriot money onward, the candidates will continue to spend most of their money on sound-bite appeals on hot-button issues. Patriotic finance will redistribute the sound bites, emphasizing themes with greater resonance for ordinary citizens. But we will still be living in a sound-bite democracy, and this isn't good enough. The next challenge is to provide citizens with the tools they need to move beyond the media blitz and engage in thoughtful political discussion. An exemplary model is the American jury. Twelve men and women begin in total ignorance, but they learn a lot during the course of the trial. After hearing competing arguments, and reasoning together, they regularly—if not invariably—come up with perfectly sensible conclusions.

The task is to design a similar format for politics. Stanford political scientist Jim Fishkin and I have come up with a practical proposal based on a new technique, deliberative polling, which has been field-tested in thirty-five settings throughout the world—from Australia to Bulgaria, China to Denmark, Baton Rouge to Philadelphia.

Each poll invites a few hundred citizens to spend a weekend deliberating on major issues of public policy. Before they arrive, participants respond to a standard questionnaire that explores their knowledge about, and positions on, the issues. They then answer the same questionnaire after completing their deliberations. Comparing these before and after responses, social scientists have rigorously established that participants greatly increase their understanding of the issues and often change their minds on the best course of action. Ten percent swings are common. No less important, participants leave with a more confident sense of their capacities as citizens.

These experiments suggest a new way of thinking about democratic reform. Fishkin and I urge the creation of a new national holiday: Deliberation Day, which will be held two weeks before presidential elections. It will replace Presidents' Day as an official holiday; Americans will no longer honor Washington and Lincoln by searching for bargains at Presidents' Day sales. Instead, ordinary business will come to a halt, and citizens will be invited to gather at neighborhood centers to discuss the central issues raised by the leading candidates for the White House. Nobody will be forced to attend, but as with jury service, participants will be paid a stipend for the day's work of citizenship. DDay would begin with a nationally televised debate between the presidential candidates, who would discuss the leading issues in the traditional way. But then citizens would deliberate in small groups of 15 and later in larger plenary assemblies. The small groups begin where the televised debate leaves off. Each spends an hour defining questions that the national candidates left unanswered. Everybody then proceeds to a 500-citizen assembly to hear their questions answered by local representatives of the major parties. After lunch, participants repeat the morning procedure. By the end of the day, citizens will have moved beyond the top-down television debate by the leading candidates. They will have achieved a bottom-up understanding of the choices confronting the nation. Discussions begun on DDay will continue during the run-up to Election Day, drawing tens of millions of other citizens into the escalating national dialogue.

If Deliberation Day succeeds, sound-bite democracy would come to an end. Candidates would have powerful incentives to create longer and more substantive infomercials. Newscasts would be full of exit polls determining the extent to which citizen discussion had changed voting preferences—framing the intensifying debate that culminates on Election Day. While there will always be plenty of room for a politics of personality, the new system would put the focus where it belongs: on the crucial issues determining the future of the United States. Our initiative took an important step forward during the 2004 presidential elections, when seventeen PBS stations throughout the country assembled scientific samples of citizens from their regions to engage in a pilot Deliberation Day. Larger media efforts in the future will help to dramatize the proposal further, serving as a vital preliminary for the great leap forward to the new national holiday.

For now, it's more important to place the proposal into the larger context defined by the patriot dollar initiative. In our present sound-bite democracy, voters are bombarded by hot-button slogans generated by well-financed special interests. The point is to arouse knee-jerk reactions, not informed judgments. So it's no surprise that most Americans go to the polls with only the vaguest understanding of the issues. But once they are provided with new tools for engagement, Americans will be in a position to take their citizenship seriously. From the very beginning of the presidential campaign, candidates will be reaching out to them with great vigor—if only to pick their pockets and get at their patriot dollars. As citizens begin to "vote with their dollars," Deliberation Day will loom on the horizon. Candidates no longer will spend most of their money on ten-second sound bites. They will be beaming longer infomercials to enable partisans to state their case intelligently on DDay. By the time Election Day arrives, voters will be going to the polls with a far better sense of the stakes before the nation and of the nature of the rival responses proposed by the candidates.

I have no need to exaggerate. I am not conjuring some mythic version of Periclean Athens. I am not asking Americans to don togas, but to march with credit cards to their ATM machines and talk to their neighbors at local centers—this time acting as citizens, not consumers. I am not longing for some brave new world, but one where ordinary citizens can compete with big money on more equal terms.

Real reform in politics comes cheap. Patriot dollars will cost about $2 billion on an annualized basis ($6 billion during presidential elections, $2.5 billion during midterm elections). DDay will be even cheaper. Running the facilities will cost about $2 billion if 50–70 million Americans show up (plus a citizen stipend for those attending). Once again, this cost won't be incurred every year. Until DDay proves itself, let's start small and only schedule the holiday for presidential elections.

But once we move from political to economic citizenship, we confront big price tags. Only a large initiative has the chance to stop the spiraling inequalities that endanger the future of democratic life. There can be no disputing the basic facts: Since the 1970s, the average annual salary in the United States has only risen $4,250—from $32,500 in 1970 to $36,750 in 2002. That's about a 13 percent increase. But the pay of the top 100 chief executives went from $1.3 million to $18.5 million—from 39 times to more than 500 times that of an average worker. Such radical disparities in income have had a big impact on the distribution of wealth. Over the eighteen years from 1983 to 2001, the share of disposable wealth owned by the top 1 percent has moved up from 33 to 39 percent. The United States could be a poorly disguised oligarchy by 2020, with the top 1 percent controlling an enormous share of the disposable wealth, with more and more billionaires following the Bushes and Bloombergs into the public sphere.

Below the oligarchs, the United States has become a three-class society. About 30 percent of America's children will graduate from four-year colleges and move into the ranks of the symbol-using class. But the vast middle class, who graduate high school or a two-year college, will fail to share in the prosperity of the symbol users. To be sure, they won't confront the long-term unemployment that will threaten the bottom fifth who drop out of high school. But that is small consolation.

Over the last half century, progressive lawyers have fashioned one new legal tool to struggle against these forces of economic exclusion: civil rights law. They have spent numberless hours seeking to pry open more good jobs for blacks, women, and other subordinated groups. For all the half-steps, the result has been a great triumph for economic citizenship. But by itself, this does nothing to address the widening gap among the oligarchs, the minority of privileged symbol users, and the broad middle class in the United States.

If we don't do anything to confront these gaps, conservatives will continue to use them to generate middle-class hatred against a welfare state that seeks to help the bottom fifth of Americans sustain a minimal economic livelihood. There is a big hole here in the progressive vision of economic citizenship, and Anne Alstott and I have tried to fill it in *The Stakeholder Society*. Our idea is simple: As a birthright of citizenship, each American should be guaranteed a stake of $80,000 as he or she confronts the challenges of life as a young adult.

This stake will cover four years of tuition at a good private college, allowing the typical college graduate to start off life without a crippling debt burden.[2] But the initiative will yield even greater gains for the seven out of ten Americans who never gain the economic autonomy that a four-year degree provides. An $80,000 nest egg will provide middle-class Americans with a rough-and-ready sense of economic independence, permitting them to confront the labor market with their heads held high.

Stakeholding creates a new institution—citizenship inheritance—to compete with traditional family inheritance. In contrast to right-wing efforts to eliminate the "death tax" on the rich and super-rich, the citizenship agenda offers a more democratic vision. The nation's wealth, after all, is the product of generations of work by all Americans—the police officer on the beat and the teacher in the school, no less than the financial wizards on Wall Street. Stakeholding recognizes this basic point by granting all citizens a share of the nation's wealth as they start out in life, when they need it most.

In order to lay claim to their $80,000, Americans will have to complete high school. The 15 percent who drop out will only receive the interest on their stake, not the principal. But for the rest, there will be no strings attached. For the first time in a long time, ordinary Americans will have the real taste of economic freedom.

Some might throw away their $80,000 on frivolities. But the abuse of freedom by a few should not deprive the many of genuine opportunities to shape their lives while they are young. Thomas Jefferson's promise of the pursuit of happiness will no longer be reserved for Fourth of July declamations. It will describe the living truth of American life. The stakeholder society expands the progressive vision of economic citizenship. It gives a head start to the young and most vital elements of American society, while continuing to provide a safety net for the poor and elderly.

All this comes, of course, with a new tax, but one that gets to the heart of the problem, hitting only Americans in the top 10 or 15 percent in the wealth distribution and forcing the top 1 percent to pay about 40 percent of the total. Using data from 2001, Alstott and I show that an annual wealth tax of 2 percent, with a family exemption of $450,000, will finance our initiative—even assuming 30 percent tax evasion. The upshot is a new social contract, in which those who succeed in the market economy provide a citizen's inheritance for all Americans in the next generation.

Writing in the midst of the Republicans' ongoing campaign against the death tax, stakeholding may seem a pipe dream. But the idea is already taking off in Great Britain. Tony Blair made the citizen's inheritance into the "big idea" of his successful reelection campaign in 2001, and his Labour government followed through by enacting a variant of stakeholding into the law of the land.

As of September 1, 2002, all children born in Britain are provided with a bank account. Every child starts with £250, and kids get an extra £250 if their parents are in the lower third of the income distribution. This small stake accumulates with interest until the children reach eighteen, when the citizens receive their inheritance. The government plans to add additional amounts when children reach seven and perhaps at later ages as well. Starting in 2020, young Britons reaching eighteen each will be receiving a couple of thousand pounds—maybe more—as they start out in life.

To be sure, a few thousand pounds isn't $80,000. But the Blair example suggests that our vision of a citizenship agenda for 2020 shouldn't be entirely obscured by the darkness that has presently descended on the United States. We *will* recover from the politics of fear that the Bush administration has exploited with such great skill. Nothing lasts forever: The future will continue to be surprising; the day after tomorrow will bring new opportunities.

But will we be able to seize the moment by bringing dynamic new ideas to the table, or will we content ourselves with rehashing noble-but-tired variations on twentieth-century themes?

The year is 2020. Citizens have voted with their patriot dollars; they have debated stakeholding at Deliberation Day; and they have voted for a dynamic progressive president who has pledged to outdo the British in creating a substantial citizen's inheritance for every American. Or maybe progressive debate has left these initial proposals far behind, and we have come up with a more attractive and effective citizenship agenda to bring before the American people.

In any event, it is only within this context that we can expect the Supreme Court to get serious about the Citizenship Clauses. With a progressive president and Senate sending a new generation of justices onto the bench, the notion that citizenship has its privileges will no longer be derided, in Borkish terms, as constitutional nonsense. The unfulfilled promise of the Fourteenth Amendment will instead be viewed as a central challenge for interpretation of the twenty-first century; the "citizenship agenda" enacted by Congress may, over time, be understood as part of every American's constitutional birthright.[3]

But we have now moved far beyond 2020 to the next generation's struggle to redeem the promise of American life.

Notes

1. Robert Bork, *The Tempting of America* 166 (New York: Free Press, 1990).

2. According to the College Board, the average, private, nonprofit, four-year college charged $21,235 in 2005–2006. Multiplied by four, that's $84,940. See http://www.collegeboard.com/press/releases/48884.html.

3. See Bruce Ackerman, *The Holmes Lectures: The Living Constitution*, 120 Harv. L. Rev. 1737 (2007).

❧ 11 ❧

National Citizenship and the Promise of Equal Educational Opportunity

GOODWIN LIU

FIFTY-PLUS YEARS AFTER *Brown v. Board of Education*, it would probably surprise most Americans to learn that education is not a right guaranteed by the U.S. Constitution. For all that *Brown* said about the importance of education, its primary legacy has been the elimination of overt racial discrimination, not the creation of genuinely equal educational opportunity. The U.S. Supreme Court said as much in 1973 when it held that wide spending differences between school districts due to local wealth disparities do not violate the Equal Protection Clause. Today, too many poor and minority schoolchildren still receive a separate and unequal education.

Although this problem has gone unaddressed by federal courts, it has garnered substantial attention in state courts, where lawsuits since the 1970s have challenged school funding inequities under state constitutions. But a national goal of equal educational opportunity cannot be realized by addressing only inequality within states. The reason is simple: The most significant component of educational inequality nationally is not inequality within states but inequality *between* states. Even if intrastate disparities were eliminated, substantial disparities across states would remain. This fact casts a long shadow over the ideal of equal opportunity.

Since *Brown*, the Equal Protection Clause has played a leading role in the struggle for equality. But the problem of educational inequality between states calls for a different approach—one whose centerpiece is not judicial enforcement of the negative prohibition against state discrimination, but rather *legislative enforcement of the affirmative guarantee of national citizenship*. Before the Fourteenth Amendment mentions "equal protection of the laws," it says that all persons born or naturalized in the United States are "citizens of the United States" and that "citizens of the United States" have certain "privileges" and "immunities." Further, the Fourteenth Amendment assigns to Congress the power to enforce its provisions, including the national citizenship guarantee.

Wide interstate disparities in educational opportunity stand in tension with the guarantee of national citizenship, and ameliorating those disparities is a constitutional duty of the federal government. This constitutional vision, rooted in the Citizenship Clause, animated legislative efforts to establish a robust federal role in public education soon after the Fourteenth Amendment was adopted. Recovering that vision and applying it to current inequalities are vital steps toward realizing the promise of *Brown*.

The Problem

Although disparities in educational opportunity still exist within and between districts in each state, disparities across states are more severe. Table 11.1 shows each state's per-pupil spending in 2003–2004 in rank order. These data have been adjusted for regional variation in educational costs and for interstate differences in the number of children who are poor, disabled, or limited in English proficiency (LEP). The top ten states on average spend 60 percent more per pupil than the bottom ten states. Low-spending states are found in the South, Southwest, and far West, while high-spending states are clustered in the Northeast, Mid-Atlantic, and Midwest.

We can better see the magnitude of these disparities with data on per-pupil spending by school districts at the 10th percentile, 90th percentile, and median level of spending in each state. Figure 11.1a shows that the median district in nineteen low-spending states spends less than

Table 11.1   Cost-adjusted spending per weighted pupil, 2003–2004

Vermont	$9,149	Maryland	5,923
Wyoming	7,941	Illinois	5,603
New Jersey	7,692	Oregon	5,491
Maine	7,581	Missouri	5,391
New York	7,428	Arkansas	5,307
Alaska	7,236	Colorado	5,267
Pennsylvania	7,027	Louisiana	5,228
Montana	6,981	Virginia	5,216
Connecticut	6,835	Georgia	5,191
Delaware	6,754	South Carolina	5,188
New Hampshire	6,674	New Mexico	5,119
Wisconsin	6,656	Kentucky	5,097
Massachusetts	6,635	Idaho	5,097
North Dakota	6,608	Alabama	4,875
Nebraska	6,459	Washington	4,798
Ohio	6,331	Mississippi	4,786
West Virginia	6,330	Florida	4,777
Michigan	6,309	Oklahoma	4,773
Rhode Island	6,238	Tennessee	4,693
Iowa	6,226	North Carolina	4,638
Indiana	6,224	Texas	4,629
South Dakota	6,149	California	4,551
Hawaii	6,076	Arizona	4,314
Kansas	6,025	Nevada	4,279
Minnesota	5,967	Utah	3,812

The data are adjusted for geographic cost differences using 2004 state-level values of the Comparable Wage Index and for special needs by assigning weights of 1.9 to students with disabilities, 1.6 to students from poor families, and 1.2 to English-language learners. Source: U.S. Census Bureau.

the 10th percentile district in eighteen high-spending states. Figure 11.1b shows that the median district in fourteen high-spending states spends more than the 90th percentile district in fifteen low-spending states. Indeed, disparities across states account for roughly two-thirds of interdistrict variation in spending nationwide.[1]

Large interstate disparities exist not only in spending but also in education standards and outcomes. Under the No Child Left Behind (NCLB) Act, states may establish their own learning standards and assessments, but they must participate annually in the National Assessment of Educational Progress (NAEP), a widely respected test of knowledge and skills. Figure 11.2a compares the percentage of fourth-graders scoring "proficient" on the 2005 NAEP math test with the percentage of fourth-graders scoring "proficient" on state tests. The solid line shows where the dots would line up if state standards of proficiency matched those of the NAEP.

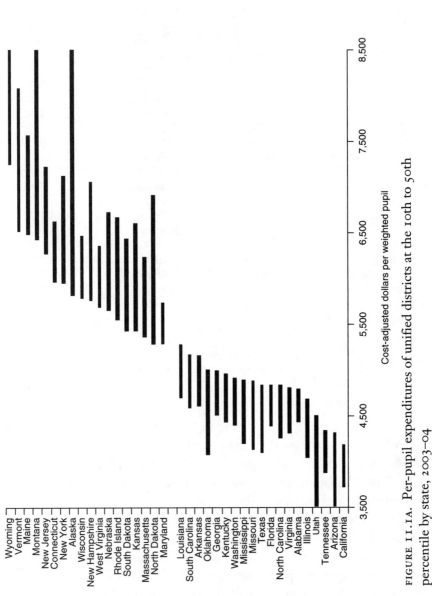

FIGURE 11.1A. Per-pupil expenditures of unified districts at the 10th to 50th percentile by state, 2003–04

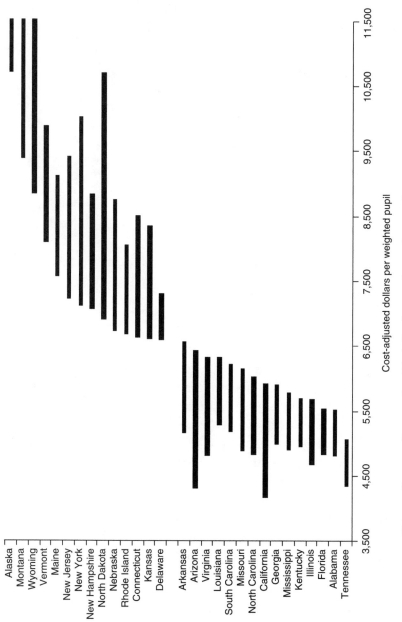

FIGURE 11.1B. Per-pupil expenditures of unified districts at the 50th to 90th percentile by state, 2003–04

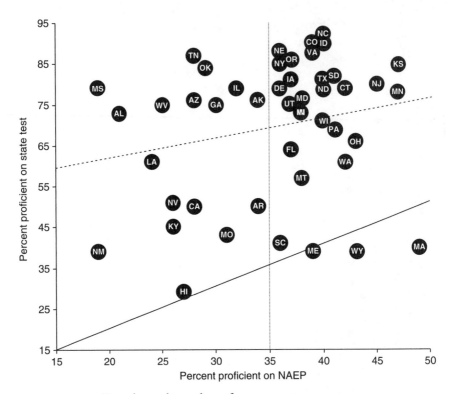

FIGURE 11.2A. Fourth-grade math performance, 2005

This graph tells us three things. First, state standards are literally all over the map and almost always less rigorous than the NAEP's. In Alabama, for example, 73 percent of students were proficient on state tests, but only 21 percent were proficient on the NAEP. Second, student performance varies considerably from state to state when measured against a common standard. While 35 percent of fourth-graders nationwide achieved proficiency on the NAEP, state figures ranged from 49 percent in Massachusetts to 19 percent in Mississippi and New Mexico. Third, the states below the national average are almost all low-spending states in the South, Southwest, and far West. A similar story can be told about fourth-grade reading (figure 11.2b), eighth-grade math, and eighth-grade reading.

These performance disparities reflect not only resource disparities but also student demographics. As table 11.2 shows, the student body in the top half of states in terms of spending is only 28 percent nonwhite, 14 percent poor, and 4 percent LEP, while the student body in the bottom half is 49 percent nonwhite, 19 percent poor, and 12 percent LEP. In short, children with the greatest educational needs live disproportionately in states with the lowest education spending.

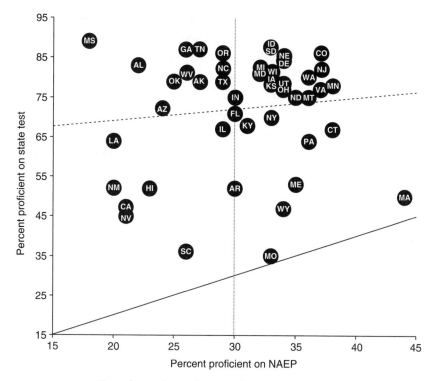

FIGURE 11.2B. Fourth-grade reading performance, 2005

We might ask low-spending states to address the problem themselves were it mainly due to their unwillingness, not inability, to devote more resources to education. But the fact is that state education spending is more highly correlated with state fiscal capacity than with state and local effort. In real terms, high-spending states like Connecticut and Maryland have as much as 50 percent more income per pupil than low-spending states like Arizona and Arkansas. Only the federal government can narrow these inequalities in the near term.

Table 11.2   Demographics of school-age children, 2003–2004

	(percentages)				
	White	Black	Latino	Poor	LEP
United States	58.3	17.0	18.4	17.3	8.9
States in top half of spending	71.6	13.9	8.9	14.4	4.2
States in bottom half of spending	51.1	18.7	23.5	18.9	11.5

Sources: U.S. Census; National Center for Education Statistics; National Clearinghouse for English Language Acquisition and Language Instruction Educational Programs (2006).

Yet Congress has not acted. NCLB created a federal framework for testing and accountability, but it did not establish national education standards nor expand the federal role in school finance. The federal share of the national education budget has never exceeded 10 percent. Very little interstate equalization can be achieved with such small sums. What's worse, the largest program of federal education aid—Title I of the Elementary and Secondary Education Act of 1965—tends to reinforce, not reduce, interstate inequality. By statute, each state's Title I aid is determined not only by its share of poor children but also by its per-pupil spending.[2] Although low-spending states have relatively more poor children, high-spending states receive more federal aid per poor child. In 2003, for example, Massachusetts had roughly the same number of poor children as Oklahoma but received more than twice as much Title I aid. Title I thus replicates rather than ameliorates interstate inequality.

The Guarantee of National Citizenship

As a policy matter, it is hard to see how the current patchwork of educational standards and resources can offer all children equal opportunity to become effective citizens and productive workers on a national and international scale. Yet the problem goes beyond policy. As a *constitutional* matter, it is hard to see how this approach to public education can be reconciled with the Fourteenth Amendment guarantee of national citizenship.

By its terms, the Citizenship Clause overruled the Supreme Court's 1857 holding in *Dred Scott* that blacks could not be citizens of a state or of the United States. But its significance goes much further. Before the Civil War, leading authorities on constitutional law denied the existence of a national citizenship separate and apart from citizenship in a particular state. National citizenship, if it existed at all, was thought to flow from state citizenship. Against this backdrop, the 1868 adoption of the Fourteenth Amendment transformed American political identity. It established a national political community—"citizens of the United States"—independent of the laws of any state.

The constitutional text and history reveal three important things about national citizenship. First, the grant of citizenship was meant to secure not only a legal status but also substantive rights; thus, the Fourteenth Amendment refers to the "privileges or immunities of citizens of the United States." Although the framers did not say what those rights were, they understood citizenship to mean, at a minimum, equal standing in the national political community. The citizenship guarantee thus encompasses substantive rights essential to realizing this equality.

Second, section 5 authorizes Congress to enforce the guarantee of national citizenship. Under this authorization, Congress may determine what civil and political rights and what social and economic entitlements are necessary to make national citizenship meaningful and effective. Neither the Fourteenth Amendment's text nor its history limits Congress to protecting national citizenship rights only against state abridgment. The Citizenship Clause is an *affirmative* recognition of national citizenship and its essential rights. Congress may protect those rights regardless of state action or inaction.

Third, the grant of congressional power to enforce citizenship rights implies a constitutional *duty* of enforcement. Unlike any other constitutional provision up to that time, the Civil War amendments expressly assigned enforcement power to Congress, reflecting the framers' belief that "appropriate legislation," not merely judicial enforcement, would be needed to make the newly created rights fully effective. Senator Jacob Howard of Michigan, introducing the Fourteenth Amendment in 1866, said that section 5 "casts upon Congress the *responsibility* of seeing to it, for the future, that all the sections of the amendment are carried out in good faith.... [I]t thus imposes upon Congress this power and *this duty*."[3]

If this reading of the Fourteenth Amendment seems unfamiliar, it is because the Supreme Court perverted the amendment's essential meaning from the start. As Bruce Ackerman explains in chapter 10, a 5–4 majority in the *Slaughterhouse Cases* read the Citizenship Clause to preserve state citizenship as primary, while severely limiting the rights of national citizenship[4]—precisely the opposite of what the framers intended. Ten years later, the Court ignored the Citizenship Clause in declaring a federal law banning racial discrimination in public accommodations to exceed Congress's power to enforce the Fourteenth Amendment.[5]

Because of these doctrinal errors, we have grown used to treating the Fourteenth Amendment as a vehicle for judicial enforcement of negative rights against governmental denial of formal equality (the classic example is *Brown*) and not for legislative enforcement of positive rights to governmental provision of what is necessary for equal citizenship. Yet this latter view was an important foundation of post–Civil War efforts to establish a federal role in public education. Early on, Congress understood national citizenship as a guarantee that it had the power and duty to enforce. That understanding led Congress then, and should lead us now, to see the task of narrowing educational inequality between states as a constitutional imperative.

Lessons from Congress, 1870–1890

During the two decades after the Fourteenth Amendment was adopted, Congress repeatedly sought to enforce the national citizenship guarantee through ambitious bills to provide leadership and funding for public education. The precursor to these efforts was an 1867 statute establishing a federal Department of Education.[6] Congress charged the committee that drafted the statute to create an agency "to enforce education, without regard to race or color, upon the population of all such States as shall fall below a standard to be established by Congress."[7] Although the department was ultimately limited to data collection and reporting, its creation signaled an emerging federal responsibility for ensuring that "every child...receive[s] a sufficient education to qualify him to discharge all the duties that may devolve upon him as an American citizen."[8]

In 1870, Representative George Hoar of Massachusetts introduced the first-ever federal proposal for public elementary education.[9] The bill required states to provide common schools for children aged six to eighteen, with instruction in reading, writing, arithmetic, geography, and history. The president was authorized to determine whether the schools of each state were adequate. Where they weren't, the bill proposed "national schools" run by federal officials and financed with a federal tax.

In Congress, critics assailed the bill's heavy-handed approach, and it did not reach a vote. But the bill drew attention to the problem of education and the basis for Congress's power and duty to make schooling universally available. Invoking the Fourteenth and Fifteenth amendments, Hoar stressed the nationalizing and equalizing effect of the new citizenship guarantees:

> The Constitution, as now completed, provides that every person born or naturalized in the United States shall be a citizen thereof, and that the right of any citizen to vote shall not be abridged by reason of race, color, or previous servitude.... The vote of the humblest black man in Arkansas affects the value of the iron furnace in Pennsylvania, the wheat farm in Iowa, or the factory in Maine as much as does the vote of its owner.[10]

With this premise, Hoar stated his central claim: "Among the funda-mental civil rights of the citizen is, by logical necessity, included the right to receive a full, free, ample education from the Government, in the administration of which it is his right and duty to take an intelligent part. We neglect our plain duty so long as we fail to secure such provision."[11]

In practice, Hoar's proposal would have targeted the South, where no state had a well-developed school system in 1870. In this respect, the bill would have been a step toward completing Reconstruction, but not a foundation for a truly *national* federal role in education. Yet the bill's underlying notion of federal responsibility gave way to an 1872 proposal by Representative Legrand Perce of Mississippi, chair of the new House Education and Labor Committee.[12] Perce sought to fund education with revenue from public lands, with half going into a perma-nent "national educational fund" and the other half, plus interest from the fund, given to states offering free education to children aged six to sixteen. His bill had genuinely national scope and would have allocated funds on the basis of illiteracy, directing more aid to states with greater need and less fiscal capacity.

As its supporters explained, the Perce bill aimed to ensure that "the children of [each] State, who will be called on to discharge the duties of citizens of the United States, shall be educated" to a national standard of literacy.[13] Like the Hoar bill, it sought to discharge "the obligation we took upon ourselves" to ensure that "those we clothed with the bal-lot should have the means of casting that ballot intelligently."[14] As one proponent observed, federal aid to public education was consonant with advances in commerce, transportation, and communications: "[W]e are becoming by means of these forces one people and one nation."[15]

The bill passed the House but died in the Senate. Nevertheless, the Hoar and Perce bills set the stage for the most significant education aid proposal of the postbellum period. Introduced by Senator Henry Blair of New Hampshire in 1882 and extensively debated throughout the 1880s, the proposal passed the Senate with broad support from north-ern Republicans and southern Democrats in 1884, 1886, and 1888, and it would have been signed by President Chester Arthur in 1884 had it not been blocked by a reactionary House minority.[16]

The Blair bill introduced the idea of granting federal aid through direct appropriations from the national treasury. Like the Perce bill, it envisioned an equalizing federal influence across the states through a distribution of funds based on illiteracy. Further, the bill advanced the notion of state and local administration of public schools within a framework of federal funding conditions. Although it did not outlaw segregation, the bill required schools to "giv[e] to each child, without distinction of race or color, an equal opportunity for education."[17] It also required each state to spend at least as much from its own funds as it received in federal aid, a simple model of cooperative federalism.

In the Senate, much of the debate examined Congress's spending power. But Blair centered his defense on Congress's power and duty to give meaning to the Citizenship Clause:

> Our leading proposition is that the General Government possesses the power and has imposed upon itself the duty of educating the people of the United States whenever for any cause those people are deficient in that degree of education which is essential to the discharge of their duties as citizens either of the United States or of the several States wherein they chance to reside.[18]

Invoking the necessity of education to "the public life of an American citizen,"[19] Blair argued that "the nation has the power, which implies the duty of its exercise when necessary, to educate the children who are to become its citizens."[20]

The Blair bill and its predecessors left important guideposts for the federal role in public education. They linked education to national citizenship with the recognition that Congress had a duty to act. And Congress's duty was not to guarantee absolute equality, but rather equal standing in the national community. In promoting basic literacy, the proposals sought to ensure what Blair called "the indispensable standard of education" for "the duties and opportunities of citizenship"[21]—a standard we might now call *educational adequacy for equal citizenship*.

Looking Ahead

In pursuing this constitutional vision today, it is important to acknowledge a sober reality. Throughout U.S. history, citizenship has had a darker side involving subordination and exclusion rather than equality and inclusion. For example, even as Congress debated the Blair bill, citizenship did not entail full membership in the national polity for women, blacks, and many other groups. We must be careful to ensure that the ideal of national citizenship does not infuse public education with nativism, cultural conformity, or chauvinistic nationalism. And we should not use the concept of citizenship to deny education to noncitizen children, not least because the Equal Protection Clause extends to "persons" not only to citizens.[22] At the same time, as Richard Ford observes in chapter

13, we should be thoughtful but not bashful in forging the political solidarity necessary for redistributive mutual aid.

With those caveats in mind, here are three recommendations for advancing educational adequacy for equal citizenship. First, it's time to create national education standards that define what all children should know and how well they should know it. As more and more students achieve "proficiency" on state tests under NCLB, continuing variation in state NAEP performance will highlight the illogic of having disparate state standards rather than coherent national standards guide education policy.

Importantly, *national* standards do not mean federal standards, *voluntary* standards obviously do not mean mandatory standards, and national *standards* do not mean a national curriculum.[23] Some version of the federal GOALS 2000 legislation, enacted in 1994 but never fully implemented, seems an appropriate model.[24] That statute envisioned an independent board of educators and citizens in the role of certifying standards developed by nongovernmental organizations in various subjects and made available to states for voluntary adoption. Although the idea may have been premature a decade ago, now is a good time to revisit the issue.

Second, Title I should be reformed to allocate funds only on the basis of child poverty, adjusted for regional cost differences. Because Title I aid is too small to incentivize state education spending, there is no defensible policy rationale for giving less aid per poor child to low-spending states. Title I should treat all poor children not as citizens of the states where they reside, but as citizens of the United States.

Third and most far-reaching, Congress should establish a new program of federal aid to bring the poorest states up to a base funding level that reflects a national standard of educational adequacy. Putting a dollar amount on educational adequacy is not easy, but many courts, policymakers, and scholars are now grappling with the challenge in informative ways. The key feature of such a program would be the distribution of aid to states in inverse proportion to their fiscal capacity, much as federal Medicaid funds are distributed.[25] The program also must ensure that federal aid reaches the neediest districts within each state and that states put more of their own resources into education where low spending is due in part to low effort.

These reforms will not be cheap. But even if we doubled federal spending on K–12 education, the federal share of school funding would still be less than 20 percent. We routinely spend billions on law enforcement, courts, and national defense to enforce our constitutional rights to liberty and security. Isn't it time we made a modest investment to enforce the one provision that literally *constituted* us as a nation over a century ago? Then and now, an ambitious education policy agenda furthers the constitutional imperative of securing the promise of national citizenship.

Notes

1. See Sheila E. Murray, William N. Evans, and Robert M. Schwab, *Education-Finance Reform and the Distribution of Education Resources*, 88 Am. Econ. Rev. 789, 799, table 1.2 (1998).

2. See 20 U.S.C. §§ 6333(a)(1), 6334(a)(2), 6335(b)(1).

3. Cong. Globe, 39th Cong., 1st sess., 2768 (1866) (emphases added) (Sen. Howard).

4. 83 U.S. 36 (1873).

5. *The Civil Rights Cases*, 109 U.S. 3 (1883).

6. Act of Mar. 2, 1867, ch. 158, 14 Stat. 434.

7. Cong. Globe, 39th Cong., 1st sess., 60 (1865).

8. Cong. Globe, 39th Cong., 1st sess., 3044–45 (1866) (Rep. Samuel Moulton); see *id*. at 2967 (Rep. Ignatius Donnelly); *id*. at 3049 (Rep. Selucius Garfield).

9. H.R. 1326, 41st Cong. (1870).

10. Cong. Globe, 41st Cong., 2d sess., app. 479 (1870).

11. Cong. Globe, 42d Cong., 1st sess., 335 (1871).

12. H.R. 1043, 42d Cong. (1872).

13. Cong. Globe, 42d Cong., 2d sess., 794 (1872) (Rep. Washington Townsend).

14. *Id*. at 861 (Rep. Henry Dawes).

15. *Id*.

16. 15 Cong. Rec. 2724 (1884); 17 Cong. Rec. 2105 (1886); 19 Cong. Rec. 1223 (1888).

17. S. 149, 49th Cong., § 10 (1886).

18. S. Rep. 101, pt. 2, 48th Cong., 1st sess., 1–2 (1884), reprinted in 17 Cong. Rec. 1240 (1886).

19. 15 Cong. Rec. 2000 (1884) (Sen. Blair).

20. S. Rep. 101, pt. 2, 48th Cong., 1st sess., 28 (1884), reprinted in 17 Cong. Rec. 1248 (1886).

21. *Id*. at 2000 (Sen. Blair).

22. See *Plyler v. Doe*, 457 U.S. 202 (1982).

23. See Diane Ravitch, *National Standards in American Education: A Citizen's Guide* (1995).

24. See GOALS 2000: Educate America Act, Pub. L. No. 103-227, 108 Stat. 125 (1994).

25. See 42 U.S.C. § 1396d(b).

❧ 12 ❧

Terms of Belonging

RACHEL F. MORAN

ONFRONTED WITH THE civil rights reversals of the 1980s and
1990s, progressive reformers are worried that the crusade for
racial equality has largely run its course. The rhetoric no longer
mobilizes popular support, and the principle no longer promises judicial
victories. Eager to overcome a series of setbacks before the bench, at the
ballot box, and in the media, progressives are searching for a new ral-
lying cry, and a number of them have latched on to the concept of citizenship. Citizenship, they say, has textual support in the Constitution,
and it speaks to the public's need to affirm national identity, rather than
apologize for national sin. Wrongly ignored and righteously resurrected,
citizenship can tell a new morality tale, one of triumphant renewal and
progressive possibilities in the United States.

I think of myself as a good citizen, and yet I am skeptical of pinning
my hopes to citizenship. My own family history and the history of the
nation give me pause, for it is clear that the power of citizenship lies in
its capacity not just to include but to exclude. To achieve our country,[1]
we need terms of belonging that run deeper than citizenship alone. The
poet Walt Whitman wrote eloquently about the promise of "We, the
People." For him, the challenge was to perfect democratic participation and the conditions for human flourishing: "I speak the password
primeval...I give the sign of democracy; / By God! I will accept nothing

which all cannot have their counterpart of on the same terms."[2] Today, in the early twenty-first century, we as progressives must accept nothing less than Whitman's vision, a faith in our collective possibilities more profound than citizenship alone can capture.

Like so many generations of immigrants before them, my grandparents came to the United States in search of a better life. While working in California, they had two children, my mother, Josefina, and her sister, Raquel. According to the U.S. Constitution, both daughters were citizens of the United States; this was their birthright. When hard times came during the Depression, the family returned to Mexico. There, my grandparents had another child, my uncle Oscar. Unlike his sisters, Oscar was a Mexican citizen. A few years later, my grandmother died in a charity ward in Mexico, too weak from malnutrition to push another child through her loins. Afterward, the authorities found her three children quietly starving to death at home. Hunger had not distinguished between the American daughters and the Mexican son. For my mother and her sister, the promise of birthright citizenship had become nothing but a mess of pottage.

If my mother's story were an aberration, it would simply be a sad part of my family history. In truth, her experience is part of a large-scale tragedy that casts serious doubt on the power of citizenship to protect against grave abuses. According to available estimates, between 500,000 and 1 million Mexicans were repatriated by the United States during the 1930s.[3] Of these, approximately 60 percent were children like my mother and aunt, who were U.S. citizens by birth.[4] Despite this inconvenient fact, citizenship was used to divide the deserving from the undeserving during the mass deportations, a development that surprised many Mexicans. After all, "[i]t had never been a factor before, either in getting work or for those who had served in the military during World War I. Mexican immigrants had served their adopted country well. Now it was the nation's obligation to respond in kind. Unfortunately, Americans did not see the situation in the same light."[5]

When Mexican parents sought welfare assistance during the Depression, they pointed out that their children were birthright citizens entitled to aid on the same terms as other Americans. Instead, entire families faced deportation because they had become public charges. Officials of the United States showed little compassion for the citizen children. In a June 1939 memorandum, Vice Consul Leon L. Cowles denied any responsibility for the desperate condition of repatriates in Matamoros: "[I]n a sense, I suppose it is no concern of ours whether these Mexican nationals are properly treated upon their return to their own country." Still, Cowles hesitated:

[I]t is obvious that there are humanitarian considerations involved, and it is probably the case that some of these so-called repatriates are citizens of this country by birth. Therefore, we are at least morally interested in an attempted solution of the plight of the people involved when such a solution [that is, repatriation to and colonization in Mexico] threatens to be no solution at all.

The consul resolved the dilemma by deciding that "for the moment there is nothing to do but observe developments," and no steps were ever taken to relieve the suffering of the repatriates, whether citizens or not.[6]

The consul's decision to "observe developments" is one of the cruelties perpetrated in the name of citizenship when the national project changes. Americans are not immune to the impulse to ignore the suffering of others. Somehow, we convince ourselves that "they" are not like "us"—though they have toiled, contributed, and lived among us.[7] Our detachment reflects the hubris that comes of wrongly privileging our citizenship over our humanity. The Constitution does not make this mistake. As legal scholar Alexander Bickel points out, "[T]he original Constitution presented the edifying picture of a government that bestowed rights on people and persons, and held itself out as bound by certain standards of conduct in its relations with people and persons, not with some legal construct called citizens."[8] For Bickel, this choice was an artful one because "[i]t has always been easier, it always will be easier, to think of someone as a noncitizen than to decide that he is a nonperson."[9]

Nearly twenty years after my mother's abrupt departure to Mexico, she came back to the United States to study, obtained her bachelor's degree, met and married my father, and raised her children as Americans. Despite her birthright, my mother found herself relegated to second-class citizenship. When my parents decided to marry in the early 1950s, the minister took my father aside and warned that he was making a terrible mistake. The marriage bordered on miscegenation, he and my mother would pay a terrible price, and their children would surely be misfits. My father could not be dissuaded, and eventually the minister agreed to perform the wedding. Many years later, Amparo, a friend of the family who had interpreted for my father's Spanish-speaking clients in criminal trials, would remark to my mother in astonishment: "Josefina, I don't think your husband even thinks of you as Mexican." Amparo could hardly believe that my father could bridge the social divide between whites and Mexicans to embrace my mother in her full humanity.

Amparo's reaction should not come as a surprise, given the United States' repeated failures to live up to its own ideals where race and ethnicity are concerned. Today, Latinos often live under conditions of "social apartness," and meaningful social interaction with non-Hispanic whites is a rarity.[10] Latino students are, by some measures, the most segregated in the United States,[11] and the promise of residential integration has yet to reach many Latino neighborhoods.[12] In an earlier era, citizenship was used to justify the exclusion of Latinos from middle-class communities. During the 1920s, for instance, a Los Angeles realtor remarked that restrictions were necessary to "maintain our high standard of American citizenship" in Glendale, California.[13] The persistent isolation of Latinos has brought stigma and misunderstanding. Despite the gains of the civil rights movement, politicians feel free to whip up nativist sentiment by proclaiming that there are too many immigrants, particularly Mexicans.[14]

As U.S. history shows, there are many types of exile from the American dream, whether through expulsion from our borders or relegation to second-class status within them. In light of these transgressions, progressives' enthusiasm for citizenship bewilders me. My anxieties are particularly acute, given that the 2000 Census showed that over one in ten Americans was born outside the United States, and, of these, over half come from Latin America.[15] Already, there are popular fears that the United States is undergoing a "reconquest"[16] and that Latino immigrants will "Hispanicize" the nation.[17]

Of course, progressives insist that their use of citizenship will be different. Citizenship, they say, can be abused—but so can any other concept. Fair enough, but a close examination shows that these purportedly new and improved approaches have almost nothing to say to immigrants. The proposals to reinvigorate citizenship fall into two categories: those that revitalize the democratic process through incentives to participate in federal elections; and those that decrease the class divide through the redistribution of resources. Whatever the inclusionary aspirations, both types of reform threaten to widen the gap between citizens and noncitizens.

Let me begin with the suggestions to enhance democratic participation. Professors Bruce Ackerman and James Fishkin have proposed Deliberation Day, a forum for dialogues about presidential candidates that would take place in local communities. Deliberation Day would be held instead of Presidents' Day, two weeks before national elections, and would be a federal holiday. Citizens could gather voluntarily at neighborhood centers to view a televised debate between the candidates, discuss the issues in depth, and move beyond "sound-bite democracy."[18] In addition, Ackerman and Ian Ayres have suggested the creation of patriot dollars to counter the problem of big money in politics. Every voter in a federal election would receive $50, which could be spent only on favored candidates and political organizations. Because noncitizens cannot vote in federal elections, they would be ineligible to participate.[19]

The exclusive focus on national elections obscures contemporary experiments with immigrant voting at the municipal level as well as the historical use of state and local elections to incorporate newcomers into the political life of the nation.[20] Modern-day efforts to enfranchise noncitizens began in the 1970s and gained momentum in the 1990s. As a result, some cities have allowed permanent resident aliens to vote on issues that clearly affect their interests. The most common example is school board elections. Because immigrant parents have a strong stake in their children's public education, noncitizens can participate in selecting board members in New York City, Chicago, and some municipalities in Maryland.[21] Under our federalist system, local experiments with immigrant voting can continue, even if Deliberation Day and patriot dollars target the federal electoral process and exclude noncitizens. Yet, there is a real danger that these high-profile initiatives will send a symbolic message, one that casts doubt on the propriety of including immigrants in elections of any kind.[22]

Moreover, the calls for Deliberation Day and for patriot dollars make no provision for the political incorporation of immigrants. This omission is a serious one. Professor Irene Bloemraad has documented the naturalization gap between the United States and Canada, which emerged in the 1970s. Until then, foreign-born people in both countries tended to become citizens at comparable rates. Beginning in 1971, however, the naturalization rates in Canada remained robust and even increased, while those in the United States steadily declined. As a result, in 1997, barely 35 percent of the foreign-born population in the United States had obtained citizenship, while 70 percent of those in Canada had done so.[23] The rates in the United States were not always so low. In 1950, for example, the proportion of foreign-born residents who naturalized peaked at 79 percent.[24]

Some have attributed the drop in U.S. naturalization to the reluctance of Latino immigrants, particularly Mexicans, to become citizens. As Bloemraad points out, however, the gap between Canada and the United States is significant for groups from a wide range of countries.[25] In her view, this persistent disparity is due in substantial part to distinct philosophies of political incorporation. In the United States, the decision to naturalize is treated as an individual choice, so there is little in the way of government support for acquiring English, learning about U.S. history, participating in civic institutions, and becoming a citizen. In Canada, by contrast, the government provides resources to local organizations that enable immigrants to adapt to their new home and prepare for citizenship.[26]

The proposals for Deliberation Day and patriot dollars recognize the challenges to political mobilization that citizens face, yet wholly ignore the needs of immigrants who seek to naturalize and engage in civic life. A truly progressive platform would promote immigrant incorporation. For instance, Deliberation Day should be open to noncitizens who wish to be part of the democratic dialogue, even if they cannot vote. The neighborhood forums at a minimum should include individuals in the process of naturalizing, who need to prepare for the day when they will be casting ballots. Because patriot dollars will go only to citizen voters (perhaps out of a concern that payments to noncitizens would be politically controversial), monies should be separately allocated to community-based organizations that support immigrants seeking to naturalize. This funding would prevent the undervaluation of institutions that serve foreign-born residents, a population that must pay taxes to help finance the award of patriot dollars yet will receive no benefit from them. Steps like these are essential to avoid further diminishing immigrants' already limited prospects for political voice.

Now, let me turn to proposals for expanded social welfare benefits based on a principle of national citizenship. Bruce Ackerman and Anne Alstott hope to counteract the corrosive effects of class inequality on U.S. democracy by creating a stakeholder society. Under this plan, the federal government would pay $80,000 to any native-born or naturalized citizen at the age of twenty-one, so long as he or she had resided in the United States for at least eleven years.[27] Also motivated by concerns about the detrimental impact of material insecurity and inequality, William Forbath calls for social citizenship, which would establish rights to education, training, and decent work.[28] Finally, Goodwin Liu invokes federal citizenship to demand recognition of a right to education.[29]

Although globalization often is blamed for widening the class divide in the United States, none of these redistributive proposals attends much to immigrants, and when they are mentioned, the language is cautionary. Ackerman and Alstott, for instance, fear that excessive generosity to naturalized citizens would prompt restrictive immigration policies, so the stakeholder society is carefully limited to those who have spent most of their youth in the United States.[30] Although Ackerman and Alstott concede that those ineligible for a stake will feel some natural resentment, their proposal ignores the ways in which siblings and peers will be divided into haves and have-nots. The realities of transnational migration mean that many immigrants now live in mixed-status families and neighborhoods.[31] Children who have grown up together as equals will find themselves facing very different futures based on accidents of birth and times of arrival. These disparities will not necessarily reflect any differences in the potential to be good citizens and responsible stakeholders.

Because the proposals neglect immigrants, any implications for their future are adventitious rather than deliberate. For example, the manner in which benefits would be distributed is highly significant in protecting the rights of noncitizens. Direct federal transfers, such as the payment of an $80,000 stake at age twenty-one, are not subject to any constitutional limits on discrimination because Congress commands plenary power over immigration policy.[32] By contrast, if state and local governments are required to improve services like schooling based on a federal right, noncitizens will be entitled to due process and equal protection under the Fourteenth Amendment. These constitutional guarantees apply to persons, not just citizens.[33]

At a minimum, progressives should prefer programs administered by state and local authorities to unmediated federal intervention for precisely this reason: Personhood can curb the exclusionary tendencies of national citizenship. Moreover, alarmist claims that a principle of personhood will require the United States to minister to the world can be readily rebuffed.[34] After all, any sensible interpretation of due process and equal protection guarantees would limit their application to people within state or municipal boundaries. Ohio hardly seems likely to be operating neighborhood schools for the benefit of children residing in Bosnia.

Public education offers an excellent example of the interplay of citizenship and personhood. The Constitution forbids public schools from instituting a deluxe national curriculum for citizen students while denying it to their immigrant classmates. Congress is authorized to discriminate in the name of nation building, but that power cannot be conferred on state and local governments that might entrench a shadow population, marked by poverty and powerlessness, in the midst of U.S. communities. Under the Fourteenth Amendment, an absolute deprivation of education thwarts the personhood of noncitizen children who grow up illiterate and innumerate, unfit to participate in the civic and economic life of either the United States or their home countries.[35] Yet, even a grossly unequal education for immigrant students can constitute the kind of relative deprivation that undermines human flourishing. After all, in *Brown v. Board of Education*, black children were going to school, but it was their relegation to inferior treatment that damaged their hearts and minds in ways unlikely ever to be undone.[36] If the Constitution were to permit communities to create a permanent underclass of noncitizens, we as a democratic people would have lost our way, even as we aimed to secure the future of the nation-state.

Any call to reinvigorate citizenship must be sensitive to the dangers that nativist impulses will be unleashed and dehumanize those who seem foreign to the body politic. As Bonnie Honig warns, "Exhorting citizens to return to the nation and relate to it or to its good guys in unambivalent terms is not the way to (re)inaugurate a vital and magnanimous democratic politics, though it may serve the rather different cause of nationalism or patriotism."[37] The United States has seduced the world with the promise of a democracy committed to principles of liberty and equality. This promise recognizes that our country's greatness depends on respect for persons as well as solicitude for citizens. Progressives may seek comfort in the concept of citizenship as a refuge from forces of globalization that blur our national boundaries and complicate our humanitarian obligations. Unfortunately, this comfort comes at a high price by invoking "at best a simple idea for a simple government."[38] The American dream has been and always will be bigger than citizenship. That is what made my mother's birthright worth reclaiming.

I would like to thank Jack Balkin, Reva Siegel, Robert Post, and the Yale chapter of the American Constitution Society for including me in this project. I also want to express my appreciation to Dean Harold Koh for his support of this undertaking.

Notes

1. Richard Rorty, *Achieving Our Country* (1998); James Baldwin, "The Fire Next Time," in Baldwin, *The Price of the Ticket: Collected Nonfiction 1948–1985* at 333, 379 (1985).

2. Walt Whitman, *Leaves of Grass* 44 (2005).

3. Francisco E. Balderrama and Raymond Rodriguez, *Decade of Betrayal: Mexican Repatriation in the 1930s* 121–22 (1995). See also Abraham Hoffman, *Unwanted Mexican Americans in the Great Depression: Repatriation Pressures, 1929–1939* 126–27, 174–75 (1974).

4. Balderrama and Rodriguez, *supra* note 3, at 183.

5. *Id.* at 85.

6. *Id.* at 183. In 2005, Senator Joseph Dunn introduced a bill in the California legislature that would allow for reparations and civil suits by Mexicans who were wrongly repatriated during the period from 1929 to 1944. S.B. 645, Calif. Reg. sess. 2005–2006 (amended May 17, 2005).

7. Sadly, there is evidence that, following the terrorist attacks of September 11, 2001, official crackdowns on immigrants led to the deportation of families that included citizen children. Jacqueline Bhabha, *The "Mere Fortuity of Birth"? Are Children Citizens?* 15 differences: A Journal of Feminist Cultural Studies 91, 91–92 (2004).

8. Alexander M. Bickel, *Citizenship in the American Constitution,* 15 Ariz. L. Rev. 369, 370 (1973).

9. *Id.* at 387.

10. Martha Menchaca, *The Mexican Outsiders: A Community History of Marginalization and Discrimination in California* (1995).

11. Erica Frankenburg et al., "A Multiracial Society with Segregated Schools: Are We Losing the Dream?" in *Harvard Civil Rights Project, Harvard University* at 4, 32–34 (2003), available at www.civilrightsproject.reseg03/reseg03_full.php; site last visited Mar. 5, 2007; Gary Orfield and Susan E. Eaton, *Back to Segregation,* Nation, Mar. 3, 2003, at 5.

12. U.S. Census Bureau, *Racial and Ethnic Residential Segregation in the United States: 1980–2000* at chs. 1, 6 (n.d.), available at http://www.census.gov/hhes/www/housing/housing_patterns/housing_patterns.html; site last visited Mar. 5, 2007 (reporting that Latinos are the second most segregated population in the United States and that levels of segregation for this group have increased while those for African Americans have steadily declined).

13. Lisa Garcia Bedolla, *Fluid Borders: Latino Power, Identity, and Politics in Los Angeles* 43 (2005).

14. *Id.* at 27–31.

15. Luke J. Larsen, *The Foreign-Born Population in the United States: 2003: Population Characteristics* at 1, Current Population Reports P20-551, Aug. 2004.

16. Gebe Martinez and Patrick J. McDonnell, *Proposition 187 Backers Counting on Message, Not Strategy,* Los Angeles Times, Oct. 30, 1994, at A1.

17. See Samuel P. Huntingdon, *Who Are We? The Challenges to America's National Identity* 221–56 (2004).

18. Bruce Ackerman and James Fishkin, *Deliberation Day* (2005); Ackerman, this volume.

19. Bruce Ackerman and Ian Ayres, *Voting with Dollars* (2004); Ackerman, *supra* note 18.

20. Alexander Keyssar, *The Right to Vote: The Contested History of Democracy in the United States* 32–33 (2000); Jamin B. Raskin, *Legal Aliens, Local Citizens: The Historical, Constitutional and Theoretical Meanings of Alien Suffrage,* 141 U. Pa. L. Rev. 1391, 1399–1417 (1993).

21. Keyssar, *supra* note 20, at 310; Raskin, *supra* note 20, at 1460–62.

22. For a description of the benefits of progressive localism, see Richard T. Ford, this volume.

23. Irene Bloemraad, *Becoming a Citizen: Incorporating Immigrants and Refugees in the United States and Canada* 17–18 (paperback ed., 2006).

24. *Id.* at 27.

25. *Id.* at 33–40.

26. *Id.* at 102–37.

27. Bruce Ackerman and Anne Alstott, *The Stakeholder Society* (paperback ed., 1999); Ackerman, *supra* note 18.

28. William E. Forbath, *Caste, Class, and Equal Citizenship,* 98 Mich. L. Rev. 1, 90 (1999); Forbath, *Why Is This Rights Talk Different from All Other Rights Talk?* 46 Stan. L. Rev. 1771, 1805 (1994); Forbath, this volume.

29. Goodwin Liu, *Education, Equality, and National Citizenship,* 116 Yale L.J. 330, 341–48, 399–406 (2006); Liu, this volume.

30. Ackerman and Alstott, *supra* note 27, at 47.

31. Jeffrey S. Passel, *Unauthorized Migrants: Numbers and Characteristics* 18–20 (2005).

32. See T. Alexander Aleinikoff, "Policing Boundaries: Migration, Citizenship, and the State," in *E Pluribus Unum? Contemporary and Historical Perspectives on Immigrant Political Incorporation* 277–78 (G. Gerstle and J. Mollenkopf, eds., 2001); Hiroshi Motomura, *Immigration Law after a Century of Plenary Power: Phantom Constitutional Norms and Statutory Interpretation*, 100 Yale L.J. 545, 550–60, 583–85 (1990).

33. David Jacobson, *Rights across Borders? Immigration and the Decline of Citizenship* 101–2 (1996).

34. Ford, this volume.

35. *Plyler v. Doe*, 457 U.S. 202 (1982).

36. *Brown v. Board of Education*, 347 U.S. 483, 493–95 (1954). See generally Liu, *Education, Equality, and National Citizenship*, *supra* note 29, at 346–47 (arguing that education is a relative good).

37. Bonnie Honig, *Democracy and the Foreigner* 121 (2001).

38. Bickel, *supra* note 8, at 387.

❧ 13 ❧

Hopeless Constitutionalism, Hopeful Pragmatism

RICHARD T. FORD

I DOUBT THAT constitutional law as typically conceived will do much to better the most severe social injustices that face us in the early twenty-first century. In fact, I think the Constitution is as likely to be an impediment to positive social change, not only because an increasingly conservative federal judiciary will use constitutional law to block or limit progressive legislation on everything from gun control to school integration, but also because the Constitution will seduce the Left away from the more daunting but more direct avenue to social justice offered by popular politics.

By way of explanation, I'd like to focus on one particularly serious social justice problem. Here's a description of one U.S. city—worse than many, but still representative:

Locals call the street the "Berlin Wall," or the "barrier," or the "Mason-Dixon Line." It divides the suburban Grosse Pointe communities, which are among the most genteel towns anywhere, from the East Side of Detroit, which is poor and mostly black. The Detroit side is studded with abandoned cars, graffiti-covered schools, and burned out buildings. Two blocks away, within view, are neatly-clipped hedges and immaculate houses—a world of servants and charity balls, two car garages and expensive clothes. On the one side, says John Kelly, a Democratic state senator whose district awkwardly straddles both neighborhoods, is "West Beirut," on the other side, "Disneyland."[1]

If I had to identify only one social injustice that most cries out for redress, it would be the plight of the disproportionately black urban underclass. Residential segregation is the most intractable legacy of America's struggle with racism. And unfortunately, it makes many other problems—poverty, unemployment, crime, educational disadvantage— harder to address. Isolated from mainstream society, ghettoized minorities suffer under several burdens: They are unable to establish the social networks that might alert them to better job opportunities. They remain unfamiliar with the social norms of the mainstream—hence, they have difficulty favorably impressing employers—exacerbating employment discrimination. They eventually become socialized to a ghetto subculture in which employment in the mainstream doesn't seem to be a viable option: They lack role models who work in mainstream jobs and become acculturated to norms that are functional only inside the ghetto environment.

These conditions don't just attach to neighborhoods within cities; increasingly, entire municipalities are characterized by ghetto-like conditions. In any metro area, one can identify the poor cities and the rich ones. This reinforces ghetto neighborhood poverty by making cities compete with rich suburbs for rich residents and lucrative tax bases by offering tax breaks and improved services—at the expense of the poor populations within their borders.

Background Rules

I and many others have argued that the black ghetto is kept in place by public policy, including policies such as local taxation and revenue distribution (school finance), the delegation of land use authority to local governments (exclusionary zoning), and the organization of U.S. states into localities with a franchise restricted by strict territorial borders and a residency requirement.

Typically, localities collect and retain the revenues collected through taxes levied against property in their territorial boundaries. This provides a fiscal incentive for residents of wealthier jurisdictions to resist integration. After all, because taxes levied against local property are retained for the benefit of schools exclusive to local residents, any merger with poorer districts effectively dilutes the fisc of the wealthier districts and makes them financially worse off. The resulting inequities and incentives for class and race segregation effectively undermine the constitutional promises of integration.

The power of localities to use land use planning as an effective immigration policy also predictably perpetuates segregation. By restricting moderate and low-income housing, localities can and do effectively screen out lower-income residents, who are often disproportionately racial minorities. In some cases, the desire to eliminate low-income housing may be motivated by classic land use considerations such as a desire for open space and low-density development generally or a desire to avoid traffic burdens and environmental impacts. In many cases, the policies are driven by fiscal concerns: The background rules that allow localities to restrict the use of public services to residents and that allow localities to retain locally collected property and sales tax revenue give localities a powerful incentive to exclude low-income residents (who will require expensive public services but contribute little to the tax base) in favor of upper-income residential, commercial, and industrial uses (that will improve property values or generate taxable sales). Local land use decisions are, of course, laws; moreover, the ability of localities acting autonomously (as opposed to through regional or state government or through shared or negotiated land use authority) to make such decisions is itself a revisable legal rule. Needless to say, a racially segregated municipality will, in most cases, have racially segregated public schools: Although school district boundaries do not always match the municipal boundaries of local governments with zoning power, they rarely diverge so much as to take in communities of significantly different race or class demographics.

Desegregation is by and large limited by the territorial boundaries of local governments. Most U.S. cities fund public services primarily through property taxes. They also are entitled to and with very rare exceptions do limit access to local services to residents of the jurisdiction. This means that cities have an overwhelming incentive to encourage in-movers with resources, who will invest in real estate and thereby increase the value of property (and tax revenues) while requiring relatively little in terms of public services, and to discourage in-movers without resources, who will need a lot of public services. It scarcely needs to be said that the heavily minority urban poor fit the latter description. And although local governments in the United States do not have explicit immigration policies, they do have quite broad powers to restrict land uses. By excluding all or most high-density or multifamily housing, middle-class and wealthy suburbs can and do effectively screen out low-income (again, disproportionately minority race) potential residents by prohibiting the housing that they can afford. And suburban local governments can and do resist regional public transportation, halfway houses, group living arrangements, and rehabilitation centers—all services that many low-income people require.

These background legal rules are a fail-safe recipe for racially segregated neighborhoods. They are not the only reason that segregation remains, but they alone are enough to keep U.S. neighborhoods segregated indefinitely.

Pessimism (and Optimism)

For constitutional lawyers, the next step follows pretty easily: The policies that perpetuate ghetto segregation are unconstitutional. But these arguments have not moved the federal courts. And I'm very skeptical that, by the year 2020, any significant durable successes in terms of egalitarian distribution of social resources can be achieved through federal constitutional litigation. I'm only slightly less skeptical that constitutional litigation will offer real gains in terms of civil rights for minorities or members of stigmatized groups: Equal protection litigation, for as long as I've been an adult, has been as likely to stall or reverse racial justice gains achieved in popular politics as to advance them beyond what can be achieved there, and this trend shows few signs of reversal. The Supreme Court's 2007 decision in *Parents Involved in Community Schools v. Seattle School District No. 1* is only the most recent citation in this respect. There, the Court, astonishingly yet predictably, held that the Fourteenth Amendment not only does not require, but in fact *prohibits* the most commonly used and efficacious policies for promoting integration in the public schools. *Parents Involved* is not a fluke nor an aberration—it is simply the latest in a long line of Supreme Court cases that have steadily eroded the integrationist spirit of *Brown v. Board of Education*. The process began in 1971 with *Milliken v. Bradley*, which held that federal courts could not require interdistrict desegregation remedies unless each district had been found to have engaged in de jure segregation in the past, and it continued apace with *Missouri v. Jenkins*, which severely limited the authority of federal courts to require milder desegregation policies of even those districts that had been segregated by force of law and remained segregated in fact. Having effectively undermined the commonsense integrationist meaning of the Fourteenth Amendment guarantee under *Brown*, the Court was poised to apply a strictly formal interpretation of that guarantee to prohibit even voluntary integrationist policies.

My point here is not to lament the erosion of *Brown*'s integrationist mandate. Although I do lament it, it's plausible that more forceful integrationist mandates imposed by federal courts would have been politically unworkable and retreat was the prudent course of action. My point is that constitutional litigation is now part of the problem; it's in the way of the integrationist policies that *are* politically workable and that have been endorsed by state and local majorities in the political process. And this can't be explained away as an aberration or as judicial overreaching or even as bad jurisprudence. Let's face it: The interpretation of the Fourteenth Amendment as a requirement of formal color blindness is plausible; it fits nicely with a traditional legalistic preference for high principle and neat formalism over messy sociology and policy-like argumentation, and it is consistent with a widespread, if oversimplified, view that the evil of Jim Crow was the formal codification of racial hierarchy. We can spend the next forty years complaining that the conservatives are wrong as a matter of constitutional theory, but as long as they dominate the federal judiciary, their theory is the only one that matters.

But all is not despair. In many states and localities, there are plenty of encouraging developments, including political movements and tangible victories centered on specific problems and bolstered by a powerful, if small, sense of political solidarity. States from California to Texas (the site of the *Rodriguez* litigation) to New Hampshire have required the equalization of public funding between rich and poor localities. The New Jersey Supreme Court famously invalidated exclusionary zoning under the state constitution, and eventually the state legislature passed innovative legislation to require localities to implement more inclusive land use policies. Cities in Massachusetts are governed by anti–"snob zoning" laws, and many states require localities to accommodate low-income housing in their land use planning.

Localities such as Portland have pioneered land use planning that can put an end to urban sprawl and make cities livable and humane. And such "smart growth" land use planning has an incidental benefit: It prevents the migration of industry to the suburbs and hence preserves the tax base of more racially and economically diverse inner cities. Localities have pushed back against the exploitation of workers by passing living wage ordinances and have worked to preserve local quality of life by controlling the location of big box retailers. Local governments have—beyond what's required by state or federal mandates—made serious efforts to provide for the indigent, not only by providing minimum cash grants but also by making real efforts to bring the homeless and jobless into the mainstream through job training, substance abuse rehabilitation, and supportive housing.

These state and local success stories capitalize on the classic advantages of localism: detailed, context-specific analyses that come from proximity to specific problems and a popular sense of solidarity that comes from an inchoate, but I think real, sense of belonging to community and place. The decisions are less abstract and principled than conventional constitutional law; and they're more down and dirty, more context-bound, more political. That's what makes Washington Beltway politicians (and elite law professors) dismiss them as anomalous or inconsequential. For instance, New Jersey's *Mount Laurel*[2] case was constitutional litigation, but much of the opinion focused on specific local facts: housing markets, changing patterns of urbanization, and the postwar suburbanization of industry and hence of the traditional urban job and tax base. *Mount Laurel* didn't look like typical constitutional litigation: It wasn't formal, conceptual, principled. Similarly, the school finance litigation in California, Texas, and New Hampshire focused on the brute facts of school segregation and the distribution of resources. But these decisions have had a more profound effect than most federal constitutional litigation, albeit on a smaller scale; for instance, some states have significantly revised their tax structures to meet school finance equalization mandates.

Constitutional Concerns

The Constitution as traditionally conceived actually can impede such progressive politics in three ways.

First, as I have suggested, the federal Constitution can be and is deployed to hinder progressive agendas at the state and local level. The Equal Protection Clause now limits or forbids affirmative action, school desegregation, race-sensitive electoral reapportionment, and public contracting set-asides for women- and minority-owned businesses. An expansive Takings Clause could undercut efforts to regulate land uses in the public interest and might even block living wage ordinances. The Second Amendment thwarts local efforts to reduce gun-related violence in our nation's most dangerous and crime-prone urban areas. The Constitution is as likely to reverse gay rights as to advance them as conservatives push for a "defense of marriage" amendment. These and many others are good reasons for liberals and progressives to reconsider our long-standing defense of judicial supremacy and perhaps even to try to curtail the power of the federal bench.

Second, progressive constitutionalism—epitomized by the important civil rights decisions of the Warren Court—can seduce us into believing that political victories are best achieved through abstract conceptual arguments rather than concrete political struggles. Conservatives have dominated national popular politics for decades—as Barack Obama noted,[3] for better and (more often) for worse, the Republican Party has been the party of ideas since the 1980s. In these circumstances, it's tempting to hope for a shift to a more favorable arena of struggle: from the ballot box to the courtroom. It's especially warm and cozy for people who did well in school to imagine that there's a place where sound arguments always prevail over half-baked rhetoric and raw power, a place where buckling down and doing your homework brings just rewards, a place where the values of Socrates, Daniel Webster, and Hermione Granger triumph over those of P. T. Barnum, Karl Rove, and Draco Malfoy. But it's a fantasy to think that fancy conceptual arguments and debate club skills can substitute for the more raw and rugged, street-level persuasion of popular politics. The stymied antipoverty aspect of the civil rights movement is one of many cautionary examples: A conceptual commitment to "equal protection of the laws" could not somehow underwrite, much less *mandate*, the egalitarian redistribution of wealth from rich suburbs to poor inner cities.

Third, sometimes the arguments that lawyers have to make in court distort the real political stakes of an issue. This is especially true in the case of equal protection arguments, where the language of bigotry and invidious discrimination is almost obligatory. It's often necessary in litigation to, in essence, claim that one's opponents are irrational chauvinists. But it's dangerous politically to believe this. The litigation-influenced idea that those who disagree with us about, say, affirmative action, immigration, or same-sex marriage are just bigots whose views are beneath engagement or consideration can become a shabby psychological consolation prize when we lose in popular politics. How often have you heard someone say, after losing a political struggle: "Well, *of course*, our position is unpopular because so many people are prejudiced; that's why we need the courts." This combination of defeatism and smug condescension is a recipe for continued failure in popular politics.

I don't want to suggest that there's no role for courts or that we should abandon judicial review altogether—only that liberals in particular have been far too willing to place their fondest hopes with the federal judiciary, an institution that, let's not forget, has historically been a bastion of conservative reaction against popular progressive politics. Based largely on the significant but limited historical period marked by the Warren Court and its progeny in lower federal courts, we have come dangerously close to an implicit assumption that the federal courts are somehow intrinsically more liberal than the popular branches. But that interlude between periods of judicial conservatism has been over for a long time, and given the decades-long dominance of conservative politicians and conservative ideas in the popular political culture from which judges ultimately draw their inspiration and legitimacy, a pioneering liberal judiciary is unlikely to reemerge anytime soon.

Liberals and conservatives alike have participated in creating an elaborate mystique for the federal courts, which insulates their many bad decisions from appropriate scrutiny and encourages the type of faith in judicial rescue from popular politics that now too often paralyzes progressive legal thought. I think this has happened, in part, because many fear that, without such a mystique, there would be no sound justification for judicial review, and we'd be left to the mercies of mob rule. I'd like to propose an unsentimental defense of a modest judicial role, one that doesn't rely on a belief either that the Constitution as a document can control judicial decision making, nor that there is one correct set of constitutional principles that judges could apply to the specific disputes and which would guide their hand.

The federal courts are a political branch of government, one of the purposes of which is to occasionally temper the excesses of representative government and even more occasionally to jump-start needed but stalled political reform. The purpose of judicial review is to allow well-educated and (hopefully) civic-minded elites who are relatively insulated from short-term politics to overrule the popular branches on occasion. Provided the elites are good enough at couching their interventions in terms that look principled, maintaining the charisma and mystique of the judiciary (hence no cameras in court or revealing autobiographies— attention Justice Thomas!—and hence the otherwise somewhat quaint attachment to archaic props like black robes, gavels, etc.), and limiting their interventions to those that most people will eventually accept, the system, such as it is, will "work." Of course, the legal elites have their own internal norms of self-discipline which keep them from intervening too often or in ways that are too blatantly political, and for the most part these internal norms (reinforced by their peers within and outside the judiciary, such as law professors and professional legal commentators) keep the elites from going too far in the direction of naked legislation from the bench long before the legitimacy of the system is even close to crisis.

One doesn't need a substantive theory of constitutional interpretation to have this view. In fact, this view arises from a sort of disenchantment with constitutional theory; it's what you wind up with once you've lost faith in the idea that there's a "right" way to do constitutional analysis (there is still, of course, a wrong way, which is to do it so that it's conspicuously political and undermines the legitimacy of the courts). We need to temper the excesses of popular rule—too much democracy can be a very bad thing, not only for minorities but also for sound policies that require tough choices, sacrifices (always unpopular), or specific expertise that's beyond the average voter. Of course, the decisions of the federal courts are "political," but that doesn't mean they should be subject to the short-term preferences of majorities. This is one of the defining features of constitutional democracy; it might not play well on CNN, but we needn't be ashamed of it.

So far, this argument doesn't take the Constitution as a document all that seriously. It sounds as if the Constitution is just a fig leaf behind which elite judges hide their own political preferences. But it's more than that. *Given the customs of legal argument and interpretation*, some outcomes can be justified by the text and many simply cannot. That's a result of a tradition of textual interpretation in which all good constitutional lawyers and scholars engage. Of course, this tradition evolves in reaction to changing social circumstances and political pressures, and so the meaning of the Constitution evolves—so much for original intent or strict textualism. And the tradition is, again, largely an elite enterprise—whether it's Ed Meese and the Federalist Society plotting the reinstallation of the Constitution in exile or a bunch of liberal law professors and lawyers meeting in New Haven to discuss the Constitution in 2020. At the same time, this elite conversation is informed by popular politics—and the more sensitive it is to popular politics, the more likely it is to be successful and long-lived.

Solidarity

Any successful political program requires a popular story that gives it meaning and legitimacy. I suspect that the best—perhaps the only—way to frame a broad constitutional vision that will both appeal to a majority of Americans and satisfy traditional left-liberal objectives (egalitarian redistribution of wealth, either in kind or through socially progressive legislation and policy; more humane workplace relationships; social esteem for racial, religious, and sexual minorities; and so on) will be to tell a story that emphasizes what joins us as a political community.

In order to build support for a meaningful social safety net, we'll have to build opportunities for common experiences and build communities that a majority of people will want to join, communities whose members will be willing to aid the needy because the needy will show by their actions that they merit the aid. In a world that is increasingly interconnected and "flat," as Thomas Friedman[4] would put it, we, more than ever, need a good rationale for a political ethic of sharing that can underwrite a social safety net and a commitment to civil rights. Liberal humanism isn't sufficient because it doesn't explain why we owe a greater duty to people in the nation than to those, equally in need, outside its borders. For instance, given the ease of trade in agricultural products across national borders and the multinational interests of many nominally "American" corporations, why do we owe a free public education and minimum social services to noncitizens who do seasonal agricultural labor in the United States but not to noncitizens who do similar work in other countries producing goods for export to the United States? True, we benefit from the labor of migrant farmworkers every time we buy produce from the San Joaquin Valley of California, but we also benefit from the labor of foreign farmworkers whenever we buy imported produce. American agribusiness directly employs migrant labor but increasingly it also directly employs labor forces that remain entirely offshore. I suspect (and share) a strong, inchoate sense that migrant laborers—even those who send much of their earnings to foreign countries and reside in the United States only seasonally—are still "us" whereas people residing and working exclusively in a foreign country are not. But without a reasonably coherent and convincing account of who "we" are, I think defending this inchoate sense to a skeptic will be very rough going.

It's a truism, but not less true for it, that nations with strong social safety nets (the caricature of European social democracy) tend to have a strong sense of social solidarity. This doesn't mean, as is often suggested, that ethnic or cultural homogeneity is a prerequisite. (It's another caricature that European nations are ethnically and culturally homogeneous; a glance at the history of almost every European nation reveals a host of distinct regions, principalities, and ethnicities, which have been joined as a single nation relatively recently and not without much political effort.) Nor does solidarity necessarily involve the brutal suppression of difference: Even the modern stereotype of ambitious and aggressive national centralization—republican France—was successful not as much because of the violent suppression of ethnic difference (not that this didn't occur) as because of the (coincidental and deliberate) creation of economic incentives to assimilation (here, I think of Eugen Weber's account of French nationalism in *Peasants into Frenchmen*) and the emergence of a robust narrative of republican citizenship (here, Benedict Anderson's *Imagined Communities* comes to mind).[5]

This does suggest, however, that whenever possible our legal and policy interventions should not be premised on strong presumptions of subgroup difference. Some of this is a question of framing. A characteristic of the New Left has been a volatile and often unrequited romance with identity politics. This romance has matured into an obsessive and dysfunctional relationship; today, it often seems that progressives deliberately frame political questions in terms of identity politics, even when substantially similar ends could be achieved by framing the question in more universal terms. For instance, Kenji Yoshino[6] has argued, quite convincingly, that many arguments for gay rights could be more usefully framed in terms of liberty—a universal interest—rather than equality, which in our constitutional tradition comes with the group-focused apparatus of "suspect classes." Not only do I think Yoshino is right about this as a matter of constitutional theory, but (dare I say, more important) I also think his insight is valuable to political organizing and popular persuasion. For instance, support for gay rights rises as voters come to see that the issue involves resistance to governmental or employer intrusion into intimate relationships; it falls when opponents are able to recast the debate as one over "special rights."

To return to my earlier example, I believe we can address the seemingly intractable problem of the ghetto underclass if we abandon the idea—untrue since at least the 1980s—that all good things come from the center and must be forced on the provinces. Local governments have some good ideas about reversing segregation and improving life in poor neighborhoods, and in many cases what they need most is help—financial help and help in terms of additional authority—not top-down limitations and pressure.

Local experiences also suggest that we'd be well served to drop feel-good multiculturalism and take a hard look at the subculture of the ghetto, with an eye toward accommodating what can be socially productive and changing what can't. Abstract constitutional theory arguments too often suggest that popular opposition to the cultural traits of racial or ethnic groups is a form of invidious prejudice. But solidarity in common institutions requires common cultural norms: It's unlikely that we'll see durable integration in the public schools if we deprive them of their historical capacity to advance a common set of social and cultural values. A realistic program of integration will necessarily entail an assertive attempt to reform the dysfunctional aspects of inner-city culture—indeed, such reform is a big part of the value of integration to the inner-city poor. If assimilation to mainstream norms and values is made an explicit goal of integrated schools and is aggressively pursued, there might be less resistance to integration among middle-class families (of all races), who would have less reason to fear the potentially negative peer influences too often associated with inner-city schools. It's easy to dismiss resistance to busing as simple bigotry from the lofty perspective of constitutional litigation—and it's just as easy to dismiss local efforts to achieve integration as lazy reverse discrimination. But from the local perspective of families with kids, neighborhoods with problems, and communities with real if fragile senses of solidarity, the situation is a complex mix of reflexive prejudice and realistic assessment, indefensible selfishness and understandable self-preservation.

Such solidarity will of necessity entail some restrictions that may strike outsiders as overbearing: Communities may demand work or changes in lifestyle or the embrace of common values or commitment to master a common language as a condition of membership in a community. Group-focused constitutional litigation can stymie these attempts to create solidarity. But the alternative to solidarity is not freedom and tolerance; it's anomie and alienation. Tell the local school district that its dress code banning gangbanger fashions is "culturally discriminatory," and the result will not be integrated schools with students of diverse cultural affectations. It will be resistance to integration in the form of strident demands for neighborhood schools, litigation to block even modest attempts to achieve integration, and of course, exit from the public schools altogether in favor of private alternatives.

Conclusion

Perhaps the greatest risk of constitutionalism as it's currently understood is that it substitutes abstraction for practicality and prefers lofty and abstruse moral rhetoric to commonsense morality. If we suspend what I'm tempted to call the constitutional lawyer's mind-set, we'd be much more likely to settle on something messier, more incomplete, less intellectually satisfying, but also more likely to create real and durable solidarities, if only by fits and starts. In other words, I'm suggesting an inversion of the conventional constitutionalism, wherein the Constitution—interpreted and imposed from above—informs and improves the retrograde politics of the provinces, and I'm suggesting that the sloppy, trial-and-error virtues of local popular politics could usefully inform the meaning of the Constitution.

Notes

1. Kenneth T. Jackson, *Crabgrass Frontier: The Suburbanization of the United States* 278 (1985).

2. *Southern Burlington County NAACP v. Township of Mount Laurel*, 67 N.J. 151 (1975); *Southern Bulington County NAACP v. Township of Mount Laurel*, 92 N.J. 158 (1983).

3. See Clinton Obama Slugfest, FactCheck.org (January 22, 2008), http://www.factcheck.org/elections-2008/clinton-obama_slugfest.html

4. Thomas Friedman, *The World Is Flat* (2006).

5. Eugen Weber, *Peasants into Frenchmen: The Modernization of Rural France, 1870–1914* (1976); Benedict Anderson, *Imagined Communities: Reflections on the Origin and Spread of Nationalism* (1993).

6. See Kenji Yoshino, Gerken-Yoshino Discussion of Liberty and Equality, *Convictions*, May 21, 2008, http://www.slate.com/blogs/blogs/convictions/archive/2008/05/21/gerken-yoshino-discussion-of-liberty-and-equality.aspx

PART IV

Democracy and Civil Liberties

❧ 14 ❧

Voting Rights and the Third Reconstruction

PAMELA S. KARLAN

AT THE SIGNING ceremony for the Voting Rights Act of 1965, President Lyndon B. Johnson called the act "one of the most monumental laws in the entire history of American freedom."[1] The act is rightly celebrated as the cornerstone of the Second Reconstruction: Within two years of its passage, more African Americans had been added to voting rolls in the South than had managed to register in the entire preceding century. As a result of the original act and its amendments, politics in jurisdictions with significant numbers of black, Latino, and Native American voters has been significantly transformed, and the number of minority elected officials has skyrocketed. But that we *needed* a Second Reconstruction is a disquieting fact about U.S. history: The First Reconstruction, which at one point saw levels of voter turnout and black electoral success that would be the envy of any state today, ended with cynical political compromises, concerted vote suppression, and judicial indifference. It took the civil rights movement of the 1950s and 1960s to resuscitate the Fourteenth and Fifteenth amendments' promise of political integration.

In a number of unfortunate ways, the twenty-first century has seen a reprise of cynical political compromises, concerted vote suppression, and judicial indifference to voting rights that has undermined some of the promise of the Second Reconstruction. In Georgia, for example, Democratic incumbents of both races agreed to a redistricting plan that decreased the number of districts from which black voters could elect the representatives of their choice in an ultimately fruitless attempt to retain Democratic control of the state legislature. (Indeed, some of the white Democratic legislators whose reelection depended on black support actually switched parties after the election.) In many states, an ostensible concern with fraud has led to the imposition of draconian voter identification requirements that make it difficult for poor, elderly, disabled, and urban voters, who often do not have the requisite documents, to cast their ballots. Despite the conceded lack of any evidence of in-person vote fraud, in 2008 the Supreme Court upheld an Indiana law, finding that it protected public confidence in the election system and downplaying the burdens it imposed. The United States remains the only country in the Western world to disenfranchise millions of its citizens on the basis of criminal convictions, and the courts have repeatedly rejected challenges to this punitive practice, despite public opinion surveys finding that over 80 percent of Americans support allowing offenders to regain their right to vote and that more than 40 percent of the public would also allow offenders on probation or parole to vote.[2]

So, we need a Third Reconstruction. And this time around, two goals must be to transform the constitutional conception of the right to vote and to recognize that voting—while it expresses a critical recognition of individual dignity and full membership in the community—is also a fundamental structural element of our constitutional democracy. While a Third Reconstruction must achieve the full enfranchisement that has so far eluded us, it needs also to look beyond voting as an atomistic, individual act. It needs to consider political structure as well in order to provide fair, effective, and responsive representation after Election Day is over.

The Constitution is honeycombed with provisions regarding political participation; most of the amendments ratified since the original Bill of Rights deal with elections or voting in one way or another. But the most explicit protections of the franchise are phrased in the negative— that is, as prohibitions on particular forms of disenfranchisement. The Fifteenth Amendment, for example, forbids denial of the right to vote "on account of race"; the Nineteenth, "on account of sex"; and the Twenty-Fourth, "by reason of failure to pay any poll tax." Still other constitutional provisions simply bootstrap off of states' decisions about the franchise; for example, the right to vote in congressional elections is protected for individuals who have "the qualifications requisite for electors of the most numerous branch of the State legislatures."[3] In light of this phraseology, the Supreme Court long ago expressed itself "unanimously of the opinion that the Constitution of the United States does not confer the right of suffrage upon any one."[4] And it reinforced this view in the notorious *Bush v. Gore* decision, with its almost offhanded declaration that "[t]he individual citizen has no federal constitutional right to vote for electors for the President of the United States unless and until the state legislature chooses a statewide election as the means to implement its power to appoint members of the Electoral College."[5]

That the right to vote is expressed in negative terms is not entirely surprising. The entire Constitution is characterized by negative rights. Even the Fourteenth Amendment, the centerpiece of the First Reconstruction, largely acts to restrict government action: "nor shall any State deprive any person of life, liberty, or property, without due process of law; nor deny to any person within its jurisdiction the equal protection of the laws." This conception can work well enough when the right at issue can fairly be framed as a right to be left alone: The right to privacy, for example, can be vindicated in large part simply by telling the government to stay out of our bedrooms, away from our e-mail, and off our property. But a negative conception doesn't work nearly so well when the ability to exercise a right depends on governmental action. A citizen who is handed an official ballot written in a language she does not understand is effectively denied the right to vote. A citizen who lives in a county that uses antiquated voting machines that frequently break down may effectively be prevented from voting by the press of other responsibilities that make it impossible for him to wait in line for hours to cast a ballot.

Moreover, the right to vote, while it is an important symbol of an individual's full membership in our political community, should not be seen as solely an individual right. Voting gets much of its meaning from the way individual votes are aggregated to determine election outcomes. If punitive offender disenfranchisement statutes bar over 1 million black men from voting, their disenfranchisement is not just their own business: It deprives the black community as a whole of political power and can skew election results sharply to the right, creating legislative bodies hostile to civil rights and economic justice for the franchised and disenfranchised alike. If four-hour lines to vote in urban precincts in Ohio deter voters there from casting their ballots, their absence can swing a presidential election, thus impairing the political interests of voters across the country. Although we stand by ourselves in the voting booth casting a secret ballot, no one really votes alone.

What would it mean to develop an affirmative conception of the right to vote, one in which the government has an obligation to facilitate citizens' exercise of the franchise? One concrete context involves voter registration. It's a bedrock principle of the Fourteenth Amendment with respect to other government-recognized or -created entitlements that the kind of notice the government must give someone before it deprives her of life, liberty, or property should be the sort that "one desirous of actually informing" the individual "might reasonably adopt." A "mere gesture" is not enough.[6]

What would happen if we applied this view to voting and treated the right to vote as a kind of liberty or property that was inherent in the very notion of citizenship? When the government really cares about whether a citizen fulfills an obligation—ranging from registering for the draft to staying clean on parole to showing up for jury duty—it acts quite differently than it does with respect to political participation. It makes affirmative efforts to ensure that citizens are informed about their obligations. For example, the government mails jury summonses to individuals' homes with prepaid mailers for returning the forms, and it follows up with individuals who do not respond. It makes the forms for Selective Service registration available at every post office, and it conditions eligibility for government programs, such as student loans, on individuals' registration. By contrast, when it comes to voting, the government relies largely on individual initiative. And some states have created a series of hurdles that make registration difficult and time con-suming. For example, one out of six individuals who tried to register to vote in Maricopa County, Arizona (the state's most populous county), had his registration papers rejected for failure to comply with the state's restrictive new voter identification bill.

If we treated voting as an affirmative right of citizenship, this could also help to reframe the way courts, legislatures, and the public think about the relationship between voter participation and vote fraud. Conservatives often claim that there is an inevitable tradeoff between making it easier for citizens to vote and increasing the likelihood of fraud. And the Supreme Court in its opinions seems to see a related tradeoff between government-imposed barriers that preclude some citi-zens from casting ballots and a sort of disillusionment effect in which qualified voters stay away from the polls because they think their votes are being canceled out by ballots cast by unqualified individuals.[7] While, as a theoretical matter, these tradeoffs might exist, the available evi-dence suggests that the number of qualified citizens who are barred from the polls by so-called voter integrity measures exceeds many times over whatever fraud is actually prevented,[8] and there is no evidence whatsoever that voters stay away from the polls because they believe unqualified individuals are voting. (Indeed, there is a far more structural explanation for low turnout: Many voters believe, with a fair amount of justification, that the present system is rigged, through gerrymandering and other incumbent-protective devices, to produce foreordained outcomes. The available evidence shows that turnout is significantly higher in competitive races.)

Just as important as the evidence, though, is the way the potential tradeoff is discussed. In the criminal justice system, where individuals' freedom is at stake, the public understands that protections such as the requirement that a defendant be proven guilty beyond a reasonable doubt before he is convicted may occasionally result in acquitting guilty people. But our system is willing to bear that risk in order to protect the innocent—hence the phrase "better a hundred guilty men go free than that one innocent person be convicted." By recognizing that voting, like physical freedom, is a fundamental constitutional right, perhaps we can move toward a similar perspective with respect to the franchise.

Beyond easier registration, recognizing that voting is an affirmative right and that the government must therefore provide individuals with the means to exercise their right could also serve as a springboard for attacking, both politically and through litigation, states' failure to construct efficient, fair, and reliable voting systems. The "reforms" instituted in the wake of the 2000 election often fail to deliver on this promise. For example, the Help America Vote Act (almost as euphemistic a moniker as the USA PATRIOT Act) requires states to provide provisional ballots to individuals who appear at a polling place only to find that their names are somehow missing from the rolls, but it says nothing about whether states must ultimately count those ballots, and many elections officials have refused to count such ballots even if the voter was entirely qualified to vote but simply showed up at the wrong polling station. Similarly, the electronic voting machines that many jurisdictions adopted in the wake of the butterfly ballot/hanging chad disasters can be difficult for elderly and disabled voters to use and may lack audit trails that allow the public to be confident that votes are being accurately counted.

Finally, remaining mindful that the right to vote is not only an affirmative right but is also a collective right offers at least a starting point for rethinking fundamental questions about who deserves representation and how our representative institutions should be constructed. The Second Reconstruction embraced a commitment to ensuring that members of traditionally excluded racial and ethnic minority groups, such as

African Americans, Latinos, and Native Americans, achieve representation on elective bodies. That representation has been accomplished largely through the use of geographic districts, making lemonade out of the sorry fact that the United States remains deeply residentially segregated. But the use of geographic districts does nothing to enhance the electoral prospects of female candidates or candidates representing numerical minorities who do not live in discrete communities. Moreover, it can make it more difficult for liberal, progressive, and moderate white voters to elect candidates. One of the striking facts about the emergence of democracies in the former Soviet bloc, in South Africa, and in the developing world is that, while all these nations have adopted features of the U.S. Constitution such as a bill of rights and judicial review, *none* has adopted our system of winner-take-all single-member districts as the sole means of electing national and provincial legislatures. Instead, they have all adopted systems that are more explicitly proportional. By their nature, these systems are more democratic, since they leave to voters, rather than to those who draw the districts, the decision about how to affiliate themselves. There's a traditional Korean saying that one should never let one's skill exceed one's virtue. One of the lessons we have learned since the reapportionment revolution that occurred during the Second Reconstruction is that the gerrymanderers' technical skill in manipulating district lines now exceeds the power of our current legal doctrine to assure fair elections. Part of the task of the Third Reconstruction must be to develop new principles that can constrain the blatant manipulation of elections, which has replaced elections where the people choose their rulers with redistricting processes in which the rulers choose their constituents.

While some activists and legislators have suggested the need for a new constitutional amendment recognizing the affirmative right to vote, my own view is that the existing constitutional provisions are sufficient. A better tactic, it seems to me, lies in reviving—as conservatives have done for their own ends—Charles Black's approach to constitutional reasoning from the structure and relationship of constitutional provisions.[9] The federalism revolution of the later Rehnquist Court relied on this approach in using the language in the Tenth and Eleventh amendments to expand state sovereignty and to constrain congressional power to vindicate civil rights. It is time for liberals and progressives to make similar arguments with respect to the contours of the right to vote. The entire Constitution presupposes free and fair elections in which all qualified citizens can participate. The individual amendments that have expanded the electorate should be read to express a more general principle. The decision in the Seventeenth Amendment to take the selection of U.S. senators away from the state legislatures should be seen as fundamentally inconsistent with a decision to turn the selection of U.S. representatives into the province of the state legislatures, as the current hands-off approach to redistricting has done. The decision in the Twenty-Fourth Amendment to abolish poll taxes should be seen as reflecting a fundamental commitment to eliminating barriers to registration and to ensuring that wealth plays less of a role in our politics.

And even beyond our politics, arguing for an affirmative conception of the right to vote can perhaps serve as an opening wedge in arguing for affirmative conceptions of other rights. In part, if we can persuade the public that the government has a responsibility to enable all citizens, including poor people, people with disabilities, and members of minority groups, to participate fully in the electoral process, then perhaps we can also persuade them that the government has a responsibility to provide all individuals with the tools necessary to participate fully in other arenas of American life. But there is a more concrete way in which voting can contribute to a more affirmative politics. The politics we have is itself a function of who votes. That was the point of Dr. Martin Luther King's great Give Us the Ballot speech in 1957. Once the U.S. electorate is more representative of all its people, the people themselves will push for legislation that more fully serves their needs. One of the great victories of the Second Reconstruction was the way in which the Voting Rights Act of 1965 transformed black Americans' lives. The act's ambition separated it from preceding civil rights laws: It sought to transform black southerners into active participants in the governance process rather than simply recipients of congressionally or judicially conferred fair treatment in some discrete arena.[10] The aim of the Third Reconstruction must be both to preserve the gains the Second Reconstruction produced for racial minority groups and to expand those gains to reach other communities as well.

Notes

1. David J. Garrow, *Protest at Selma: Martin Luther King, Jr., and the Voting Rights Act of 1965*, 132 (1978).

2. See Pamela S. Karlan, *Convictions and Doubts: Retribution, Representation, and the Debate over Felon Disenfranchisement*, 56 Stan. L. Rev. 1147 (2004); Brian Pinaire, Milton Heumann, and Laura Bilotta, *Public Attitudes toward the Disenfranchisement of Felons*, 30 Fordham Urb. L.J. 1519, 1540 (2003); Jeff Manza, Clem Brooks, and Christopher Uggen, *"Civil Death" or Civil Rights? Public Attitudes towards Felon Disfranchisement in the United States* 21–23 (2003), available at http://www.socsci.umn.edu/~uggen/POQ8.pdf.

3. U.S. Const. amend. XVII; see also U.S. Const. Art. I, § 2, cl. 1.

4. *Minor v. Happersett*, 88 U.S. 162, 178 (1875).

5. 531 U.S. 98, 104 (2000) (per curiam).

6. *Mullane v. Central Hanover Bank and Trust Co.*, 339 U.S. 306, 315 (1950).

7. See *Purcell v. Gonzalez*, 549 U.S. 1 (2006); see also *Crawford v. Marion County*, 128 S. Ct. 1610 (2008).

8. See, e.g., Spencer Overton, *Stealing Democracy: The New Politics of Voter Suppression* (2006).

9. See Charles L. Black, Jr., *Structure and Relationship in Constitutional Law* (1969).

10. See Samuel Issacharoff and Pamela S. Karlan, *Groups, Politics, and the Equal Protection Clause*, 58 Miami L. Rev. 35 (2003); Karlan, *Loss and Redemption: Voting Rights at the Turn of a Century*, 50 Vand. L. Rev. 291, 316 (1997); Karlan, *The Rights to Vote: Some Realism about Formalism*, 71 Tex. L. Rev. 1705, 1719 (1993).

～ 15 ～

Political Organization and the Future of Democracy

LARRY KRAMER

A Puzzle

The twentieth century ended with a spectacular surge of democracy, the greatest by far since the end of the eighteenth. In simple numbers of people getting their first taste of self-government, the spread of the democratic sentiment across the globe today dwarfs the tiny American and French revolutions. In the United States and Western Europe, the cradle of modern democracy, democratic institutions have never been healthier. Government is more responsive than ever. Politicians are less corrupt, better educated, and more devoted to public service than at any time in the past. The free press flourishes, with greater access and far more resources, and the battle to create political and economic opportunities for women, minorities, and the poor, while far from over, is steadily advancing. Liberal democracy looks better than ever.

Except for one thing. Apart from a handful of historically minded academics, no one else seems to think so. As remarkable as the late twentieth-century spread of democratic institutions throughout the world has been the simultaneous swell of cynicism in the places where democracy is oldest and that have seen its benefits most. Signs of this phenomenon are all around us. Voter turnout in the United States continues to drop, despite occasional bounces. In Europe, splinter parties with extremist agendas and depressingly thin commitments to democracy are making hair-raising gains. Scandals abound, even as politicians become cleaner under the ceaseless glare of public scrutiny. On both continents, the electorate willingly embraces extravagantly implausible amateur politicians, while polls report persistently rising levels of mistrust in leadership and skepticism about the ability of politics to make life better. Here, then, is a puzzle worth pondering. How can democracy do so well and so poorly at the same time? And why are people losing faith in political institutions even as those institutions are, in fact, becoming healthier?

Taking the Long View

The most beneficial use of history is not, as the familiar canard would have it, that without understanding history we are destined to repeat it. Rather, studying history gives us distance and perspective from which to see things that may otherwise be obscured. The concerns of the day and convictions of the moment too easily fill our perceptions of problems and solutions. In looking at our own cultures at an earlier time, we may discover otherwise imperceptible forces that shape events.

The struggle for democracy in modern times achieved its first triumph in the United States, during the years 1763–1800. The popular misperception that this victory was complete with the Declaration of Independence in 1776 or that it was secured by the adoption of the Constitution in 1789 is just that: a misperception. The American founders had a terribly difficult time devising institutions capable of supporting popular government, and the infant republic came perilously close to collapse during its first decade. These early struggles to build a successful democracy are worth revisiting, if only briefly, to see what light they cast on our problems today.

Although the war for independence from England was effectively won by 1781, the new United States lacked the institutional and political infrastructure to survive as a nation. The 1780s are known for good reason as "the critical period," for even contemporaries appreciated that a crisis was at hand. The usually sober and restrained George Washington thus wrote despairingly in 1786, "From the high ground we stood upon, from the plain path which invited our footsteps, to be so fallen! so lost! it is really mortifying."[1] The reform movement to adopt a new Constitution in 1787 was first and foremost a movement to create a stronger, more "energetic" national government.

Opponents of the new system shrieked that popular government was impossible on a national scale. No matter how dedicated, no matter how faithful its representatives, they urged, the government of a society as large and diverse as the United States would be unable to maintain "the confidence of the people." Faith in government would erode, and the system would eventually collapse. Instead, they counseled, governing should be left mainly to the states, with a modest national organization arranged along the lines of a league among coequals—a model closely akin to the existing European Union.

At its heart, this Anti-Federal argument rested on a shrewd evaluation of the conditions necessary for democratic politics. Democracy is not just a matter of rational debate about the best policy, nor solely a question of interests or even principles. It is also a matter of what Enlightenment philosophers referred to as "affection" or "attachment." A democratic system must engage people's emotions and imaginations as well as their interests. It must make them believe, truly feel, that the government acts for them, that it follows their wishes and can be controlled by them—that it is, in a word, theirs.

Opponents of the Constitution insisted that a national government could never secure this sort of affection and confidence. Why? Because, they explained, popular government requires an intimacy and connection between rulers and ruled that will never exist in a large republic, where government officials and institutions must necessarily be distant and remote from the average citizen. Under the then-existing state systems, voters were "acquainted with" their representatives and had "personal knowledge" of their characters; constituents could "make known their wants, circumstances, and opinions"[2] because elected officials were friends, neighbors, or patrons who "mixed" with them and whom they regularly encountered while going about their daily business. It was this sort of relationship that made government by representatives acceptable without force or tyranny—a kind of intimacy that would be impossible for officials in a continent-sized republic. Relying on reputation or expecting voters to be satisfied with reports and editorials in newspapers simply would not suffice.

This is why Anti-Federalists were so troubled by the Constitution. If you remove the props on which faith in popular government has rested, they asked, what will support it when things get rough, as they assuredly will? How will government retain the confidence of the people if you weaken the foundations on which that confidence has been based? When lawmakers adopted measures that were controversial or that called for unequal sacrifices—something inevitable in a diverse, eclectic society—the government would be unable to manage the political strains that would emerge. The nation would, eventually, either erupt in civil war or dissolve under the collective weight of the people's apathy.

The Constitution's supporters thought they had an answer to this quandary. Giving people better government was one way to earn their support and affection. "I believe it may be laid down as a general rule," Alexander Hamilton wrote in *Federalist* 27, that the people's "confidence in and obedience to a government, will commonly be proportioned to the goodness or badness of its administration." More fundamentally, the Federalists offered an ingenious structural solution in the form of federalism. No sensible Federalist denied either that substantial differences existed among the states or that the legislature in a unitary national system would be hard-pressed to take all of them into account. Instead, they denied that such a thing was necessary—pointing to the Constitution's federal division of labor, which confined the national government to objects of a general nature that would not need to be adjusted to suit the particular circumstances of every community. By thus limiting the responsibilities of national representatives, federalism itself became an integral component of the Federalist theory of republicanism and democracy.

This decentralizing strategy was, as it turned out, exceedingly useful (a point to which I will return below). But it was also incomplete—and for reasons the Anti-Federalists anticipated. Even with federalism, they said, the national government must do things that will touch people where it counts, that will affect their lives and their pocketbooks and stir their emotions. That the objects of federal law are general does not make them insignificant in the lives of ordinary citizens, and Congress's actions must often rouse passionate conflict in the community. The problem of governing a pluralistic society is not merely the technocratic one of tailoring laws appropriately to suit dissimilar local circumstances. It also includes finding a way to engage the polity: enabling citizens to embrace and take possession of a distant government that must often make decisions with which they disagree or whose content they do not fully grasp. Federalism is no help when national policy is at stake. Nor can political stress be relieved by "good government" when it is precisely whether the government is good that is at issue.

The clairvoyance of these Anti-Federalists was apparent from the start. The United States experienced one of the greatest economic booms of its history during the first decade under the Constitution, yet the 1790s were still a time of "vicious party warfare" and "almost hysterical fear." Although Federalists delivered precisely the kind of good government they had promised, domestic political debate achieved a level of violence and alienation exceeded only by the Civil War. By the decade's end, talk of disunion and secession was rife, the commander of the U.S. Army (who happened to be Alexander Hamilton) was musing about whether to invade Virginia, while the governors there and in Pennsylvania were anxiously preparing to mobilize their militias in anticipation of a possible civil war.

The new nation weathered the crisis, due in large part to the emergence of the world's first political parties. With each new controversy, even as the emerging Federalist and Republican parties exacerbated popular discontent, they helped simultaneously to channel that discontent back into the system. When disgruntled citizens began murmuring about secession and civil war, party leaders were able to encourage them instead to turn to the polls by offering supporters a national organization capable of formulating positions, managing election campaigns, and arranging the government to ensure that their party's program was implemented. It was the replacement of traditional forms of face-to-face politics with the new rituals of party politics that made constitutional democracy on a large scale functional. Parties gave public debate on a continental scale the structure and coherence needed to create tolerable consensus on an agenda, while offering citizens opportunities to participate at the local level, which facilitated their acceptance of the system and its laws.

The crucial insight of the Anti-Federalists in 1787 was thus the same insight as former Speaker of the House Tip O'Neill's familiar line about how in a democracy "all politics is local." Because popular government depends on the affection and good will of the citizenry, for democracy to work it must be experienced as something vital and immediate. But this means more than meekly submitting to policies dictated from above or dutifully trudging down to the local high school to cast a vote every few years. A democratic system must engage its citizens where they live—not abstractly or passively, not through watching television or reading newspapers or sending checks, but in forms and on planes that are personal and feel efficacious.

Federalism helps to do this by relocating the situs of political decision making closer to home, putting it at a level where most people feel a greater sense of familiarity and control than is likely to be true of national politics. But national politics cannot be avoided, and a solution is needed to bring politics home from this level as well. For most of the nineteenth and twentieth centuries, in both the United States and Europe, it was political parties that filled the gap, connecting people to government by traversing and mediating the space between politicians and their constituents.

Back to the Future

Even in this sketchy form, the story related above highlights some important lessons about the nature of democracy. First, democracy has an emotional and affective side as well as a rational one. Second, we must tend to democracy's affective side through political stratagems capable of nourishing a vibrant political life for ordinary citizens. More particularly, the story points to two very different sorts of institutional devices that are worth reexamining in this regard. And, as we shall see, it provides a possible partial explanation for rising public cynicism about government while suggesting some ways to think about how to turn that cynicism around.

Federalism

Federalism was out of favor among progressives for most of the twentieth century, particularly in the United States, where it was blamed for perpetuating racism and for a variety of other evils. This tendency peaked around 1964, when William Riker concluded a comparative study of federalist systems around the globe by observing that federalism was good only for shielding powerful groups from surrendering their privileged status. Put in other words, Riker mused sardonically, "if...one approves of Southern white racists, then one should approve of American federalism....If one disapproves of racism, one should disapprove of federalism."[3]

Not so, conservatives, who continued to champion federalism and who have spent the last quarter of a century busily investigating and finding ways to return authority to the states (albeit with a countervailing centralizing trend in the George W. Bush administration)—accompanied by an equally incessant chorus of praise for the genius of federalism. Items listed in the inventory of claimed benefits for federalism include everything from enhancing freedom to fostering participatory democracy, facilitating regulatory diversity, protecting individual liberty, promoting responsible fiscal policy, and providing a laboratory for testing novel legislative programs.

To be sure, some of the items included in this litany reflect nothing more than thoughtless repetition of theoretical justifications that experience has disproved or called into question. The view that federalism enhances freedom, for example, was first voiced in the late eighteenth century, at which time it rested on a "civic humanist" understanding of liberty that was group rather than individually oriented. The argument may have made sense in this context, but if anything seems clear today, it is that central governments generally (though not invariably) do a better job than local governments when it comes to protecting individual liberties and the rights of subordinated minorities. Similarly, an abundance of studies have refuted the notion—first articulated by Justice Louis Brandeis—that state and local governments provide valuable laboratories of democracy.[4]

Such qualifications aside, two centuries of experience have vindicated the conviction of the American founders that federalism can contribute to the political health of a democracy. Because state and local electorates are smaller, elected representatives are more immediately accountable to individuals and their concerns. Government is closer to the people, and democratic ideals can be more fully realized. The paradigmatic model of democracy remains the legendary Greek polis or New England town meeting, a setting in which the whole electorate deliberates and decides, and elected representatives have essentially managerial responsibilities. Of course, direct democracy of this sort is not only impossible, but ultimately undesirable. There is much truth in James Madison's famous quip in *Federalist* 55 that "had every Athenian citizen been a Socrates, every Athenian assembly would still have been a mob." Nevertheless, the aspect of direct democracy that retains a hold on our imaginations is the way in which it engages ordinary citizens in political decision making. There is overwhelming evidence to support the proposition that our most local governing structures—school boards, county commissions, city government, and so forth—are also our liveliest and most vital. Government close to home enables people to participate in ways that feel more vivid and fulfilling than is ever possible for decisions made at the national or multinational level.

Progressives have been far too quick to run away from local politics, far too quick to assume that these forums are controlled by ordinary citizens who are hopelessly reactionary and need to be gotten around— something more easily accomplished at the national level or in court. But if this seems to be so, might that not be because conservatives have *not* run away and have *not* shared these attitudes, but have instead been willing to put their energy and political capital into winning at the local level? Successful progressive grassroots movements are a staple of U.S. history—from the Revolution itself to abolition, women's suffrage, civil rights, and the movement for equal rights for women. Progressives need to rediscover the advantages and desirability of state and local politics and must begin the slow, hard process of winning people's hearts and minds at these levels by taking them (and the ordinary citizens who participate in and control them) seriously.

It does not follow that all decisions should be made at the state or local level. There are powerful and essential justifications favoring national legislation: the demand for a country to speak with one voice on important matters, the need to prevent spillover effects among the different states or regions of a nation, the desires to achieve economies of scale and to protect individual rights, and so forth. What is wanted, then, is a genuine commitment responsibly to allocate political authority among different levels of government, together with appropriate devices to ensure that national lawmakers leave suitable decisions to lower levels.

As to political commitment, there seems everywhere to be a renewed willingness on the part of public officials and party leaders to explore decentralizing strategies. Nevertheless, the reflex among progressives to address every new problem at the national level or through litigation remains strong and must be watched and resisted where it is inappropriate. The process of sensibly rethinking how big to make big government is still just beginning. It has been and should be an important part of the progressive agenda.

The problem of discovering means to achieve an optimal allocation of authority is more difficult, but also more exciting. The first impulse among scholars is invariably to think in constitutional terms, which means looking ultimately to courts for answers. But while this surely is a possible strategy, articulating legally enforceable limits on national authority has proved to be exceedingly difficult in practice. The German courts have been somewhat successful in this venture, whereas U.S. courts have experienced nothing but controversy and trouble. In any event, legal solutions have actually been less common and less prominent than political ones. In the United States, the Supreme Court has historically played an insignificant part in defining the boundaries of national power (with unfortunate results when it has intruded, though this has not stopped the present Court from trying). Instead, the allocation of power between the federal government and the states, and between state and local governments, has been fought and decided through ordinary politics.

Moreover, legal strategies have generally been less successful than political ones. International dialogue is important in this respect, for among the different nations that use federalism we have already seen and tested a wide variety of possible approaches. These include various ways of giving state or provincial governments a voice in national politics, sharing legislative and administrative authority at different levels, innovative efforts to foster "home rule," and the formation of novel cross-governmental funding and other inventive structures to shape policy. We have only just begun to explore the full potential of what has come to be known as "cooperative federalism": arrangements for sharing power among officials at different levels rather than allocating exclusive responsibility in any particular area to one or another authority. Early efforts at cooperation, such as the Great Society programs of President Lyndon Johnson, failed badly. But there is room to build on the lessons of these failures, as well as on subsequent successful efforts in the United States and elsewhere. The space for creative thinking and innovative leadership remains enormous.

Beyond Parties

Having said all that, there are nevertheless limits to what can be accomplished through decentralization and the dispersal of power. As noted above, many political choices can only be made at the national level: choices about war and peace, foreign relations, trade and commerce—in other words, all the most important and controversial choices in society. Pressure for national legislation will continue to intensify, moreover, as the process of globalization accelerates, demanding national and multinational solutions for an ever-expanding range of economic and social problems. Indeed, the creeping alienation so characteristic of contemporary democracy is surely at least partly attributable to this trend. It is hardly surprising that people would become more removed from politics as politics becomes more removed from them.

During the nineteenth and early twentieth centuries, it was political parties that kept politics from becoming too remote. This was mostly a matter of technology. Learning what people wanted, whom they favored, or what issues mattered to them could be done only through face-to-face encounters—a method of intelligence gathering that demanded a presence in the community that only political parties could manage. Campaigning was labor-intensive activity, requiring nothing so much as bodies to hand out pamphlets; to canvass door to door; to stage rallies and torchlight parades; and to make stump speeches in parks, on corners, or near polling places. With armies of volunteers obtained through their extensive patronage networks, it was the parties that supplied these services, nurturing a style of politics that engaged citizens on a personal level.

Nor were party activities confined to elections and electioneering only. Absent government welfare systems, political parties managed private welfare networks: In exchange for loyal support, ward bosses or precinct captains would help constituents to find jobs in the neighborhood or arrange for them to receive food and shelter during a bad stretch. The parties also provided entertainment at a time when cheap forms of amusement were scarce. The famous debates between Abraham Lincoln and Stephen Douglas attracted immense crowds not only because the issue of slavery was so pressing, but also because their contest was the best entertainment around. Parties sponsored dances and social events and organized a wide variety of other neighborhood activities, thus becoming important institutions in people's daily lives. And because the parties' agendas were never far from the surface, these full-service organizations made active engagement with politics an important aspect of everyday life.

In the United States, successive waves of well-meaning reform progressively maimed this system over the course of the twentieth century's first six decades. In the United States and elsewhere, a still more crushing blow was delivered by new technology: the invention and spectacular growth of television, computer-based polling and survey techniques, and direct mail and other sophisticated means of reaching voters with minimal labor. Even as greater numbers of political decisions were being made at higher levels of government, politicians and government officials were becoming more distant as they abandoned the traditional forms of party politics. Leaders in the twenty-first century reach out to constituents primarily through the national media, apparently content to establish "personal" contact through forms of address that are, in fact, one-sided and anything but personal.

Politics today has thus become a remote, passive activity for most of us. We read newspapers or watch TV; we discuss the issues with friends; we vote and maybe give some money to a party or other organization. But apart from that, we leave the management of our political affairs to others working in a businesslike manner in or closely with government agencies. Is it really any wonder that ordinary citizens have become progressively more alienated and mistrustful?

Obviously, it is too late to think about resurrecting old-style political parties, even in Europe, where these forms have retained more of their traditional flavor and salience. Nor is it clear that we should want to do so. Mass party politics in the United States was, indeed, a sinkhole of corruption, and the fascist and communist parties of midcentury Europe made the potential dangers of demagoguery and excessive party control abundantly clear. In focusing on dangers and downsides, however, we may have paid too little attention to the important constitutive role the parties played in maintaining a healthy democracy. We allowed these critical institutions to atrophy without giving adequate thought to alternative means or institutions to fill the resulting gap. We became content to address the public from a distance without seeing how this might affect the long-term vitality of democratic politics.

Here, then, is an even more important item demanding the attention of responsible leaders concerned for the future of democracy. The process of globalization has just begun to hit full stride. No matter how much energy we invest trying to preserve spheres of local autonomy, the pressures for greater centralization will be irresistible, for the simple reason that increasing numbers of issues really can be addressed only at a national or international level. As this happens, it is incumbent on political leaders to devise new means and new forms of political organization to draw the public in, to give ordinary citizens a sense not merely that the policies being adopted are good, but that these policies are also theirs.

Conservatives have responded to these changes brilliantly by establishing new and alternative institutions that knit politics and the conservative political agenda into the lives of ordinary citizens—institutions capable not only of reaching existing supporters, but also of drawing in and persuading potential new supporters. They have created a network of think tanks and intellectual societies to train future leaders and assure proper networking. They have established media outlets, including newspapers, magazines, talk radio, and even a TV network, to develop and disseminate their intellectual agenda in a manner accessible to the average person. Most important, they have used churches and religious organizations to engage and involve large numbers of citizens and make conservative politics part of the local culture and social fabric of everyday life.

These efforts have been coordinated and well considered. And effective. Progressives, in the meantime, have done nothing similar. Older organizations that once served this purpose, like unions, have atrophied, while liberal media have either been cowed into striving for a "balance" that makes their message disappear or converted into elite outlets that do not even attempt to speak to most Americans. If there is a critical agenda for progressives as we look ahead, then first and foremost, it must be to address this fatal shortcoming: Progressives must devise new and effective institutions capable of doing what parties used to do. The stakes are greater than just advancing a substantive progressive agenda. The health of our democracy more broadly speaking demands a richer, more effective array of institutions capable of actively engaging Americans in politics and restoring their sense that what they want and believe is worthy and actually matters.

Notes

1. Letter from George Washington to John Jay, May 18, 1786, in 28 *The Writings of George Washington* 431–32 (John C. Fitzpatrick, ed., Washington, D.C.: GPO, 1938).

2. The Federal Farmer, An Additional Number of Letters to the Republican (letter VII), December 31, 1787, in 17 *The Documentary History of the Ratification of the Constitution* 265, 281–82 (John P. Kaminski and Gaspare J. Saladino, eds., Madison: Wisconsin Historical Society Press, 1984).

3. William H. Riker, *Federalism: Origin, Operation, Significance* 145 (Boston: Little, Brown, 1964).

4. *New State Ice Co. v. Liebmann*, 285 US 262, 311 (1932) (Brandeis, J., dissenting).

A Progressive Perspective on Freedom of Speech

ROBERT C. POST

FIRST AMENDMENT PROTECTIONS for freedom of speech have long been the darling of the Left. Since the 1930s, these protections have sheltered the speech of labor activists, civil rights advocates, and revolutionaries. But since the late twentieth century, First Amendment rights have been used to undermine campaign finance reform, hate speech prohibitions, and the suppression of pornography, and commercial speech doctrine has evolved into a shield against market regulation. These developments have diminished the First Amendment's progressive shine. The Left has divided bitterly, with some maintaining the old-time First Amendment religion and others attacking freedom of speech as the last refuge of a reactionary libertarianism. In the face of such dissensus, what protections for freedom of speech should progressives aspire to defend in the year 2020?

Constitutional rights of freedom of speech are protected for many reasons, but historically the most important, and what ought to be most central to a progressive jurisprudence, is the protection of the communicative processes necessary for the maintenance of democracy. The First Amendment should be interpreted to ensure free participation in the formation of public opinion, which in a democracy guides the conduct of government. The central importance of this basic First Amendment value has grown increasingly central in the face of an imperial presidency that has sought to criminalize our associations, to penalize our speech, and to constrict our access to information. A progressive jurisprudence should work toward First Amendment doctrine capable of safeguarding the principle that a democratic government cannot control and censor public opinion, but must on the contrary be responsive to it.

The most fundamental implication of this jurisprudence is that the First Amendment does not protect speech as such, but only such speech as is necessary for democracy. This principle is essential in preventing the First Amendment from generating *Lochner*-type immunities from government regulation. In the early years of the First Amendment, protections were sought for speech that was obviously political; emblematic was the prosecution of Eugene Debs for what was effectively seditious libel. But since the 1970s, the idea has grown that constitutional rights extend to all speech. Because almost all human transactions occur through speech, government efforts to regulate transactions can always be recharacterized as restrictions on speech. If the First Amendment did protect speech as such, it could be used very effectively to prevent all forms of salutary government regulation.

Conservatives have become especially adept at promoting this form of argument in the context of commercial speech. The right wing of the Court has been very aggressive in using the First Amendment to strike down regulations designed to control commercial transactions. As Justice Clarence Thomas explained in 1997 in the context of compelled contributions to advertisements for California summer fruit: "Although the Constitution may not 'enact Mr. Herbert Spencer's Social Statics,'...the First Amendment—does enact a distinctly individualistic notion of 'the freedom of speech,' and Congress may not simply collectivize that aspect of our society, regardless of what it may do elsewhere."[1] Thomas's reference to *Lochner* is explicit and provocative.

Progressives should not allow First Amendment doctrine to be perverted in this way. They should be clear that advertising products for sale is not a form of participation in the creation of democratic public opinion. It may be true that commercial advertisements disseminate information that is useful for the formation of public opinion, and this is the theory on which the Supreme Court initially extended a "subordinate" form of constitutional protection to commercial speech.[2] But because commercial advertisements are primarily about selling products rather than participating in the formation of public opinion, they do not themselves merit full-bore First Amendment protection.

If this distinction is to be maintained—and without it First Amendment protections will inevitably proliferate and undermine important and desirable forms of state regulation—a progressive constitutional vision for 2020 must advance a robust theory of democracy that can identify the forms of speech and association that deserve constitutional protection because they are essential to the formation of democratic public opinion.

The first major theorist systematically to advance a democratic interpretation of the First Amendment was Alexander Meiklejohn. He argued that democracy requires freedom of communication so that citizens can receive the information necessary to exercise the franchise in an informed way and thus intelligently to direct the actions of government. There are two major difficulties with this theory. The first is that virtually all communications, including commercial advertisements, provide information, so that virtually all speech fulfills the democratic function that Meiklejohn identified as essential. The second is that Meiklejohn's theory justifies protecting speech because of the right of an audience to receive the substance of a message, rather than because of the right of a speaker to communicate that substance. As Meiklejohn famously observed, "What is essential is not that everyone shall speak, but that everything worth saying shall be said."[3] In fact, solicitude for the circulation of information, rather than for the rights of speakers, is exactly the subordinate form of constitutional protection that the Supreme Court originally extended to commercial advertisements.

A progressive constitutional vision for 2020 ought to embrace the importance of freely circulating information, but it also ought to identify core First Amendment rights on the basis of a different criterion. Democracy has a deeper rationale than merely informed public decision making. Democracy is most fundamentally about self-government. It is about ensuring that the people are sovereign, that government is responsive to their wishes, and that citizens experience the government as their own. This view of democracy implies that First Amendment jurisprudence must ultimately be based on the political ground of popular sovereignty, rather than on the cognitive ground of accurate popular decision making.

Popular sovereignty, however, is a difficult concept. In any modern democracy, "the people" consist of a hopelessly diverse and heterogeneous collection of individual persons. How can this agglomeration be "sovereign"? How can government be responsive to so many individuals who disagree with one another? How, for example, can the U.S. government, which at this writing is dominated by ideological conservatives, be said to be responsive to someone like myself, who vigorously disagrees with many if not most of the policies pursued by the Bush administration? If democracy requires that a minority of 49 percent yield to a majority of 51 percent, in what sense is the minority self-governing?

The answer, surely, is that the minority, and the individuals who comprise it, continue to identify with their government because they believe that their government is *potentially* responsive to them. So long as I can continue to believe that the policies and direction of the government would change if I could persuade others of the correctness of my views, it is possible for me to maintain my sense that this government is mine. There are many factors that contribute to this identification, but one necessary (although not sufficient) condition is that I am guaranteed the right freely to participate in the formation of public opinion. If the Bush administration were to prevent me from associating and communicating in ways designed to alter public opinion, my government would eventually come to feel to me as something alien and imposed; I would cease to identify with it. It would cease to be *mine*. It would lose, with respect to me, democratic legitimacy.

It is in this precise sense that the Court has celebrated the First Amendment, which negates otherwise valid majoritarian enactments, as "the guardian of our democracy."[4] The First Amendment safeguards the ability of persons to participate in the formation of public opinion so as to preserve the democratic legitimacy of our government. Because we understand commercial advertising as an effort to sell goods rather than to alter public opinion, commercial advertising should not receive core First Amendment protection, even though it may contribute information that is valuable for those who wish to transform public opinion. In this chapter, I shall use the term *public discourse* to refer to speech that ought to receive core First Amendment protection because it constitutes participation in the formation of public opinion.

In a modern democracy, public opinion is formed in what sociologists have called the "public sphere," which is a social formation in which strangers extend and receive communications from people whom they otherwise do not know. The public sphere should be contrasted to the face-to-face world of gossip. The public sphere is sustained by recognized media that facilitate communication among strangers, like books, newspapers, magazines, cinema, broadcast media, mail, and so on. Public opinion emerges through discussions and debates that occur in the pages, columns, and frames of these media. A democratic understanding of the First Amendment will closely scrutinize all regulation of such media to ensure that the state does not compromise their capacity to sustain a healthy public sphere. Impairment of such media is typically measured against the baseline of their traditional communicative functions.

Early democratic theorists of the First Amendment, like Robert Bork, imagined that constitutional protections extend only to communications that are explicitly about governmental decision making. But this is a mistake. In a democracy, the state is responsive to public opinion. Any speech that participates in the formation of public opinion, therefore, should be protected by a First Amendment that safeguards democracy. Even speech that seems on its surface irrelevant to politics, like debate about the reputation of a celebrity (such as Mel Gibson), serves to focus and clarify public values and commitments. That is why constitutional protection should be extended to media of communication, like art, music, and ballet, which may not concern overtly political subjects and which may not even contain propositional content. These media undeniably focus and clarify the formation of public opinion within the public sphere.

Keeping an eye firmly on the importance of a healthy public sphere will help progressives to clarify First Amendment jurisprudence. At present, First Amendment doctrine is notoriously scattered and confused, a jumble of incompatible and indeterminate tests, like those for "content neutrality" or "time, place and manner." Lacking a clear sense of the values that the First Amendment is meant to serve, the Court has applied these tests arbitrarily and inconsistently. It is for this reason that libertarian values have been able to infiltrate constitutional decision making, converting the First Amendment into an instrument for the protection of large business enterprises, like cable companies wishing to resist the policies of the Federal Communications Commission.

The ideal of self-governance is an essential progressive value. The First Amendment has come into disrepute on the left not merely because it has been interpreted in ways that advance libertarian rather than democratic ideals, but also because the value of self-governance can sometimes conflict with another important progressive value, equality. The tension is now especially inflamed in the area of campaign finance reform. Many on the left argue that all persons ought to have an equal opportunity to influence the development of public opinion, and they urge that campaign contributions and expenditures be accordingly regulated. The Court's opinion in *Buckley v. Valeo*, however, invoked the First Amendment to prohibit much of this regulation.

A democratic interpretation of the First Amendment would begin with the premise that free debate about the election of candidates is necessary in order to ensure the democratic legitimation of the state. Fundamental constitutional difficulties would thus be raised by government regulations that, in the name of equality, prevented persons from participating in public discourse in ways that they believe to be necessary to make public opinion responsive to them. Speakers might well experience more extensive participation in public discourse to be necessary as the intensity of their convictions increases. If participation were truncated so as to ensure equality, the function of democratic legitimation would be impaired; those with relatively more intense convictions would not experience their participation in public discourse as adequate to their need to alter public opinion. Regulation in the name of equality would thus be in tension with the value of self-government.

This does not imply, however, that a democratic interpretation of the First Amendment would prohibit all forms of campaign finance regulation. If persons came to believe that the structure of public debate was so skewed, so unfairly dominated by wealthy speakers, that the formation of public opinion could not in fact be potentially responsive to their participation, a democratic interpretation of the First Amendment would allow regulation necessary to preserve the function of democratic legitimation. A democratic interpretation of the First Amendment would require, however, that any such regulation be justifiable in terms of the logic of democratic legitimacy, rather than that of equality.

A similar tension between the ideal of self-governance and the ideal of equality has arisen in other contexts, most notably in the old debates about prohibiting racist speech or pornography. Racist speech and pornography surely contribute to inequality, and for this reason many on the left urged some time ago that they be severely regulated. Yet the suppression of racist speech and pornography within public discourse would prevent public discourse from serving to establish democratic legitimacy with respect to those who wish to speak in these ways. This suggests that there may be occasions in which progressives will have to choose between the value of equality and the value of self-governance.

Counting in favor of the latter is the fact that modern democracies consist of large and heterogeneous populations who no doubt hold very diverse views about the proper meaning of "equality." If modern democracies enact laws enforcing one or another vision of equality, like laws prohibiting employment discrimination or requiring wealth redistribution, such laws possess democratic legitimacy only so long as dissenting citizens believe that they can participate in public opinion in order to render it responsive to their own differing visions of equality. When statutes are enacted that deploy egalitarian principles to circumscribe participation in public discourse itself, the democratic legitimacy of such statutes cannot be sustained in the same way. If democratic legitimacy starts to unravel because of constraints on public discourse, all state actions suffer, including those that seek to instantiate egalitarian values. So long as progressives wish to sustain a government that is democratically legitimate with respect to all citizens, including those who are not progressive, they must allow for free participation in public discourse.

Interpreting the First Amendment to protect the ability of persons to participate in the formation of public opinion has a number of important implications for a progressive vision of the Constitution in 2020. Most important, it invites progressives normatively to clarify the forms of participation that they believe are essential for a healthy public sphere. This question has particular bite in the context of emerging new media that do not yet have traditional communicative functions. The Internet, for example, is rapidly becoming an extremely important medium for the formation of public opinion. But exactly how the Internet actually serves this function very much depends upon subtle regulations of its architecture, economic structure, protocols, etc. Because the relationship between the Internet and the formation of public opinion is new and continuously changing, it is difficult to argue that particular state interventions will impair traditional communicative functions. For this reason, constitutional argumentation in the context of the Internet will characteristically be conducted through debate about how the Internet ought as a normative matter to contribute to a healthy and flourishing public sphere. Progressives ought to be important contributors to that debate.

In the coming decades, issues such as net neutrality or the installation of centralized (versus decentralized) filters will hugely impact the precise ways in which the Internet will contribute to the formation of public opinion. Progressives will need a convincing normative vision of a healthy public sphere in order to assess the constitutional implications of potential government interventions. They will need this vision as much to shape a progressive regulatory policy as to litigate for the maintenance of progressive constitutional rights.

A strong normative vision of a healthy public sphere will enable progressives to make visible important constitutional questions that are simply invisible when seen through the lens of received First Amendment doctrine. The Court has virtually given Congress a free pass to enact copyright legislation, for example, without seriously analyzing the effects of such legislation on the formation of public opinion. As communication becomes increasingly digital, and as copyright legislation correspondingly diminishes the capacity of persons to participate in the public sphere, the insensitivity of current doctrine will have ever more significant effects. This insensitivity is, of course, encouraged by the fact that large and powerful economic interests benefit from ever more stringent copyright legislation.

If progressives succeed in modifying First Amendment jurisprudence to focus clearly and sharply on the relevant constitutional value of maintaining democratic legitimation through free participation in the formation of public opinion, anomalies like the immunity of copyright legislation from close judicial scrutiny will disappear. The First Amendment will become an effective counterweight to the undue privatization of the public sphere through intellectual property rights, which allows large economic interests to control public discussion and in this way threatens the ongoing legitimacy of our democracy.

Notes

1. *Glickman v. Wileman Bros. & Elliot, Inc.*, 521 U.S. 457,505 n.3 (1997) (Thomas, J., dissenting).

2. *Bd. of Trs. v. Fox*, 492 U.S. 469, 477 (1989).

3. Alexander Meiklejohn, *Political Freedom: The Constitutional Powers of the People* 26 (1960).

4. *Brown v. Hartlage*, 456 U.S. 45, 60 (1982).

❧ 17 ❧

Information, Structures, and the Constitution of American Society

YOCHAI BENKLER

T HE CONSTITUTION OF liberty and justice—the actual set of constraints and affordances that makes human beings more or less free, capable, and flourishing in life as they actually live it—is less affected by "the Constitution" as a formal legal category than by the confluence of formal rules within the economic, social, and technical structures that make up the actual context within which human action, alone and with others, occurs. Even after *Lawrence v. Texas*, individuals are not as free to live a gay life in Alabama as they were in New York City or San Francisco even while *Bowers v. Hardwick* was law. A democratic agenda truly concerned with human freedom, equality, and flourishing must conceive of itself in terms broader than the Constitution as law. It must be concerned with the constitution of U.S. society, rather than with the U.S. Constitution. I will illustrate this idea through examples from Internet communications, copyright issues, and telecommunications. In the process, I will make, in addition to the point that "private law" and economic arrangements are important to core democratic commitments, a more specific claim: Between now and 2020, one major policy area through which the construction of the public sphere and the constitution of liberty will be determined will be information policy. Policy choices in this area will have implications well beyond the United States. A democratic agenda should be humanistic, and therefore global, rather than formal rights–based and particular.

Consider the following stylized account of the *Pentagon Papers* affair. In a high point of American journalism and press freedom, the *New York Times* received from Daniel Ellsberg documents showing that the Pentagon early realized the dim prospects of the war in Vietnam, but the administration hid these assessments in an effort to sustain support for a losing proposition. The *Times* reporters spent weeks pouring over the materials, analyzed them, and ultimately published excerpts and analyses that would sound the beginning of the end for the Nixon administration. The government obtained an injunction on national security grounds. The *Washington Post* picked up the story for a while, but it too was subject to injunction. Both newspapers appealed to the U.S. Supreme Court, which in short order removed the injunction and permitted publication.

This is the classic optimistic story of twentieth-century media. First, the powerful commercial mass media organization is committed to journalistic ethics and vigorously investigates the administration. By doing so, the press uses the independence that market-based revenues give it to fulfill its watchdog function and fight to preserve public access to the truth. Second, the Constitution as formal law is the critical linchpin and is enforced by the Court to protect the public sphere from an overreaching administration.

Now, let me tell you a different story. Here, the public sphere is constructed by individuals and groups, using radically decentralized nonmarket forms of production, sometimes known as *peer production*. Freedom is sustained by actions and resistance is made feasible by a set of technical and economic conditions, which in turn are imperfectly affected by law, and not primarily by constitutional law.

Electronic voting machines were first substantially used in the United States in 2002. Media coverage of these machines was limited. In January 2003, Bev Harris, an activist focused on electronic voting machines, found an open site where Diebold Election Systems, a major electronic voting machine manufacturer, stored files about its systems. In early February of that year, Harris published two initial accounts on an online journal in New Zealand, *Scoop*, and created space on her Web site for technically literate users to review and comment on the files. In an editorial note published in July entitled *Bigger than Watergate, Scoop* invited its readers to action, in words that go to the heart of how the networked information economy can use peer production to play the role of watchdog:

> We can now reveal for the first time the location of a complete online copy of the original data set. As we anticipate attempts to prevent the distribution of this information we encourage supporters of democracy to make copies of these files and to make them available on websites and file sharing networks: http://users.actrix.co.nz/dolly.
>
> As many of the files are zip password protected you may need some assistance in opening them, we have found that the utility available at the following URL works well: http://www.lostpassword.com.
>
> Finally some of the zip files are partially damaged, but these too can be read by using the utility at: http://www.zip-repair.com.
>
> At this stage in this inquiry we do not believe that we have come even remotely close to investigating all aspects of this [*sic*] data, i.e., there is no reason to believe that the security flaws discovered so far are the only ones. Therefore we expect many more discoveries to be made. We want the assistance of the online computing community in this enterprise and we encourage you to file your findings at the forum HERE.[1]

Several characteristics of this call would have been simply unworkable in the mass media environment. They represent a different mindset about how news and analysis are produced and how censorship and power are avoided. First, the ubiquity of storage and communications capacity means that public discourse can rely on "see for yourself" rather than "trust me." The first move was to make the raw materials available for all to see. Second, the editors anticipated that the company would try to suppress the information. They did not possess a big media company's muscle to protect the materials. Instead, they leveraged the widespread distribution of information—about where one could find the files and the tools to crack passwords and repair bad files—matched with a call for action: Copy the files, store them in many places, so they cannot be squelched. Third, the editors did not rely on large sums flowing from being a big media organization to hire experts and interns to scour the files. Instead, they posed a challenge to whomever was interested—there are more scoops to be found, this is important for democracy, good hunting! Finally, they offered a platform for collecting the findings. This short paragraph outlined a radically distributed system for storage, distribution, analysis, and reporting on the Diebold files.

As the story unfolded over the next few months, this basic model—the peer production of investigation, reportage, analysis, and communication—worked. It resulted in the decertification of many Diebold machines in California and contributed to a shift in the requirements of other states. The first analysis of the Diebold system was published by computer scientists at Johns Hopkins. The online debate that followed prompted Maryland to commission two further reports, which found flaws in the systems and required modifications.

Meanwhile, in early August, a whistleblower provided *Wired* magazine with thousands of internal Diebold e-mails. *Wired* reported on the e-mails, emphasizing this as another example of Diebold's lax security. But the magazine provided neither analysis of the e-mails nor access to them. Bev Harris received the same cache and posted the e-mails and memos on her site. Diebold threatened litigation. Claiming copyright in the e-mails, the company demanded that the e-mails be removed by Harris, her Internet service provider, and a number of other sites where the materials had been posted. The e-mails were indeed removed. But the strategy of widely distributed replication and the storage of data in diverse topological and organizational settings rendered Diebold's efforts futile. The protagonists from here on were college students. First, two students at Swarthmore College and then students in other universities began storing the e-mails and scouring them for evidence of impropriety. Diebold wrote to universities whose students were hosting the materials, invoking "notice and take down" provisions of the Digital Millennium Copyright Act, which require Web-hosting companies to remove infringing materials when notified of their presence. The universities obliged, requiring the students to remove the materials from their sites. The students, however, did not disappear quietly into the night. Instead, they launched a multipronged campaign of what they described as "electronic civil disobedience." First, they moved the files from one student's to another's machine, encouraging students around the country to resist the efforts to eliminate the material. Second, they injected the materials into Freenet, an anticensorship peer-to-peer publication network, and into peer-to-peer file-sharing systems like eDonkey and BitTorrent. Finally, supported by the Electronic Frontier Foundation, the students sued Diebold, seeking a judicial declaration that posting the materials was privileged. They won both the insurgent and formal campaigns. As a practical matter, the materials remained publicly available throughout this period. As a matter of law, the court ultimately awarded the students damages and attorneys' fees because it found that Diebold had "knowingly and materially misrepresented" that the publication of the e-mail archive was a copyright violation.[2]

The court victory was, however, insignificant from the perspective of the dynamics of the networked public sphere. It came a year after most of the important events had already unfolded. The critical fact was the efficacy of the students' persistent publication in the teeth of cease-and-desist letters and the willingness of universities to comply with them. The strategy of replicating the files everywhere made it impractical to keep the documents from the public eye. And the public eye, in turn, scrutinized. The e-mails seemed to have played at least some role in California's investigation, and ultimate decertification, of many Diebold machines.

The twenty-first-century structure of public inquiry, debate, and collective action exemplified by this story is fundamentally different than the structure of public inquiry and debate in the mass-mediated public sphere of the twentieth century. The initial investigations and analyses were done by a committed activist, operating on a low budget with no financing from a media company. This is not yet radically different, though the low costs significantly increase the efficacy of the committed individual. The output of this initial inquiry was not only, or even most importantly, respectable analysis by a media voice in the public debate. The output was access to the raw materials and initial observations about them, which were enough to start a conversation. Analyses emerged from a widely distributed process undertaken by Internet users of many different types and abilities. They included academics studying electronic voting systems, activists, computer systems practitioners, and mobilized students. When the pressure from a well-financed corporation mounted, it was not the prestige and money of a *New York Times* that protected the integrity of the information and its availability for public scrutiny. It was the radically distributed cooperative efforts of students and peer-to-peer network users around the Internet. These efforts were, in turn, nested in other communities of cooperative production: the free software community that developed some of the applications used to disseminate the e-mails and the semi-legal file-sharing networks. There was no single orchestrating power—neither party nor professional commercial media outlet. There were, instead, a series of uncoordinated, mutually reinforcing actions by individuals in different contexts, operating under diverse organizational restrictions and affordances, to expose, analyze, and distribute criticism and the evidence for it. The networked public sphere that was utilized here does not rely on advertising or capturing large audiences to focus its efforts. What is observed, stated, and achieves salience is what intensely interests the active participants, not what moderately interests large groups of passive viewers. Instead of the lowest common denominator, each individual and group can—indeed, most likely will—focus precisely on what is most intensely interesting to its participants. Instead of iconic representation built on the scarcity of time slots or space on the air or on the page, we see the emergence of a see-for-yourself culture. Access to underlying documents and statements and to the direct expression of the opinions of others has become a central part of the medium.

In this story, freedom, personal and collective, is a condition characterized by the system of constraints and affordances under which people interact with existing information, knowledge, and culture, and how they produce and exchange their own. At the individual level, there is a new freedom to engage in new kinds of production. The basic enabling conditions go well beyond the use for political criticism: from writing your own blog, to contributing to a free online encyclopedia like Wikipedia, to developing software, to constructing an immersive video experience. In the past, it was practically infeasible for individuals to do many of these things without a business model. The costs of collecting the information, producing a communication of acceptable quality, and communicating it were simply too high for anyone who did not operate within one of three business models: commercial, government- or tax-funded, or large-scale philanthropic grants.

Liberals do not usually think of high costs or the lack of tools as constraints on individual freedom. But that is because we choose to take a very particular view: a partial systems analysis view, rather than either a first-person view or a more expansive systems view. We focus on the system of law and government power. If we took either a first-person humancentric view—that is, what actually makes actions possible and impossible, or at least hard and easy, for individual human beings—or, in the alternative, if we took a genuine systems analysis view and looked at all system affordances and constraints, we would see economic, technical, and social constraints together with state power as relevant. The networked information environment is a significant improvement in individual freedom because of its technical affordances and because it enables users to act together in loose affiliation to leverage their respective capabilities and to achieve common outcomes.

From the perspective of public discourse, the case is even easier to make. The coordinated efforts of the individual players in this story came to play the role of the Fourth Estate for a mass media largely absent from the debate. And in this case, because the Fourth Estate was actually the universe of the citizenry at large, it was not merely a new estate but a new state of mind for citizenship. As we learn that, with as small a contribution as making a copy of e-mails and posting them or reading through some to look for tidbits, we can make an impact on public debate, our very conception of the possibilities of citizenship changes. Instead of walking through life knowing that, if we observe something, all we can do is whine about it to friends, we begin to observe our environment knowing that we are potential reporters and contributors to public discourse, and our efforts could actually result in action.

The same underlying affordances are giving rise to new cultural practices. Individuals and cooperative peer efforts are beginning to write encyclopedias and to make their own richly rendered online games, film sites, music, and photographic images. Culture is becoming both more transparent and more available for users to make for themselves and others. The public sphere has always encompassed a much wider range of communicative moves than those that are focused on the explicit exchange of information and opinions on matters that all participants understand to be about politics. Instead, it is being constructed through a much broader range of conversational moves within the society and cultural groups, through which we understand what the state of the world is, how it might be different, and the various courses of action open to us as individuals and as a society. These now come to be made in a radically more open and egalitarian way than was possible in the mass-mediated environment.

As the new freedom to create and exchange information increases, it has come to threaten several incumbent businesses of the industrial information economy. Here is where politics and the future constitution of U.S. society meet. We are going now through a battle over the institutional ecology of the digital environment. The battle is being waged over whether law will be optimized for industrial information production on the model of Hollywood and the recording industry, or whether it will be open to new forms of social production—both individual nonmarket and cooperative peer production. This battle is not being primarily played out in the domain of constitutional law. It is, instead, played out in areas as diverse as copyright and new paracopyright technology regulations, software patents, telecommunications, wireless systems design, database protection rights, and technical standards setting. If we take the Diebold story as paradigmatic, we can see most obviously how the pompously named Digital Millennium Copyright Act was used as a sword to silence criticism, which, but for the students' resistance, would have delayed debate until it would have been too late to matter. More subtly, we see the role of telecommunications law. The e-mails could be replicated in many places because there was no single point that Diebold could use to shut down the information. Where there was a sole provider, as in the case of Swarthmore, the students were in fact shut down. It was only the diversity of providers that allowed the e-mail archives to stay in play politically. Yet, the current broadband regulation in the United States trends toward an unregulated duopoly over broadband access to homes. The law of copyright itself, in the form of fair use, ended up providing the students with protection from Diebold, but only because they were supported in litigation by a nonprofit, the Electronic Frontier Foundation. The majority of individuals facing litigation simply fold, rather than risk tens or hundreds of thousands of dollars in statutory damages, even absent actual damage. The consequences of these legal battles to the freedom of individuals to act in the information economy as they will, to be creative and expressive, to form meaningful associations in the domain of information and culture, whether for explicitly political purposes or otherwise, will be profound.

These, then, are my two points. In an immediate and specific sense, we are currently engaged in a battle over the future shape of information, knowledge, and cultural production. On one side stand some of the incumbents of the industrial information economy. Their business models depend on rendering consumers as passive recipients of finished information goods provided in a market dependent on government-granted exclusive rights—like copyrights and spectrum licenses. On the other side are the beneficiaries of the newly emerging networked information environment. These include individuals who want to be creative, informative, and inquisitive and who, alone or in diverse associations, are coming together to make and share all of the conceivable informational, cultural, and knowledge goods under the sun, and many new ones that were not there before. But they also include businesses that have realized that this new explosion of curiosity and creativity offers new opportunities. Toolmakers like computer and software companies, platform creators who enable individuals to connect with each other and be creative in new ways, and businesses that have learned to integrate the outputs of peer production into their supply chain are also onboard. At stake in this battle is not whether there will or will not be some form of Internet in the future. Of course, there will. What is at stake is whether it will be easy for individuals to be creative users, participants in a public discourse, and creators of the public sphere, or whether it will be hard and expensive, as it has been in the mass-mediated environment to the detriment of freedom, both individual and collective.

The broader point is also by now obvious. The sources and constraints on liberty are not purely a matter of the Constitution as law. Perhaps, they are not even primarily a matter of the Constitution as law. They are, instead, a matter of human action and constraint, of patterns of human communication and expression. As lawyers and law students aiming for a more democratic society in 2020, we must avoid a narrow focus on "the Constitution" and a narrow legal and Americancentric view of our goals and targets of reform and analysis. Instead, the freedom of human beings as human beings, rather than as Americans, depends on a wide range of constraints which interact with a wide and historically contingent set of legal battles. As we strive for a more democratic society, where individuals are ever more free and equal citizens, we must train ourselves to think of the constitution of society, of the totality of the sources of freedom and constraint, equality and inequality, and to think of law in terms of its role in that broadly defined system of freedom and constraint.

Notes

1. See Scoop, *Sludge Report #154—Bigger Than Watergate!*, July 8, 2003, 6:13 pm, at http://whatreallyhappened.com/WRHARTICLES/biggerthanwatergate.html.

2. *Online Policy Group v. Diebold, Inc.*, 337 F. Supp. 2d 1195 (2004).

❧ 18 ❧

The Constitution in the National Surveillance State

JACK M. BALKIN

L ATE IN 2005, the *New York Times* reported that the Bush administration had ordered the National Security Agency (NSA) to
eavesdrop on telephone conversations by persons in the United
States in order to obtain information that might help combat terrorist
attacks. The secret NSA program operated outside of the restrictions
on government surveillance imposed by the 1978 Foreign Intelligence
Surveillance Act and was thought to be only one of several such programs. In 2007, Congress temporarily amended FISA to increase the
president's power to listen in on conversations where at least one party
is believed to be outside the United States, and in June 2008, Congress
passed a series of amendments to FISA, which allow the president to
engage in a broad range of electronic surveillance without seeking warrants against particular individual targets of surveillance. At the same
time, Congress effectively immunized telecommunications companies
that participated in the secret NSA program.

In 2007, New York City announced that it planned to mount thousands of cameras throughout Lower Manhattan to monitor vehicles and
individuals. Some cameras will be able to photograph and read license
plates and send out alerts for suspicious cars. The system of cameras

will link to a series of pivoting gates installed at critical intersections, giving government officials the ability to block off traffic through electronic commands. New York's new plan—called the Lower Manhattan Security Initiative—is based on London's "ring of steel," a security and surveillance system around London's central core that features thousands of surveillance cameras. New York is hardly alone; the Department of Homeland Security has been quietly channeling millions of dollars to local governments around the country to create high-tech camera networks that can be linked with private surveillance systems.

The secret NSA program and New York's Lower Manhattan Security Initiative reflect a larger trend in how governments do their jobs that predates the September 11, 2001, attacks and the Bush administration's declaration of a war on terror. During the last part of the twentieth century, the United States began developing a new form of governance that features the collection, collation, and analysis of information about populations both in the United States and around the world. This new form of governance is the national surveillance state.

In the national surveillance state, the government uses surveillance, data collection, collation, and analysis to identify problems, to head off potential threats, to govern populations, and to deliver valuable social services. The national surveillance state is a special case of the information state—a state that tries to identify and solve problems of governance through the collection, collation, analysis, and production of information.

The war on terror may be the most familiar justification for the rise of the national surveillance state, but it is hardly the sole or even the most important cause. Government's increasing use of surveillance and data mining is a predictable result of accelerating developments in information technology. As technologies that let us discover and analyze what is happening in the world become ever more powerful, both governments and private parties will seek to use them.

The question is not whether we will have a surveillance state in the years to come, but what sort of surveillance state we will have. Will we have a government without sufficient controls over public and private surveillance, or will we have a government that protects individual dignity and conforms both public and private surveillance to the rule of law?

The national surveillance state is a way of governing. It is neither the product of emergency nor the product of war. War and emergency are temporary conditions. The national surveillance state is a permanent feature of governance and will become as ubiquitous in time as the familiar devices of the regulatory and welfare state. Governments will use surveillance, data collection, and data-mining technologies not only to keep Americans safe from terrorist attacks but also to prevent ordinary crime and deliver social services. In fact, providing basic social services and protecting key rights—like rights against employment discrimination—is already quite difficult, if not impossible, without extensive data collection and analysis. Moreover, much of the surveillance in the national surveillance state will be conducted and analyzed by private parties. The increased demand for—and the increased use of—public and private surveillance cannot be explained or justified solely in terms of war or emergency.

The national surveillance state grows naturally out of the welfare state and the national security state; it is their logical successor. The welfare state governs domestic affairs by spending and transferring money and by creating government entitlements, licenses, and public works. The national security state promotes foreign policy through investments in defense industries and defense-related technologies, through creating and expanding national intelligence agencies like the CIA and the NSA, and through the placement of U.S. military forces and weapons systems around the globe to counter military threats and project national power worldwide.

The welfare state created a huge demand for data-processing technologies to identify individuals—think about all the uses for your Social Security number—and deliver social services like licenses, benefits, and pensions. The national security state created the need for effective intelligence collection and data analysis. It funded the development of increasingly powerful technologies for surveillance, data collection, and data mining, not to mention increasingly powerful computer and telecommunications technologies. American investments in defense technologies spurred the electronics industry, the computer industry, and, eventually, the birth of the Internet itself.

By the time the Internet went commercial in the mid-1990s, the national surveillance state was already well in gear. Telecommunications, computing, data storage, and surveillance technologies have become ever more potent, while their costs have steadily declined. It is unthinkable that governments would not seek to use these technologies to promote the public good; it is even more unthinkable that private parties would not try to harness them as well. In fact much, if not most, surveillance and information collection in the early twenty-first century is in private hands. Corporations invest heavily in security and surveillance, especially to protect sensitive information in their computer networks.

Private security cameras still outnumber those operated by the government. Many businesses make money from collecting, analyzing, and selling consumer data; governments increasingly purchase information from corporations instead of collecting it themselves.

In the national surveillance state, the line between public and private modes of surveillance and security has blurred if not vanished. Public and private enterprises are thoroughly intertwined. The NSA program would be impossible without the assistance of telecommunications companies; the government now requires that new communications technologies be designed with back ends that facilitate government surveillance. Federal programs encourage linking private security cameras with comprehensive government systems like those planned in Manhattan. Corporate data collectors and commercial data-mining operations are major sources of information on individuals' tastes, preferences, histories, and behaviors that governments can harness. Governments and businesses are increasingly partners in surveillance, data mining, and information analysis. Moreover, the architecture of the Internet—and the many possible methods of attack—requires governments, corporations, and private parties to work together to protect network security and head off threats before they occur.

Increased focus on surveillance and prevention becomes inevitable once digital information technologies become widely dispersed. Criminal organizations and terrorist groups use many of the same information and surveillance technologies that governments and legitimate businesses do. Terrorist groups that lack fixed addresses can use new information technologies to communicate and plan assaults. Hackers can attack networks from afar. A new breed of criminals employs digital networks to commit old-fashioned crimes like embezzlement and to commit new crimes like identity theft and denial-of-service attacks. Cyber attacks can not only bring down financial institutions; they can also target the nation's defense systems. Digital technologies simultaneously pose new problems for governments and create new opportunities for identifying threats and meeting them in advance.

Older models of law enforcement have focused on the apprehension and prosecution of wrongdoers after the fact and the threat of criminal or civil sanctions to deter future bad behavior. The national surveillance state supplements this model of prosecution and deterrence with technologies of prediction and prevention. Computer security tries to identify potential weaknesses and block entry by suspicious persons before they have a chance to strike. Private companies and government agencies use databases to develop profiles of individuals who are likely to violate laws, drive up costs, or cause problems, and then deflect them, block them, or deny them benefits, access, or opportunities. The government's No Fly and Selectee watch lists and its still-planned Secure Flight Screening program collect information on passengers and create profiles that seek to block dangerous people from boarding planes. Governance in the national surveillance state is increasingly statistically oriented, ex ante, and preventive rather than focused on deterrence and ex post prosecution of individual wrongdoing. Such tendencies have been around for at least a century, but new technologies for surveillance, data analysis, and regulation by computer code and physical architecture have made them far easier to put into effect.

The national surveillance state seeks any and all information that assists governance; electronic surveillance is not its only tool. Governments can also get information out of human bodies, for example, through collection and analysis of DNA, through locational tracking, and through facial recognition systems. The detention and interrogation practices used by George W. Bush's administration sought to get information out of human bodies through relatively old-fashioned methods, including some techniques that were tantamount to torture. In the national surveillance state, bodies are not simply objects of governance; they are rich sources of information that governments can mine through a multitude of different technologies and techniques.

Decades ago, Michel Foucault argued that modern societies had become increasingly focused on watching and measuring people in order to control them, normalize their behavior, and make them docile and obedient. His famous example was Jeremy Bentham's idea of a panopticon—a prison designed so that the prisoners could always be watched even if they did not know exactly when. By making surveillance ubiquitous, governments and private organizations could discourage behavior that they deemed unusual or abnormal.

Today's national surveillance state goes beyond Foucault's panoptic model. Government's most important technique of control is no longer watching or threatening to watch. It is analyzing and drawing connections between data. Much public and private surveillance occurs without any knowledge that one is watched. More to the point, data-mining technologies allow the state and business enterprises to record perfectly innocent behavior that no one is particularly ashamed of and draw surprisingly powerful inferences about people's behavior, beliefs, and attitudes. Over time, these tools will only become more effective. We leave traces of ourselves continually, including our location, our communications contacts, our consumption choices—even our DNA.

Data mining allows inferences not only about the direct subjects of surveillance, but about *other people* with whom they live, work, and communicate. Instead of spying on a particular person, data about other persons combined with public facts about a person can allow governments and private businesses to draw increasingly powerful inferences about that person's motives, desires, and behaviors.

The problem today is not that fear of surveillance will lead people to docile conformity, for even the most innocent and seemingly unimportant behaviors can increase knowledge about ourselves and others. Normal behavior does not merely acquiesce to the state's power; it may actually amplify it, adding information to databases that make inferences more powerful and effective: Our behavior may tell things about us we may not even know about ourselves. In addition, knowledge about some people can generate knowledge about others who are not being directly watched. Individuals can no longer protect themselves simply by preventing the government from watching them, for the government may no longer need to watch *them* in particular to gain knowledge that can be used against them.

Equally important, the rise of the national surveillance state portends the death of amnesia. In practice, much privacy protection depends on forgetting. When people display unusual or embarrassing behavior, or participate in political protests in public places, their most effective protection may be that most people don't know who they are and will soon forget who did what at a certain time and place. But cameras, facial recognition systems, and location tracking systems let governments and businesses compile continuous records of what happens at particular locations, which can be collated with records of different times and places. The collation and analysis of events allows public and private actors to create locational and temporal profiles of people, making it easier to trace and predict their behaviors. Older surveillance cameras featured imprecise, grainy images; and the recordings were quickly taped over. New digital systems offer ever greater fidelity and precision, and the declining cost of digital storage means that records of events can be maintained indefinitely, copied, and distributed widely to other surveillance systems around the country or even around the globe. Ordinary citizens can no longer assume that what they do will be forgotten; rather, records will be stored and collated with other information collected at other times and places. The greatest single protector of privacy—amnesia—will soon be a thing of the past. As technology improves and storage costs decline, the national surveillance state becomes the state that never forgets.

The national surveillance state poses three major dangers for our freedom. Because the national surveillance state emphasizes ex ante prevention rather than ex post apprehension and prosecution, the first danger is that government will create a parallel track of preventive law enforcement that routes around the traditional guarantees of the Bill of Rights. The Bush administration's military detention practices and its NSA surveillance program are two examples. The administration justified detaining and interrogating people—including U.S. citizens—in ways that would have violated traditional legal restraints on the grounds that it was not engaged in criminal law enforcement. It sought intelligence that would prevent future attacks and it wanted to prevent terrorists from returning to the battlefield. Similarly, the administration defended the warrantless surveillance of people in the United States by arguing that the president was not engaged in criminal prosecutions but in the collection of military intelligence designed to fight terrorism.

The second danger is that traditional law enforcement and social services will increasingly resemble the parallel track. Once governments have access to powerful surveillance and data-mining technologies, there will be enormous political pressure to use them in everyday law enforcement and for the delivery of government services. If data mining can help us to locate terrorists, why not use it to find deadbeat dads, or even people who haven't paid their parking tickets? If surveillance technologies signal that certain people are likely threats to public order, why not create a system of preventive detention outside the ordinary criminal justice system? Why not impose sanctions outside the criminal law, like denying people the right to board airplanes or use public facilities and transportation systems? And if DNA analysis can identify people who will likely impose high costs on public resources, why not identify them in advance and exclude them from public programs and other opportunities? The more powerful and effective our technologies of surveillance and analysis become, the more pressure the government will feel to route around warrant requirements and other procedural hurdles so that it can catch potential troublemakers more effectively and efficiently before they have a chance to cause any harm.

Private power and public-private cooperation pose a third danger. Because the Constitution does not reach private parties, government has increasing incentives to rely on private enterprise to collect and generate information for it. Corporate business models, in turn, lead companies to amass and analyze more and more information about people in order to target new customers and reject undesirable ones. As computing power increases and storage costs decline, companies will seek to know more and more about their customers and sell this valuable information to other companies and to the government.

If some form of the national surveillance state is inevitable, how do we continue to protect individual rights and constitutional government? Today's challenge is similar to that faced during the first half of the twentieth century, when government transitioned into the welfare state and the national security state. Americans had to figure out how to tame these new forms of governance within constitutional boundaries. It is no accident that this period spawned both the New Deal—with its vast increase in government power—and the civil rights revolution. The more power the state amasses, the more Americans need constitutional guarantees to keep governments honest and devoted to the public good.

We might begin by distinguishing between an authoritarian information state and a democratic information state. Authoritarian information states are *information gluttons* and *information misers*. Like gluttons, they grab as much information as possible because this helps maximize their power. Authoritarian states are information misers because they try to keep the information they collect—and their own operations—secret from the public. They try to treat everything that might embarrass them or undermine their authority as state secrets, and they multiply secret rules and regulations, which lets them claim to obey the law without having to account for what they do. In this way, they avoid accountability for violating people's rights and for their own policy failures. Thus, information gluttony and information miserliness are two sides of the same coin: Both secure governments' power by using information to control their populations, to prevent inquiry into their own operations, to limit avenues of political accountability, and to facilitate self-serving propaganda.

By contrast, democratic information states are *information gourmets* and *information philanthropists*. Like gourmets, they collect and collate only the information they need to ensure efficient government and national security. They do not keep tabs on citizens without justifiable reasons; they create a regular system of checks and procedures to avoid abuse. They stop collecting information when it is no longer needed, and they discard information at regular intervals to protect privacy. When it is impossible or impractical to destroy information—for example, because it is stored redundantly in many different locations—democratic information states strictly regulate the data's subsequent use. If the information state is unable to forget, it is imperative that it be able to forgive.

Democratic information states are also information philanthropists because they willingly distribute much of the valuable information they gather and create to the public, in the form of education, scientific research, and agricultural and medical information. They allow the public access to information about their laws and their decision-making processes so that the public can hold government officials accountable if they act illegally or arbitrarily or are corrupt or inefficient. They avoid secret laws and secret proceedings except where absolutely necessary. Democratic states recognize that access and disclosure prevent governments from manipulating their citizens. They protect individual privacy because surveillance encourages abuses of power and inhibits freedom and democratic participation. Thus, being an information gourmet and an information philanthropist are also connected: Both help keep governments open and responsible to citizens; both further individual autonomy and democracy by respecting privacy and promoting access to knowledge.

You might think that the Fourth Amendment would be the most important constitutional provision for controlling and preventing abuses of power in the national surveillance state. But courts have largely debilitated the Fourth Amendment to meet the demands of the regulatory and welfare state, the national security state, and the war on drugs. Much government collection and use of personal data now falls outside the Fourth Amendment's protection—at least as the courts currently construe it. Courts have held that there is no expectation of privacy in business records and information that people give to third parties like banks and other businesses; in the digital age, this accounts for a vast amount of personal information. Most e-mail messages are copied onto privately held servers, making their protection limited if not nonexistent. Courts have also held that the Fourth Amendment poses few limits on foreign intelligence surveillance, which is largely regulated by FISA. As a result, the executive branch has increasingly justified domestic surveillance by asserting that it is a permissible by-product of foreign intelligence gathering.

Currently, governments are free to place cameras in public places like streets and parks because there is no expectation of privacy there. Governments can also collect information that people leave out in the open, like their presence on a public street, or abandon, like fingerprints, hair, skin cells, or DNA samples. Moreover, because the Fourth Amendment focuses on searches and seizures, it places few limits on collation and analysis, including data mining. The Fourth Amendment does not require governments to discard any information they have already lawfully collected. Digital files once assembled can be copied and augmented with new information indefinitely for later analysis and pattern matching. Finally, whatever constitutional limits might restrain government do not apply to private parties, who can freely collect, collate, and sell personal information back to the government free of Fourth Amendment restrictions, effectively allowing an end-run around the Constitution.

We should try to change some of the weaknesses in current Fourth Amendment doctrine. But legislative, administrative, and technological solutions may be far more important means of guaranteeing constitutional freedoms in the national surveillance state. These laws and technologies will probably do far more to enforce the constitutional values underlying the Fourth Amendment and the Due Process Clause.

Congress must pass new superstatutes to regulate the collection, collation, purchase, and analysis of data. These new superstatutes would have three basic features. First, they would restrict the kinds of data that governments may collect, collate, and use against people. They would strengthen the very limited protections of e-mail and digital business records and rein in how the government purchases and uses data collected by private parties. They would institutionalize government "amnesia" by requiring that some kinds of data be regularly destroyed after a certain amount of time unless there were good reasons for retaining them. Second, the new superstatutes would create a code of proper conduct for private companies that collect, analyze, and sell personal information. Third, the new superstatutes would create a series of oversight mechanisms for executive bureaucracies that collect, purchase, process, and use information.

Oversight of executive branch officials may be the single most important goal in securing freedom in the national surveillance state. Without appropriate checks and oversight mechanisms, executive officials will too easily slide into the bad tendencies that characterize authoritarian information states. They will increase secrecy, avoid accountability, cover up mistakes, and confuse their interest with the public interest.

Events in the Bush administration suggest that legislative oversight increasingly plays only a limited role in checking the executive. Meaningful oversight is most likely to occur only when there is divided government. Even then, the executive will resist sharing any information about its internal processes and about the legal justifications for its decisions. A vast number of different programs affect personal privacy, and it is unrealistic to expect that Congress can supervise them all. National security often demands that only a small number of legislators know about particularly sensitive programs and how they operate, making it easy for an administration to co-opt the legislators. The Bush administration's history demonstrates the many ways that presidents can feign consultation with Congress without really doing so.

Judicial oversight need not require a traditional system of warrants; it could include a system of prior disclosure and explanation and subsequent regular reporting and minimization. This is especially important as surveillance practices shift from operations targeted at individual suspected persons to surveillance programs that do not begin with identified individuals and focus on matching and discovering patterns based on the analysis of large amounts of data and contact information. We need procedures that translate the values of the Fourth Amendment (with its warrant requirement) and the Fifth Amendment's Due Process Clause into a new technological context. In the early twenty-first century, however, we have excluded more and more executive action from judicial review on the twin grounds of secrecy and efficiency. The Bush administration's secret NSA program is one example; the explosion in the use of administrative warrants that require no judicial oversight is another. Yet an independent judiciary plays an important role in making sure that zealous officials do not overreach. If the executive seeks greater efficiency, this requires a corresponding duty of greater disclosure before the fact and reporting after the fact to determine whether its surveillance programs are targeting the right people or are being abused. Judges must also counter the executive's increasing use of secrecy and the state secrets privilege to avoid accountability for its actions. Executive officials have institutional incentives to label their operations as secret and beyond the reach of judicial scrutiny. Unless legislatures and courts can devise effective procedures for inspecting and evaluating secret programs, the presidency will become a law unto itself.

Given the limits of legislative and judicial oversight, oversight within the executive branch will prove especially crucial. Congress can design institutional structures that require the executive to police itself and make regular reports about its conduct. For example, if Congress wants to bolster legal protections against warrantless surveillance, it might create a cadre of information ombudsmen within the executive branch—with the highest security clearances—whose job is to ensure that government deploys information collection techniques legally and nonarbitrarily. Unfortunately, the Bush administration has made extreme claims of inherent presidential power that it said allowed it to disregard oversight and reporting mechanisms. Rejecting those claims about presidential power will be crucial to securing the rule of law in the national surveillance state.

Finally, technological oversight will probably be an indispensable supplement to legal procedures. The best way to control the watchers is to watch them as well. We should construct surveillance architectures so that government surveillance is regularly recorded and available for audit by ombudsmen and executive branch inspectors. Records of surveillance can, in turn, be subjected to data analysis and pattern matching to discover any unusual behavior that suggests abuse of proper procedures. These technological audits can automate part of the process of oversight; they can assist ombudsmen, executive officials, Congress, and the courts in ensuring that surveillance practices stay within legal bounds. We can prevent some kinds of abuse by technological design; at the very least, technology can force disclosure of information that executive officials would otherwise keep hidden.

The administrative and welfare state raised problems not only for the Constitution, but also for the rule of law itself. The same is true for the national surveillance state. Changing methods of governance demand new strategies to preserve constitutional values and democratic self-government. We mastered at least some of the problems caused by the rise of the administrative and welfare state; we must hope that we can do the same for the national surveillance state, which is already here.

❧ 19 ❧

The Progressive Past

TRACEY L. MEARES

A PROGRESSIVE CONSTITUTION FOR today must consider how race deeply impacts—indeed, infects—the U.S. criminal justice system. There are the obvious facts: The rate of American punishment is significant as a general matter, but the African American punishment rate is staggering. African Americans comprise about 44 percent of the state and federal prison population.[1] There is increasing evidence that unacceptable numbers of these people are wrongfully imprisoned. There is an endless stream of complaints by many African Americans and Latinos of police stopping them because of their race.

Less obviously, there is evidence that, when law enforcement officials treat people of color differently from others, those actions broadly impact all minority group members. Survey evidence is crystal clear regarding the gap between the levels of confidence that minority group members and whites have in the police and the courts,[2] and research notably shows that the more negative opinions of people of color are durable without regard to group members' specific experiences with legal authorities.

Of course, racial injustice in the U.S. criminal justice system is not a new problem. We've tried to fix it before. Most recently, in the late 1960s and early '70s, the Supreme Court reworked state criminal procedures by implementing new constitutional rules in an attempt to ensure that criminal defendants—especially minority ones—are treated fairly. But the constitutional architecture of that moment has proven no match for the racial unfairness we continue to see in the twenty-first century.

Many have noted in both the scholarly and popular press that there is too little judicial policing of criminal defendants' constitutional rights. Too few commentators have noted, though, that courts play a vanishingly small role in the very important task of shoring up a diverse community's confidence in the legitimacy of the criminal law and its operation.

It was not always so. In the early twentieth century, a set of cases about the functional conception of constitutional criminal procedure outlined a notion of fundamental fairness demanded by the Due Process Clause of the Fourteenth Amendment that took seriously the public's interest in fair criminal procedures. The opinions reflect what so many of us know intuitively to be true: Public perceptions of fairness are critical to the proper operation of the criminal justice system. These early cases are important for another reason. The public-regarding vision of fairness articulated in them is inextricably intertwined with the racial dynamics of the cases. That is, the Court set out the boundary lines of constitutional fairness specifically by reference to southern racial injustice.

My argument is that it is time to rethink constitutional criminal procedure in a way that enhances the legitimacy of criminal law and its administration for all groups with particular emphasis on African Americans. As Lani Guinier and Gerald Torres have poignantly noted, issues pertaining to race in the United States are the "miner's canary" that alert us to problems in society that ultimately impact everyone.[3] We will not make headway in dispensing justice for *all* until we take seriously the promotion of the legitimacy of law in the eyes of the African American public. This means that courts must consider the interests of the public as well as defendants when engaging in constitutional decision making.

I want to make clear that I do not believe that the interests of criminal defendants and the minority public balance each other out in a zero-sum game. Rather, I simply believe that one cannot properly conceive of fundamental fairness without taking into account the interests of all the stakeholders in the system. The interests of law-abiding minority citizens have been ignored all too often, and African Americans—especially those in disadvantaged urban areas—bear the brunt of more than their fair share of both crime and the law enforcement strategies designed to combat it. A legitimate Constitution would pay more attention to this group.

While I am focusing primarily upon the interests of African Americans here, let me emphasize that other groups can and will benefit from a search for fundamental fairness. Any group that has a focused interest in fair criminal justice proceedings through greater involvement in it as a defendant, a victim, or a relative or friend of one of the former should welcome the approach I describe here.

I start by tying together the idea that public perceptions of fairness matter to the legitimacy of criminal law and also to compliance with a snapshot of the early criminal procedural cases. It turns out that the Supreme Court's first forays into substantial review of state criminal convictions in the late 1920s and early '30s can teach us a great deal about public-regarding justice. The language and ideas in these opinions both reflect and are congenial to the modern social science of legitimacy and procedural justice. I hope that dusting off these cases and bringing them together with modern social science research inspires a dialogue about the ways that a reimagined criminal procedure might inspire a more fair criminal justice system.

That the criminal justice system operates fairly is a good in and of itself; nonetheless, fair processes can lead to instrumental benefits. Increased public confidence in the criminal justice system is one benefit. Psychologists have demonstrated that the public is much more likely to support and participate in the criminal justice system and to support those officials who run it when the public believes that the system is just and fair. People want to be treated with dignity. They want decision makers to act without bias. In general, they expect authorities to behave in ways that inspire trust. If these things do not happen, then negative public perceptions follow. Public perceptions that the system is unfair can result in low levels of public support, which, in turn, can lead to diminished respect for the law. Research connects diminished respect for the law to less compliance with it.[4]

Because people want to be held in high esteem by members of groups with which they identify, they use the fairness of procedures as a method of evaluating their status.[5] Individuals tend to believe that how an authority treats them is an important indicator of how that authority views the group to which the person believes she belongs, the status of that group relative to others, and the status of the person within that group.[6] When a person experiences fair procedures or is treated well by legal authorities, she feels that her group has high status and that others think well of her within her group. Researchers think that people rely on procedures for these status cues because formal sources of treatment are more stable over time than informal ones, and thus provide more reliable cues.[7]

Perceptions of fairness, in turn, support compliance with rules and laws. So, when people think they have been treated fairly—with dignity in ways that inspire trust and cooperation—people appear to be more likely to obey the law because they are motivated to defer to authorities they believe to be legitimate.[8] Research suggests that, when a person believes that an authority enforcing the law has the right to do so, she is more likely to obey the law than she would be if she were simply presented with a threat of formal punishment.[9]

Unfortunately, studies consistently document that minority communities perceive higher levels of bias in the legal system than do nonminority communities.[10] Minority respondents have been shown to be more likely to say that they had received unfair outcomes in their experiences with authorities, to say that the procedures used by authorities were unfair, and to express low levels of trust in the motives of authorities.[11] Yet, members of minority groups care deeply about process issues.[12] That is, the evaluations of both minority and nonminority groups of police and courts (and, presumably, prosecutors) depend a great deal on the fairness of the treatment—as opposed to outcomes—that people feel they receive from these authorities.

This research explains why racial profiling, for example, is not just a problem for the particular African American motorist who has been stopped. Theories of group value suggest that, when a police officer harasses an African American, the officer damages that person's sense of status, but the treatment also communicates disdain for the group as a whole.[13] As a result, the treatment impacts the relationship of that group with specific authorities and with government in general.

One can imagine many helpful strategies to address racial inequality in treatment that would take this research seriously. Elsewhere, I have described some of them,[14] but our task here is to reimagine constitutional procedure in ways that more fairly treat all citizens. I believe that a return to public-regarding notions of fundamental fairness is one potential path.

A quick review is in order. In the late 1920s and continuing throughout the 1930s, public-regarding ideas of fundamental fairness were prominent in cases in which the Supreme Court began to interpret the Due Process Clause of the Fourteenth Amendment to invalidate state criminal convictions—the birthplace of constitutional criminal procedure. In many of these cases, the Court emphasized that public perceptions of the fairness of proceedings and of police actions were critical in order to establish constitutional standards for due process.[15] For example, in one case, the Court held that Alabama was required to appoint counsel for the defendants because the right to a lawyer is a "fundamental principle of liberty and justice which lie[s] at the base of all our civil and political institutions,"[16] and the "ends of public justice" required the trial court to appoint counsel for the defendants, "however guilty."[17]

Addressing racial injustice was an important imperative as the Court specified normative constitutional values in the criminal procedure arena. It was by reference to southern racial injustice in cases such as *Powell v. Alabama*[18] and *Norris v. Alabama*[19] (cases dealing with the Scottsboro Boys episode) and *Brown v. Mississippi* (where a local sheriff, in order to obtain a murder confession from a black defendant, beat him bloody with a belt buckle and then testified that the beating was not "too much for a Negro")[20] that the Court was able to articulate what constitutional fairness was *not* and, therefore, provide some purchase on what it is.

Today, however, there is little room in criminal procedure decision making to consider racial injustice explicitly. For example, when the Supreme Court unanimously upheld pretextual traffic stops in *Whren v. United States*,[21] it paid no attention to the impact of the practice on the minority public. For the Court, the decision was a simple one based on the motorist's traffic violation. The motives of the police officer who made the stop were irrelevant. Similarly, in a case involving suspect flight from a police officer, *Illinois v. Wardlow*,[22] the Court focused upon (or tried to) how reliably flight indicates guilt. That inquiry is a good place to start, but the ultimate question that the Court did not answer is: How good an indicator of guilt does flight from police have to be to satisfy Fourth Amendment reasonableness? This normative question obviously is informed by the question that the Court attempted to answer in *Wardlow*, but a real answer requires the Court to consider additional factors: law enforcement needs, police and public safety, and social realities, such as race relations between the police and the policed in the disadvantaged neighborhoods that were the factual context of the case.[23] Today's approach to interpreting the Fourth Amendment, with its emphasis on eighteenth-century history, leaves little room for this kind of analysis. An approach to constitutional interpretation inspired by due process and fundamental fairness, with its emphasis on public-regarding fairness, just might.

How might this be done? A couple of examples will demonstrate how promotion of the public's interest in system fairness through constitutional law could also address racial unfairness. Let us start with race-based jury exclusion.

It was practically impossible for a criminal defendant to challenge jury discrimination until the Supreme Court decided in *Batson v. Kentucky*[24] that the Equal Protection Clause of the Fourteenth Amendment prohibits prosecutors from exercising peremptory challenges to exclude potential jurors on the basis of race and that evidence of race-based jury selection from a single case is sufficient to establish a constitutional violation.

Although *Batson* is about a defendant's right to a jury free from discrimination, it is obvious that *jurors* have an interest in not being excluded from service on the basis of their race. The Court, picking up on this idea, noted, "The harm from discriminatory jury selection extends beyond that inflicted on the defendant and the excluded juror to touch the entire community. Selection procedures that purposefully exclude black persons from juries undermine public confidence in the fairness of our system of justice."[25]

This is the essence of public-regarding justice. Excluding a juror because of her race is a problem whether or not the defendant shares the excluded juror's race. It is a problem whether or not the exclusion somehow impacts the outcome of the case by impacting the jury's decisional skew. Illegal and unconstitutional jury selection procedures cast doubt on the integrity of the whole judicial process. They create the appearance of bias. They create unfair tribunals. They ought not to be tolerated.

But a constitutional foundation for addressing racial bias in jury selection has not been articulated by the Court in this way. Instead, real redress of this kind of discrimination is hampered by an anemic equal protection doctrine and commonsense-defying third-party-standing gymnastics. It would be much more straightforward to recognize, as a public-regarding due process approach would, that excluding a juror because of her race creates a structural defect that *all* members of the public have an interest in correcting. This way of framing the issue also finds support in the social science of procedural justice.

Selective prosecution claims present another example of the benefits of a procedural justice-infused fundamental fairness approach. Selective prosecution claims have proven to be an extremely difficult issue for courts to address. One problem with selective prosecution claims is that courts tend to think about them solely from the perspective of the defendant to be prosecuted. Thinking about the problem in this way creates a conundrum when it comes time to deliver a remedy, for selective prosecution cases present factual scenarios in which a defendant is likely guilty, while the likely remedy is that the defendant should be free from prosecution because of the prosecutor's bias.

What the courts fail to see is that selective prosecution claims can harm the public just like juror exclusion claims do. In some ways, the procedural justice argument is clearer here. I think that the harm of racialized jury exclusion is that a person is wrongfully excluded because of her race—regardless of any impact on the jury's ultimate decision that exclusion might have—but that exclusion *could* have an impact on the outcome of the case, and so it is a bit harder to identify a pure procedural justice argument that has little regard for outcomes. With respect to selective prosecution claims, though, one can argue that, notwithstanding the defendant's guilt, the prosecution is defective because the methods and procedures the prosecutor used to single out the particular defendant were unfair, and they were unfair in ways that harm racialized groups. If a prosecutor selects someone for prosecution, even someone who is guilty, on the basis of an irrelevant factor such as race, observers might conclude that the prosecutor cannot be counted on to act fairly and benevolently in the future. Specifically, members of the group to which the selected defendant belongs may very well interpret the prosecutor's act as a message about the level of esteem in which the prosecutor holds the group.

The last case in which the Supreme Court dealt with a selective prosecution claim is *United States v. Armstrong*.[26] There, five black defendants were charged in federal court for distribution of cocaine base, or crack. At the time that these defendants were indicted in the Central District of California, federal law provided for a minimum penalty of ten years in prison with a maximum penalty of life if a defendant were convicted of distributing more than fifty grams of crack. Simultaneously, California law punished the identical conduct with a three- to five-year prison term. The *Armstrong* defendants contended that federal prosecutors in the Central District of California targeted them for prosecution because of their race, and they sought discovery of the criteria by which the U.S. Attorney's Office for the Central District of California chose crack cases for prosecution in federal court.

The Supreme Court overturned the Ninth Circuit's decision, stating that the defendants had "failed to show that the Government declined to prosecute similarly-situated suspects of other races,"[27] and therefore that they had failed to clear the threshold showing for discovery. The defendants had presented the district court with affidavits summarizing evidence that white offenders were prosecuted in state court rather than in federal court, but the Court held that this evidence was insufficient to entitle the defendants to discovery.

One of the key aspects of procedural justice is its attention to procedure, not outcomes. Accordingly, in *Armstrong*, the important issue in the case was not whether the *Armstrong* defendants should have ultimately succeeded on their substantive claim; rather, the issue was whether their discovery request should have been granted. The *Armstrong* Court set the bar for access to discovery very high. After *Armstrong*, in order to obtain discovery, a defendant must provide some evidence of similarly situated unprosecuted people—a requirement that is almost unattainably high.

The most likely explanation for the *Armstrong* Court's high discovery bar is its desire to radically limit selective prosecution claims, but this desire misconceives the importance of promoting public-regarding justice. The *perception* of selective prosecution is a real problem regardless of the actual offense, as the studies reviewed here suggest. In light of these perceptions, prosecutors could do well by promoting transparency and turning over the evidence that selective prosecution claimants seek. By being more open, prosecutors would communicate to the public that they have nothing to hide. They might also by their actions signal their regard for the members of the group to which the complaining defendant belongs.

Constitutional criminal procedure was born out of an interpretation of fundamental fairness that began to establish procedures protective of criminal defendants. Importantly though, the Court, in relying on fundamental fairness, recognized that the Due Process Clause is a constitutional guarantee that includes the interests of *the whole public*, not just defendants. Taking seriously in the modern era the public-regarding justice ideas developed in those early cases might lead to the right path to achieve a better quality of justice in our criminal process.

Notes

1. See Human Rights Watch, *Human Rights Watch Backgrounder, Incarcerated America*, Apr. 2003, http://www.hrw.org/backgrounder/usa/incarceration.

2. See Richard R. W. Brooks and Haekyung Jeon-Slaughter, *Race, Income, and Perceptions of the U.S. Court System*, 19 Behav. Sci. & L. 249, 251 n. 7 (2001) (collecting cases).

3. Lani Guinier and Gerald Torres, *The Miner's Canary: Enlisting Race, Resisting Power, Transforming Democracy* (2002).

4. See Tracey L. Meares, *Norms, Legitimacy, and Law Enforcement*, 79 Ore. L. Rev. 391 (2000).

5. See generally Allan E. Lind and Tom R. Tyler, *The Social Psychology of Procedural Justice* (1988).

6. See Tom R. Tyler and Steven L. Blader, *Cooperation in Groups: Procedural Justice, Social Identity, and Behavioral Engagement* 169–178 (2000).

7. See *id.* at 178.

8. See generally Tom R. Tyler, *Why People Obey the Law* (1990).

9. Tom R. Tyler and Yuen J. Huo, *Trust in the Law: Encouraging Public Cooperation with the Police and Courts* 204–8 (2002).

10. See Brooks and Slaughter, *supra* note 2.

11. See Tyler and Huo, *supra* note 9, at 148–49.

12. See *id.* at 155–56 ("White respondents are especially likely to rely on their assessments of the process, in comparison to minority respondents.... [However,] as with whites, the favorability of outcomes is not the most important determinant of the willingness to accept decisions in either of the two minority groups").

13. See Tyler and Blader, *supra* note 6, at 170.

14. See, e.g., Tracey L. Meares, Dan M. Kahan, and Neal Katyal, *Updating the Study of Punishment*, 56 Stan. L. Rev. 1171 (2004); Meares, *Norms, Legitimacy and Law Enforcement*, 79 Ore. L. Rev. 391 (2000).

15. See Tracey L. Meares, *Everything Old Is New Again: Fundamental Fairness and the Legitimacy of Criminal Justice*, 3 Ohio St. J. Crim. L. 117 (2005); Meares, *What's Wrong with Gideon?* 70 U. Chi. L. Rev. 215 (2003).

16. *Powell v. Alabama*, 287 U.S. 45, 67 (1932). The same language had previously been quoted in *Brown v. Mississippi*, 279 U.S. 278, 286 (1936).

17. *Powell*, 287 U.S. at 52, 72.

18. 287 U.S. 45 (1932).

19. 294 U.S. 587 (1935).

20. 297 U.S. 278, 284 (1936).

21. 517 U.S. 806 (1996).

22. 528 U.S. 119 (2000).

23. See Tracey L. Meares and Bernard E. Harcourt, *Transparent Adjudication and Social Science Research in Constitutional Criminal Procedure*, 90 J. Crim. L. & Criminology 733 (2000).

24. 476 U.S. 79 (1986).

25. *Id.* at 87.

26. 517 U.S. 456 (1996).

27. *Id.* at 458.

PART V

Protecting Religious Diversity

❧ 20 ❧

The Framers' Church-State Problem—and Ours

NOAH FELDMAN

FOR ROUGHLY 1,400 years, from the time the Roman Empire became Christian to the American Revolution, the question of church and state in the West always began with a simple assumption: The official religion of the state was the religion of its ruler.[1] All this changed with the radical idea, introduced during the American Revolution, that the people were sovereign. The United States was religiously diverse: How could the state establish the religion of the sovereign when the sovereign people in the United States belonged to many faiths—Congregationalist, Episcopalian, Presbyterian, Baptist, Quaker, Jewish—not one?

Faced with the problem of how religious diversity could be reconciled with national cohesion in a democratic polity, the framers of the U.S. Constitution designed a federal government that, for the first time in recorded history, had no official religion at all. In this chapter, I want to ask whether the solution that the framers adopted, and the principle on which it was based, can still afford us direction for solving the problem ourselves. If it can, then we will have a better sense of how the Constitution should look in 2020 with respect to church and state.

The Framers' Religion Clauses

The framers' church-state solution combined principle and politics.[2] The principled reason behind the religion clauses of the First Amendment was to protect the liberty of conscience of religious dissenters—and everybody involved in the process understood that fact. The political reason for the clauses was that no one in the new United States opposed the idea of religious liberty, and given the religious diversity among Americans, no one denomination seriously believed it could establish a national religion of its own.

Ironically, James Madison believed and argued that religious diversity at the national level meant that a constitutional amendment on religion was unnecessary. Without religious diversity to ensure nonestablishment from the practical standpoint, he reasoned, a constitutional amendment would do no good, since it would be ignored by the majority. Religious diversity, he maintained, would guarantee religious freedom by itself: "For where there is such a variety of sects, there cannot be a majority of any one sect to oppress and persecute the rest."[3] It was pointless to prohibit what no one group could ever hope to accomplish.[4]

Brilliant though it was (or perhaps *because* of its brilliance), this argument went nowhere; religious dissenters were experiencing the entrance into a meaningful union as a threat to religious liberty, not a guarantor. Madison had the political sense to give up his objection and take on the cause of a constitutional amendment guaranteeing religious liberty, pursuing it with characteristic vigor in the First Congress. But Madison's first insight was still right in an important sense. Religious diversity was indeed the best guarantor of nonestablishment and religious liberty because it became the mechanism for the passage of the religion clauses in the First Amendment. The dissenters got the guarantees of religious liberty that they wanted—but they got them for a political reason that only Madison fully understood.

The new constitutional amendment guaranteed two things. The Establishment Clause guaranteed that the government would not compel anybody to support any religious teaching or worship with which he conscientiously disagreed. The Free Exercise Clause guaranteed that the government would not stop anybody from worshipping or practicing his religion as he chose. Both clauses were necessary because the framers understood that there was a difference between making somebody do something against his will and stopping him from doing something he wanted to do. Prohibiting establishment protected citizens from being placed in the position where they would have to act against conscience in the realm of religious exercise. Guaranteeing free exercise protected them to worship in the way their consciences told them they must.[5]

Reduced to their core, these original constitutional principles can be captured in a simple phrase: no coercion and no money. If no one is being coerced by the government, and if the government is not spending its money to support religious institutions and practices, then the religion clauses of the Constitution are not violated. Notice that the framers were not especially concerned with public religious symbolism. They would certainly not have approved of the use of federal public funds to erect churches or support religious teaching, because they would have understood the taxes involved to be obtained through coercion of conscience. But they were largely untroubled by norms like the opening of legislative sessions with symbolic prayers. The main reason the framers did not react to public symbols of religion with horror is that they were not secularists in the modern sense. They did not think that the state needed to be protected from the dangers of religious influence, nor were they especially concerned with keeping religious symbolism out of the public sphere. Madison himself, as president, followed all his predecessors except Jefferson in issuing proclamations of prayer and thanksgiving.

Church and State, Then and Now

In successive eras, repeated infusions of religious diversity into American life brought new constitutional answers to the challenge of preserving unity in the face of expanding diversity. The Second Great Awakening of the early nineteenth century split old sects and created new ones, and the response was the identification of "nonsectarian Christianity" as the basis for common morality, which would be taught in the new public schools and produce the republican virtue needed to hold the country together. Yet as soon as the nonsectarian idea was put into practice, it ran headlong into a wave of Catholic immigration from famine-stricken Ireland. For many Catholics, nonsectarianism was nothing more than Protestant sectarianism, forcibly imposed— and instead of fostering unity, it generated a half century of intense and sometimes violent fighting over state funding of parochial education and the role of the Bible in the public schools, culminating in a proposed constitutional amendment barring states from funding Catholic education. Although the amendment failed at the federal level, by and large Catholics lost the fight against nonsectarianism and accommodated themselves to it even as nonsectarianism sought to assimilate them to itself.

Next, in the last quarter of the nineteenth century, Darwin-inspired agnosticism and atheism entered the picture, further adding to religious diversity by fueling a strong secularism that denied religion's truth and proceeded to the conclusion that religion should be banished from all aspects of life—government affairs included. As mainstream Protestantism liberalized itself in response to the new teachings on evolution, fundamentalism was born in reaction to the liberals, and strong secularism faded from the U.S. political scene. Reacting against the elitism associated with strong secularism and goaded by the idiosyncratic political genius of the aging William Jennings Bryan, the new fundamentalism sought to combine political populism with exemplary legislative enactments that would keep secularism at bay, enshrine the faith, and keep ordinary, believing people united in their faith, not divided by modern heresy. From the ideal of religious populism were born dozens of antievolution statutes and the extraordinary spectacle of the *Scopes* monkey trial.

Then, an increase in Jewish immigration created diversity of a new sort and, with it, a movement for a new kind of secularism that was not antireligious but rather legal, nominally neutral toward religion, and devoted only to keeping religion out of the governmental sphere. Legal secularists believed that unity could never be achieved in an America that felt like a Christian country, so long as some Americans were not Christians. Looking to the courts to instantiate its ideal of secular government, this movement had great success in the years after World War II, until the tide began to turn again.

Fundamentalism, it turned out, was not out of the picture. Impelled by what some sociologists would call America's Third Great Awakening, it returned to the political scene in a blaze of frustration at the successes of legal secularism under the banner of the Moral Majority and, later, the Christian Coalition. Reconfigured fundamentalism gave rise to what is today one of the two camps that dominate the church-state issue: values evangelicalism, a movement devoted to disseminating its moral values, grounded in religion. Unlike earlier fundamentalists, values evangelicals claim to advocate not their own particular creeds but values that could be shared by all persons of faith and so produce national unity; in this sense, they draw on the rhetoric that made nonsectarianism such a success. Not content with popular politics, values evangelicals have pushed for judicial appointments and developed their own innovative legal strategy, depicting religious people as a persecuted minority in need of the courts' protection.

This compressed history brings us to our present predicament. Today, there is a deep divide in U.S. life over the role that belief should play in the business of politics and government.[6] The divide is reflected in the courts, where the doctrines beloved by legal secularists—the secular purpose test and its offspring, the endorsement test—remain good law, even as government funding of religion through nominally neutral programs like vouchers has come to be held constitutional—in a concession to the values evangelicals. This state of play is the result of the compromise position of Justice Sandra Day O'Connor, now retired. The other eight justices on the Rehnquist Court thought that government funding of religion and state-sponsored religious symbolism should be treated the same way: Either both are permissible, or both aren't. But since those justices were split 4–4 on whether to allow more of each or less of both, Justice O'Connor's compromise—allowing some government financing of religion but no government endorsement of religious symbols—has been the law of the land since the 1980s.

The resulting doctrine is a mess. In 2004, for instance, when a California atheist pressed the Court to find that the words "under God" in the Pledge of Allegiance impermissibly endorses religion, the Court ducked the issue: The more liberal justices seemed afraid to rule the pledge unconstitutional yet were unwilling to embrace the view (advanced awkwardly by O'Connor, given her usual opposition to endorsing religious symbols) that old and ubiquitous religious symbolism should not count as endorsement. During the same Supreme Court term, a student asked the Court to require Washington state to let him use his public scholarship money to pay for his studies as a theology major at an evangelical college. But the Court, including Chief Justice William Rehnquist, refused to overturn Washington's policy against paying for religious courses of study, even though Joshua Davey was as much the victim of "discrimination" as were earlier evangelical plaintiffs whom the Court had granted access to government funds to pay for their student publications. In the Ten Commandments cases in 2005, the Court again reached a compromise that expressed the national division by allowing a granite monument outside the Texas state house (5–4) while banning displays inside two Kentucky courthouses (again, 5–4). This time, Justice Stephen Breyer was the swing voter, and in his opinion he all but said outright that the purpose of the compromise was to resist divisiveness on a national scale.

Original Meaning and Constitutional Choice:
A Way Forward

If the Constitution in 2020 is to reflect a coherent perspective on church-state questions, one option is to return to the framers' solution: no money and no coercion. Offer greater latitude for religious speech and symbols in public debate, but also impose a stricter ban on state funding of religious institutions and activities. Such a solution would both recognize religious values and respect the institutional separation of religion and government as an American value in its own right. This would mean abandoning the argument that religion has no place in the public sphere, while simultaneously insisting that government must go to great lengths to dissociate itself from supporting religious institutions. It would mean acknowledging a substantial difference between allowing religious symbols and speech in public places (so long as there is no public funding involved) and spending resources to sustain religious entities.

Following the model of no coercion and no money in a serious way would ensure an end to programs that fund faith-based entities, such as religious schools, through nominally neutral voucher programs. A religious charity seeking access to government funds would have to create a separate entity free of religious content to qualify. These results would no doubt seem attractive to many progressives, but the same model would also require progressives to concede that the government may constitutionally endorse religion so long as it does so through purely symbolic and noncoercive means, without spending a penny of the taxpayers' money. Prayers to open legislative sessions are just fine, provided they are not offered by government-paid chaplains like those who currently serve the U.S. Congress.

But *why* should we go back to the framers' approach? Just as the framers' solution derived from principle and politics, it would make sense for us to adopt it only if principle and politics lead us toward the same answer. Here, we encounter one of the toughest questions we can face in constitutional decision making: What should we do when the fit between principles and political practices is different today than it was in the late eighteenth century?

In some ways, of course, our principles are the same as ever. The framers were committed to the liberty of conscience, and so are we. They opposed coercion in religion, and so do we. So the no-coercion part of the approach I am suggesting may be pursued for the most appealing reason that can ever be given for following the framers' principles the way they intended: The framers hit on an excellent and true moral principle, and we do right morally and legally by adhering to that principle today.

When it comes to "no money," things are a bit more complicated. The framers considered that government taxation for religious purposes violated conscience. Do we still think the same, especially since today's state taxes us all the time to pay for activities we may loathe and to support government speech we may consider to violate conscience? Many of us still balk at the idea of paying to support religious teachings with which we disagree or even which we abhor; and to that extent, we still follow the framers' impulse. But on the whole, it is today difficult fully to credit the argument that my tax dollars should express my conscience when it comes to religion, and to nothing else. The government does many things with our taxes that we do not like, yet we do not generally believe this violates our conscience.

Yet we may follow the framers' legal conclusions for reasons different from that of the framers, provided that those reasons make sense to us. We can, for example, favor the no-money principle on the ground that debates over government funding are likely to lead to political polarization—an especially great risk in our vibrantly diverse society. It is true that symbols can spur division too, but the essence of politics in the modern welfare state lies in the distribution of resources. (In fact, the same is true in most kinds of states in the real world, which is why politicians usually care more about resource allocation than about symbolic action.) If money is the substructure that lies beneath political reality, then it is advisable today, as it was for the framers, to keep religion out of the competition for the state's financial largesse if we wish to reduce the divisive effects of religion in public life.

One apparent difficulty with the no-money and no-coercion approach is that the framers were not concerned with the effects of symbolic religion on religious minorities—perhaps because their United States was 95 percent Protestant. Today, with our much greater religious diversity, we have much greater concern for the potential marginalization of minorities from public life. Perhaps that should lead us to adopt a constitutional posture more restrictive of government endorsement of religion than the framers would have imagined, adding a third principle, like no symbolic endorsement of religion, to their two. It could well be argued that our increased diversity means we should keep government from endorsing religion.

The problem with this endorsement approach is that it assumes that there really is a neutral position that the government can take with respect to such symbols. But in a democracy in which citizens take religion seriously, some will want to base their political choices on their religious values and beliefs. To block them from having their government express their preferred symbols is to disqualify those citizens from full political participation. And symbols amount to acknowledgments of the role of values in public life. To allow the state to endorse labor (Labor Day) or nonviolence (Martin Luther King Day) or liberal humanism (school curriculums) while blocking the endorsement of religious values amounts to the exclusion of religiously inspired citizens from public participation.

The point, then, is not to deny that religious symbols may be marginalizing, because they may. So indeed may other political symbols that the state may choose to adopt or express. The point is to notice, rather, that the impossibility of choosing neutrally between religious and non-religious symbols is a reason to confer the choice on the democratic polity, rather than making the decision in the courts. If *any* judicial decision will marginalize *some* constituency, then there is no principled basis for the courts to choose among them. Furthermore, if religious citizens are marginalized by judicial decisions that ban their preferred symbols from public life, they will not simply give up, but will redouble their efforts to extend their dominance through other spheres of politics—with results too familiar to recount here.

The framers did not think this through. They were unconcerned with symbolism because they tended to converge on symbols, not because they realized that the judiciary could not neutrally limit the symbolic field. So favoring "no coercion" as a limiting principle beyond which religious liberty will not extend is only originalist in a narrow sense. We would be choosing to follow the framers' principle, but for reasons of our own. And those reasons are not restricted to principle. Expanding a sense of inclusion in the polity is a political aspiration, not just a theoretical one.

The trick to successful constitutionalism, then, is not an unreasoned following of the dead hand of the past. It is, rather, the reexamination of original principles and politics in contemporary terms. When it comes to church and state, our own predicament is very different from that of the framers. We have a rich history of church-state debates on which to draw and historical lessons to learn. Our diversity and theirs are not identical, nor are all the applications of long-held principles unchanged in the light of circumstance. It so happens, though, that in this case, the framers' model may still work for us. It ought to be readopted—so that our children and theirs can choose afresh whether to continue this course or chart a new one.

This chapter builds on material that I presented in *Divided by God: America's Church-State Problem—and What We Should Do about It* (New York: Farrar, Straus and Giroux, 2005), which I first developed in two articles, *The Intellectual Origins of the Establishment Clause*, 77 N.Y.U. L. Rev. 346 (2002), and *The Transformation of the Establishment Clause*, 90 Cal. L. Rev. 673 (2002). I have drawn freely on language from these sources without further footnoting.

Notes

1. On the history of state religion, see Harold Berman, *Law and Revolution: The Formation of the Western Legal Tradition* (Cambridge, Mass.: Harvard University Press, 1983).

2. This is by necessity a summary of arguments detailed and supported elsewhere, with which some other writers disagree.

3. John P. Kaminski and Gaspare J. Saladino, eds., 10 *Documentary History of the Ratification of the Constitution (Virginia)*, 1223–24 (Madison: State Historical Society of Wisconsin, 1990).

4. Cf. *Federalist* 51, at 324 ("In a free government the security for civil rights must be the same as that for religious rights. It consists in the one case in the multiplicity of interests, and in the other in the multiplicity of sects. The degree of security in both cases will depend on the number of interests and sects; and this may be presumed to depend on the extent of country and number of people comprehended under the same government"). In both points, Madison owed something to David Hume, who had also struggled with the question of religious faction.

5. This dual formulation did not clarify whether the guarantee of free exercise of religion entitled the citizen to an exception from a duly enacted law if he objected for reasons of conscience.

6. I am therefore not taking issue with sociologist Alan Wolfe, who has argued that Americans' religious faith is not in itself a source of deep division. See Alan Wolfe, *The Transformation of American Religion: How We Actually Live Our Faith* (New York: Free Press, 2003); Wolfe, *One Nation, after All* (New York: Penguin, 1998). My claim is that the division is over the role that religious values should play in political choices.

❧ 21 ❧

Progressives, the Religion Clauses, and the Limits of Secularism

WILLIAM P. MARSHALL

T HE UNITED STATES is a deeply religious country. Ninety-one percent of Americans believe in God.[1] Three of four Americans pray at least once per week,[2] and 66 percent of Americans belong to a church.[3] Sixty percent of Americans report that religion is "very important" in their daily lives while only 14 percent claim that it is "not very important."[4]

Against this background, it is not surprising that conservatives have tried to portray themselves as the defenders of religion, protecting the country against a rampant and hostile secularism. After all, purporting to carry the cause of an unfairly besieged constituency is always good politics, particularly when that constituency is a vast and overwhelming political majority. It is also not surprising, then, that these efforts have played well.

Progressives, however, are the true protectors of religious liberty. The progressive agenda is to protect the religious liberty of all and to guard against the divisiveness and intolerance that inevitably follows when religion and government become unduly entwined. The religious freedom that some conservatives seek to protect, on the other hand, seems more geared to fostering the ability of their constituencies to enlist government support for particular sectarian agendas. Of course, conservatives understandably do not desire their efforts to be understood in this manner. Framing the debate as one between proreligion conservatives, on one side, and antireligion secularists, on the other, better suits their political purpose.

What is less understandable is why progressives have let the constitutional debate be framed in these terms. Secularism has an important place in First Amendment jurisprudence, and in many cases its principles should appropriately guide the constitutional inquiry. But the values of secularism are only instrumental. Secularism has no independent constitutional value, and a too-rigid secularism raises its own set of constitutional difficulties. Until progressives understand this position, they will continue to lose the public debate—even if they win the occasional constitutional case.

The first section of this chapter identifies the values in a secular approach to religion clause issues. The second section sets forth its weaknesses. The third section briefly discusses how progressives should apply this understanding of secularism and its weaknesses to specific contemporary constitutional issues. The fourth section offers a brief conclusion.

The Values of Secularism

The secularist position is that government should be entirely secular and must not use its powers to promote, advance, or endorse religion. The state should not, for example, endorse religion by displaying religious symbols, and it should not provide financial support for religious exercise or to religious institutions.

Three overarching policy considerations support the secular approach. First, government support of religion harms religion generally. Second, government support of one or some religions harms those religious traditions outside government's favor. Third, government support of religion harms the government. Notably, the first two of these policies are explicitly religion-protective rationales and the third also directly supports religious freedom.

The Harms to Religion Generally

That government support of religion harms the religion it purports to serve has long been recognized. Indeed, this understanding comes originally not from progressive thought but from the early American evangelical position that the separation of church and state is necessary to preserve religion's purity and integrity. As Roger Williams and others maintained, state support of religion would only weaken religion by fostering its dependence upon the state and subjecting it to "worldly corruptions."[5] Brought forward to the modern welfare state, this rationale is only more compelling. Because government aid programs typically come with strings attached, recipients must conform their practices to government standards in order to maintain their good standing. Religious organizations receiving government funds may therefore find themselves pressured to sacrifice their principles in order to meet government demands. Additionally, the availability of government funds places considerable pressures even on those religious organizations whose tenets oppose government subsidy. A religious organization providing food and housing to the poor might find it hard to turn down needed funds, particularly when other religious and nonreligious organizations are accepting the government's largesse—even when so doing would require it to abandon its preexisting religious beliefs.

Further, even when government does not attempt to aid particular religious institutions but strives only to benefit religion generally, harms to religion will again accrue. If the government truly intends to act in a nondenominational matter in promoting religion, its product is likely to be so watered-down that it may demean rather than advance the religious enterprise. Moreover, any attempt by the government to support religion generally, no matter how well conceived, will invariably fail. The number of religious traditions in the United States is immense, and finding commonality among all of the differing belief systems is virtually impossible.

Finally, permitting the state to get involved in fostering religion raises the problem of the government getting it wrong. Conservatives, who are so willing to criticize the government in other areas, should be questioned as to why they are so willing to let the government become involved in a subject as delicate and complex as religion.

The Harms to Other Religions

Government support of religion also, not surprisingly, harms those religious groups outside the ambit of government beneficence. The use of one sect's prayer to begin the school day, for example, not only bestows a state-granted legitimacy upon that particular religion but also suggests that other religions are not equally valid. Similarly, granting state aid to only one or a few religious entities sends a message of government approval of the selected beneficiaries and disapproval of the others. The concern, moreover, is not just perception. In both the school prayer and government funding cases, the government has enhanced the ability of the favored religion to disseminate its message and attract new adherents while weakening the relative ability of the nonfavored sects to do the same.

Sect preferences can also impose substantial social costs. As Justice Sandra Day O'Connor recognized, favoring only some religious traditions may alienate members of those groups outside the ambit of government support.[6] Such action tells the nonfavored religious traditions that they are outsiders, potentially breaking the bonds of social community.

Finally, prohibiting state-sponsored sect preferences serves as a check on government power being used to harm other religious traditions. If history is any example, the most cogent threats to religion come from other religions—not secular states (communism being the notable exception). Empowering favored religions through selective government assistance can easily be turned into empowering favored religions by discriminating (or worse) against competing belief systems.

The Harms to Government (and Religion)

Government support of religion harms government by diverting its resources to religious matters and involving government officials in matters over which they may not have competence. How is a state's antidrug program administrator, for example, supposed to determine which religion's antidrug program is the most effective? Can she consider a religious organization's antidrug program to have succeeded if its clients are still using drugs but are devoting their time and energies toward worship and good works rather than scouring for contraband? Government is well served (as is religion) when its employees are not required or allowed to make such choices.

Keeping religion out of government also helps both government and religion in a more fundamental way. One of the problems in allowing government support of religion is that it suggests that government is a prize that can be won through political action. Committed religious believers, then, may see it as a test of their faith to prevail in the political arena. This, in turn, may motivate other believers who may not have felt so disposed to also enter the fray because in viewing the actions of others they may become persuaded that political action *is* properly a test of divine commitment. The result of this increased political action at the behest of religious conviction is a politics imbued with religious divisiveness and acrimony. Consider what school board politics might look like if school prayer were allowed and government officials were empowered to decide which religion's prayer should begin the school day. Would candidates run on the all-Methodist ticket? Would office seekers suggest that a vote for their opponent is a vote for heresy? What would the rough and tumble of political campaigns do to the dignity and integrity of the religions that are placing their principles up for popular vote? What would it do to the respect of the democratic process?

Finally, entwining religion and government harms both religion and government because, if history again is any indication, the juxtaposition of these two powerful forces can be lethal. When church and state are combined, the state often turns into a tool of oppression. The primary targets of that oppression are often people of other faiths.

The Limits of Secularism

Although, as the previous section demonstrates, the policies underlying secularism are compelling, progressives should understand that there are considerable weaknesses in a First Amendment jurisprudence that too rigidly attempts to enforce a secular ideal. Three, in particular, deserve mention. First, secularism suffers from unavoidable internal inconsistencies that cause it inevitably to undermine the policies it is designed to serve. Second, secularism is not neutral between religion and non-religion and therefore conflicts with general constitutional notions of equality. Third, adherence to secularism runs up against a public culture that is replete with religious symbols, names, and references. Each of these concerns will be addressed in turn.

The Internal Contradictions of Secularism

The secular position that government should not depend on divine authority for its legitimacy is itself a religion-laden precept.[7] The notion, for example, that morality can be derived from nonreligious sources and taught in the public schools without religious reference is a theological proposition. Secularism, in short, is not completely secular. Accordingly, treating secularism as if it presents the correct view of the relationship of government and morality is, in effect, to create its own establishment.

Additionally, secularism's tenet that the state must be neutral among religions is not neutral—particularly with respect to those religious belief systems that believe otherwise. Government neutrality among religions conforms to the beliefs of those religions that believe in state neutrality, but it rejects those religions that believe that state neutrality is improper. To those religions, the state has favored the religious beliefs of others.[8] To be sure, some may respond to this point by contending that the fact that some religions may view neutrality as "religious" does not make it so. It is "religious," they might contend, only from one idiosyncratic perspective. Perhaps so, but a complete commitment to true neutrality cannot allow differing views or perspectives to be summarily dismissed or discounted. True neutrality should mean that there is no privileged standpoint from which to make universal observations of what is neutral and what is not.

Moreover, a too-rigid application of secularism can lead to self-defeating results. Enforcing the rule that the government should never display religious symbols, for example, appears like a constitutional endorsement of secularism rather than merely a rule that furthers strong instrumental policies. Thus, like a religious believer of one faith witnessing her government endorse the beliefs of another, those opposed to secularism are likely to be offended and alienated by what they perceive as government's support of a secular regime that, to them, is no more than a competing faith system. In this manner, secularism creates and exacerbates some of the very problems that it should assuage.

Secularism's Non-Neutrality

Secularism is also potentially problematic because it is not neutral between religious and nonreligious entities. This concern has particular play in the context of state funding issues because to the extent that a regime of secularism excludes religious organizations from participation in programs available to nonreligious organizations, it creates real inequalities. A religiously affiliated drug treatment program, for example, that is prohibited from receiving state funds is placed at a disadvantage compared to the nonreligious drug treatment program down the street that can receive state funds.

Such disparate treatment, as we have discussed, is supported by important policy concerns. Among other harms, state aid to religion can damage religion's integrity, lead to improper sect preferences, and promote a divisive politics as religious organizations compete for greater and greater resources. But there are also strong constitutional concerns on the other side. Consider, for example, the university policy at issue in *Rosenberger v. Rector and Visitors of the University of Virginia,*[9] which authorized state university funding for a variety of student publications but excluded religious publications from eligibility. That policy, informed by secularist values, enhanced the ability of nonreligious organizations to disseminate their messages as compared to the religious organizations that received no university support. As such, the policy contradicted the essential Free Speech Clause principle that government must remain neutral among competing belief systems in the marketplace of ideas. Whether constitutional law should vindicate the values of secularism or those of free speech in this circumstance is neither obvious nor straightforward.[10]

Moreover, even when a potential religious recipient of government funds cannot raise a free speech claim (because its activities are not speech related), its exclusion from funding that is available to parallel nonreligious organizations raises significant concerns. After all, excluding religious organizations from government programs solely because they are religious at least superficially appears as discrimination against religion. And if secularism is rightly concerned about the message of disfavor that is sent when government supports some but not all religious entities, it should also recognize that there is a similar concern when government supports all entities *except* those that are religious. There is considerable tension, in short, between principles of secularism and principles of equality.

Secularism and Public Culture

A full constitutional embrace of secularism is prevented by still another factor. Religion is deeply embedded in our public life and institutions; ours is not a secular culture. Countless cities, counties, and parks have religious names. Christmas and Thanksgiving are national holidays. The Supreme Court begins each session with "God bless this honorable Court." Congress employs a full-time chaplain. Presidents routinely invoke religious themes in their speeches. The national motto is "In God We Trust." The list is endless.

Constitutional law, of course, has not ignored and cannot ignore this reality. Indeed, even the most liberal justices have recognized that applying a rigid secular approach to all religious vestiges in the public culture is unrealistic. As Justice William Brennan once stated, "[S]ome official 'acknowledgment' is inevitable in a religious society if government is not to adopt a stilted indifference to the religious life of the people."[11]

A too-rigid secularist approach to religious references in the public culture, moreover, can be affirmatively counterproductive. As Justice Breyer noted in the Texas Ten Commandments case, excising ingrained religious symbols or practices from the public culture may be perceived as hostility toward religion and may engender religious divisiveness[12]— two results the secularist approach is designed to avoid.

Secularism, Its Limits, and a Progressive Religion Clause Jurisprudence

As the previous sections demonstrate, the value of a secular approach to religion clause issues must be tempered by an acknowledgment of its limitations. How then should this understanding be applied in constructing a progressive approach to contemporary religion clause issues? The following provides an overview of this approach.

Identifying a Progressive Approach to Funding Issues

Without doubt, Establishment Clause jurisprudence has moved away from a secularist approach, which would deny state aid to religious entities, toward an approach that allows the government to treat religious and nonreligious beneficiaries equally. Thus, in *Zelman v. Simmons-Harris*,[13] the Court upheld a controversial program allowing parents to use state-funded vouchers to send their children to parochial schools, and in *Mitchell v. Helms*,[14] the Court overturned contrary precedent and approved the state's provision of educational equipment, such as computers, laboratory equipment, maps, and globes, to parochial schools. The Court's approach can be summarized as follows: As long as the program in question does not favor religion and is available to a broad class of beneficiaries that includes religious and nonreligious entities, it is likely to be upheld. The question is: How should progressives react to this trend?

The answer, as the previous sections suggest, is not obvious. The reasons for excluding religious organizations from government funding are weighty—but excluding only religious organizations from government programs is also troublesome in that it both contradicts equality norms and appears hostile to religion by singling it out for disfavored treatment. Because of this, progressives should not frame their objections to financial aid programs on the simple ground that aid to religiously affiliated organizations is forbidden per se. That objection alone suggests that there is something about religion that justifies disfavored treatment. Rather, if the objection is to be made at all, it should be made on grounds that these programs affirmatively harm religion. Thus, for example, any objection to the state's funding of a religiously affiliated drug treatment program should be raised on the grounds that such aid may adversely affect the religious organization by fostering its dependence on government and subjecting it to government evaluation and monitoring rather than solely on the grounds of the religious affiliation of the organization.

And it may be that progressives should understand that such arguments can best be made in the legislative arena as policy objections rather than in courts claiming that such programs are unconstitutional. The Court's jurisprudence currently suggests that legislatures are free to either include or exclude religion in financial aid programs (as long as the free speech rights of religious organizations are not implicated, as in the *Rosenberger* case).[15] Given the strength of the competing interests involved, this may be the optimum approach.

Progressives should, however, draw the line in three respects. First, progressives should steadfastly oppose efforts to exempt religious organizations from regulatory requirements connected to funding programs. Some conservatives have argued that not only should religious organizations be eligible for public funds, but they should also be exempt from certain regulatory strings attached to those funds. For example, they have contended that religious groups should be free from program restrictions prohibiting recipient organizations from discriminating in employment, on the grounds that religious organizations should be able to require their employees to share their religious faith in order to preserve the enterprise's religious identity and mission. They have also argued that religious organizations should not have to comply with monitoring and disclosure requirements because forced compliance would infringe upon their rights of religious autonomy. These arguments should be rejected. If the raison d'être for allowing funding is that religious and nonreligious organizations should be treated equally, that policy is not served if religion is provided special advantages that nonreligious organizations are denied.

Second, progressives should require that ostensibly neutral aid programs be truly neutral in application. A state substance abuse program whose only eligible recipient in a wide geographical radius is a religious provider, for example, is constitutionally problematic because it both uniquely subsidizes a religious entity and effectively directs program beneficiaries to a particular religious outlet—even though such beneficiaries may have deep religious and nonreligious objections to affiliating with the sect sponsoring the drug treatment program. Aid programs, accordingly, must have viable nonreligious alternatives available to program beneficiaries.

Third, progressives should raise constitutional objections to programs that fund purely religious activity. The state has no legitimate reason to fund religious exercise for its own sake and quite obviously cannot claim that, in so doing, it is merely treating religion and nonreligion equally.

Identifying a Progressive Approach to Public Religious Displays and References

Progressives should also exercise caution before taking the position that long-standing public religious displays and religious references are unconstitutional. As we have seen, constitutional attacks on such symbols and practices can foster religious divisiveness and send messages of perceived hostility toward religion, thus undercutting progressive concerns. This is not to suggest that all religious vestiges in the culture should receive a carte blanche. School prayer, after all, had a considerable historical pedigree at the time it was struck down. But the simple criticism that an aspect of the public culture is religiously laden, whether it be the national motto or the Pledge of Allegiance, does not end the constitutional argument. It is only a starting point for further analysis.

At the same time, government attempts to initiate new displays of religious symbols or new forms of religious reference present an entirely different constitutional calculus. First, such efforts suggest that the state has been captured by sectarian interests, not just that religion has had an important historical role. They thus provide a powerful immediacy to antiestablishment concerns. Second, by raising the possibility that the state is open to additional efforts to endorse religion, they provide impetus for religions to continue to seek additional government favor, thereby triggering a politics divided along religious lines. (To be sure, allowing religion to receive funding can also encourage its seeking rents from the state, but the political rhetoric in seeking money for programs that benefit all religions and nonreligion alike is likely to be different in tone and substance than a religion's seeking a narrow, symbolic, and inevitably sectarian-tinged endorsement for itself.) Third, and most important, opening the government to battles over religious symbols is likely to be particularly destructive because symbolism excites human behavior in a uniquely powerful manner. "[Humanity] may possess thought," Max

Lerner wrote, "but symbols possess [humanity]."[16] Indeed, because, as Sanford Levinson noted, symbols "[establish] relationships of hierarchy and domination,"[17] their use by government to endorse religion raises the highest levels of antiestablishment concerns.[18] Progressives, accordingly, should oppose such actions.[19]

Conclusion

The progressive approach to religion clause issues does not demand a rigid adherence to secularism. Instead, it requires the understanding that secularism is not of constitutional value in and of itself but only has value for its instrumental role in protecting religion from corruption and debasement, limiting religious divisiveness, and promoting the freedom of religion of all citizens. This means that progressives should not take absolutist positions with respect to such issues as government funding or the display of religious symbols. Rather, these issues should be addressed in light of how they affect the policies that secularism is designed to serve. Most important, progressives should not surrender to the claim that conservatives are the allies of religion and progressives its opponents. The progressive approach to the religion clauses is the one that is protective of religious liberty; the conservative vision is more akin to the Old World experience from which the founders were trying to escape.

Notes

1. Jon Meacham, *Is God Real?* Newsweek, Apr. 9, 2007, at 54.

2. Statistics are from a poll conducted by Baylor University and the Gallup Organization in September 2006. See also Terry Lee Goodrich, *How Do You Pray? Study Shows Americans Are Very Different—and Similar—in Prayer*, News-Sentinel (Ft. Wayne, Ind.), Nov. 23, 2006, available at http://www.fortwayne.com/mld/newssentinel/living/16083542.htm.

3. From a poll conducted by CNN, *USA Today*, and the Gallup Organization on Dec. 9 and 10, 2002. For this and other related statistics, see *Religion* (2002), available at http://www.pollingreport.com/religion2.htm.

4. The Pew Research Center for the People and the Press, *Religion: A Strength and Weakness for Both Parties*, question 39 (Aug. 30, 2005), available at http://people-press.org/reports/print.php3?PageID=991.

5. Mark DeWolfe Howe, *The Garden and the Wilderness* 6 (1965).

6. Justice O'Connor originally raised this concern in *County of Allegheny v. ACLU*, 492 U.S. 573 (1989) (O'Connor, J., concurring in part and concurring in the judgment).

7. Larry Alexander, *Liberalism, Religion, and the Unity of Epistemology*, 30 San Diego L. Rev. 763 (1993).

8. Indeed, as some leading commentators have noted, the feeling that they have lost their country to a competing ideology is one of the major reasons behind the rise of the religious Right. See John C. Jeffries, Jr., and James E. Ryan, *A Political History of the Establishment Clause*, 100 Mich. L. Rev. 279, 341–42 (2001).

9. 515 U.S. 819 (1995).

10. In *Rosenberger* itself, the Court, in a 5–4 opinion, ruled on the free speech side.

11. *Lynch v. Donnelly*, 465 U.S. 668, 714 (1984) (Brennan, J., dissenting).

12. *Van Orden v. Perry*, 545 U.S. 677, 704 (2005) (Breyer, J., concurring).

13. 536 U.S. 639 (2002).

14. 521 U.S. 203 (1997), overruling *Meek v. Pittenger*, 421 U.S. 349 (1975).

15. See *Locke v. Davey*, 540 U.S. 712 (2004).

16. Max Lerner, *Constitution and Court as Symbols*, 46 Yale L.J. 1290, 1293 (1937).

17. Sanford Levinson, *Freedom, Politics, They Whisper: Reflections on Flags, Monuments, and State Holidays, and the Construction of Social Meaning in a Multicultural Society*, 70 Chi.-Kent. L. Rev. 1079, 1107 (1995).

18. For an opposing view, see Noah Feldman, *Divided by God: America's Church-State Problem—and What We Should Do about It* (2005).

19. Even here, however, there needs to be a caveat. As I have elsewhere argued, there may be highly extraordinary circumstances, such as the New York City memorial services for the victims of 9/11, where the nation may need a collective religious outlet and where, because of the obvious place of religion in memorial services, its exclusion from public recognition would constitute secularism in the extreme. See William P. Marshall, *The Limits of Secularism: Public Religious Expression in Moments of National Crisis and Tragedy*, 78 Notre Dame L. Rev. 11 (2002).

PART VI

Families and Values

❧ 22 ❧

A Liberal Vision of U.S. Family Law in 2020

WILLIAM N. ESKRIDGE, JR.

AMILY LAW IN the United States underwent a revolution in the twentieth century. Before the revolution, family law focused on marriage as the only legitimate situs for love, sex, and children, while at the same time it defined marital eligibility narrowly and its inescapable duties broadly. In 1900, for example, it was illegal almost everywhere in the United States for two adults to enjoy sexual intercourse or to cohabit sexually unless they were married to one another; children born outside of marriage were legal as well as social bastards. To enjoy the advantages of marriage, Americans were required to accept obligations of support and sexual fidelity, as well as other duties that could not be waived as a matter of law; these obligations were usually for life, as divorce was difficult in 1900. Ironically, adults wanting to legitimate their sexual activities or children by marrying were often not permitted to do so; the law prohibited the marriage of many disabled people, persons of different races, and same-sex couples.[1]

American family life and its norms changed in the twentieth century. Family law has, on the whole, liberalized, offering adults a lot more choices. First, Americans now enjoy the freedom to find love, sex, and family outside of marriage. Not only do states allow adults to have nonmarital sex, but they provide legal methods for regulating cohabiting relationships and protecting children born outside of marriage. Second, Americans can create families of choice. Most adults in this country enjoy substantial freedom to marry the person they choose, freely adopt children, and even engage third parties to assist in childbearing. Third, Americans unhappy with their marriages have escape options. The old rule of marriage-for-life has been supplanted by essentially no-fault divorce across the United States.[2]

What connection does the Constitution have with the legal revolution in U.S. family law? Surprisingly little. State legislatures and judges have accomplished most of the liberalization of U.S. family law, with the Supreme Court playing mostly a cleaning-up role. The most salient principles have been *autonomy* (pro-choice) and *equality* (inclusion). While these principles have taken the positive law quite far, they are now under siege in debates about lesbian and gay families. Embodying both autonomy and equality principles, same-sex marriage has been a piñata for cultural conservatives. Liberals should respond with a third principle supporting lesbian and gay, as well as straight, households: responsible commitment. This principle should become the third leg of a liberal constitutionalism that offers couples of all orientations a menu of relationship choices, while at the same time encouraging committed relationships, including adults' responsibility toward children.

Liberal Principles: Autonomy, Equal Treatment, Responsible Commitment

The autonomy and equality principles have worked together to liberalize U.S. family law. Women's equality as partners in relationships, rather than their roles as mothers and homemakers under the governance of husbands, was a prerequisite to a conception of the family as entailing the partnership of autonomous adults. Once policymakers viewed the family this way, the autonomy principle has supported expanded eligibility rules, greater sexual freedom within and outside of marriage, and broader exit options. Equality was front and center for the momentous struggle to recognize different-race marriages.

Liberals should recognize the limits of these principles as traditionally applied. For example, the autonomy principle supports the freedom of infertile couples to have resort to alternative reproductive technologies and of same-sex couples to raise children within their households, but it does not help society decide how to resolve disputes when those households dissolve. As the Supreme Court has ruled, the autonomy principle assures priority for the blood parent, but that often runs athwart the best interests of the child. In many cases, say social psychologists, the child suffers if wrenched from his not-related caregiver. Shouldn't those interests be important?

When the autonomy principle imposes third-party costs, especially upon children, it loses much of its moral authority. This critique applies to some liberalizations that have already been accomplished, like no-fault divorce. From case studies and preliminary empirical examinations, scholars argue that parental divorce has terrible effects upon children. Feminists criticize easy divorce on equality grounds, as it typically leaves wives worse off than before, but the effect-on-children criticism cuts more deeply. The most vulnerable persons, with no direct say in the parental decision to divorce, bear sometimes devastating consequences. Those consequences are primarily psychic, although they also include the economic hardships following many divorces.[3]

Another criticism is that the liberalization of family law has altered the nature of intimate relationships. Marriage is a treasured institution because its committed-for-life culture is a training ground for altruism; mutually committed adults sacrifice temporary pleasures for one another and for the welfare of the family. A society which validates cohabiting relationships, tolerates adultery, and permits no-fault divorce is a society that has moved away from a traditionalist philosophy—demanding self-sacrifice, permanent mutual commitment, and the family as a collective unity—toward a consumerist philosophy of self-satisfaction, mutual cooperation, and the family as a collection of pleasure-seeking individuals. Ours is a society where sex, relationships, and even children are morphing into hedonic goods, that is, sources of pleasure and sites of consumer choice.

This critique has come out of the closet during the same-sex marriage debate. Same-sex marriage is a liberal gimme. If two women love each other and want to commit to one another for life, both the autonomy and equality premises suggest that the state should recognize their relationship as a marriage—yet this obvious resolution is not the one that U.S. law has thus far taken. Why not? Although much opposition to same-sex marriage is inspired by antihomosexual prejudice and irrational stereotyping, not all of it is. Many cultural conservatives argue that same-sex marriage will be a fatal tipping point for the institution, its Maginot Line. Once that line is crossed, choice will be all that's left in marriage; it will lose its ability to inspire partners to make sacrifices for one another and the children they are raising.[4]

In most of the United States, conservative arguments like this have sent liberals running for cover, but same-sex marriage offers liberals a third principle that complements the ones that swept the field in the twentieth century. Lesbian and gay couples who have been leading the same-sex marriage parade in the last decade are not hedonistic home wreckers. Rather, they are responsible adults committed to one another and to the children that about one-fourth of the couples are raising. Same-sex marriage is not about selfish choices, for Americans today can enjoy sex outside of marriage with no legal worries and few social sanctions. Same-sex marriage is all about *responsible commitment*. The state should be encouraging that norm for same-sex as well as different-sex couples, at the same time that it should allow considerable choice in family recognition.

What is most distinctive about civil marriage is the legal duties it entails. Couples do not receive most of the benefits of marriage unless they accept its obligations. Civil marriage reinforces the long-term nature of the couple's interpersonal commitment. Deciding to get married requires conversations between the partners about that commitment, and marriage is a public signal to family, friends, and co-workers that the partners have undertaken these commitments. Liberals should value the commitment feature of marriage and childrearing. The mutual altruism it entails enriches the lives of the partners, is beneficial for their children, and bears significant social insurance and other benefits for the larger community. The case for same-sex marriage then becomes a synthesis of three liberal principles: Like different-sex couples (equality), same-sex couples ought to have the choice (autonomy) to accept the duties as well as the rights of marriage and, increasingly for lesbian and gay couples, childrearing (responsible commitment).

In same-sex marriage, the gay rights movement offers progressive constitutionalism a cutting-edge issue where it can again prove the worthiness of liberal values *and* offers liberalism an opportunity to deepen its values. To be sure, public opinion remains unpersuaded of the case for same-sex marriage. Popular hostility to a norm often triggers a race by progressives to the U.S. Supreme Court to constitutionalize their norm. Progressives should *not* follow such a strategy for same-sex marriage. What we have learned from family law evolution in the United States and the same-sex marriage experience all over the world is that the best way to proceed is incrementally, legislatively, and locally.[5]

In the near future, the main audience for constitutional arguments will be state judges in jurisdictions (mainly in the Northeast and on the

Pacific Coast now) where grassroots movements have prepared citizens to accept the legitimacy of lesbian and gay families. In such states, judges can place equal marriage rights on the public agenda, can reverse the burden of legislative inertia, and can sometimes (as the Massachusetts Supreme Court did in 2003–2004) create conditions under which irresponsible predictions made by gay rights opponents can be falsified. By 2020, the U.S. Constitution ought to be ripe for a national constitutional requirement that states must provide some legal structure for same-sex relationships (e.g., marriages, civil unions, domestic partnerships).

Toward a Menu of Equally Available Relationship Options

In most states, by 2020, marriage will no longer be the only option for different-sex as well as same-sex couples. Adults in Western countries have demanded more choices within their romantic relationships. Responding to this demand, postindustrial Western nations have already legalized sexual cohabitation outside of marriage, and most grant some legal rights and duties to cohabiting couples. The same-sex marriage debate has generated yet more new legal institutions, which are noted below. What is emerging is a regime where the state will offer a menu of options for couples desiring state recognition of their relationships.

I do not know what the menu will look like in 2020, and the options will vary by nation or state. Here is a stylized list of options, ordered from least to most like "traditional" marriage:[6]

1. *Domestic partnership.* By signing a form identifying a significant other (of any sex), many corporate and municipal employees can add that person to the health care, life insurance, and other benefits provided by the employer to married employees. Being someone's domestic partner typically signals a level of commitment only slightly greater than being a close friend.

2. *Cohabitation.* Sexual cohabitation suggests greater commitment and interdependence, which the state both rewards and obligates. Thus, a cohabitation regime will generally impose duties of support on the couple, especially if there is specialization within the household. European and Canadian laws also provide legal presumptions of joint property ownership and tenancy, family and bereavement leave, and sometimes wrongful death claims for cohabiting partners.

3. *Cohabitation-plus.* Hawaii and France have created new kinds of cohabitation-plus regimes, reciprocal beneficiaries and *pactes civils*, respectively. These new forms presume a greater level of commitment but allow dissolution through a summary process. In addition to duties of mutual support, the state provides a wider array of unitive rights, namely, rules treating the partners as coupled and granting them financial and other benefits that reflect their unity as to matters like health care decisions when one partner is incapacitated.

4. *Registered partnerships (Scandinavia) or civil unions (New England).* Under these new legal forms, the state provides most of the legal rights and duties of marriage, but without the name and its interjurisdictional portability. In addition to mutual support and fidelity and with the added difficulty of legal divorce proceedings in the event of a breakup, the state will reinforce family ties by giving the partners mutual rights over their adopted or biological children.

5. *Marriage.* The state provides all the traditional rights and benefits, but with exit easier (albeit not costless) through no-fault divorce. In addition to the cultural and religious significance the name carries with it, "marriage" is much more likely to be recognized in other jurisdictions.

6. *Covenant marriage.* Some U.S. jurisdictions offer an option that is more like traditional marriage, because it is harder to exit. Louisiana's covenant marriage law requires husbands and wives in unhappy marriages to go through compulsory mediation and a longer waiting period before they can divorce. This is the closest any state now comes to "traditional" marriage-for-life.

No U.S. state or European nation offers this complete menu of options, and only a handful of jurisdictions offers same-sex couples the same menu as that available to different-sex couples. The menu tells us where we are going. Its main normative virtue is that it respects people's autonomy. Couples choose among an array of state regulatory regimes keyed to the level of commitment they want to signal or create. So couples uncertain if they want to live together permanently might choose domestic partnership or cohabitation regimes, which are easy to exit. Committed couples will choose civil union or marriage, which is harder to exit but offers a larger array of legal rights and benefits. Couples rearing children will also often choose either marriage or civil union. In my view, the menu regime must also be equally accessible to same-sex and different-sex couples, but equal treatment will come unevenly and perhaps slowly, for the reasons suggested earlier.

An objection to the emerging menu is that it might derogate from the principle of responsible commitment. A menu that includes cohabitation-plus and civil union options will siphon more couples away from marriage, a signal that some would take to be an abandonment of altruistic, committed relationships. Indeed, increasing numbers of scholars argue that the state should get out of the marriage business entirely and just offer couples civil unions or domestic partnerships.[7]

The effect of such a menu on committed relationships remains to be seen. A menu that offers civil union *and* marriage to lesbian, gay, and straight couples is in some respects more in line with responsible commitment than a regime that excludes loving same-sex couples as well as couples suspicious of the patriarchal, exclusionary, and sectarian features of marriage. Moreover, a menu that also includes covenant marriage is a move toward *greater* commitment, not less. Relatedly, something like the menu sketched above might facilitate communication about the precise expectations in a relationship. A person deciding how much to invest in a relationship receives valuable information when her romantic partner tells her that she or he is willing to cohabit but not marry. *Responsible* commitment means not rushing into marriage thoughtlessly, and commitment itself might flourish in a regime that allows couples to experiment.

The Challenges of the New World of Mix-and-Match Parenting

With no-fault divorce, nonmarital children, and adoption common-place rather than exceptional, the typical family is no longer one where two spouses owe marital duties to one another, and both owe parental duties to the children. Person A, for example, may be the cohabiting partner or spouse of person B, with whom he is raising child C, conceived with the aid of person D, a surrogate or a sperm donor; A may also be the stepparent (with B) of child E, have joint custody (with former spouse F) of child G, and have support obligations for child H, conceived in a nonmarital relationship with person I. This fracturing of responsibilities is a consequence of freedom of choice (overwhelmingly preferred by straight Americans), but the costs of it are borne primarily by dependent partners and children. Those costs include insufficient nurturing and financial support for those partners and children. What

I call *mix-and-match parenting* also may be exacting psychological and other costs on nondependent partners, some of whom may feel regret, confusion, or role overload because of their multiple and fractured responsibilities.[8]

The decline of the nuclear (mom, dad, and biological kids) family generates understandable anxiety among Americans, for they see that their own desired regime may be having a lamentable effect not only on children's tangible welfare, but upon the family as a refuge of altruism and mutual support. Liberal constitutionalism should be responsive to this anxiety, but not in ways that disrespect choice and equality norms without evidence that particular choices actually undermine responsible commitment.

On the one hand, liberal constitutionalism should support rights of lesbian and gay couples to adopt children and to bear children within their relationships, typically through artificial insemination (for lesbian couples) and surrogacy (for gay couples). State discriminations against lesbian and gay families should be subject to skeptical scrutiny, for they typically reflect prejudice and stereotypes rather than the genuine needs of children. Generally, liberal constitutionalism should be open to new reproductive technologies, though liberals should be attentive to issues of free choice and inequality that present themselves in surrogacy. Indeed, a liberal approach to surrogacy would provide useful information to the participants, create contract default rules, and perhaps insist upon mandatory rules, such as waiting periods, to minimize regret.

On the other hand, the evidence is strong that children suffer when their parents break up. This is certainly a cost of no-fault divorce, and perhaps of cohabitation regimes as well. Liberal constitutionalism should emphasize the creation and strict (interstate) enforcement of fair support formulas, especially as they relate to the support of children. The liberal agenda might also borrow some ideas from covenant marriage: Without making divorce substantively harder to achieve, the state should require family counseling and perhaps waiting periods before spouses with children end their marriages.

Anxiety about nonmarital children fuels opposition to same-sex marriage. Opponents correctly perceive that there is a correlation between high rates of nonmarital children in a society and its willingness to recognize same-sex unions, but incorrectly claim that same-sex marriage then correlates with *and causes* the family instability that harms children. The data from Scandinavia refute the latter claim. Moreover, because approximately one-fourth of U.S. lesbian and gay couples are rearing children within their households, state recognition of their committed unions (including divorce requirements that make it harder to split up) could benefit rather than harm their children.[9]

Liberals should support Martha Fineman's suggestion that family law devote more resources to support parent-child relationships. The Family Medical Leave Act of 1993 requires employers to give parents time off from their jobs for child care and other family responsibilities. Liberals should consider nationalizing the California approach, which requires that such leaves be paid. This is a start. A liberal family law should consider other ways to support working-class and poor parents and to educate their children more effectively.[10]

Like same-sex marriage, little of the positive liberal agenda for children can or should be imposed by judges interpreting the U.S. Constitution. (State judges interpreting state constitutions, on the other hand, are more likely to insist on same-sex marriage, civil unions, and nondiscriminatory adoption rights.) The primary role for federal judges is cleaning up clearly outdated discrimination that remains from earlier eras. A prime candidate is Florida's blanket exclusion of lesbians, gay men, and bisexuals from adoption. This exclusion originated in the political hysteria accompanying Anita Bryant's antihomosexual Dade County campaign in 1977, rests upon no serious evidence regarding lesbian and gay capabilities, and in practice operates *against* children's interests, as revealed in 2004 litigation.[11] No other state has an adoption restriction that explicitly targets lesbian and gay parents, and it is likely that the Florida exclusion will not survive, in its present from, in 2020. Nor will presumptions survive against lesbian and gay parents involved in child custody disputes with former spouses. Found mainly in the southern states that long discriminated against different-race couples, these antigay discriminations are objectionable mainly because they violate the responsible commitment features of the liberal agenda for the Constitution in 2020.[12]

Notes

1. See generally Nancy F. Cott, *Public Vows: A History of Marriage and the Nation* (2000).

2. See generally Jana B. Singer, *The Privatization of Family Law*, 1992 Wis. L. Rev. 1443–1568.

3. See, e.g., Sara McLanahan and Gary D. Sandefur, *Growing Up with a Single Parent: What Hurts, What Helps* (1994); Judith Wallerstein et al., *The Unexpected Legacy of Divorce: A 25 Year Landmark Study* (2000).

4. See, e.g., Maggie Gallagher, "A Reality Waiting to Happen," in Lynn D. Wardle et al., eds., *Marriage and Same-Sex Unions: A Debate* 11–12 (2003).

5. On the incremental process by which states have come to recognize same-sex marriages and unions, see William N. Eskridge, Jr., *Equality Practice: Civil Unions and the Future of Gay Rights* (2002); Robert Wintemute and Mads Andenaes, eds., *Legal Recognition of Same-Sex Partnerships: A Study of National, European, and International Law* (2001); Kees Waaldijk, *More or Less Together: Levels of Legal Consequences of Marriage, Cohabitation, and Registered Partnership for Different-Sex and Same-Sex Partners: A Comparative Study of Nine European Countries* (2005).

6. The menu of options is drawn from Eskridge, *Equality Practice*, 121–26.

7. E.g., Brenda Cossman and Bruce Ryder, *The Legal Regulation of Adult Personal Relationships: Evaluating Policy Objectives and Legal Options in Federal Legislation* (May 2000), available at www.lcc.gc.ca/research_project/00_regulations_1-en.asp.

8. See Katharine Bartlett, *Rethinking Parenthood as an Exclusive Status*, 70 Va. L. Rev. (1984).

9. On the evidence that the recognition of same-sex marriages or unions has no depressive effect upon different-sex marriages, see William N. Eskridge, Jr., and Darren R. Spedale, *Gay Marriage: For Better or for Worse? What We've Learned from the Evidence*, chap. 5 (2006).

10. See Martha Albertson Fineman, *The Neutered Mother, the Sexual Family, and Other Twentieth Century Tragedies* (1995).

11. *Lofton v. Secretary, Dep't of Children & Social Services*, 377 F. 3d 1275 (11th Cir. 2004) (Barkett, J., dissenting from denial of rehearing en banc).

12. See *Bottoms v. Bottoms*, 457 S.E. 2d 102 (1995) (Keenan, J., dissenting) (powerfully arguing against the validity of antilesbian presumption in custody cases).

❧ 23 ❧

A Progressive Reproductive Rights Agenda for 2020

DAWN E. JOHNSEN

Since the 1970s, the issue of abortion has pervaded U.S. law and politics. The Supreme Court's decision in *Roe v. Wade* continues to be both celebrated and reviled with an intensity rarely inspired by a Court decision.[1] Responses have ranged from a torrent of legislation and litigation, to mass demonstrations and marches, and even to the bombing of health care clinics and the murder of abortion service providers. Whether abortion will remain legal has loomed large—too large, some charge—in electoral politics and judicial nominations.

What will the next decades bring? The editors of this book challenged the contributors to be proactive and visionary, to look ahead to the year 2020 and contemplate the constitutional change we hope to promote between now and then. This chapter asks: What vision of reproductive justice, and what objectives and strategies to achieve that vision, should progressives adopt? This book was inspired in part by *The Constitution in 2000*, a 1988 Department of Justice report that, along with others in a series, set forth a blueprint for radically remaking constitutional law on the great issues of the day, including by overruling dozens of Supreme Court opinions.[2] Although the substance of the Reagan administration's agenda was terribly wrong, its breathtaking ambition and subsequent successes demonstrate the value of having a vision and a long-term strategic plan. Progressives similarly should take the long view and formulate ambitious goals that are informed by deep ideological commitments and not unduly constrained by present realities. In short, progressives should think big—and then devise effective strategies for moving toward their objectives.

The progressive agenda should aspire to protect genuine reproductive health and liberty for all. Toward this ideal, I would suggest the following three shifts in strategic priorities to augment ongoing efforts to persuade courts to invalidate abortion restrictions. First, focus more on persuading the public to support meaningful reproductive options through political action, grassroots organizing, and public education. Second, focus relatively less on the threat of criminal abortion bans that would be enforceable if the Court overruled *Roe* and more on existing and forthcoming abortion restrictions, both legislative and extralegal, which cumulatively deprive a growing number of women of access to abortion services. Finally, situate abortion within the full range of progressive policies essential to genuine reproductive health and liberty, policies that empower women and men to prevent unintended pregnancies and to bear and raise healthy and wanted children.

These recommendations entail not radical changes, but significant shifts in emphasis. They will be familiar to prochoice advocates, who long have led efforts against all manner of abortion obstacles and in favor of pregnancy prevention. Yet in the public's eye, the prochoice effort is associated far more with extremism and "abortion on demand" than with healthy childbearing and reductions in unintended pregnancies. Effective strategies must target public misperceptions and emphasize political action, preventing harmful incremental abortion obstacles and instituting a broad range of policies that promote reproductive choice and health. Finally, even while broadening this political agenda, progressives must counteract new strategies to stigmatize and induce shame into a woman's decision to terminate a pregnancy, by affirming the vital place of legal and accessible abortion services on that agenda and by resisting any temptation to avoid the controversy of abortion.

Reproductive Rights in the Courts

The concerted attack on *Roe v. Wade* began in earnest in the late 1970s and accelerated with the election of Ronald Reagan. The Reagan constitutional blueprint targeted the Supreme Court and *Roe*, as well as earlier landmark cases that protected fundamental liberties through substantive due process analysis. Under the Reagan view, the constitutional guarantee of "liberty" created no obstacle to laws that ban abortion during the earliest stages of pregnancy, criminalize the use of contraception,[3] or forcibly sterilize people as a form of punishment.[4] The Reagan agenda also warned against expansions of liberty, for example, to protect same-sex physical intimacy. It situated this opposition to fundamental liberties within a broad framework that sought both diminished judicial protection for rights and liberties (justified by the "original intent" of the framers) and judicial enforcement of a "federalism" that would narrow Congress's authority to safeguard rights.

One way to formulate a progressive reproductive rights agenda for 2020 would similarly identify Supreme Court decisions as consistent or inconsistent with the desired vision of reproductive liberty. This list should start by acknowledging losses—principally, that *Roe v. Wade* no longer governs the constitutionality of abortion restrictions. Instead, the Court's 1992 decision in *Planned Parenthood v. Casey* controls.[5] Best known for its reaffirmation of *Roe*'s "essential holding," *Casey* confounded expectations that the Court would overrule *Roe* expressly and completely, bringing tremendous relief to *Roe*'s supporters—and disappointment and outrage to its opponents.

Far less noted, *Casey* allowed the government substantially greater authority to interfere with women's reproductive choices. The Court overruled protective rulings from the 1980s and upheld the very types of restrictions it previously had held to be unconstitutional.[6] Chief Justice William Rehnquist's *Casey* dissent noted, "*Roe* continues to exist, but only in the way a storefront on a western movie set exists: a mere facade to give the illusion of reality."[7]

The Court's 2007 *Gonzales v. Carhart* decision confirmed and extended *Casey*'s damage to *Roe*. Justice Anthony Kennedy, a swing fifth vote in both cases, emphasized in *Carhart* that *Casey* "struck a balance" that centrally included the government's "substantial interest in preserving and promoting fetal life" from the outset of pregnancy; he omitted any mention of women's essential interests, which were so eloquently described in his joint opinion in *Casey*.[8] Using antichoice terminology, *Carhart* upheld a criminal ban on a method of abortion that intentionally omitted any exception for women's health. The dissent charged that the majority "dishonors our precedent" and that "the Act, and the Court's defense of it, cannot be understood as anything other than an effort to chip away at a right declared again and again by this Court."[9] *Casey*—and even more, *Carhart*'s reading of *Casey*—is inconsistent with a progressive notion of liberty.

The list of wrongly decided cases also should include several that upheld harmful and deceptively reasonable-sounding restrictions on access to abortion services: decisions that upheld the exclusion of abortion from government-provided health care for the poor, the prohibition of abortion services at publicly funded medical facilities (even when no public funds subsidized the services), and parental notice and consent requirements.[10] Progressives should also anticipate future controversies, including those that might arise from medical and scientific advances.

Most critical, just as conservatives promoted "federalism" and "originalism" in the courts and, more effectively, in political arenas, progressives should develop improved understandings of the constitutional bases for reproductive liberty. Progressives need to rethink *Roe's* theoretical underpinnings—and what remains after *Casey* and *Carhart*. The *Carhart* dissent, for four justices, made significant progress in this regard. It responded to the majority's shocking reliance on gender stereotypes about women's natural role as mothers by describing reproductive liberty in terms of equal protection and equal citizenship: "Thus, legal challenges to undue restrictions on abortion procedures do not seek to vindicate some generalized notion of privacy; rather they center on a woman's autonomy to determine her life's course, and thus to enjoy equal citizenship stature."[11]

Priority One: Enhance Public Education and Political Action

To date, litigation has served as the primary and most effective weapon against dangerous abortion restrictions. Progressives should continue to secure whatever protections are achievable from judicial enforcement of both state and federal constitutions and to develop constitutional theory for the long haul. Litigation, however, should not remain the principal means of safeguarding reproductive rights. The Supreme Court is unlikely in the near future to overrule *Casey's* undue burden test in favor of *Roe's* more protective approach (or a new protective theory), let alone overrule earlier rulings that upheld onerous parental consent requirements and discriminatory funding provisions. A Court-centered strategy for the coming decades would be dangerously inadequate.

Some progressives have criticized *Roe* on the grounds that (over)reliance on the Court has inadvertently energized opponents and falsely reassured supporters of *Roe*. In my judgment, *Roe's* enormous and immediate benefits to women and families—and its positive effect on expectations about women's rights—outweighed any resulting loss in political momentum since the 1970s. Regardless of differences in judgments about the past, progressives should agree in the coming decade to dedicate relatively greater resources to build public and political support at every level of government.

Progressives also should agree—and should endeavor to persuade others—that restrictive abortion laws do violate women's constitutional rights, whether or not the Court protects those rights. Even in political arenas, prochoice aspirations can be strengthened by appeals to the Constitution and to the notion that compulsory pregnancy and childbirth are beyond the government's authority. Given *Roe*'s stature and the Court's prior vigorous protection of reproductive liberty, an appeal to the Constitution in political battles over abortion seems particularly helpful. It is far more effective (and, to my mind, more accurate) to emphasize that the Court protected the constitutional right to choose until the ideological Right took over the Court, than it is to argue that the Court went too far and that the debate is now where it belongs, in the legislatures.

Prochoice advocates, with national organizations headquartered in Washington, D.C., and New York, have done more to supplement litigation with national political work than they have expanded efforts at the state and local levels. Notwithstanding the good work of the affiliates of Planned Parenthood, the American Civil Liberties Union, and NARAL Pro-Choice America throughout the country, the greatest reproductive rights need for 2020 is the building of strong grassroots political organizations with public education capabilities. Progressives must work effectively outside the courts in state legislatures, local communities, political parties, and elections at every level of government. Electing representatives who will safeguard reproductive health and liberty also promotes a more protective judiciary, both directly through judicial appointments and less directly, for history instructs that the courts will not stray very far from political and public opinion. The dramatic political, legislative, and judicial successes of opponents of *Roe* have resulted directly from their decades-long attention to public persuasion and grassroots organizing.

My two remaining recommendations elaborate on the desirable content of the largely political reproductive rights agenda, but first a caution. As attention to state and local politics increases, progressives should take care not to condone gross inequalities determined by a woman's physical location. A 2006 *New York Magazine* article illustrates the danger. It celebrates a state court decision that declined to find a right to same-sex marriage, suggesting that the court had avoided the *Roe* problem of getting too far ahead of the public. The article concluded: "With the right ascendant, it's clear that states' rights is an essential American principle without any inherent ideological tilt. . . . If letting Georgia and Indiana and Utah go their own way is the price for Massachusetts and California and New York's being free to go ours, I'm willing to pay it."[12] As a former New Yorker now living in Indiana, I am not willing to accept this view of "states' rights." Fundamental liberties essential to equality should not vary state by state, despite the necessity for state-by-state efforts to protect them. States' rights should entail the opportunity to expand, not curtail, rights guaranteed by the federal Constitution. Progressives should aim for uniform nationwide protection of the fundamental right of all women to meaningful access to legal contraception and abortion services.

Priority Two: Oppose Incremental Obstacles

One question has drowned out virtually all others in the abortion debate since the Republican Party began calling for the appointment of anti-*Roe* justices and President Reagan began replacing justices in the *Roe* majority: Will the Court overrule *Roe*? And the natural follow-up: Will states again criminalize abortion, forcing many women to risk their lives and health with illegal "back-alley" abortionists? That was the proper focus for the 1980s, but it is increasingly inadequate.

With each appointment, the Court's support for *Roe* diminished, from *Roe*'s solid, bipartisan seven justices, to a bare majority of five in 1986. But *Roe* proved resilient. Many court watchers expected *Roe*'s demise in the 1989 *Webster* case. The Court upheld all the restrictions before it, but the justice in the middle—Sandra Day O'Connor—declined to join the four justices who wanted to go further and strike at *Roe*'s heart. Justice Harry Blackmun, *Roe*'s author, warned in dissent that the reprieve likely was temporary and that "a chill wind blows." By 1992, Presidents Reagan and George H. W. Bush had replaced five of the seven justices in the *Roe* majority, and *Planned Parenthood v. Casey* was widely expected to deliver the final blow. The *Casey* Court's partial (and eloquent) reaffirmation of *Roe* shocked supporters and opponents of *Roe* alike.

Looking ahead to 2020, the risk remains real that the Court will overrule *Roe*. But more likely is a continued death by a dozen decisions, with no express overruling (if at all) until after the Court has rendered the formal protections practically useless. At least since *Casey* authorized increased governmental restriction while purporting to reaffirm *Roe*, the preoccupation with whether the Court will expressly overrule *Roe* has proven misplaced. It has worked to the detriment of women and to the advantage of opponents of reproductive liberty.

Since *Casey*, states have adopted literally hundreds of abortion restrictions, reflecting an incremental, multitiered strategy to create "abortion-free" states and to deter women from having abortions, often through deception. (With its 2003 ban on so-called partial birth abortions, Congress joined the effort, which previously had been justified with appeals to federalism and states' rights.) Cumulatively, these efforts—restrictive legislation that the courts will uphold, diminished abortion training in medical schools, stigmatization of women who have abortions and physicians who perform them, harassment and violence directed at health care providers at work and at home—have dramatically reduced the number of abortion providers. In many parts of the country, abortion services are unavailable for hundreds of miles, while antichoice "crisis pregnancy centers" flourish (often with the assistance of public funding). Legislative and extralegal obstacles combine to thwart women's access to the clinics that do remain open: Mandatory forty-eight-hour waiting periods translate into multiple long-distance trips often over weeks, "informed consent" requirements amount to state-mandated antichoice propaganda, and two-parent consent requirements for minors thwart the wishes not only of the pregnant girl but of her custodial parent. As of 2008, abortion services were less available in the United States than at any time since 1974. Three states were just one clinic away from being abortion-free.

One single-clinic state, South Dakota, achieved fame when it outlawed abortion in all cases except when necessary to save a woman's life: No exceptions were allowed even for rape, incest, severe fetal abnormalities, or threats to a woman's health. The fact that only one abortion clinic existed in the entire state was far less publicized. The abortion ban was controversial even among some strong opponents of legal abortion (and ultimately was repealed by a November 2006 ballot measure) because of its lack of a rape or incest exception and also because it faced almost certain judicial invalidation (at least absent the appointment of one additional anti-*Roe* justice). Prominent national antichoice organizations even refused to endorse the ban, favoring instead the incremental approach of more reasonable-sounding and limited restrictions tailored to shut down the one remaining clinic.

A 2005 *Frontline* documentary, *The Last Abortion Clinic*, illustrates the effectiveness of the incremental approach. Antichoice efforts reduced Mississippi, like South Dakota, to just one clinic that provides abortion services.[13] *Frontline* interviewed Mississippi women who described their utter lack of any meaningful right to decide whether to terminate a pregnancy. They lived many hours of travel from the nearest clinic. As in the pre-*Roe* years, women who most suffer from legal and practical obstacles to safe abortion services are those without resources and the ability to travel. These include women who never have traveled out of their home towns, who cannot afford the travel, who do not own cars or have access to any other transportation, who would lose their jobs if they missed the days of work required to make multiple long-distance trips, who cannot arrange child care, or who have abusive husbands they cannot escape. The litany is familiar: Poverty, location, and abuse are the circumstances that, prior to *Roe*, determined which women had to risk their lives to terminate a pregnancy.

The *Frontline* episode also described efforts to close that last Mississippi clinic, including TRAP, or "targeted regulation of abortion providers," laws that impose medically unnecessary, extremely expensive regulations, such as hallway widths and room sizes that mirror those in hospitals. Another restriction would require physicians who perform abortions at the clinic to have admitting privileges at the local hospital, a requirement that is both medically unnecessary (the clinic already has a transfer agreement with the hospital) and, as those who devised the restriction well know, unattainable: The hospital will not confer admitting privileges to an out-of-state physician, and no in-state physician is willing to work at the clinic because of the continual antichoice protests and harassment.

Given the effectiveness of ingenious, reasonable-sounding options, why bother with a highly contentious abortion ban? In Indiana, antichoice legislators introduced two bills in 2006: one to ban abortion and one TRAP law that would have closed every abortion clinic in the state, unless and until they could implement expensive renovations or relocate. The criminal ban went nowhere, but the legislature nearly enacted the TRAP law. That law would have shut down every one of Indiana's nine clinics, located in just five of the state's ninety-two counties—clinics that devote the overwhelming majority of their resources to preventing unintended pregnancies (thereby decreasing the need for abortion) and other non-abortion health care. Opponents of reproductive choice in Indiana responded by working county by county to try to enact ordinances that would close down those same clinics through local ordinances.

Activists on both sides understand the true intent and serious costs behind such reasonable-sounding regulations. Prochoice advocates, however, have not found effective ways to communicate those harms to a public that favors keeping abortion legal, but not too easily available. Some progressives speculate that preserving meaningful access to abortion would be easier if the Court expressly overruled *Roe* and galvanized prochoice Americans to act and vote accordingly. The speculation continues that this is precisely what many self-proclaimed antichoice politicians most fear (and therefore secretly resist). In my view, an express overruling of *Roe* would be far worse than existing restrictions, particularly for the most vulnerable of women who cannot manage to travel to faraway clinics.

The most underappreciated obstacles to abortion, though, are those already in place or soon to come: the protests, harassment, and violence directed at abortion clinics, providers, and their families; the lack of abortion training opportunities in medical schools; and the hundreds of state abortion restrictions that are designed both to sound reasonable and to stop the performance of abortions as effectively as a criminal ban.

Priority Three: Advance a Comprehensive Reproductive Choice Agenda

As progressives plan for 2020, the agenda must include meaningful access not only to abortion services, but also to the full range of policies essential for genuine reproductive choice and health. Advocacy for the right to decide whether to continue or terminate a pregnancy—for keeping the government out of highly personal, life-altering decisions about when and whether to have a child—should be paired explicitly with policies that support women in all their reproductive decisions. Being prochoice means not only keeping the government out of people's private lives, but also defining and promoting the right role for government and society in supporting women and families.

The progressive reproductive rights agenda should include policies that support healthy pregnancies and healthy families, including universal health care, affordable child care, paid family leave, and other workplace support for employees who need to care for children and other family members. Prochoice progressives also should address the full range of economic justice issues, from the minimum wage to taxation policy to financial support for struggling families. Also key are efforts to protect women from violence, including in their own homes.

Reproductive liberty also encompasses the ability to prevent unintended pregnancy. Progressive priorities should include support for comprehensive and age-appropriate sexuality education, universal access to reproductive health care, and new contraceptive technologies. Also critical is opposition to all politicization and distortion of reproductive health care information and services: inaccurate abstinence-only programs that mislead and endanger children, government support for deceptive crisis pregnancy centers, restrictions on the over-the-counter availability of emergency contraception, protocols that omit any mention of emergency contraception for the treatment of rape victims, pharmacists' refusals to fill prescriptions for contraception, biased reproductive health counseling, and the costly TRAP laws that burden reproductive health clinics. All of these so-called conservative policies actually increase the rate of unintended pregnancy and thus abortion—not coincidentally, because many abortion opponents also oppose contraceptive use.

Major prochoice organizations have worked in these broader directions—especially to champion pregnancy prevention. Eighty-one percent of Planned Parenthood clients receive services to prevent unintended pregnancy, while 10 percent receive abortion services.[14] This work has borne real fruit, including significant reductions in unintended pregnancy and abortion rates and the enactment of the Family and Medical Leave Act. Organizations that work for reproductive justice, however, should expand their emphasis to include the range of issues essential to healthy childbearing and healthy families. Moreover, it remains an essential task to convey continually that prochoice candidates and advocates are not pro-abortion, but pro-prevention and pro-family. This is a promising message, for it substitutes a true picture for a caricature, offers an affirmative agenda around which to organize, and addresses antichoice sentiment in ways that empower rather than burden vulnerable women and families.

With greater emphasis on pregnancy prevention and healthy childbearing, some cautions are warranted. First, progressives must not portray all abortions as tragedies. Beginning in 1992, President Bill Clinton popularized the saying "abortion should be safe, legal and rare," which reflects a worthy aspiration for policies that emphasize prevention and make abortion less necessary. Senator Hillary Clinton, in a 2005 speech commendable for setting forth a prochoice, pro-prevention, pro-family agenda, took the aspiration a step in the wrong direction when she called for policy changes so that abortion "does not ever have to be exercised or only in very rare circumstances."[15] But absent unforeseen technological and medical changes, abortion is unlikely to become truly "rare" and certainly not nonexistent. An estimated one-third of all women will choose to terminate a pregnancy by age forty-five. Our nation can and should significantly reduce that number by reducing unintended pregnancies (roughly half of all pregnancies). But abortion will remain a necessary option, for example, when contraception fails and a woman is not ready to have a child, when women conceive following rape or incest, when pregnant women develop serious medical problems that require pregnancy termination, and when severe fetal abnormalities are detected.

Abortion undoubtedly is a complex, important, highly personal issue—often a difficult and painful decision with which many women struggle. But describing any and all abortions as terrible tragedies stigmatizes women who have abortions. To be sure, some abortions involve tragic circumstances and many women do consider abortion a personal tragedy. But many do not, especially when the abortion is performed early in pregnancy, as about 90 percent are. Certainly, many rape and incest victims would consider a government-compelled childbirth a much greater tragedy than terminating the criminally caused pregnancy.

The tragedy label also promotes shame and silence, while protecting choice critically depends instead upon women's willingness to talk about their personal experiences. Stigmatizing abortion also feeds increasing antichoice efforts to portray women as victims who are harmed by terminating pregnancies and who make such deeply tragic and wrong choices only because they are misled by physicians, clinics, and laws that promote abortion—a view irresponsibly promoted by the Supreme Court in *Carhart*.

Progressives also should oppose inaccurate and incomplete abstinence-only sex education and other treatments of sexuality issues that instill negative attitudes about sexuality itself. A century ago, Margaret Sanger, in opposing government restrictions on contraception for married couples, proclaimed that a "mutual and satisfied sexual act is of great benefit to the average woman."[16] Such frank recognition of the natural, healthy, and valuable role of sex in a loving relationship rarely is heard in today's public debate over issues of sexuality. Instead, what we teach our young people in sexuality education courses often can be summarized as "Sex is dirty, nasty, and dangerous. Save it for the one you love and marry." When nonprocreative sex, even within marriage, is not valued as one of humanity's gifts, government-compelled pregnancy and childbearing can seem more reasonable. Progressives should affirm Planned Parenthood's first-listed value: "Sexuality is a natural, healthy, lifelong part of being human."[17]

Conclusion: Reproductive Justice for All

None of the recommendations outlined above is a silver bullet or a prochoice version of the wildly successful—and intentionally deceptive—partial birth abortion ban. Far from it. Effective advocacy and reform inescapably will require hard work over time, in the face of great challenges. Nor do my suggestions directly address many of the women most devastated by antichoice policies in many places across the globe, where contraception and abortion services are illegal or unavailable, health care is nonexistent, AIDS is rampant, and rape is routine. More than a half million women die each year because of unsafe abortions and childbirth practices. To conclude, I offer a final recommendation for beyond U.S. borders. Progressives must address the harms inflicted by our nation's foreign policy and support the important work of non-governmental organizations abroad, even as we struggle to avert similar tragedies here at home. Wherever they call home, women's ability to participate fully and equally in public and private life and even their very health and lives depend on being able to control when and whether to have children to raise and to love.

Notes

1. *Roe v. Wade*, 410 U.S. 113 (1973).
2. Office of Legal Policy, U.S. Dep't of Justice, Report to the Attorney General, *The Constitution in the Year 2000: Choices Ahead in Constitutional Interpretation* (1988).
3. See *Griswold v. Connecticut*, 381 U.S. 479 (1965).
4. See *Skinner v. Oklahoma*, 316 U.S. 535 (1942).
5. *Planned Parenthood of Southeast Pennsylvania v. Casey*, 505 U.S. 833 (1992).
6. See *Thornburgh v. American College of Obstetricians & Gynecologists*, 476 U.S. 747 (1986); *City of Akron v. Akron Center for Reproductive Health, Inc.*, 462 U.S. 416 (1983).
7. *Casey*, 505 U.S. at 954 (Rehnquist, C.J., dissenting).
8. *Gonzales v. Carhart*, 127 S. Ct. 1610 (2007).
9. *Id.* at 1653 (Ginsburg, J., dissenting).
10. See, e.g., *Ohio v. Akron Center for Reproductive Health*, 497 U.S. 502 (1990); *Hodgson v. Minnesota*, 497 U.S. 417 (1990); *Webster v. Reproductive Health Services*, 492 U.S. 490 (1989); *H.L. v. Matheson*, 450 U.S. 398 (1981); *Harris v. McRae*, 448 U.S. 297 (1980); *Bellotti v. Baird*, 428 U.S. 132 (1976).
11. *Gonzales v. Carhart*, 127 S. Ct. at 1641 (Ginsburg, J., dissenting).
12. Kurt Andersen, *The Gay-Wedding Present*, New York Magazine, July 24, 2006.
13. Frontline: *The Last Abortion Clinic* (PBS television broadcast, Nov. 8, 2005), available at http://www.pbs.org/wgbh/pages/frontline/clinic.
14. *Planned Parenthood at a Glance*, available at http://www.plannedparenthood.org/about-us/who-we-are/pp-services-5552.htm.
15. Senator Hillary Rodham Clinton, *Remarks to the New York State Family Planning Providers* (Jan. 24, 2005), available at http://clinton.senate.gov/~clinton/speeches/2005125A05.html.
16. Margaret Sanger, *Family Limitation* 6 (1914).
17. Planned Parenthood Federation of America, *We Believe* (2003).

PART VII

State, Nation, World

❧ 24 ❧

What's Federalism For?

JUDITH RESNIK

T HE WORD *federalism* does not appear in the text of the U.S. Constitution. This fact may come as a surprise, given that the American Revolution is said to have invented this form of government and that the U.S. Supreme Court has come to use the term federalism as an explanation of why Congress, or the executive, or states do—or do not—have certain kinds of power.

The Constitution does, however, create a federal structure in which states are the linchpin. States are the source of senators, members of the House of Representatives, and, via the Electoral College, the president. The Constitution also recognizes states' lawmaking powers, which are separate from those of the national government. States can structure their own court systems, legislatures, and executive branches. Further, states can make their own laws, even if their rule making is at odds with those of other states and the national government. The result is a complex, redundant, and in some ways deliberately inefficient form of government, celebrated for separating powers, respecting local autonomy, and generating diverse practices about how to order interdependent and connected legal, political, social, and economic regimes.

But the diversity that federalism engenders is also constrained. The predicate proposition is that some basic commitments are so foundational as to permit no deviation. The perennial issue is specifying what national norms trump local choice. Thus, although federalism may seem to be a dry facet of political theory, the Supreme Court's federalism docket repeatedly features many of the pressing and politically freighted topics of a given era.

The present is no exception. Decisions in the late twentieth and early twenty-first centuries parsed the constitutional clauses regulating commerce, providing equal protection, and giving some immunity to states from lawsuits, as the Court decided questions such as whether Congress can authorize individuals to seek money damages from states for violating federal rights to fair labor standards (it can't),[1] for violating federal protections against discrimination based on age or disability (it can't),[2] or for violating rights to take family leaves (it can).[3] Other famous federalism cases have involved a state's power to execute people who committed crimes when under age eighteen (prohibited),[4] a state's capacity to ban the import of liquor from out-of-state producers (also prohibited),[5] and a state's authority to limit its own purchase of goods from Burma, where laborers work in horrid conditions (again, prohibited).[6]

The Ideology of Separate Spheres

In federalism opinions, the decisions typically posit states to be singular actors, sometimes in competition but rarely understood to act in concert. Further, the Supreme Court often speaks in essentializing terms, as though certain categories of law belong intrinsically to separate spheres that are naturally governed by what we have come to call "state" or "federal" law but which did not have those labels until several decades after the United States was founded.[7] For example, the Court has intervened to prevent federal "interference" with state governance of tort, family law, crime, and education. Yet, at other points, the Court has preempted state lawmaking, even when states are engaged in activities that could also be categorized as traditionally theirs, such as protecting consumers from commercial fraud.[8]

The Court's weaving back and forth demonstrates the unworkability of its categorical enterprise. The flip-flops have been particularly vivid since the late 1980s. What were once nationally regulated income supports and speed limits on highways became areas claimed better suited to state governance. And, while education and marriage were once specially identified as within state prerogatives, national laws (with titles such as No Child Left Behind[9] and the Defense of Marriage Act[10]) now impose federal regulations.

The Progressive Potential of Interdependent Realities

The actual autonomy—of states vis-à-vis each other or the nation, and of states and the nation vis-à-vis the world—is vastly overstated. The Constitution itself recognizes that states may join together in compacts sanctioned by Congress.[11] Twentieth-century examples include the Tennessee Valley Authority and New York's Port Authority. Further, under the aegis of the National Conference of Commissioners on Uniform State Laws, representatives of states meet to draft laws that are then brought to state legislatures, which independently adopt the same provisions, perhaps with modifications, on issues ranging from extradition to commercial law. Many federal laws, in turn, rely on state implementation, prompting political scientists to use the metaphors of a marble cake,[12] picket fences,[13] and matrixes[14] to capture the interdependencies of local, state, and national governance.

But even those terms no longer suffice, as technology and globalization further interrupt a tidy narrative of federalism. Forms of jurisdiction bending are everywhere, as private sector nongovernmental organizations (NGOs) seek to bring about translocal changes that range from bans on abortions, same-sex marriage, or immigration to the regulation of handguns and caps on greenhouse gases. Further, subnational and transnational collectives regularly defy conventional federalism's assumptions that interactions are either horizontal (state to state) or vertical (nation to states or cities). State and federal judges join forces to deal with lawsuits involving harms from mass torts and environmental hazards that respect no jurisdiction lines. Executive officials of state and local governments work in conjunction with their counterparts elsewhere as they formulate standards to apply around the country.

A new institutional infrastructure reflects these changes through the development during the twentieth century of national organizations of local officials (such as the National League of Cities, the U.S. Conference of Mayors, and the National Governors Association). These translocal organizations of government actors (which are private organizations deriving political capital from being composed of public officials or employees) help to weave common agendas for cities and states on topics ranging from trade and antitrust to the environment and personal liberties. They regularly cross national borders as well, such that issues once characterized as foreign affairs can become matters of domestic obligations. While political scientists have focused on what they term special interest groups ("SIGs") and public interest groups ("PIGs") as well as NGOs, less attention has been paid to the structural and political import of these translocal organizations of government actors, which I think are aptly denoted "TOGAs" to capture the civic roots and agendas of these entities.[15]

This translocalism ought to prompt progressive Americans to reassess attitudes toward federalism. Progressives need to reread the history of the United States to remember that the abolition of slavery was nurtured at the state level before gaining national currency, and that women voted in states (Wyoming was the first that lasted in 1869) some fifty years before getting the national franchise. Moreover, the protection of twentieth-century rights, from welfare and employment to access for the disabled, depends heavily on protection at the state level. Of course, states have also been sites of radical racism and nativism. One needs thus to be keenly aware that no jurisdiction is intrinsically generative or oppressive, and those seeking to make good on constitutional promises of equality and liberty need to be both fans and skeptics of federalism and of nationalism.

The Freight of Federalism

Federalism in the United States has a painful history. The nation was founded on a constitutional agreement to split "the atom of sovereignty"[16] and thereby to enable the survival of slavery. States claimed a sovereign prerogative to determine which persons were entitled to the sanctity of their bodies and the fruits of their labors. The Civil War represented a victory of force rather than a shared moral imperative. While Reconstruction aimed briefly to implement some promises of equal treatment, backlash and retrenchment followed, putting into place multiple forms of subordination of blacks.

During the middle of the twentieth century, national policies shifted. Responding to the Depression, two world wars, the needs of a national economy, and then renewed commitments to equality, all three branches of the federal government pressed for enhanced national power. "States' rights" and "federalism" became euphemisms for assertions of freedom from national regulation and, in many instances, for the provision of less equality, less access to well-being and safety, and fewer protections for black individuals. Even after *Brown v. Board of Education* nationalized one aspect of education policy by banning segregated schools, state leaders opposed national interference at other sites of segregation, such as housing and the criminal justice system.

Federalism continues to be used to constrain various forms of equality claims. In 2000, a five-person majority in *United States v. Morrison*[17] held that Congress lacked the power to redress violence against women by giving victims the right to seek money damages from their assailants through lawsuits in federal court. According to the opinion's author, Chief Justice William Rehnquist, the problem of violence against women was "truly local" rather than "truly national."[18] Similarly, when efforts are made to convince the United States to join international human rights conventions, including the Convention on the Elimination of All Forms of Discrimination Against Women (CEDAW),[19] opponents rely regularly on their conceptions of U.S. federalism to argue that foreign influences ought not disturb either the democratic processes represented by local governance or the dominion of states over interpersonal relations.

This freighted history has prompted many progressives to look to the national government to bring about new understandings of rights and social welfare. Such faith in national elaborations has sometimes been rewarded. In the nineteenth century, vindication came through the Civil War, the aftermath of which produced amendments to the Constitution and civil rights remedies in federal courts. In the twentieth century, New Deal legislation focused on the regulation of national markets and the provision of social benefits while, in the 1960s and 1970s, congressional mandates prohibited discrimination in employment, voting, housing, and credit, thereby shaping a Second Reconstruction. In addition, new kinds of rights came into view through the development of national standards for clean air, clean water, and the protection of endangered species. Prompted by social activists and joining with Congress and the executive branch, the Supreme Court shared in this elaboration of rights. The Fourteenth Amendment was reread to prevent certain kinds of discrimination based on sex, and the Bill of Rights came to be seen as curbing the power of state prosecutors, police, and judges.

Federalism Revisited: A Complex Past and Present

But during the latter part of the twentieth century, the national arena became much less hospitable to many rights-seekers. Opponents of the particular substantive powers exercised and of the accrual of power to the national government shaped their own social movement, flying the banner of federalism and calling for power to return to the states. Relying in part on claims that states were the natural holders of power and that federal authority was constitutionally suspect, this social movement has succeeded on many metrics. The national commitment to progressive rights enhancement (i.e., openness to redistribution and to recognition of status inequalities) has waned, as administrations with different agendas and Congresses with other aspirations have come to power.

Further, because the two political branches nominate and confirm life-tenured judges, many of those selected for that branch are of the view that federal courts' enforcement of certain kinds of rights is illicit. The national government under the presidency of George W. Bush became increasingly committed to deregulation and privatization, as it also reduced the transparency of governance practices and campaigned to limit the obligations and liabilities of public and private sector actors. One technique of particular import for constitutionalists is the erosion of the jurisdiction and remedial powers of federal judges.[20] Concurrent with the narrowing of federal rights has come the preemption of personal rights protected under state laws. Federal judges have read statutes to preclude state-based claims and thus constricted the remedies that had been available to tort victims and to consumers.

It is thus time for progressives to look again at the federalist structure and to reassess a narrative that assumes that national leadership alone has produced the rereading of the Constitution to embrace rights-holding by women and men of all colors. States and localities have been and are important sites of social change. While the Internet has facilitated the ease of connections across localities, transjurisdictional human rights work (of all political stripes) has a long history of coordinated action. That work began with eighteenth-century international efforts to end slavery and enhance women's rights and continues under the contemporary nomenclature of human rights. Today's translocalism and transnationalism run the political gamut as they embrace issues from environmental protection and climate control to the protection of family values and of individual liberties to own property and guns.

Translocal Transnationalism

One contemporary example involves the Convention on the Elimination of All Forms of Discrimination Against Women, entered into force in 1981. This convention has been ratified by 185 countries, but not the United States. Opponents to ratification recognize that, in some respects, CEDAW is more expansive than current interpretations of U.S. constitutional guarantees of equal protection. CEDAW is focused on impact, rather than discriminatory intent, and its precepts apply to private as well as public actors. Further, counter to the current retrenchment on affirmative action in the United States, CEDAW encourages such "temporary measures" to respond to women's subordination in the "political, social, economic, and cultural fields."[21]

Although the United States has yet to ratify CEDAW, a few cities have adopted aspects of it as local law. For example, reflecting principles of CEDAW, San Francisco requires reports on the role that gender plays in the delivery of municipal services, employment practices, and budget allocations. The goal is to understand "systematic and structural discrimination" against women and girls.[22] This kind of analysis is what the United Nations, the Council of Europe, and the Commonwealth Secretariat all call "gender mainstreaming," which is aimed at ensuring that all policy decisions are made with attention to their effects on both women and men.[23]

The decision by San Francisco to adopt CEDAW measures needs to be understood as not simply a "local" initiative undertaken by a notably progressive community. Rather, San Francisco's provisions are the outgrowth of a social movement that has formed around CEDAW. More than 150 civic and religious organizations built a coalition to provide model resolutions for localities to adopt to combat sex-based discrimination. As of 2004, forty-four cities, eighteen counties, and sixteen states have legislation relating to CEDAW. Most of those provisions are expressive, calling upon the national government to ratify the convention. But, as illustrated by San Francisco, a few jurisdictions have done more, incorporating these precepts as local law.

A second example of local interventions generating self-imposed obligations comes from the U.S. Conference of Mayors Climate Protection Center. That project responds to the national government's refusal to participate in the Kyoto Protocol on Climate Change. In the spring of 2005, a group of 9 mayors from a diverse set of cities agreed to their own climate protection program.[24] After that resolution gained approval by the U.S. Conference of Mayors, more than 900 mayors representing some 80 million people joined the effort. Thus, while at a formal level, only the U.S. Senate can ratify a treaty, at the subnational level, the principles of the Kyoto Protocol have been adopted around the United States.[25]

Translocalism through Transnational Organizations of Government Actors: The Roles of TOGAs

The local interest in CEDAW and the Kyoto Protocol results from networks built through transjurisdictional organizations of government officials and employees. Organizations such as the National League of Cities, the U.S. Conference of Mayors, the National Conference of State Legislatures, the National Governors Association, and the National Conference of Commissioners on Uniform State Laws are conduits for border crossings, city to city, state to state, and transnationally.

In many respects, these organizations are artifacts *of* U.S. federalism. They were formed during the twentieth century as government-based interest groups to protect localities from national encroachments and to forward municipal agendas in Washington. With the nationalization and globalization of the economy, they have broadened their horizons. They are, in the language of social movement theory, "norm entrepreneurs," using their institutional voices to shape policies and define the parameters of their own concerns. But unlike classic NGOs or the SIGs and PIGs in the political science literature, these TOGAs—private organizations of public officials—straddle public and private sectors.[26] Further, they are now forging links to other national and subnational entities around the world in a fashion beyond the ability of the national government to "control, supervise, or even monitor."[27]

Judicial Crossings of Federalism's Jurisdictional Borders

Boundary bending does not only occur through the actions of local executives of state governments. State and federal judges, presumed to be landlocked, are also actively involved in practices sometimes described as "judicial federalism," which reflect the interdependencies of federal and state court systems.

Global trading, national and transnational companies, national law firms, the Internet, and a population in which millions move annually do not fit into territorial boxes; persons and activities do not belong either singularly to one state or exclusively to any one national government. Pressures from large-scale aggregated litigation, such as environmental litigation or mass torts, prompted some of this innovation. While formally based either in state or federal court, participants in these cases often aspire to global peace—a settlement that includes all pending cases, whether filed in state or in federal courts. In other kinds of cases, incentives to coordinate come from prisoners' filings from cross-jurisdictional issues in criminal, immigration, and bankruptcy cases, and from efforts to regulate attorneys.

During the 1980s, federal and state judges began to cross jurisdictional lines simply to talk. In 1990, the Conference of Chief Justices and the Judicial Conference of the United States authorized the creation of Federal-State Judicial Councils, resulting in 1992 in the first-ever national conference aimed specifically at bringing state and federal judges together. In various parts of the country, judges of both kinds of courts set up regular meetings to address shared problems—from how to transfer prisoners to how to deal with mass torts. The consequences of judicial federalism became visible through the press, law reviews, and occasionally case law. Despite the formal statements of statutes and doctrine (that federal and state judicial systems are distinct, with few mechanisms for interjurisdictional consolidation), informally, federal and state judges have co-ventured. For example, federal and state judges in charge of the Brooklyn Navy Yard asbestos cases literally sat in the same room, jointly convening a "state and federal court" and ruling together on issues. In the *Exxon Valdez* oil-spill litigation, federal and state judges coordinated scheduling and discovery. On the criminal side, the cross-designation of federal and state agents and prosecutors makes permeable the lines between state and federal crime enforcement.

We Are All Federalists Now

This brief overview has revealed the need to reevaluate attitudes toward localism and nationalism in U.S. constitutional law. Take the National League of Cities, whose name is the shorthand in the jurisprudence of the federal courts for a Supreme Court decision recognizing a locality's (short-lived) Tenth Amendment exemption from federal regulation of fair labor laws.[28]

In addition to equating the National League of Cities with local prerogatives, we should also associate that name with energetic support for network building, both local and global, and with a nascent equality agenda. In the 1950s during the Cold War, the National League of Cities developed the Sister-Cities program aimed at people-to-people diplomacy. More recently, it has created projects to reduce racism and to promote women as decision makers in government, locally and globally. In 2005, the National League of Cities called for full funding of the federal Violence Against Women Act as well as "efforts which support the abolition of international systematic cultural and state-sanctioned physical, sexual and psychological human rights abuse and oppression of women throughout the world."[29] The organization also raised concerns about federal use of the USA PATRIOT Act in a resolution arguing that its "sweeping law enforcement and intelligence gathering powers...would dilute, if not undermine, many basic constitutional rights," and the NLC has called for "equal treatment and due process for all immigrants."[30]

State constitution writers themselves have ventured abroad. The legislative history of New Jersey's 1947 constitutional amendment to recognize women's equality refers to the attention paid at the United Nations to women's rights and the worldwide demand for equal rights.[31] Puerto Rico's 1951 Constitution, inspired by the United Nations' Universal Declaration of Human Rights, protects individual "dignity," as does the Constitution of Montana, which in 1972 also incorporated that language.[32]

The Legality of Local Transnationalism

Many of the transnational projects of organizations like the National League of Cities enable law's migration. They domesticate various non-U.S. precepts or create interactions across borders in a manner that has few economic effects and relatively low visibility. Some measures are more evocative—such as calling for an end to the use of land mines or the ratification of CEDAW. But sometimes, states or localities do more—for example, by creating rights of recovery for war victims, banning the purchase of goods from a certain country because of disapproval of its labor policies, forbidding investments in a particular country because of its policies, or refusing to recognize property claims of foreigners if their home nations do not reciprocate for Americans. Through an inversion of ordinary federalism discourse, which is protective of *state* decision making, federal judges have held these efforts to be illegal. Judges conclude that various state and city initiatives have violated national authority to speak with one voice on anything related to foreign affairs, foreign commerce, war, and national security.

Some of these decisions rest on a legal doctrine called "foreign affairs preemption." Writing in the 1940s for the Court, Justice William O. Douglas read the Constitution to provide, implicitly, for expansive federal authority over issues posited as foreign and opined that the power "over external affairs is not shared by the States; it is vested in the national government exclusively."[33] In two more recent decisions—*Crosby v. National*

Foreign Trade Council[34] (addressing efforts in Massachusetts to refuse to purchase products from Burma) and *American Insurance Association v. Garamendi*[35] (involving a California statute seeking to help Holocaust victims by requiring insurance companies doing business in California to disclose policies sold by them or their affiliates in Europe between 1920 and 1945)—the Court again insisted on national control.

While the *Crosby* decision relied in part on the existence of a congressional act that empowered the president to calibrate sanctions against Burma, in *Garamendi*, a bare majority of the Court held that state powers had to cede to an executive interest in its negotiated settlement with the German government. The dissenters argued that the state's disclosure obligations did not harm general federal interests in settling victims' claims. The Court was thus particularly solicitous of the executive when it claimed that what it categorized as foreign policy or national interests were at stake. Thus, courts have implied that the national government has dormant powers that preempt state lawmaking. This doctrinal development ought, from a progressive conception appreciating the democratic iterations of federalism, be met with dismay. Long ago, Herbert Wechsler counseled that courts should generally leave the allocation of power to what he called the "political safeguards of federalism."[36] His idea was that states should go to Congress rather than to the courts to protect their prerogatives. Today, however, the national government and private parties are going to court to get protection from state laws affecting investments in countries like Burma or the Sudan.

Given the commitments to federalism and the complexity of the issues, we should be leery of claims of the singular authority of the national government. Instead of asking courts to find new ways to preclude local lawmaking, those insisting on a uniform federal rule ought to make their arguments in Congress, which can be responsive to the needs to safeguard both federalism and nationalism. Judges ought not void local or state actions on CEDAW, the Kyoto Protocol, Burma, the Holocaust, or Darfur absent either a specific showing of direct congressional intent to locate all authority in the national government or facts demonstrating exactly how a national interest is in jeopardy. One reason comes from the history here recounted. The norms of the United States have repeatedly been shaped through translocal and transnational dialogues, with localities in the forefront as importers.

Such local efforts embody a second reason for courts to be reluctant to intervene, for they represent what democratic federalism has to offer: efforts to affect national rules or to express local variations through popular initiatives debated in the public sphere. As San Francisco's CEDAW ordinance and the mayors' climate initiatives illustrate, through majoritarian localism, the global is regularly collapsed into the local, turning problems that could have been dealt with as foreign affairs on the national level (for example, by entering into treaties) into domestic policies about how cities run themselves.

In 2007, the form of political action that I commend produced new federal legislation through interactions among the various sectors of the U.S. polity. During the first years of the twenty-first century and in the wake of revelations of genocide in Darfur, many localities and states—prompted by transjurisdictional NGOs and sometimes working through translocal organizations—decided to withdraw their investments from the Sudan. The words used to capture the point were, "not on our dollar," as state officials insisted that government pension funds or other forms of equity not be held in companies that did business in the Sudan.[37] Some members of the business community, however, objected, and the same trade association that had challenged the refusal of Massachusetts to buy goods produced through the labor system in Burma asked a federal court to enjoin Illinois from divesting from the Sudan. A judge did so by relying on the implied exclusivity of the foreign affairs authority of the national government.[38] But Senator Richard Durbin of Illinois introduced national legislation to permit such local action. The outcome was the 2007 Sudan Accountability and Divestment Act (SADA), a federal statute that empowers local authorities to divest assets, subject to detailed rules of notice and comment to companies and safe harbors for asset managers.[39]

Resisting a Jurisdictional Romance—Federated or Otherwise

I do not suggest that local initiatives are always to be celebrated by progressives. While I have provided examples aimed at expanding rights, local activism is regularly a site of efforts to constrain such rights. Contemporary examples include proposed bans on abortion and same-sex marriage. Since the 1960s, mobilization by conservative groups has wrought an impressive transformation at both the local and global levels, and their focus has also shifted to exporting such precepts abroad. Coming from conservatives or progressives, locally based initiatives have been proven able to make powerful inroads on national rights regimes.

Further, while the early twenty-first century's national agendas were dominated for several years by conservative policymakers, they were once shaped by progressives creating the New Deal and a Second Reconstruction, which were aimed at ending forms of racial and gender subordination. The 2008 election of Democrat Barack Obama and of a Congress in which his party has majorities marks the potential for another shift in policy. Moreover, with the fifty states come an array of positions. Many famous federalism cases—including *Printz v. United States*[40] (about local implementation of national gun control laws), *New York v. United States*[41] (about a state's refusal to participate in a federal statute requiring state cooperation in the disposal of low-level nuclear wastes), and *Morrison* (about congressional power to create a private damage remedy for victims of gender-motivated violence)—are instances in which state actors can be found on both sides, for and against the national action. In short, institutional voices in a host of jurisdictions, public and private, can and do shift their tones.

My purpose thus is to refocus the U.S. constitutional conversation about federalism to understand the many ports of entry for rights and the mechanisms by which rights come to be shaped and internalized. The diversity of arrangements among and between state and federal actors that I have sketched stands in contrast to the federalism described in case law and in a good deal of legal commentary, which is both formalistic and unresponsive to an array of efforts—both within the United States and beyond its borders—to reformat arrangements crafted in earlier eras. For more than a century, institutions have developed that recognize the need to cross state lines without becoming instruments of the U.S. government. Horizontal federalism is no longer only about state-to-state interactions but now includes another facet—national but not federal organizations—as well as another focus, transnational localism.

Thus, it is time to depart from the history of dichotomous alternatives (of either a state or a federal domain) and of essentialized images (of both states and the federal government) so as to investigate ongoing, and to imagine new, institutional arrangements that embody the interdependence of participants within and beyond the United States. Neither the kind of jurisdiction nor the territorial space occupied by a polity produces rights of a particular kind. Renouncing a claim of a jurisdictional imperative, this chapter is likely to disappoint nationalists and federalists, sovereigntists and internationalists alike.

Jurisdictions do not make rights, but people do—through collective action and repeated iterations, some democratic and some not. Moreover, only when many actors, at national and local levels, in and outside formal legal structures, fully embrace propositions like racial and gender equality do such understandings become constitutive, even if the question of what obligations flow from commitments to equality remains contested.

This chapter builds on my discussions in a series of essays, including *Ratifying Kyoto at the Local Level: Sovereigntism, Federalism, and Translocal Organizations of Government Actors (TOGAs)* (with Joshua Civin and Joseph Frueh), 50 Ariz. L. Rev. 709 (2008); *Foreign as Domestic Affairs: Rethinking Horizontal Federalism and Foreign Affairs Preemption in Light of Translocal Internationalism,* 57 Emory L. Rev. 31 (2007); *Categorical Federalism: Jurisdiction, Gender, and the Globe,* 111 Yale L.J. 619 (2001); and *Afterword: Federalism's Options,* 14 Yale L. & Pol'y Rev. 465 (1996) and 14 Yale J. Reg. 465 (1996). Thanks are due to Dennis Curtis, Vicki Jackson, Reva Siegel, and Josh Civin for years of conversations about both constitutional parameters and inventions, as well as to Adam Grogg and Joseph Frueh for thoughtful research assistance with the issues of this chapter.

Notes

1. *Alden v. Maine,* 527 U.S. 706 (1999).
2. *Board of Trustees of the Univ. of Ala. v. Garrett,* 531 U.S. 356 (2001); *Kimel v. Fla. Bd. of Regents,* 528 U.S. 62 (2000).
3. *Nevada Dep't of Human Res. v. Hibbs,* 538 U.S. 721 (2003).
4. *Roper v. Simmons,* 543 U.S. 551 (2005).
5. *Graham County Soil & Water Conservation Dist. v. United States ex rel. Wilson,* 545 U.S. 409 (2005).
6. *Crosby v. Nat'l Foreign Trade Council,* 530 U.S. 363 (2000).
7. For example, as late as 1875, the Supreme Court self-consciously noted that it would use the term "Federal question"—relied upon "for the sake of brevity, though not with strict verbal accuracy"—to capture the part of its discussion devoted to issues that involved the construction of the "Constitution, treaties, statutes, commissions, or authority of the Federal government." See *Murdock v. City of Memphis,* 87 U.S. (20 Wall.) 590, 618 (1875).
8. See, e.g., *Watters v. Wachovia Bank,* 127 U.S. 1559 (2007); *Crosby,* 530 U.S. 363.
9. No Child Left Behind Act of 2001, Pub. L. No. 107-110, 115 Stat. 1425 (codified at 20 U.S.C. §§ 6301 et seq. (2006)).
10. Defense of Marriage Act, Pub. L. No. 104-199, 110 Stat. 2419 (1996) (codified at 1 U.S.C. § 7 and 28 U.S.C. § 1738C (2006)).
11. See U.S. Const. art. I, § 10, cl. 3.
12. Morton Grodzin, *The American System: A New View of Government in the United States* 3-4 (Daniel J. Elazar, ed., 1966).
13. Deil S. Wright, *Revenue Sharing and Structural Features of Federalism,* 419 Annals 100, 109-10 (1975).
14. Daniel J. Elazar, *Exploring Federalism* 37, 200 (1987).
15. I have used this term to denote these entities and analyze their import in several essays. See, e.g., Judith Resnik, *Lessons on Federalism from the 1960s Class Action Rule and the 2005 Class Action Fairness Act: "Political Safeguards" of Aggregate Translocal Actions,* 156 U. Pa. L. Rev. 1929 (2008); Judith Resnik, Joshua Civin, and Joseph Frueh, *Ratifying Kyoto at the Local Level: Sovereigntism, Federalism, and Translocal Organizations of Government Actors (TOGAs),* 50 Ariz. L. Rev. 709 (2008).
16. Justice Anthony Kennedy has used this phrase several times. See, e.g., *Alden v. Maine,* 527 U.S. 706, 751 (1999).

17. 529 U.S. 598 (2000).

18. *Id.* at 617–18.

19. Convention on the Elimination of All Forms of Discrimination Against Women, adopted Dec. 18, 1971, 1249 U.N.T.S. 20378 (entered into force Sept. 3, 1981) [*hereinafter* CEDAW].

20. See Judith Resnik, *Constricting Remedies: The Rehnquist Judiciary, Congress, and Federal Power*, 78 Ind. L.J. 223 (2003).

21. See CEDAW, *supra* note 19, at Preamble, art. 1, and art. 4.

22. See San Francisco, California, *Local Implementation of the United Nations Convention on the Elimination of All Forms of Discrimination against Women*, § 12.K (Apr. 13, 1998), available at http://www.sfgov.org/site/cosw_page.asp?id=10849. Strategic plans and annual reports from San Francisco's Department on the Status of Women are available online at http://www.sfgov.org/site/dosw_index.asp?id=16978. Gender analysis reports are available at http://www.sfgov.org/site/cosw_page.asp?id=10856.

23. See, e.g., UN Economic and Social Council (ECOSOC), Review of Economic and Social Council Agreed Conclusions 1997/2 on Mainstreaming the Gender Perspective into All Policies and Programmes in the United Nations System, ECOSOC Res. 2004/4, UN Doc. E/2004/INF/2/Add.2 (July 7, 2004). Whether this approach succeeds is another question. See Hilary Charlesworth, *Not Waving but Drowning: Gender Mainstreaming and Human Rights in the United Nations*, 18 Harv. Hum. Rts. J. 1 (2005).

24. See *Cities Working Together to Protect Our Air Quality, Health and Environment: A Call to Action*, available at http://www.seattle.gov/mayor/climate/PDF/USCM_Climate_Letter_0401.pdf.

25. See Resnik, Civin, and Frueh, *supra* note 15, at 709.

26. The structures of several TOGAs, as well as some of the political economy and legal implications of these organizations, are explored in Resnik, Civin, and Frueh, *supra* note 15.

27. Earl H. Fry, *The Expanding Role of State and Local Governments in U.S. Foreign Affairs* 128 (1998).

28. See *National League of Cities v. Usery*, 426 U.S. 833 (1976), overruled by *Garcia v. San Antonio Metro. Transit Auth.*, 469 U.S. 528 (1985).

29. See, e.g., *National League of Cities, Domestic Violence and International Human Rights Abuse*, Res. 2006-45 (Dec. 10, 2005), available at www.nlc.org/ASSETS/14929CCCB69C45A3999FB8BC26AA796C/2006resolutionspscp.pdf.

30. See *id.* at *Resolution Affirming the Principles of Federalism and Civil Liberties*, Res. 2006-46, Res. 2006-49.

31. New Jersey Joint Legislative Committee, *Proceedings before the Joint Committee of the New Jersey Legislature Constituted under the Senate Concurrent Resolution No. 19* (July–Sept. 1942), as reprinted in 16 Women's Rts. L. Rep. 69, 95 (1994).

32. See Vicki C. Jackson, *Constitutional Dialogue and Human Dignity: States and Transnational Constitutional Discourse*, 65 Mont. L. Rev. 15, 21–28 (2004).

33. *United States v. Pink*, 315 U.S. 203, 233 (1942).

34. 530 U.S. 363 (2000).

35. 539 U.S. 396 (2003).

36. Herbert Wechsler, *The Political Safeguards of Federalism: The Role of the States in the Composition and Selection of the National Government*, 54 Colum. L. Rev. 543 (1954).

37. *Combating Genocide in Darfur: The Role of Divestment and Other Policy Tools: Hearing before the S. Comm. on Banking, Housing, and Urban Affairs*, 110th Cong. (Oct. 3, 2007) (statement of Frank T. Caprio, Rhode Island general treasurer), available at http://banking.senate.gov/public/_files/caprio.pdf. One count reported more than twenty states with such provisions. See Sudan Divestment Task Force, Figures for States,

Universities, Cities, International & Religious Organizations and Countries, *available at* http://sudandivestment.org/statistics.asp (last updated on October 15, 2008).

38. See *Nat'l Foreign Trade Council, Inc. v. Giannoulias*, 523 F. Supp. 2d 731 (N.D. Ill. 2007).

39. Pub. L. No. 110-174, 121 Stat. 2516 (2007) (to be codified at 50 U.S.C. § 1701).

40. *Printz v. United States*, 538 U.S. 1036 (2003).

41. 488 U.S. 1041 (1992).

❧ 25 ❧

Progressive Constitutionalism and Transnational Legal Discourse

VICKI C. JACKSON

I N THE LAST decade, there has been considerable controversy over the Supreme Court's occasional reference to foreign or international law in resolving contested constitutional issues.[1] The debate is rhetorically lopsided and ahistoric. Opponents characterize references to foreign or international law as symbolic of all that is wrong with the Supreme Court, including its countermajoritarianism and its perceived elitism (verging on the un-American); proponents of using foreign or international law see these sources as just one part of a much larger process of constitutional interpretation, not necessarily something to crusade over. What is lost in this debate is the United States' long history of using foreign law and the 'law of nations' in constitutional interpretation.[2] It has been episodic rather than sustained, ad hoc rather than systematic. But the occasional consideration of international or foreign law is not dissimilar to the Court's occasional consideration of, for example, social science research, scholarly literature, and other elements of what David Strauss calls common-law constitutional interpretation,[3] in which our Court has long engaged.

This chapter makes three points. First, the practice of referring to foreign and international law in interpreting the U.S. Constitution is of long standing. Second, in light of the growth of foreign constitutional law, being aware of leading national courts' decisions is part of being a well-informed judge on a national high court, and it is legitimate for judges to refer to nonbinding foreign or international law—whether as positive support or as alternative approaches to be distinguished from those in the United States. Third, progressives should support this practice, but not because it will inevitably lead to results with which they will agree—it may not. Rather, they should support it because progressives ought to favor knowing more rather than less about law's possibilities and because it is important to an independent adjudicatory process for judges to be able to consider and refer to a range of sources in deciding difficult constitutional questions.

Some History

From the founding case on judicial review, the Court has drawn comparisons between our Constitution and the approaches of foreign governments. In *Marbury v. Madison*,[4] the Court emphasized the distinction between governments of limited and of unlimited powers, implicitly distinguishing our Constitution from Britain's tradition of parliamentary sovereignty. The Court also referred to British tradition as a positive example in defining the "essence of civil liberty," noting that, in England, the "king himself" could be sued. In several other early cases, justices referred to the "law of nations"—analogous to what might today be called *customary international law*—in deciding constitutional issues. Perhaps the most infamous U.S. constitutional case, *Dred Scott v. Sandford*,[5] involved extensive discussions of foreign law. While Chief Justice Roger Taney referred to foreign views at the time of the framing and deplored any effort to look to contemporary foreign law, the two dissenters—John McLean and Benjamin Curtis—discussed contemporary foreign law in arguing against the Taney Court's racist and disastrous conclusions.

In the wake of the Civil War, the Court had to decide the constitutionality of efforts to penalize those who had participated in the rebellion. In *Cummings v. Missouri*,[6] the Court analyzed British law and contemporary French law to conclude that barring someone from serving as a minister if he failed to take an oath of nonparticipation was a "punishment" and that the state law in question violated the Constitution's ban on bills of attainder and ex post facto laws. Twelve years later, the first Eighth Amendment case to address on the merits a challenge to a death penalty relied on foreign law, noting that the challenged punishment (death by shooting) was one that "prevail[s] in other countries."[7]

References to foreign practices continued in the later nineteenth century. In *Fong Yue Ting v. United States*,[8] the majority invoked the practices of other nations to argue that national sovereignty permitted racist immigration laws, while the dissenters argued that the United States "takes nothing" from the practice of foreign despots. Justice John Harlan, in his lone dissent in *Plessy v. Ferguson*,[9] appealed to the world beyond the United States at two junctures in his justly praised dissent. First, he said, the Civil War amendments were "notable additions to the fundamental law … [,] welcomed by the friends of liberty throughout the world," placing the U.S. Constitution in a more global context. Second, Harlan invoked U.S. exceptionalism to chastise the legal racism of the majority's decision upholding racial segregation in public transport: "We boast of the freedom enjoyed by our people above all other peoples. But it is difficult to reconcile that boast with a state of the law which, practically, puts the brand of servitude and degradation upon a large class of our fellow-citizens."[10]

Throughout the twentieth century, opinions in constitutional cases referred to foreign or international law in resolving interpretive questions. In 1905, the Court referred extensively to foreign law in upholding mandatory vaccinations;[11] and the famous "Brandeis brief" presented information about foreign laws to which the Court referred in 1908 in upholding a state law limiting working hours for women.[12] In *Lochner v. New York*,[13] Justice Oliver Wendell Holmes' dissent referred to foreign experience and concern over working conditions in arguing that New York's law limiting the working hours of bakers should have been upheld. Holmes invoked Australian law in his dissent from the Court's invalidation of a federal minimum wage law for women in 1923.[14] And Justice Felix Frankfurter in the 1930s and 1940s referred to foreign federalisms in cases involving constitutional tax immunities.[15]

In both the Vinson and Warren courts, a concern to distinguish the United States from European totalitarianisms was visibly reflected in constitutional decisions—on criminal procedure, equal protection, and race—and has been well documented by scholars.[16] These concerns also were invoked by Justice Robert Jackson's famous concurrence in the Youngstown Steel decision,[17] one of the most important cases dealing with constitutional limitations on presidential power. The United Nations Charter or the U.N. General Assembly's Universal Declaration of Human Rights made their way into Supreme Court justices' opinions on at least a half dozen occasions between 1949 and 1970.[18] And in *Miranda v. Arizona*,[19] the Court analyzed the laws of four other English-speaking countries dealing with the interrogation of suspects, concluding that their experience suggested that law enforcement would not suffer from providing more protections and that, given our Constitution, we should offer "at least as" much protection against abusive interrogations as they did.

In more recent decades, international and foreign law has been referred to in deciding the constitutionality of the death penalty as a punishment for particular defendants or particular crimes, and foreign practices have been noted—by majorities and dissenters—in a significant number of cases in other areas, including abortion, assisted suicide, and gay rights.

Engagement with the New World of Transnational Sources of Law

Although there is a long history of referring to foreign and international law, I do not mean to suggest that nothing has changed. The rest of the world has changed significantly since World War II. For one thing, there is simply more law; there are more countries producing law and more international agreements being negotiated and ratified. More countries have adopted written constitutions and judicial review, so that there is more constitutional law in the world. Finally, the development of international human rights law marks a fundamental change in relationships among nations, a new understanding that each has an interest in how others treat the basic human rights of those within their jurisdiction.

While this may make the prospect of considering foreign law more intimidating, it also emphasizes the need to take a position on its relevance in constitutional interpretation. On my view, foreign and international comparisons should be welcomed as a way of deepening understanding of our own Constitution and checking those impulses and traditions which, on reflection in the reasoned law of comparable countries, do not merit inclusion in the U.S. constitutional canon. It is through efforts to develop interpretive standards within communities of judging and to engage with perspectives from beyond that judges can "enlarge" their mental vision, check their own biases, and render the best account of what they are authorized to interpret for their own community.[20] Engagement with communities of judges in other locations may increase the capacity of judges for critical objectivity, which is part of the highest calling of judging.

Justice Antonin Scalia, however, accuses those who refer to foreign law of seeking convergence with transnational elite cultures, ignoring the Court's actual use of foreign law, which has been far more modest.[21] He proposes an attitude of resistance to considering foreign or international law in constitutional interpretation, for several reasons. First, he argues, these sources are irrelevant to originalism—an argument in tension with the Court's earliest interpretive practice and that can be persuasive only to those who believe that originalism, and of a very specific kind, is the only legitimate interpretive method.

Second, he and others suggest, judges' references to foreign law are undemocratic, because the United States plays no role in creating the law of another country nor in choosing or controlling their judges. This objection would have traction if foreign law were being treated as in any way binding precedent, but it is not. Judges do not feel obligated to consider foreign law, and they may refer to foreign law to contrast the situation in the United States as well as to affirmatively understand what it has in common with other countries.

Third, critics suggest that use of foreign law illegitimately expands the range of judicial discretion, because by cherry-picking "foreign law, you can find anything you want," as Chief Justice John Roberts suggested in his confirmation hearings.[22] This critique is based on an unrealistic conception of the judging process. Judicial decision making is multivectored; it typically begins with what are widely agreed to be the most important sources. When those sources align, cases are seen as easy. It is only when traditional domestic sources are not in alignment, where genuine and hard interpretive choices are presented—about how to understand what the U.S. Constitution means—that judges need to struggle with best understandings.

When an interpretive question appears straightforward to a judge based on her analysis of U.S. law, foreign law is unlikely to make a difference, whether cited or not. When an interpretive question seems difficult to a judge, foreign law might matter—but in a way that is not the same as being "determinative" or "dispositive." Judges, like other people, do not make decisions using mathematical models or formulas to identify the impact of various factors. Rather, the process of coming to judgment is one in which facts and theories interact with each other in a drive toward ultimate coherence in the decision maker's mind. Judges in difficult cases may find it helpful to consider foreign or international law; judges also may in those cases want to reflect on understandings of human psychology, based on scientific data, literature, and their own experience, and on their views of the practical consequences of different interpretations. Although it is possible that looking at foreign decisions might increase the range of possibilities a judge would consider as a solution to an interpretive problem, so do other judicial experiences (for example, reading law reviews). Foreign law does not have the same authority as domestic sources, whatever its persuasive value may be; ideas developed from judges' confrontations with foreign law will necessarily be tested against their understanding of domestic sources and will be rejected if found remote or contradictory. The judge in the end is always deciding what she thinks is the best interpretation of U.S. law.

The appropriate model for U.S. consideration of foreign law is not one of resistance to foreign law, nor of convergence with foreign or nonbinding international law, but of engagement with foreign law: mindful of the views and practices of others, open to reconsidering what we think we know, but also able to insist that our own commitment to an understanding of human rights may differ from others'. We share common problems, common government functions, and many common commitments to rights and a vision of human freedom and dignity as central to the purpose of constitutional government. The idea that we have nothing to learn about our own commitments from other nations is foolishness; the suggestion that U.S. judges would be "brainwashed" by foreign judges sounds more in science fiction than familiarity with the actual process of judging. Far more likely is that judges who speak only with other judges on their own court will be isolated from the possibility of improved understandings that comes with experience—in Holmes' view, "the life of the law." Experience is not all there is to law, but law that is developed without regard for experience is unlikely to work well or last long.

Progressives and Foreign Law

Progressives should favor knowledge of foreign and international law, but not because it is inevitable that foreign or international law will point in the directions believed to be progressive by any given generation.[23] To be sure, U.S. history does give progressives some reason to think that consideration of foreign law may help to constrain egregious errors. When totalitarian government arose in Europe in the mid-twentieth century, there was no rush by the Court to dilute existing constitutional standards in the United States but rather an effort to distinguish ourselves in comparison with Europe. Dissenters in cases widely regarded as grave mistakes—*Dred Scott, Plessy, Lochner*—invoked comparisons with foreign laws, experience, or values.

Yet in the important U.S. debate over incorporation, foreign law was invoked to argue that rights guaranteed as against the federal government were not so essential to a well-ordered polity as to justify incorporating them as against the states.[24] In *Hurtado v. California*,[25] the Court concluded that the Fifth Amendment guarantee of a grand jury did not mean that the Due Process Clause of the Fourteenth Amendment required states to proceed by way of indictment rather than information. Rejecting arguments that the meaning of the U.S. Constitution was governed by prior common-law understandings, the Court wrote:

> The Constitution of the United States...was made for an undefined and expanding future, and for a people gathered and to be gathered from many nations and of many tongues. And while we take just pride in the principles and institutions of the common law, we are not to forget that in lands where other systems of jurisprudence prevail, the ideas and processes of civil justice are also not unknown.... There is nothing in Magna Charta, rightly construed as a broad charter of public right and law [and predecessor to the Due Process Clause], which ought to exclude the best ideas of all systems and of every age; and as it was the characteristic principle of the common law to draw its inspiration from every fountain of justice, we are not to assume that the sources of its supply have been exhausted. On the contrary, we should expect that the new and various experiences of our own situation and system will mould and shape it into new and not less useful forms.

That foreign law may be invoked on behalf of more narrow understandings of some individual rights is not of merely historic interest. Many Western democracies afford somewhat less protection to freedom of expression than does U.S. First Amendment jurisprudence; allow more state regulation of a woman's decision to have an abortion; and permit greater governmental involvement in the support of religion than our Establishment Clause case law does.

Nor is international law itself necessarily "progressive" in its content, as debate over U.N. Security Council antiterrorism resolutions shows. Moreover, contests are inevitable over what it means to be "progressive," when different forms of rights recognized in international law come into conflict. For example, the "right of self-determination" possessed by "all peoples," as two leading human rights covenants declare,[26] may conflict with rights of gender equality or of religious minorities. Determining the "progressive" solution is difficult and may be contested. It would not be surprising, as Karen Knop anticipates, for international law itself to be what she calls "multivocal," establishing something far less than a uniform standard and functioning more like the way foreign law can be used comparatively—as a point of reference, not binding authority.[27]

Rather, progressives should support appropriate references to foreign and international law for three reasons.

First, any progressive approach should hold that it is better, generally, to know more than to know less, and to make decisions with an accurate, not distorted, understanding of the facts (including "legal facts" about other nations), about what is and is not workable and legitimate in the "free society" we imagine ourselves to be. Given the inevitability of pseudo-knowledge—of mistaken beliefs about the superiority, or inferiority, of a practice in the United States as compared with other nations, or the inconsistency of a practice with a free government—it is important that understandings that influence decision makers' interpretations be accurate. Transparency by judges in identifying their reasons for decisions, including their understandings of foreign or international law where relevant, will contribute to greater accuracy and accountability.

Second, progressives should support looking to the practices of other nations for insight because, for the most part, progressives understand that originalism (narrowly understood) is not an adequate theory for constitutional development, and under virtually any other significant interpretive theory, knowledge about foreign law can be helpful. For example, in applying John Hart Ely's concern for representation reinforcement, it would be valuable to know how other democracies approach, for example, campaign finance; if one is concerned for "active liberty," as is Justice Stephen Breyer, awareness of approaches in foreign countries that share that value once again may be helpful.[28] Or, if one believes that the Fourteenth Amendment infuses the Constitution with a commitment to antisubordination, the jurisprudence of a country like South Africa may be illuminating on the possibilities and limitations of such an approach.

Third, progressives should protect the judiciary from attacks on its adjudicatory independence. The fight over judicial independence is real, not merely symbolic. Efforts to dictate to judges what they can and cannot refer to in their opinions plainly violate the Constitution, but these efforts are related to a much broader attack on the courts and on their independence. They are, in a sense, of a piece with Congress' unseemly effort to intervene, as a legislature, in the judicial determinations in the tragic Terri Schiavo case, and in the threats some years ago against a district court judge in New York who determined that evidence of an arrest should be suppressed. Questions of judicial independence also were raised by changes Congress made in 2003 in the sentencing guidelines, which required the reporting—to Congress—of the names of individual judges who had departed from the guidelines, an implicit threat (possibly of impeachment) thus added on to the more appropriate provisions for appellate review of sentences outside the guidelines, and in attacks on the federal courts' efforts to identify gender and race bias within the court system in the early to mid-1990s.

Attacks on judges are not at all new in U.S. history; they have, for the most part, not succeeded, and for good reason. It is widely agreed among comparative scholars that the single most influential contribution that the U.S. Constitution has made to the world has been the idea of a written set of rights enforced by independent courts. At the core of judicial independence is adjudicatory independence, which must include what sources to consider. Nowhere is that independence more important than in interpreting the Constitution as a limit on other branches of government. Mistakes by judges, if exposed to view, can be corrected through the usual processes—in the case of the lower courts, through appeals, and in the case of the Supreme Court, through disagreement with other judges on the Court, through lawyers' arguments, public discussion and debate, and—ultimately—the appointment or amendment processes.

We do not want judges independent of law. What we want them to have independence from are the prevailing powers of their time, for lacking that, courts cannot serve as a check on other branches. As Nedelsky's work suggests, to the extent that it is the responsibility of judges, in a system of constitutional review, sometimes to say no to their governments, being aware of other communities' knowledge and learning can be of real importance in providing a critical footing. Awareness of foreign and international law will not avoid the sometimes painful choices with which conscientious judges are confronted but may provide judges with resources and, as Nedelsky puts it, a sufficiently "enlarged" frame of reference,[29] to have the judicial courage to "speak law to power," to insist that no one—including the president of the United States—is above the law.

1. For a description of political responses, including proposals to prohibit the Court from citing contemporary foreign or international materials in constitutional cases and questions at confirmation hearings, see Mark C. Rahdert, *Comparative Constitutional Advocacy*, 56 Am. U. L. Rev. 553, 556–60 (2007).

2. See, e.g., Vicki C. Jackson, *Constitutional Comparisons: Convergence, Resistance, Engagement*, 119 Harv L. Rev. 109 (2005).

3. David A. Strauss, *Common Law Constitutional Interpretation*, 63 U. Chi. L. Rev. 877 (1996).

4. 5 U.S. 137 (1803).

5. 60 U.S. 393 (1857).

6. 71 U.S. 277 (1867).

7. *Wilkerson v. Utah*, 99 U.S. 130, 135 (1879).

8. 149 U.S. 698, 757 (1893).

9. 163 U.S. 537 (1896).

10. *Id.* at 555, 562.

11. *Jacobson v. Massachusetts*, 197 U.S. 11 (1905).

12. *Muller v. Oregon*, 208 U.S. 412 (1908).

13. 198 U.S. 45 (1905).

14. *Adkins v. Children's Hospital*, 261 U.S. 525, 570–71 (1923).

15. See, e.g., *New York v. United States*, 326 U.S. 572, 583 n.5 (1946); *Graves v. N.Y. ex rel. O'Keefe*, 306 U.S. 466, 491 (1939).

16. See Mary L. Dudziak, *Cold War Civil Rights* (2000); Richard A. Primus, *The American Language of Rights* (1999); Kim Lane Scheppele, *Aspirational and Aversive Constitutionalism*, 1 Int'l J. Const. L. 296 (2003).

17. *Youngstown Sheet & Tube Co. v. Sawyer*, 343 U.S. 579, 634, 651-52 (1952).

18. See Vicki C. Jackson, *Transnational Discourse, Relational Authority and the U.S. Court: Gender Equality*, 37 Loy. L.A. L. Rev. 271, 307 n. 127 (2003).

19. 384 U.S. 436, 489 (1966).

20. See Jennifer Nedelsky, *Communities of Judgment and Human Rights*, 1 Theor. Inq. L. 245 (2000).

21. Although Justice Scalia has complained that the Court was "'imposing foreign moods, fads or fashions'" on the American people, see *Lawrence v. Texas*, 539 U.S. 558, 598 (2003) (Scalia, J., dissenting and quoting Justice Thomas), the Court's use of foreign law in constitutional cases has been quite modest—and may be contrasted with the Court's occasional practice of adopting a common-law rule in use in some states and imposing it as a constitutional norm on all others. See, e.g., *New York Times v. Sullivan*, 376 U.S. 254, 280–82 and n. 20 (1964) (adopting Kansas rule on malice as constitutional standard).

22. Rahdert, *supra* note 1, at 559 (quoting Roberts).

23. But cf. Jeremy Waldron, *Foreign Law and the Modern Ius Gentium*, 119 Harv. L. Rev. 129 (2005) (arguing that if foreign nations reach a consensus on a point of law, there is reason to treat that position as having some authority, because consulting the results of repeated testing and trying of solutions is more likely to prevent than to cause errors). Waldron's argument applies only when a genuine and (and multiply) deliberated consensus has emerged. Given the diversity of nations in the world, such consensus is likely to be relatively rare.

24. See, e.g., *Twining v. New Jersey*, 211 U.S. 78, 113 (1908) (privilege against self-incrimination "has no place in the jurisprudence of civilized and free countries outside the domain of the common law").

25. 110 U.S. 516, 530–31 (1884).

26. International Covenant on Civil and Political Rights, § 1; International Covenant on Economic, Social, and Cultural Rights, § 1.

27. Karen Knop, *Here and There: International Law in Domestic Courts*, 32 N.Y.U. J. Int'l L. & Pol. 501, 507 (2000) (discussing "international law as a force for multivocality").

28. See John Hart Ely, *Democracy and Distrust* 86–88, 101–04 (1980); Stephen Breyer, *Active Liberty: Interpreting Our Democratic Constitution* (2005).

29. Nedelsky, *supra* note 19, at 265–66, 274.

❧ 26 ❧

"Strategies of the Weak"

Thinking Globally and Acting Locally toward a Progressive Constitutional Vision

DAVID COLE

S OMETIMES, DESPITE THEIR best intentions, bureaucrats manage to say something truly revealing. In March 2005, the Department of Defense issued *The National Defense Strategy of the United States.*[1] At page 5, the document warns, "Our strength as a nation state will continue to be challenged by those who employ a strategy of the weak, using international fora, judicial processes, and terrorism."

This is a remarkable statement, as it not only dismisses the rule of law, and especially international law, as a strategy of the weak, of no interest to the "strong" United States, but likens it to terrorism itself. When a nation is attacked, as the United States was on September 11, 2001, by fanatics willing to commit suicide in order to inflict untold suffering on thousands of innocent civilians, one might think that the rule of law would be on the nation's side. Yet, to the Bush administraton's Defense Department, the rule of law was merely a tactic of the enemy, akin to terrorism itself.

The Defense Department's sentiment echoed the early warning of then Attorney General John Ashcroft in his first testimony before Congress after 9/11, in which he insisted that those who raised "phantoms of lost liberties … only aid terrorists."[2] But those were the words of a contentious and often impolitic attorney general in the heat of the moment. The Pentagon document, a formal articulation of national defense strategy issued years after the attacks, suggests that this perspective took on the status of official dogma in the Bush administration.

In fashioning a progressive vision of constitutional law, we ought to *endorse* a strategy of the weak, minus, of course, the terrorism. As progressives respond to the security threats that 9/11 has revealed in the United States (and elsewhere), we need to think about using not just constitutional law, but international forums, judicial processes, and constitutional politics—not to challenge our strength as a nation, but to restore and reinforce the principles upon which the nation's strength must ultimately rest. This would be a strategy of the weak in two senses: It insists on the importance of respecting the rights of the most vulnerable, and it is designed for those without immediate access to state power (because even when Democrats are in the majority, progressives are unlikely to be in the majority). Properly understood, however, this strategy of the weak should also be seen as a strategy of the strong, for it promotes the long-term interests of the nation-state, from the standpoint of both security and liberty, to respect human rights and the rule of law.

Any attempt to strategize about the future of constitutional law must keep three present realities in mind. First, the struggle to protect ourselves from terror is likely to continue to be a driving force of federal and state policies and laws for the foreseeable future. The Bush administration defined the struggle as a war on terror rather than a war against an identifiable *adversary*—even one as elusive as Al-Qaeda—and insisted that the war was global in scope and would not end until we vanquished all terrorist organizations of potentially global reach.[3] Such a war would by definition never end. But even if the struggle is defined more realistically as a conflict with Al-Qaeda, it is likely to continue for the foreseeable future. And because technological advances have made it increasingly possible for small groups of individuals to do widespread damage, security challenges will continue even in Al-Qaeda's wake.

More concretely, the way the Bush administration pursued the war on terror, and in particular its engagement with Iraq, has energized and expanded the forces arrayed against the United States, by sharply increasing anti-American sentiment throughout the world, and by taking the focus off defeating Al-Qaeda in its stronghold. In July 2007, the National Intelligence Estimate, reflecting the consensus views of all U.S. intelligence agencies, reported that Al-Qaeda had reconstituted itself in the border regions of Pakistan. And the threat is not limited to Al-Qaeda, but extends to independent groups of like-minded individuals, not directed or controlled by Al-Qaeda, but inspired to act against the United States and its allies out of opposition to the nation's policies and practices in Iraq, in Israel, in the Middle East generally, and toward Arabs and Muslims in particular. International terrorist incidents tripled in 2004 over 2003, and one-half of that increase was directly attributable to terrorist incidents in Iraq itself.[4] In 2005, there were 360 suicide bombings, compared to an average of about 90 a year over the preceding five years.[5] Just as the Afghanistan conflict with the Soviet Union served as a recruiting and training ground for Osama bin Laden and other Islamic fundamentalist terrorists, so, too, Iraq performed that function in more recent years. As the then-director of Central Intelligence, Porter Goss, told Congress in 2005, "[T]hose who survive will leave Iraq experienced and focused on acts of urban terrorism. They represent a potential pool of contacts to build transnational terrorist cells, groups, and networks."[6]

In a 2003 internal army memorandum, Defense Secretary Donald Rumsfeld asked, "Are we capturing, killing or deterring and dissuading more terrorists every day than the madrassas and the radical clerics are recruiting, training, and deploying against us?"[7] While it may never be possible to answer that question with certainty, it appears that, as of this writing, seven years after 9/11, we are losing ground from this vantage point, and the threat of terrorist attacks will likely loom large for the rest of our lifetimes.

While the Obama administration can be expected to take a much more respectful attitude toward human rights and the rule of law than the Bush administration did, any significant future terrorist attack will almost inevitably prompt renewed calls for more intrusive government surveillance, further restrictions on speech and associations thought to be connected with terrorism, and the like. Indeed, the revival of arguments for ethnic profiling in the United States in the wake of the July 7, 2005, London subway bombings demonstrates that the attack need not even be local to spark calls for greater security measures.[8] The need for security is, in the end, insatiable.

The second reality that progressives must confront as they think about a constitutional vision and strategy is the reality that they will face a hostile majority on the Supreme Court for the foreseeable future and that they are unlikely to see truly progressive majorities in either house of Congress. While Democrats managed to take control of Congress in 2006, and although a Democrat won the presidency in 2008, there is no necessary equation between Democrat and progressive, especially on issues of security. In August 2007, for example, a Democratic Congress enacted the Protect America Act, giving the executive branch sweeping authority to conduct warrantless wiretapping of Americans as long as the "target" of the surveillance was a person overseas. And the last Democratic president, Bill Clinton was far from progressive on matters relating to security. It was under his administration and at his urging, for example, that Congress enacted the Antiterrorism and Effective Death Penalty Act of 1996, which gutted habeas corpus review for prisoners challenging the constitutionality of their convictions, enacted a sweeping "material support" law that effectively imposed guilt by association, and authorized a special court to deport foreign nationals on secret evidence.

This suggests that it is an insufficient answer to call for "constitutionalism outside the courts," because the very reason many rights are constitutional in nature is that the ordinary political process is especially unlikely to be hospitable toward them.[9] Thus, a progressive vision of constitutional rights must confront the fact that we are not only likely to face an unfriendly Supreme Court, but are also unlikely to hold the reins of power in the political branches on these issues. This is the fundamental challenge of constitutionalism—how to advance rights protections in a democracy for those who need protection precisely because they lack access to democratic power.

Third, a progressive constitutional strategy must take into account the fact that the world is changing in ways that may be used to our advantage. We may well be in the midst of a quasi-revolutionary moment, akin to the transformations of the New Deal, but on a global scale. The rapid globalization of world markets, accelerated by the technological innovations of the Internet, has altered law and politics in fundamental ways. Transnational legal regimes are growing in number and importance, and international grassroots politics, eased by the worldwide Web, have become possible in ways that could not have been imagined only a decade ago. Meanwhile, the worldwide economic collapse of 2008 has demonstrated that the neo-liberal faith in unregulated markets is entirely unsatisfactory.

Indeed, while the analogy is far from perfect, the paradigm shift can be compared to that which the nation experienced in the New Deal. At that point, economic realities fueled a shift in basic understandings about the relative roles of federal and state governments. Before the New Deal, federal economic regulation was thought to infringe on state autonomy, or individual freedom, or both, and was therefore deemed suspect. Moreover, individual rights protection was also thought to rest largely with the states. But in the wake of the Great Depression, the nation came to see the economy as an integrated national phenomenon requiring federal regulation and also increasingly saw rights protection as the responsibility of the federal government.

The shift in the twenty-first century is from federal to transnational regulation. Global markets need transnational regulation, and a series of treaties and executive agreements have fostered the development of transnational economic regulation. At the same time, the last fifty years have seen a human rights revolution, as a multitude of human rights treaties and enforcement systems have been drafted, adopted, ratified, and implemented the world over. While these developments are not necessarily formally interrelated, in both instances as the significance of sovereign borders has broken down, regulation at the international level has become more necessary and more acceptable. Sometimes, the developments are quite closely interrelated, as for example in Europe, where entry into the European Union requires an agreement to be bound by the European Court of Human Rights, and where the European Court of Justice, which adjudicates transnational trade and economic disputes, has imposed human rights mandates on its member states. But even without such formal ties, the fact that trade and communications are becoming increasingly global puts pressure on traditional notions of sovereignty, thereby facilitating the development and implementation of international and transnational standards. While the transformation is ongoing, and not without substantial hurdles and resistance, the trend line seems inevitable, and the global extent of the 2008 economic crisis has underscored the need for coordinated transnational responses.

Any program for constitutional progress must take into consideration these three realities. I do not suggest that these are the *only* realities that must be considered,[10] but they are three of the most important factors for constitutional reformers to take into account. Any program that does not grapple with these features is virtually doomed to failure.

So what are the normative and strategic implications of these features of the political and legal landscape? The first factor—a long-term struggle to establish security from terrorism—means that government security measures are likely to pose some of the most significant constitutional challenges between now and 2020. The rights at stake will run the gamut, from freedoms of speech and association, to liberty, privacy, equality, and the right to know. Structural issues involving the separation of powers are also likely to be recurrent. Bush administration lawyers maintained that the president in his capacity as commander in chief had unilateral unchecked power to detain human beings without trial as "enemy combatants" and to disregard criminal prohibitions on torture and warrantless wiretapping.[11] While President Bush did not prevail on these contentions, and President Obama has said that he will take a less aggressive view of executive power, it is still the case that, as Franklin Delano Roosevelt's attorney general, Francis Biddle, once said, "The Constitution has not greatly bothered any wartime president."[12]

Moreover the communities whose rights have most been under attack since 9/11 have been, and are likely to continue to be, foreign nationals, and especially Arabs and Muslims. Societies beset by fear too often seem willing to sacrifice the liberties of the most vulnerable in the name of promises of security for the majority, and the United States' post–9/11 response followed this pattern.[13] Government officials repeatedly stressed that security measures were targeted at foreign nationals, not U.S. citizens, at "them," not "us."

For example, government officials chose Guantánamo Bay as a place to hold "enemy combatants," and chose to hold only foreign nationals there, in part so that it could argue that no U.S. law limited their actions. The government argued consistently that, as foreign nationals beyond our borders, the Guantánamo detainees had no constitutional rights. That argument failed in *Boumediene v. Bush*, when the Supreme Court ruled that Guantánamo detainees were constitutionally entitled to the writ of habeas corpus, but the government continues to maintain that foreign nationals outside our borders are not entitled to constitutional protections even when in U.S. custody.

The military tribunals initially established to try some of the Guantánamo detainees for war crimes applied only to foreign nationals accused of terrorism, not to U.S. citizens. The rationale? As Vice President Richard Cheney explained, foreigners who attack the United States "don't deserve the same guarantees and safeguards that would be used for an American citizen."[14] And when the Supreme Court invalidated those tribunals and ruled that, among other things, they contravened the Geneva Conventions, Congress responded by explicitly authorizing the tribunals with minor changes, again only for foreign nationals, by eliminating habeas corpus for foreign nationals deemed to be enemy combatants and by barring foreign nationals from invoking the Geneva Conventions in any lawsuit against the federal government or its officials arising out of their detention or treatment.

Detainees held at Guantánamo, in CIA "black sites," and elsewhere in the war on terror have been subjected to a wide variety of humiliating, cruel, and degrading practices designed to coerce them into providing information. They have been deprived of sleep, exposed to extreme heat and cold, bound and shackled to bare floors for so long that they have urinated and defecated on themselves, been forced to wear women's underwear and pictures of naked women, and injected with intravenous fluid and then barred from going to the bathroom, so that they urinate on themselves.[15] The government's defense of such practices was twofold: (1) It read the prohibition on torture extremely narrowly, to apply only to the most extreme forms of physical and psychological coercion;[16] and (2) it interpreted the prohibition on "cruel, inhuman, and degrading treatment" not to apply at all to foreign nationals interrogated outside our borders.[17]

These initiatives suggest that the most fundamental threats to constitutional freedoms likely to arise in the next decades will be, at least initially, selectively targeted at foreign nationals and particularly Arab and Muslim foreign nationals. If progressives are to meet those challenges, we must articulate and defend a constitutional vision that resists the temptation to sacrifice the rights of a vulnerable minority for the apparent security of the majority.

The best example of a progressive constitutional vision responsive to these challenges is found not in any Supreme Court opinion, but in the 2004 decision of the Law Lords, the United Kingdom's highest court, which declared a post–9/11 law that authorized indefinite detention without trial of foreign terror suspects to be "incompatible" with the European Convention on Human Rights.[18] What condemned the measure, according to the Law Lords, was *precisely* its differential treatment of foreign nationals and citizens. The lords reasoned that the threat an individual poses to national security does not turn on what passport he has. Nor does the interest in liberty from indefinite detention vary with citizenship; it is owed to all human beings in equal measure. Thus, if indefinite detention was not necessary to deal with British subjects suspected of terrorism, it was not necessary for foreign nationals similarly suspected. The Law Lords lack the power to invalidate legislation, but Parliament nonetheless responded to the decision by replacing the indefinite detention law with a more limited authority to impose "control orders" on terrorist suspects, equally applicable to British citizens and foreign nationals.

The significance of the Law Lords' decision goes far beyond the specific law at issue in that case. If Parliament is forced to treat British citizens and foreign nationals alike absent a good reason for distinction, it will be much harder to adopt repressive security measures. Where everyone's rights are at stake, the political process is more likely to ensure that a reasonable accommodation is reached—perhaps not in the heat of the moment, when the politics of fear is especially powerful, but over the long run. Thus, the mandate to treat foreign nationals and citizens equally will likely serve as a significant brake on rights-restrictive measures in the United Kingdom.

While the specific source of the Law Lords' opinion was the European Convention on Human Rights, the same principles can be grounded in the U.S. Constitution. The Due Process Clause provides that "no *person* shall be deprived of life, liberty, or property without due process of law." Due process analysis, like that of the Law Lords, examines the individual's interest in liberty and the state's interest in national security. Here, too, there is no legitimate basis for drawing any distinctions based on citizenship; a terror suspect poses the same dangers and has the same interests in liberty regardless of his country of passport.

The point can be generalized further. Apart from the right to vote and the elusive "privileges and immunities of citizenship," virtually all of the individual rights in the Constitution extend to "persons," "people," or "the accused" and are not limited to citizens. The Bill of Rights was understood as a list of "natural rights," given by God, and not only to Americans. That original understanding is recapitulated today in the universalist understanding of human rights that animates the various human rights treaties, which predicate their protections on human dignity. Human dignity does not turn on citizenship.

Along these lines, one of the least thought-through maxims of U.S. constitutional law is the notion that the Constitution does not protect foreign nationals beyond our borders. At one point, all law was thought to be territorially bounded, including constitutional law, so much so that U.S. citizens were not protected by the Constitution from their own government when they were abroad. But the Supreme Court long ago rejected that notion. Until *Boumediene*, however, it had clung, at least in dicta, to the idea that the Constitution did not extend to foreign nationals beyond our borders. But the cases cited for that principle are much more limited, and there is little reason that the Constitution should not constrain the federal government wherever it exerts its sovereign power, as that power is defined and delimited by the Constitution and its Bill of Rights. At a minimum, due process, which protects all persons deprived of life, liberty, or property, should restrict government actors whenever and wherever they impose the official force of the state on human beings to lock them up, subject them to water-boarding or similar measures, or render them to other countries so that others can torture them. While the precise process that is due might well vary depending on the circumstances in which government power is exercised, there is no reason that due process should be inapplicable altogether simply because the United States is acting outside rather than inside its physical borders.

Despite its deep resonance with international human rights law, U.S. constitutional law is a long way from adopting this human dignity view, in which passports are not relevant to certain basic protections. As an example, consider the Supreme Court's decision in *Hamdi v. Rumsfeld*,[19] holding that the president cannot detain a U.S. citizen captured fighting for the enemy on the Afghanistan battlefield as an enemy combatant without a fair hearing before a neutral decision maker at which the detainee has an opportunity to prove that he is not in fact an enemy combatant. The majority opinion in *Hamdi* mentioned the fact that Yaser Hamdi is a U.S. citizen forty-two times in a relatively short opinion, even though as an analytic matter, the Court gave no reason that his citizenship status should matter to the process he was due.

In addition, the Court has frequently tolerated treatment of foreign nationals that it would not find constitutionally acceptable for U.S. citizens.[20] For example, while citizens cannot be punished retroactively for conduct that was legal at the time they engaged in it, foreign nationals can be deported for conduct that was legal at the time they engaged in it, at least under some circumstances.[21] And while citizens cannot be selectively prosecuted based on their race, religion, or political associations, foreign nationals can be selectively targeted for deportation on such bases.[22]

To advance a progressive agenda in this regard, then, it is plainly not enough to articulate an appealing constitutional vision. One needs also a strategy for bridging the gulf between contemporary reality and constitutional vision. On the question of tactics, we need to consider the second and third realities noted above—namely, a conservative Supreme Court and a democratic political process that is, by design, unfriendly to minority interests, and a shrinking world in which national borders are becoming less significant. We must learn to take advantage of the latter development to offset the obvious disadvantages posed by the former.

Even though we face substantial hurdles in every arena, progressives cannot give up on legislative initiatives, litigation, or lobbying the executive branch. On particular issues and at particular times, one or another of the three branches may be more hospitable to progressive claims. Congress, for example, may be a better forum for raising issues of privacy protections in the Internet age than the courts may be. The Supreme Court's Fourth Amendment jurisprudence has long adopted the wooden and increasingly unacceptable notion that, once one shares information with a third party, one no longer has any expectation of privacy vis-à-vis government efforts to obtain that information from the third party.[23] Congress has frequently responded to those decisions by creating statutory protections for privacy with respect to matters such as bank records, medical records, video store records, and the like. Because privacy concerns tend to be broadly shared, they sometimes facilitate bipartisan coalitions, and legislative avenues may prove promising.[24]

On other issues, the courts are likely to remain the most promising forum for protection, even in an era of Republican-dominated courts. Consider, for example, the enemy combatant dispute. Virtually every newspaper across the United States editorialized against President George W. Bush's position that he could lock up United States citizens as enemy combatants without hearing or trial. Yet despite this widespread criticism of this policy, Congress did absolutely nothing to stop it. It took the Supreme Court, composed predominantly of justices appointed by Republicans, to stand up to the president. When it did so, Congress responded by giving the president most of what he wanted, in the Military Commissions Act of 2006, while simultaneously seeking to strip the federal courts of habeas corpus review of the president's actions. It took the Supreme Court, in *Boumediene*, to undo what Congress had done.

The election of Barack Obama has created great hope that mainstream politics can support a progressive political vision. But part of Obama's appeal was that he eschewed an identifiably progressive message, instead seeking to unite a majority around a more abstract desire for "change." Obama may indeed prove to be a progressive president, but that remains to be seen. It is quite possible that, until there is a fundamental shift in national politics (not simply a widespread disaffection with a particular Republican president), none of the federal branches of government will be a very promising venue for advancing a progressive constitutional vision. Progressives may need to look for support elsewhere. And here is where the last of the three factors noted above offers some hope. In light of the powerful trend toward globalization, progressive constitutionalists need to take a page from the book of the late environmentalist René Dubos, who argued that one must "think globally, and act locally."[25] Progressives need to think globally and act locally on matters of constitutional rights.

What does this mandate entail? First, we should not be afraid to look to conceptions of international human rights as a way of buttressing and extending constitutional rights at home. Doing so is likely to be particularly useful in defending the rights of foreign nationals because, as noted above, human rights generally do not differentiate between citizens and noncitizens. But the appeal of international human rights law is not limited to this area of law and extends to such issues as the death penalty, criminal justice, gay rights, and economic and social rights, where international human rights standards often reflect more robust visions than does current U.S. constitutional law. Appeals to international human rights may support claims that the U.S. Constitution should be read progressively, to conform as much as possible with such principles. Even when they are not directly enforceable, international human rights norms can exert pressure on the content of constitutional law, as the Court and the country may feel some pressure to conform to broad international consensus about the fundamental character of certain rights. Skeptics often object that international law is vague and antidemocratic, but the same can be said of the Constitution itself; like international human rights, it speaks in generalities, not with the "prolixity of a legal code," as Chief Justice John Marshall famously said, and by design the Constitution is antidemocratic. In another sense, however, both constitutional rights and international human rights are profoundly democratic. They have been developed through a democratic process of consensus and ratification at the nation-state level. And they are designed to protect precisely those rights that democracies, left to their own devices, are least equipped to protect.

In addition, framing arguments in international human rights terms may facilitate the mobilization of international pressure for change at home. As Professor Mary Dudziak has shown in her historical work on civil rights during the Cold War, international concerns can facilitate domestic reforms; the fight against segregation was spurred by a desire on the part of the federal government to deflect communist criticism of racial subordination in the United States.[26] Progressives need to think self-consciously about how to harness international opinion to further their ends, at least where international standards support progressive goals. Framing arguments in international human rights terms as well as in constitutional terms can facilitate this result. When critics argued that detention at Guantánamo violated the U.S. Constitution's Due Process Clause, foreign observers may have felt ill equipped to evaluate the claim. When the arguments, by contrast, were made in terms of the Geneva Conventions, the Convention against Torture, or the International Covenant on Civil and Political Rights, observers in other countries owed no deference to U.S. interpretations and had more standing to offer their own views. And as Guantánamo itself demonstrated, international pressure can play a significant role in bringing about change in U.S. policies and practices.

Progressive constitutionalists can also learn from the tactics employed by human rights lawyers and activists. Human rights activists, after all, are accustomed to acting in settings where they have little or no access to power. Accordingly, they have developed strategies that do not rely on access to power. They stress the publication of investigative reports, the exchange of information, public education, and grassroots activism—all with the goal of shaming the powers-that-be into acting in ways more consistent with human rights principles. Often shut out of the channels of official state power, human rights activists have learned to harness civil society itself as a checking force on state power.

In appealing to international human rights, moreover, progressive constitutionalists should seek to frame arguments that appeal not just to moral concepts of justice and human dignity, but to the United States' need for legitimacy on the world stage. Human rights and the rule of law are valuable not just because they are the right thing to do, but because they are essential to security itself. As reactions to Abu Ghraib and Guantánamo have graphically illustrated, when the United States violates basic human rights principles, there is a real danger that its actions will aid the enemy, both by spurring enemy recruitment and by reducing the willingness of other nations to cooperate with us. As obvious as this may seem, the *National Defense Strategy* quoted at the beginning of this chapter suggests that the Bush administration never got it.

In addition, human rights appeals may prod action at home precisely because they appeal to norms that are, at their root, consistent with American ideals. The United States has long prided itself as a human rights leader. It played an important role in the development of the human rights tradition, and its annual State Department reports focus on human rights abuses around the world. Americans feel comfortable with that vision of their country. They are less likely to feel comfortable with a vision of the United States as a human rights violator. Accordingly, the shaming that human rights activists so heavily rely upon to do their work may have added power in the United States, precisely because of our self-conception as a rights-respecting nation.

As an example of this human rights strategy at work, consider Guantánamo. When the military first announced that it would be holding enemy combatants there, few were willing to come to the detainees' defense. The Bush administration described the detainees as "the worst of the worst." Legal challenges seemed certain to lose. The precedent was dead set against the detainees, as the Supreme Court in World War II had held that "enemy aliens" held as combatants abroad during wartime could not sue in U.S. courts.[27] The detainees lost in the district court and lost again unanimously in the court of appeals.[28]

But the detainees' claims that their treatment violated not only due process but the Geneva Conventions and international human rights guarantees resonated with the rest of the world. Guantánamo soon became a focal point of international criticism of U.S. antiterrorism policy. The fact that the United States was detaining nationals of forty-two different countries gave many countries a vested interest in the policies there. The British were especially vocal in their criticism, and President Bush was forced to negotiate a return of the British detainees at Guantánamo to their homeland.

The international opprobrium directed at U.S. policy at Guantánamo Bay very likely played a role in the Supreme Court's surprise decision to accept review of the lower courts' rulings in the cases in 2003, and in its equally surprising ruling against the government in 2004. In the first Guantánamo case to be heard by the Supreme Court, *Rasul v. Bush*, 175 members of Parliament, the Commonwealth Lawyers Association, the International Commission of Jurists, the Human Rights Institute of the International Bar Association, and the International League for Human Rights, among others, filed amicus briefs. And public criticism was heard from the British Law Lords, the European Parliament, and even the International Committee for the Red Cross, which departed from its strict policy of *not* publicly criticizing the countries whose detainees it is monitoring.[29] All three of the Court's rulings in Guantánamo cases have gone against the president. In its 2008 decision in *Boumediene v. Bush*, the Court invalidated the Military Commissions Act's repeal of habeas corpus, for the first time ever declaring invalid joint action of the president and Congress acting together on a matter of national security. While the Guantánamo litigation is ongoing, and the makeup of the Court has grown considerably more conservative, the litigation has already achieved remarkable success, pressuring the government to open up access to Guantánamo for the press, lawyers, and human rights observers; to release approximately five hundred detainees; to explain the bases for the initial detentions at Guantánamo; to modify its interrogation tactics to eliminate reliance on physically coercive tactics; and to provide hearings, albeit inadequate, to those whom the government originally claimed were entitled to no process whatsoever. President Obama promised to close the facility altogether. All of this was achieved through a litigation, public education, and organizing campaign that insisted on the basic humanity of even "the worst of the worst" and that employed the tactics of human rights to push back an administration that initially acted as if human rights and the rule of law were inconvenient obstacles to be cast aside in the war on terror.

A progressive constitutional vision for the future must take into account the continuing threat of terrorism; a conservative Supreme Court; the likelihood that neither of the political branches will be especially progressive on constitutional rights issues, even under a Democratic administration; and the fast-paced developments toward globalization and the diminished significance of national sovereignty. We will be best served by a strategy that looks outward as well as inward and that seeks to employ the rhetoric and tactics of the international human rights movement to help frame our constitutional vision. We should steer clear of appeals to citizenship in favor of the more universal claim of human dignity, which rests ultimately on personhood. While he was not a framer, the nineteenth-century Kantian philosopher Hermann Cohen had it right, in this commentary on the Bible: "The alien was to be protected, not because he was a member of one's family, clan, or religious community, but because he was a human being. In the alien, therefore, man discovered the idea of humanity."[30]

We need to rediscover the idea of humanity. If we can do that by 2020, we will have made real progress.

Notes

1. Department of Defense, *The National Defense Strategy of the United States of America* (Mar. 2005), available at http://www.globalsecurity.org/military/library/policy/dod/d20050318nds1.pdf.

2. John Ashcroft, *Testimony before the Senate Judiciary Committee* (Dec. 6, 2001), transcript available at http://www.usdoj.gov/ag/testimony/2001/1206transcriptsenatejudiciarycommittee.htm.

3. President George Bush, *Address to a Joint Session of Congress and the American People* (Sept. 20, 2001), transcript available at http://www.whitehouse.gov/news/releases/2001/09/20010920-8.html.

4. U.S. State Department, *Patterns of Global Terrorism 2004* (Apr. 27, 2005), available at http://www.state.gov/s/ct/rls/c14818.htm.

5. David Sands, *Suicide Bombing Popular Terrorist Tactic*, Washington Times, May 8, 2006.

6. Senate Select Committee on Intelligence, *Hearing on Current and Projected National Security Threats to the United States*, 109th Cong., 1st sess., Feb. 16, 2005 (testimony of Porter Goss).

7. Memorandum from Donald Rumsfeld to General Dick Myers et al., *Re: Global War on Terrorism* (Oct. 16, 2003), available at http://www.globalsecurity.org/military/library/policy/dod/rumsfeld-d20031016sdmemo.htm.

8. Michelle Garcia, *New York Police Sued over Subway Searches*, Washington Post, Aug. 5, 2005, at A3; Sarah Kershaw, *Suicide Bombings Bring Urgency to Police in U.S.*, New York Times, July 25, 2005, at A14.

9. See, e.g., Mark Tushnet, *Taking the Constitution Away from the Courts* (Princeton University Press, 2000); Larry Kramer, *The People Themselves: Popular Constitutionalism and Judicial Review* (Oxford University Press, 2004).

10. Other realities to consider include the growing power of multinational corporations, increasing global and domestic wealth disparities, global warming, the deadlock that campaign spending and redistricting practices have placed on electoral politics, and the increasing alienation of the underclass, to name but a few.

11. Memorandum from Jay S. Bybee to Alberto Gonzales, *Re: Standards of Conduct for Interrogation under 18 U.S.C. §§ 2340–2340A* (Aug. 1, 2002), reprinted in Karen J. Greenberg and Joshua L. Dratel, eds., *The Torture Papers: The Road to Abu Ghraib* (Cambridge University Press, 2005); David Cole, *Reviving the Nixon Doctrine: NSA Spying, the Commander-in-Chief, and Executive Power in the War on Terror*, 13 Wash. & Lee J. Civ. Rts. & Soc. Justice 1 (2006).

12. Francis Biddle, *In Brief Authority* 219 (Doubleday 1962).

13. See generally David Cole, *Enemy Aliens: Double Standards and Constitutional Freedoms in the War on Terrorism* (New Press, rev. ed., 2005).

14. Elisabeth Bumiller and Steven Lee Myers, *Senior Administration Officials Defend Military Tribunals for Terrorist Suspects*, New York Times, Nov. 15, 2001, at B6.

15. See, e.g., Lt. Gen. Anthony R. Jones and Maj. Gen. George Fay, *Investigation of Intelligence Activities at Abu Ghraib* (Aug. 2004), available at http://www.information-clearinghouse.info/article6784.htm; Josh White, *Abu Ghraib Dog Tactics Came from Guantánamo*, Washington Post, July 27, 2005, at A14.

16. See Memorandum from Jay S. Bybee, *supra* note 11.

17. Human Rights First, *Human Rights First's Analysis of Gonzales Testimony before the Senate Judiciary Committee and His Written Answers to Supplemental Questions* (Jan. 24, 2003), available at http://www.humanrightsfirst.org/us_law/etn/gonzales/statements/hrf_opp_gonz_full_012405.asp.

18. *A (FC) and Others (FC) v. Secretary of State for the Home Department* (2004) UKHL 56 (Dec. 16, 2004).

19. 124 S. Ct. 2711 (2004).

20. See, e.g., *Mathews v. Diaz*, 426 U.S. 67, 80 (1976) (when regulating immigration, "Congress regularly makes rules that would be unacceptable if applied to citizens").

21. E.g., *Galvan v. Press*, 347 U.S. 522 (1954).

22. See *Reno v. American-Arab Anti-Discrimination Comm.*, 525 U.S. 471 (1999).

23. See, e.g., *California v. Greenwood*, 486 U.S. 35 (1988); *United States v. White*, 401 U.S. 745 (1971).

24. For the moment, the Protect America Act of 2007 casts substantial doubt on this prediction, but it is nonetheless true over the longer term that Congress has been more protective of privacy than has the Supreme Court, at least where the privacy of the majority is potentially at stake. See Jeffrey Rosen, *The Naked Crowd: Reclaiming Security and Freedom in an Anxious Age* 13–57 (Random House, 2004).

25. René Dubos, *The Wooing of Earth* (1980).

26. Mary Dudziak. *Cold War Civil Rights: Race and the Image of American Democracy* (Princeton University Press 2000).

27. *Johnson v. Eisentrager*, 339 U.S. 763 (1950).

28. *Al Odah v. United States*, 321 F. 3d 1134 (D.C. Cir. 2003); *Rasul v. Bush*, 215 F. Supp. 2d 55 (D.D.C. 2002).

29. United Kingdom Parliament, *Publication of Report: Foreign Policy Aspects of the War against Terrorism* (Feb. 2, 2004), available at http://www.parliament.uk/directories/

house_of_lords_information_office/bplist.cfmGuantánamo; Johan Steyn, *Guantánamo Bay: The Legal Black Hole* (Nov. 25, 2003; Twenty-Seventh F. A. Mann Lecture, delivered by Law Lords to British Institute of International and Comparative Law), available at http://www.nimj.com/documents/Guantánamo.PDF; Neil A. Lewis, *Red Cross Criticizes Indefinite Detention in Guantánamo Bay*, New York Times, Oct. 10, 2003, at A1.

30. H. Freedman, ed., *Jeremiah* (Soncino Books of the Bible, rev. ed., 1985), 52 (quoting Hermann Cohen).

❧ 27 ❧

America and the World, 2020

HAROLD HONGJU KOH

W HAT WILL THE world look like in 2020? Let me offer the following, fairly safe predictions: In 2020, the globe will hold more than 7 billion people and more than 200 nation-states, perhaps 150 of them nominally democracies.

Because of our current deficit and military overstretch, the United States will be weaker, relative to other states, politically and economically, than it is today. China will be an economic superpower. Europe will extend to Moscow and Istanbul. Latin America will be a free trade zone. The Asian tigers will have fully recovered; South Asia and the Pacific will have suffered more earthquakes and tsunamis. Africa will continue to be ravaged by war and disease. Middle Eastern democratization will have advanced only marginally.

More nations will have nuclear, chemical, and biological weapons, but none will have an effective national missile defense. The World Trade Organization (WTO) will be stronger. The International Criminal Court will still exist, and will have expanded its activities.

In 2020, there will be genuinely global round-the-clock markets, and we will rely on methods of communication that we cannot dream of now. After all, in 1990, few of us were using the Internet or the World Wide Web, and blogs, cell phones, BlackBerries, Palm Pilots, and satellite television were still in the future. But the digital divide in 2020 will have grown, as will the economic gap between the world's richest people and the bottom billion.

The United Nations will still exist, having undergone modest reforms. More nongovernmental organizations will have proliferated. Oil prices will be higher. Ethnic conflict will be alive and well in places like Indonesia, Burundi, and Iraq, if a nation-state of that name still even exists.

Trafficking in drugs, persons, and weapons will continue. Osama bin Laden will be dead, but not transborder terrorism nor Islamic fundamentalism. Somewhere in the world, a human being will have been cloned, and the world's average temperature will be a few degrees higher.

In the United States, same-sex marriage will have been legalized in some states and forbidden in others, the death penalty will have been eliminated, many parts of the country will speak only Spanish, and Caucasians will be in the minority.

At age seventy-two, Clarence Thomas will be the senior justice on the Supreme Court, and the president of the United States will not be named Bush.

Whether you agree with all or none of this thought experiment, each of us must conduct our own speculation about what the world will look like in 2020. Because we cannot ask the question: What constitutional principles will govern U.S. engagement with the world in 2020? without first asking: What will the world and the United States look like when that date arrives? That means asking: What will the United States and the world look like if we just let constitutional change happen? And what will they look like if we seize this moment to push our constitutionalism and our politics in better directions?

This chapter suggests five issues that will likely shape the constitutional law framework governing America's relationship with the world in 2020: first, the broad contest between competing visions of executive power and shared power (what I call *Curtiss-Wright* versus *Youngstown*) for the guiding vision of the constitutional framework to fight the "war on terror"; second, judicial nominations; third, canons governing interjudicial comity and the incorporation of international and foreign law into national law; fourth, extraterritorial application of the U.S. Constitution and laws; and fifth, issues surrounding membership in our national community. To see why these five issues will frame America's relationship with the world in 2020, we must first ask: What has happened to our global constitutional vision since the Twin Towers fell on September 11, 2001?[1]

A World Turned Upside Down

In the late twentieth century, U.S. foreign policy was characterized by four emphases. First, diplomacy backed by force, but only as a last resort. Second, a human rights policy based on promoting universal human rights values and a growing emphasis on international criminal justice and the core principles stated in Franklin Delano Roosevelt's 1941 Four Freedoms speech (freedom of speech, freedom of religion, freedom from want, and freedom from fear). Third, a democracy-promotion policy that focused on building democracy from the bottom up. And fourth, a diplomatic approach that could be called "strategic multilateralism and tactical unilateralism."[2]

Remarkably, in two terms, the Bush administration turned each of those four ideas on its head. Instead of diplomacy backed by force, U.S. interventions in Afghanistan and Iraq have applied a policy of force first, where coalitions of the willing preserve homeland security by discretionary war making on real and potential state sponsors of terror—based on international law theories of preemptive self-defense and feared access to weapons of mass destruction. The main constraint on this strategy has not been seen as international law, but rather the constraints imposed by our finite military and economic resources.

Second, U.S. human rights policy has rejected universalism and international criminal adjudication in favor of a Cold War–style human rights double standard. The U.S. government has downplayed acts of torture, cruel treatment, and Geneva Conventions violations committed by ourselves and our allies as necessary elements of the war against terror, claiming that the overriding human rights value is now freedom from fear.

Third, the United States shifted from a strategy of democracy promotion from the bottom up to one of militarily imposed democracy promotion from the top down in Afghanistan and Iraq, coupled with weak efforts at domino democratization throughout the Middle East and reduced democracy-promotion efforts in Central and Eastern Europe (see, e.g., Russia and Ukraine), Africa (see, e.g., Kenya, Côte d'Ivoire and Zimbabwe), Latin America (see, e.g., Venezuela), and South and Southeast Asia (see, e.g., Pakistan and Thailand).

Fourth and finally, the United States shifted to a new diplomatic strategy of strategic unilateralism and tactical multilateralism, characterized by broad antipathy toward international law and global regime building through treaty negotiation. And so the United States has not signed the Rome Treaty creating the International Criminal Court, flouted the Kyoto Protocol on Global Climate Change, declined to join nascent conventions on disability rights and against forced disappearances, withdrawn from the optional protocol of the Vienna Convention on Consular Relations, and remained conspicuously outside the Law of the Sea Treaty, the Convention on the Elimination of All Forms of Discrimination Against Women, and the Convention on the Rights of the Child.

What does this foreign policy flip-flop mean for what I called some years ago "the National Security Constitution," the constitutional framework within which our national security affairs transpire?[3] After 9/11, the Bush administration shifted toward an extreme constitutional vision to enable the inverted foreign policy vision I have just described, a vision of unfettered executive power in the war on terror, human rights double standards, militarily imposed democracy, and strategic unilateralism.

In 2001, as a matter of constitutional law, national security policy was conducted within four widely accepted premises. First, executive power operates within a constitutional framework of checks and balances, resting on the vision of shared institutional powers set forth in Justice Robert H. Jackson's canonical concurrence in the *Steel Seizure Case* (*Youngstown Sheet & Tube Co. v. Sawyer*).[4] That vision of shared powers rests on the simple notion that constitutional checks and balances do not stop at the water's edge; the nation requires an energetic executive, to be sure, but one checked by an energetic Congress and overseen by a searching judicial branch. Second, there are no law-free zones, practices, courts, or persons. Third, we accept no infringement on our civil liberties absent a clear statement by our elected congressional representatives.[5] Fourth and finally—except for a few political rights, such as the right to vote or serve on a jury—aliens and citizens are treated largely the same, particularly with respect to economic, social, and cultural rights.

Yet this constitutional vision became similarly inverted. First, the Bush administration asserted a constitutional theory of unfettered executive power, based on extraordinarily broad interpretations of the Article II Commander in Chief Clause and the Supreme Court's decision in *United States v. Curtiss-Wright Export Corp.*, which famously called the president the "sole organ of the federal government in the field of international relations."[6] Under this vision, the president's Article II powers are paramount, Congress exercises minimal oversight over executive activity, government secrecy prevails, and the solicitor general urges the courts to give extreme deference to the president, citing the judiciary's "passive virtues." Second, the Bush administration rejected human rights universalism in favor of executive efforts to create law-free zones: extralegal spaces (Guantánamo), extralegal courts (military commissions), extralegal persons (enemy combatants), and extralegal practices (extraordinary rendition)—all of which, it claimed, are exempt from judicial review. In so saying, the administration opposed judicial efforts to incorporate international and foreign law into domestic legal review, so as to insulate the U.S. government from charges that it was violating universal human rights norms. Third, we increasingly heard claims that the executive can infringe on civil liberties without clear legislative statements, which relied on such broadly worded laws as the Authorization for Use of Military Force (AUMF) of September 2001 to justify secret National Security Agency surveillance, indefinite detentions, and torture of foreign detainees.[7] And fourth, the war on terror exacerbated already sharp distinctions between citizens and aliens within U.S. society with respect to political, civil, social, and economic rights, contributing to pronounced scapegoating of Muslim and Arab aliens in American life.

And finally, late in the second term of George W. Bush, came the startling notion that executive action constitutes a law unto itself. In justifying warrantless electronic surveillance[8] and harsh treatment of detainees,[9] the president's defenders argued that the policy rationale for executive action had somehow *created* the legal justification for executive unilateralism.

Looming Constitutional Battlegrounds

If this was the Bush administration's four-part constitutional vision—*Curtiss-Wright*, human rights double standards, reduced civil liberties, and driving a wedge between citizens and aliens—the major check on its implementation was the Supreme Court. The Bush administration had lost all four major terrorism cases decided there.[10] The Court's critical role in shaping the future of our National Security Constitution emerged most clearly from the landmark 2006 decision in *Hamdan v. Rumsfeld*, where, strikingly, the majority rejected all four elements of the administration's anticonstitutional vision.[11]

First, all of the justices who addressed the merits rejected the *Curtiss-Wright* framework as the starting point for analysis, invoking instead the accepted framework of shared institutional powers set forth in the *Steel Seizure Case*.[12] Second, the *Hamdan* Court rejected the government's claim that Salim Ahmed Hamdan was a person outside the law, who could be held in an extralegal zone (Guantánamo) and subjected to the jurisdiction of a noncourt (a military commission), and it treated as binding a universal treaty obligation—Common Article 3 of the Geneva Conventions.

Third, the *Hamdan* Court demanded a clear congressional statement before authorizing the commander in chief to try a suspected alien terrorist before a military commission in a manner inconsistent with the Uniform Code of Military Justice. As Justice Stephen Breyer said, in his concurrence for four justices, "The Court's conclusion ultimately rests upon a single ground: Congress has not issued the Executive a 'blank check'" in the AUMF.[13] Fourth and finally, in *Hamdan*, the Court acknowledged not only that enemy aliens have rights, but also that the government cannot discriminate against aliens by asserting an alleged dichotomy between law and war. The Court acknowledged that, once war begins, law does not end. Rather, the Court required consistent application of the *law of war* to Hamdan's case. As Justice Anthony Kennedy succinctly put it, "If the military commission at issue is illegal under the law of war, then an offender cannot be tried 'by the law of war' before that commission."[14]

Hamdan illustrates that, just as the Supreme Court in the 1950s could be divided into nationalists and federalists, the early twenty-first-century Court can be divided into a nationalist minority—Chief Justice John G. Roberts and Justices Antonin Scalia, Clarence Thomas, and Samuel Alito—and a slim transnationalist majority created by adding Justice Kennedy to Justices John Paul Stevens, David H. Souter, Ruth Bader Ginsburg, and Stephen Breyer (the group that, along with now-retired Justice Sandra Day O'Connor, formed the majority in three of the four terror cases mentioned above).[15]

The transnationalist and the nationalist philosophies differ, inasmuch as the transnationalists tend to believe in the political and economic interdependence of nations, while nationalists focus instead on preserving U.S. autonomy. The transnationalists recognize that international and domestic law are merging into a hybrid body of transnational law, while nationalists preserve a rigid division between domestic and foreign law. Transnationalists believe that domestic courts have a critical role to play in incorporating international law into domestic law, while the nationalists claim that only the political branches are authorized to domesticate international legal norms. The transnationalists argue that U.S. courts should use their interpretive powers to help develop a global legal system, while nationalists believe that courts should focus solely on the development of a U.S. legal system. And finally, transnationalists see the power of the executive branch as constrained by the concept of comity and by the institution of judicial review, while the nationalists would have federal courts give extraordinarily broad deference to executive power in matters of foreign affairs. The continuing clash between these two judicial philosophies explains much of the struggle that rages in the federal courts over the role of international and foreign law as part of U.S. law.

In the years ahead, the clash between these competing visions will play out in the confirmation hearings of future nominees to the U.S. Supreme Court. While receptivity to international and foreign law has emerged as a partisan issue, historically, it has not been. Four of the last six transnationalist justices—Stevens, O'Connor, Kennedy, and Souter—were appointed by Republicans. So in this, as in other constitutional areas, the next Court appointments will be pivotal in determining whether by 2020 our constitutional jurisprudence moves the United States in a transnationalist or nationalist direction.

In the two latest Supreme Court confirmation hearings, the nominees were openly dismissive of arguments based on international and foreign law.[16] But as Justice Harry Blackmun noted some years ago, "[I]f the substance of the Eighth Amendment is to turn on 'evolving standards of decency' of the civilized world [as the Court has held since at least 1958], there can be no justification for limiting judicial inquiry to the opinions of the United States."[17] In this day and age, we would never consider deciding what is "unusual" for global capital markets by looking only at U.S. stock exchanges, and we would never suggest that what is "unusual" for cyberspace can be determined by looking only at Web sites in Silicon Valley. So when the Eighth Amendment expressly bars "cruel and unusual" punishments, and some states in the United States persist in the increasingly rare practice of executing children or persons with mental retardation, why shouldn't the Court have examined those practices in light of global practices and deemed them "cruel and unusual" and hence unconstitutional under the Eighth Amendment?[18]

When confronted with such arguments, Justice Scalia likes to ask, "If our Supreme Court must look to foreign law, must it apply the law of Zimbabwe as part of our law?"[19] The short answer is: "No more than the courts of the early U.S. republic felt obliged to apply the law of the Barbary pirates as U.S. law." The framers' originalist vision of paying "decent respect to the opinions of mankind," as the Declaration of Independence does, supports the selective incorporation of the best practices of international and foreign law into domestic legal review.

Federal courts in the United States are no more obliged to apply the worst foreign practices today than they were obliged to apply bad state practices during the 1950s. The role of selective incorporation of foreign and international law into U.S. jurisprudence is not to surrender U.S. sovereignty, but rather to check the creation of a constitutional jurisprudence of rights that sits visibly below global human rights standards, and by doing so, bring us into inevitable conflict with our allies.

In the 1950s, the Supreme Court played a critical role in developing the federal system through the jurisprudence of the federal courts.[20] During the next few decades, a parallel phenomenon will unfold: the development of a transnationalist legal system, in part through the interpretive activities of U.S. courts in delineating the relationship between domestic courts and international and foreign tribunals. Since the late 1990s, this issue has come before the Supreme Court in a string of cases involving foreign nationals on death row who have been denied their consular rights under the Vienna Convention on Consular Relations.[21] The Court has directed that International Court of Justice rulings are "entitled only to the 'respectful consideration' due an interpretation of an international agreement by an international court," but it has not elaborated precisely what "respectful consideration" means.[22] In *Medellin v. Texas*, the Supreme Court issued the startling ruling that an International Court of Justice judgment is not self-executing and hence not federal law, thus denying it a domestic effect that is even less than "respectful consideration."[23] These cases make clear that our courts cannot afford to withdraw from this field, but rather must keep working in it to craft a set of judicial canons to govern the relationship between domestic and international tribunals in such areas as the death penalty, international trade, international business transactions, and international commercial arbitration.

Crafting judicial doctrines for managing relations among courts is hardly a new activity for U.S. courts. In the early days of the republic, U.S. courts regularly applied international and foreign law and paid "decent respect to the opinions of mankind" by framing doctrines of comity with respect to foreign courts.[24] Just as the Warren and Burger courts framed canons of abstention, avoidance, ripeness, and comity to govern the interjudicial relations between state and federal courts, in the twenty-first century, we will need a similar set of judicial canons to govern the relationship between domestic and global tribunals. In developing that doctrine, perhaps the best extant guidance was offered by Justice Blackmun in the *Aerospatiale* case. When construing laws, U.S. courts must look beyond national interest to the "mutual interests of all nations in a smoothly functioning international legal regime," he suggested, to "consider if there is a course that furthers, rather than impedes, the development of an ordered international system."[25]

So these are three obvious constitutional battlegrounds that will help to define America's relationship with the world between now and 2020: judicial nominations, judicial management of the evolving relationship between U.S. and international and foreign tribunals, and the ongoing struggle between the *Curtiss-Wright* and *Steel Seizure* visions of constitutional authority over foreign policy decision making.[26]

My discussion would not be complete without mentioning two others: the extraterritorial reach of the Constitution and how Americans define membership in the U.S. national community. The two issues revolve around the same questions: To whom does the United States owe legal duties, and to what extent are those obligations defined by U.S. citizenship? The first defines the geographical scope of U.S. human rights protections; the second delineates to whom those protections extend and whether they encompass what Roosevelt called "freedom from want" and what Cass Sunstein (in this volume and elsewhere) terms the "Second Bill of Rights."[27]

The first question—how far do U.S. laws extend?—has long been a familiar issue with regard to America's relationship to the global economy and historic controversies over the extraterritorial application of U.S. antitrust, securities, discovery, and export control rules to foreign activities.[28] But the further question—how far do our human rights and constitutional obligations extend?—has been brought into sharp relief by Abu Ghraib and the debates over extraterritorial torture, the mistreatment of detainees at Guantánamo, and the denial of habeas corpus and full trial rights to suspected enemy combatants. By the time this volume appears, one would hope that the Guantánamo detention facility has finally closed, but questions will surely linger about where the Guantánamo detainees will next be sent, with what assurances against torture, and whether the CIA's notorious "black sites" will continue to operate in the shocking manner described in journalistic accounts.[29] Far from eliminating American torture, public reaction to Abu Ghraib seems perversely to have entrenched it. Before 9/11, we treated torture as absolutely forbidden.[30] But as Mark Danner puts it, "[W]e are all torturers now."[31] Some seem to accept that our government is, and will continue to be, engaged in a widespread set of shadowy, cruel practices on unseen and unheard detainees abroad.[32]

Just before the turn of the twentieth century, the Supreme Court baldly declared that the "Constitution can have no operation in any other country,"[33] but during the Cold War, the Court retreated from that categorical declaration, at least for U.S. citizens.[34] In the late twentieth and early twenty-first centuries, the swing justice in these cases, Justice Kennedy, relied upon Justice John M. Harlan's separate opinion in *Reid v. Covert* to argue that particular constitutional limitations may be applied "overseas" even to aliens subject to U.S. authority, so long as the circumstances would not render such application "altogether impracticable and anomalous."[35] Yet precisely what it means when one says that applying a constitutional protection is "impracticable and anomalous" is an issue likely to be repeatedly tested before the Court.[36] As the war on terror wears on, we can expect the contours of that concept to be fleshed out not just in the Guantánamo cases, but more directly in judicial challenges to the conduct of U.S. officials and private contractors charged with the extraordinary rendition and abusive detention of aliens held abroad.

A final, related issue to be debated both before the legislatures and the courts will be the growing distinction between citizens and aliens *within* U.S. society. Left unchecked, by 2020, rising visa barriers and the scapegoating of aliens in American life may well divide the U.S. immigrant population into two: well-educated, visa-holding, high-tech resident aliens, who will be treated almost like citizens (lacking only the right to vote and serve on juries), and uneducated, low-tech, undocumented aliens, who will make up much of our permanent underclass. Policies that would limit the availability of old and new government benefits to only U.S. citizens will likely exacerbate these differences.[37] These policy proposals need to be tested against the Supreme Court's equal protection doctrine, which once declared aliens to be a discrete and insular minority, worthy of heightened constitutional protection.[38] Particularly in a post-Obama era, when a progressive vision of what it means to be American will embrace more mixed-race, nontraditional groups, we need to define ascending levels of membership in our national community, not treat the legal status of citizenship as an on-off switch for determining whether millions of longtime residents with deep ties to the United States have access to the most basic civil and political rights.

These are the battlegrounds in the coming struggle. Significantly, Kofi Annan's 2005 report, *In Larger Freedom*, written in response to a call for reform of the United Nations system, is organized around the topics of security issues (freedom from fear), economic and cultural rights (freedom from want), and civil and political rights (freedom of speech and religion).[39] These freedoms, the report claims, are what the twenty-first-century United Nations exists to promote. The subtext is clear: In the year 2020, the issues will be the same, but the world guardian of human rights will no longer be the United States, as it was for the previous seventy-five years, but rather the United Nations.

I support the United Nations and admire its former secretary-general, Kofi Annan, but I for one neither expect nor want this to happen.

Think back to the vision of the world in 2020 that I painted moments ago. Its main feature is that most of the likely problems—terrorism, trafficking, weapons of mass destruction, the environment, AIDS, avian flu, cloning, global warming—in a globalizing century will require global solutions. Terrorism will continue to plague the Barack Obama administration, as it has the Bush administration. To address those challenges, we must do more than simply go back to the future, both in restoring our constitutional principles and in restoring our human rights principles, which have been so dishonored since 9/11.

In 2020, the United States will still be an exceptional country, with exceptional capacity to fill global vacuums, to shape global regimes, and to generate those global solutions. But if we are to do that, we must return to a foreign policy strategy that is based not on unilateralism and a power politics of fear, but rather, on time-honored principles of democracy, human rights, and the rule of law: promoting democracy from the bottom up, then using international law and diplomacy to mobilize global cooperation among global democracies to solve global problems.

To enable that global rule-of-law strategy, we need to return to a domestic constitutional vision based on *Youngstown*, not *Curtiss-Wright*, a theory not of the imperial presidency but of constitutional powers shared among the executive, the Congress, and the courts and overseen by a transnational process in which the global media, networks of nongovernmental organizations, and ordinary citizens all play important roles.

In short, a progressive vision of U.S. public law must both maintain the integrity of constitutional argument against political manipulation and enable our Constitution to adapt to a rapidly changing world. We can move toward a just future in 2020, but only if we renovate established constitutional and human rights frameworks to embrace a world that today, we can only imagine.

This chapter grows out of remarks delivered at the Yale Constitution in 2020 Conference on Apr. 10, 2005, and at the National American Constitution Society Convention on July 27, 2007.

Notes

1. See generally Harold Hongju Koh, *Setting the World Right*, 115 Yale L.J. 2350 (2006), from which some of what follows is drawn.

2. I owe this phrase to former Deputy Secretary of State Strobe Talbott.

3. Harold Hongju Koh, *The National Security Constitution: Sharing Power after the Iran-Contra Affair* (1990).

4. 343 U.S. 579, 635–38 (1952) (Jackson, J., concurring). In *Dames & Moore v. Regan*, 453 U.S. 654, 661 (1981), a majority of the Court adopted Justice Jackson's tripartite framework.

5. Under the clear statement doctrine of *Kent v. Dulles*, 357 U.S. 116 (1958), courts must carefully scrutinize statutes cited by the executive for signs not only that Congress has consented to the president's actions, but also to determine whether the president and Congress acting together have made a clear determination to infringe on individual rights. When individual rights are at stake, courts should "construe narrowly all delegated powers that curtail or dilute them." *Id.* at 129; accord *Greene v. McElroy*, 360 U.S. 474, 507–8 (1959).

6. 299 U.S. 304, 320 (1936); Koh, *supra* note 3, at 94 ("Among government attorneys, Justice Sutherland's lavish description of the president's powers is so often cited that it has come to be known as the '*Curtiss-Wright*, so I'm right cite'—a statement of deference to the president so sweeping as to be worthy of frequent citation in any government foreign-affairs brief") (footnote omitted); see also *id.* at 93–96 (criticizing the decision).

7. Authorization for Use of Military Force, Pub. L. No. 107-40, 115 Stat. 224 (codified at 50 U.S.C. § 1541 note (Supp. III 2003)).

8. "The President has determined that the speed and agility required to carry out the NSA [National Security Agency] surveillance activities successfully could not have been achieved under FISA [Foreign Intelligence Surveillance Act]. Because the President also has determined that the NSA activities are necessary...FISA would impermissibly interfere with the President's most solemn constitutional obligation" to defend the country and therefore would be "unconstitutional as applied." U.S. Department of Justice, *Legal Authorities Supporting the Activities of the National Security Agency Described by the President* 34–35 (Jan. 19, 2006), available at http://www.fas.org/irp/nsa/dojo11906.pdf.

9. In its infamous, now-overruled August 2002 "Torture Opinion," the Justice Department's Office of Legal Counsel opined, "Any effort by Congress to regulate the interrogation of battlefield combatants would violate the Constitution's sole vesting of the Commander-in-Chief authority in the President." Memorandum from Jay S. Bybee, assistant attorney general, to Alberto Gonzales, counsel to the president, 35, 39 (Aug. 1, 2002), available at http://www.washingtonpost.com/wpsrv/nation/documents/dojinterrogationmemo20020801.pdf.

10. *Hamdan v. Rumsfeld*, 126 S. Ct. 2749 (2006); *Hamdi v. Rumsfeld*, 542 U.S. 507 (2004); *Rasul v. Bush*, 542 U.S. 466 (2004); *Boumediene v. Bush*, 128 S. Ct. 2229 (2008).

11. *Hamdan v. Rumsfeld*, 126 S. Ct. 2749 (2006).

12. 343 U.S. 579, 635–38 (1952) (Jackson, J., concurring) (followed by the Court in *Dames & Moore v. Regan*, 453 U.S. 654, 661 (1981)).

13. *Hamdan*, 126 S. Ct. at 2799 (Breyer, J., concurring) (citing *Hamdi v. Rumsfeld*, 542 U.S. 507, 536 (2004) (plurality opinion)).

14. *Hamdan*, 126 S. Ct. at 2802 (Kennedy, J., concurring).

15. The pivotal role of Justice Kennedy on these, as on so many other, issues was demonstrated in the Court's 2007 term, during which he wrote the Court's transnationalist majority opinion in *Boumediene v. Bush*, 128 S. Ct. 2229 (2008), but sided with Chief Justice Roberts's nationalist majority opinion in *Medellin v. Texas*, 128 S. Ct. 1346

(2008), which ruled that a final judgment of the International Court of Justice was not self-executing and did not constitute binding federal law.

16. In his confirmation hearings, John Roberts argued that foreign precedent provided an illegitimate means for a judge to "cloak his own views" by claiming to cite legitimate authority. In his confirmation hearings, Samuel Alito similarly opined that it would be neither "appropriate [n]or useful to look to foreign law in interpreting the provisions of our Constitution." See James W. Leary, *Foreword: "Outsourcing Authority?" Citation to Foreign Court Precedent in Domestic Jurisprudence*, 69 Alb. L. Rev. vii, viii (2006).

17. Harry A. Blackmun, *The Supreme Court and the Law of Nations*, 104 Yale L.J. 39, 48 (1994). In *Trop v. Dulles*, 356 U.S. 86 (1958), the Court specifically held that the Eighth Amendment of the U.S. Constitution contained an "evolving standard of decency that marked the progress of a maturing society," which, it suggested, should be measured not just according to American experience, but by reference to foreign and international experience as well.

18. *Atkins v. Virginia*, 536 U.S. 304 (2002) (holding "cruel and unusual" the execution of persons with mental retardation); *Roper v. Simmons*, 543 U.S. 551 (2005) (holding "cruel and unusual" the execution of minors). For further discussion of these cases, see Harold Hongju Koh, *International Law as Part of Our Law*, 98 Am. J. Int'l L. 43 (2004).

19. Emily Bazelon, *What Would Zimbabwe Do?* Atlantic, Nov. 2005, available at http://www.theatlantic.com/doc/prem/200511/supreme-court-comparativism.

20. For a compact summary of this jurisprudence, see generally *Hart and Wechsler's The Federal Courts and the Federal System* (Richard H. Fallon et al., eds., 4th ed., 2004).

21. See, e.g., *Breard v. Greene*, 523 U.S. 371 (1998); *Germany v. U.S.*, 526 U.S. 111 (1999); *Medellin v. Dretke*, 544 U.S. 660 (2005); *Sanchez-Llamas v. Oregon*, 126 S. Ct. 2669, 2675–76 (2006); *Medellin v. Texas*, 128 S. Ct. 1346 (2008).

22. *Sanchez-Llamas v. Oregon*, 126 S. Ct. at 2685.

23. *Medellin v. Texas*, 128 S. Ct. 1346 (2008).

24. See, e.g., *Hilton v. Guyot*, 159 U.S. 113, 163 (1895) (directing courts to give comity to foreign judgments and declaring that "[i]nternational law, in its widest and most comprehensive sense...is part of our law, and must be ascertained and administered by the courts of justice, as often as such questions are presented in litigation between man and man").

25. *Société Nationale Industrielle Aerospatiale v. United States District Court for the Southern District of Iowa*, 482 U.S. 522, 555, 560, 567 (1987) (Blackmun, J., concurring in part and dissenting in part).

26. See generally David Cole, *Youngstown v. Curtiss-Wright*, 99 Yale L.J. 2063 (1990).

27. Cass Sunstein, *The Second Bill of Rights: FDR's Unfinished Revolution and Why We Need It More than Ever* (2004); and Sunstein in this volume.

28. For examples of extraterritoriality controversies in the international business realm, see generally 1 Restatement (Third) of the Foreign Relations Law of the United States, sec. 403 (1986); *Timberlane Lumber Co. v. Bank of America*, 549 F. 2d 597, 608–13 (9th Cir. 1976) (linking "interest-balancing" test for extraterritoriality to "effects doctrine" of *United States v. Alcoa*, 148 F. 2d 416 (2nd Cir. 1945)); *O.N.E. Shipping Ltd. v. Flota Mercante Grancolombiana, S.A.*, 830 F. 2d 449, 451–53 (2nd Cir. 1987) (adopting a variant of the *Timberlane* test); *Data Processing Equip. Co. v. Maxwell*, 468 F. 2d 1326 (2nd Cir. 1972).

29. For a suggestion regarding how to close Guantánamo, see *Statement of Harold Hongju Koh, before the Senate Judiciary Committee, Subcommittee on the Constitution on Restoring the Rule of Law* (Sept. 16, 2008), available at http://www.law.yale.edu/documents/pdf/News_&_Events/Kohtestimony091608RuleofLaw.pdf. See generally Jane Mayer,

The Black Sites: A Rare Look inside the CIA's Secret Interrogation Program, New Yorker (Aug. 13, 2007), available at http://www.newyorker.com/reporting/2007/08/13/070813fa_fact_mayer; William Glaberson, *Hurdles Frustrate Effort to Shrink Guantánamo*, New York Times, Aug. 9, 2007, at A1 (noting concerns that detainees removed from Guantánamo will be tortured in new destinations).

30. Statement of Harold Hongju Koh, assistant secretary of state for democracy, human rights, and labor, On-the-Record Briefing on the *Initial Report of the United States of America to the UN Committee against Torture*, Washington, D.C. (Oct. 15, 1999), available at http://www.state.gov/www/policy_remarks/1999/991015_koh_rpt_torture.html ("as a country [Americans] are unalterably committed to a world without torture").

31. See generally Mark Danner, *We Are All Torturers Now*, New York Times op-ed, Jan. 6, 2005.

32. Significantly, both 2008 presidential candidates—John McCain and Barack Obama— campaigned on unequivocal platforms of banning torture by U.S. officials.

33. *In re Ross*, 140 U.S. 453, 464 (1891).

34. *Reid v. Covert*, 354 U.S. 1 (1957); *Kinsella v. United States ex rel. Singleton*, 361 U.S. 234 (1960) (holding that U.S. government must honor Article III and the Fifth and Sixth amendments before punishing civilian citizens accompanying U.S. armed forces abroad).

35. *Reid v. Covert*, 354 U.S. at 74 (Harlan, J., concurring); *United States v. Verdugo-Urquidez*, 494 U.S. 259, 277–78 (Kennedy, J, concurring) (1990) (agreeing that Fourth Amendment does not govern searches of nonresident aliens' property in a foreign country, but arguing that application of particular constitutional limitations "abroad," or in territories with wholly dissimilar traditions and institutions, would not be "impracticable and anomalous"). See generally Gerald L. Neuman, *Strangers to the Constitution: Immigrants, Borders, and Fundamental Law* (1996).

36. Indeed, this concept was central to Justice Kennedy's functional analysis, arguing for the constitutional application of the writ of habeas corpus on Guantánamo in *Boumediene v. Bush*, 128 S. Ct. 2229 (2008).

37. This is why I object to my colleagues Anne Alstott and Bruce Ackerman's suggestion that only U.S. citizens be afforded an $80,000 share in a "stakeholder society," because even if successful, their proposal will only cause the gap between citizens and aliens to grow. See Anne Alstott and Bruce A. Ackerman, *The Stakeholder Society* (2000) (arguing that all U.S. citizens with high school diplomas should be guaranteed, on their twenty-first birthdays, $80,000, no strings attached); also see Ackerman in this volume.

38. See *Graham v. Richardson*, 403 U.S. 365, 371–72 (1971) ("the Court's decisions have established that classifications based on alienage, like those based on nationality or race, are inherently suspect and subject to close judicial scrutiny. Aliens as a class are a prime example of a 'discrete and insular' minority for whom such heightened judicial solicitude is appropriate") (internal citations omitted). See generally Harold Hongju Koh, *Equality with a Human Face: Justice Blackmun and the Equal Protection of Aliens*, 8 Hamline L. Rev. 51 (1985) (describing the evolution of the Court's subsequent equal protection doctrine toward aliens).

39. Kofi Annan, *In Larger Freedom: Toward Security, Development and Human Rights for All* (Sept. 2005), available at http://www.un.org/largerfreedom.

Acknowledgments

THIS BOOK BEGAN several years ago at a planning meeting and a major conference at Yale Law School on the Constitution in 2020, supported by the Open Society Institute and by the Yale Law School, and cosponsored by the American Constitution Society.

The 2020 project grew out of conversations among faculty and students of the Yale chapter of the American Constitution Society. In organizing the conferences and an associated 2020 blog, students led by Chad Golder, Seth Grossman, Joey Fishkin, and Karen Dunn had wide-ranging discussions with the chapter's faculty board, led by Reva Siegel and including Bruce Ackerman, Jack Balkin, Drew Days, Bill Eskridge, Paul Gewirtz, Bob Gordon, Robert Post, and Judith Resnik. Discussion of the Constitution in 2020 was first prompted by the Reagan administration's Constitution in 2000 initiative, which we learned of through Dawn Johnsen's important research. From its inception, the 2020 project received crucial support from Harold Koh, Dean of Yale Law School, Gara LaMarche, then Vice President of the Open Society Institute, Lisa Brown, then Executive Director of the American Constitution Society, and John Podesta, President of the Center for American Progress. The practical execution of the conferences would not have been possible without the remarkable Renee Dematteo; Debbie Sestito gave constant and unstinting support.

As the conference participants began writing the essays collected in this volume, the Open Society Institute again stepped forward to support activities for disseminating the ideas in the 2020 book. We are especially indebted to Gara LaMarche, John Kowal, and Tom Hilbink, who have been great friends of the project throughout its various incarnations. We would also like to thank Diane Wachtell at New Press for her enthusiasm and her belief in the project.

Judy Appelbaum at the American Constitution Society worked closely with us in planning for activities related to the book. Lynn Chu of Writers' Representatives spent countless hours helping us make the book a reality. We are deeply indebted to Niko Pfund and David McBride of Oxford University Press, both of whom made publication smoother than we had any right to expect.

We are especially indebted to two friends and colleagues, Robert Post and Bruce Ackerman, who helped imagine this project at its inception and advised us throughout. The book would not be what it is without their counsel and support.

An earlier version of chapter 2 was originally published as part of Jack M. Balkin, *Abortion and Original Meaning*, 24 Constitutional Commentary 291 (2006).

Chapter 11 is adapted from Goodwin Liu, *Interstate Inequality in Educational Opportunity*, 81 N.Y.U. L. Rev. 2044 (2006), and Goodwin Liu, *Education, Equality, and National Citizenship*, 116 Yale L.J. 330 (2006).

A longer version of chapter 18 appears as Jack M. Balkin, *The Constitution in the National Surveillance State*, 93 Minn. L. Rev. 1 (2008).

Portions of chapter 27 originally appeared in Harold Hongju Koh, *Setting the World Right*, 115 Yale L.J. 2350 (2006).

About the Contributors

Bruce Ackerman is Sterling Professor of Law and Political Science at Yale University and the author of fifteen books, which have had a broad influence in political philosophy, constitutional law, and public policy. His major works include *Social Justice in the Liberal State* (1980) and his multivolume constitutional history, *We the People* (1991, 1998). His most recent books are *The Failure of the Founding Fathers* (2005) and *Before the Next Attack* (2006). His book *The Stakeholder Society* (1999, with Anne Alstott) served as a basis for Tony Blair's introduction of child investment accounts in the United Kingdom, and his book *Deliberation Day* (2004, with James Fishkin) served as a basis for *PBS Deliberation Day*, a national series of citizen deliberations produced by the *McNeil-Lehrer NewsHour* on national television for the 2004 elections. Professor Ackerman is a member of the American Law Institute and the American Academy of Arts and Sciences. He is a commander of the French Order of Merit and the recipient of the American Philosophical Society's Henry Phillips Prize for Lifetime Achievement in Jurisprudence.

Jack M. Balkin is Knight Professor of Constitutional Law and the First Amendment at Yale Law School, the founder and director of Yale's Information Society Project, and the codirector of Yale's Law and Media Program. His work ranges over many different fields, including constitutional theory, telecommunications and Internet law, reproductive rights, freedom of speech, jurisprudence and legal reasoning, the theory of ideology, and musical and legal interpretation. Professor Balkin is a member of the American Academy of Arts and Sciences and writes political and legal commentary at *Balkinization* (http://balkin. blogspot.com). His books include *Cultural Software: A Theory of Ideology* (1998), *Processes of Constitutional Decisionmaking* (5th ed. 2006, with Paul Brest, Sanford Levinson, Akhil Reed Amar, and Reva Siegel), *The State of Play: Law, Games and Virtual Worlds* (2006, with Beth Noveck), *Cybercrime: Digital Cops in a Networked Environment* (2007, with James Grimmelmann et al.), *What* Brown v. Board of Education *Should Have Said* (2001), and *What* Roe v. Wade *Should Have Said* (2005).

Yochai Benkler is Jack N. and Lillian R. Berkman Professor for Entrepreneurial Legal Studies at Harvard Law School and a co-director of Harvard's Berkman Center for Internet and Society. He is a leading scholar of Internet law and the author of *The Wealth of Networks: How Social Production Transforms Markets and Freedom* (2006). Professor Benkler's work was recognized with the Electronic Frontier Foundation's Pioneer Award in 2007 and the Public Knowledge IP3 Award in 2006. His research focuses on commons-based approaches to managing resources in networked environments. He received his law degree from Harvard Law School and clerked for Justice Stephen Breyer on the U.S. Supreme Court. His work can be freely accessed at www.benkler.org.

David Cole is professor of law at Georgetown University Law Center, a volunteer staff attorney for the Center for Constitutional Rights, the legal affairs correspondent for the *Nation*, a regular contributor to the *New York Review of Books*, and a commentator on National Public Radio's *All Things Considered*. He has litigated many significant constitutional cases, including *Texas v. Johnson* and *United States v. Eichman*, which extended First Amendment protection to flag burning, and *National Endowment for the Arts v. Finley*, which challenged political content restrictions on NEA funding. Since the 9/11 attacks, Professor Cole has been involved in many of the nation's most important cases involving civil liberties and national security. He is the author of several books, including *Justice at War: The Men and Ideas That Shaped America's War on Terror* (2008); *Less Safe, Less Free: Why America Is Losing the War on Terror* (with Jules Lobel, 2007); *Terrorism and the Constitution: Sacrificing Civil Liberties in the Name of National Security* (with James X. Dempsey, 3rd ed., 2006); *Enemy Aliens: Double Standards and Constitutional Freedoms in the War on Terrorism* (2003), which received the American Book Award in 2004; and *No Equal Justice: Race and Class in the American Criminal Justice System* (1999), which was named best nonfiction book of 1999 by the *Boston*

Book Review and the best book on an issue of national policy in 1999 by the American Political Science Association.

William N. Eskridge, Jr., is the John A. Garver Professor of Jurisprudence at Yale Law School. His primary legal academic interest has been statutory interpretation. Together with Philip Frickey, he developed an innovative casebook on legislation. In 1990–1995, Professor Eskridge represented a gay couple suing for recognition of their same-sex marriage. Since then, he has published a field-establishing casebook, three monographs, and dozens of law review articles articulating a legal and political framework for the proper state treatment of sexual and gender minorities. The historical materials in his book *Gaylaw: Challenging the Apartheid of the Closet* (2002) formed the basis for an amicus brief he drafted for the Cato Institute and for much of the Court's (and the dissenting opinion's) analysis in *Lawrence v. Texas* (2003), which invalidated consensual sodomy laws. His most recent books are *Gay Marriage: For Better or for Worse?* (with Darren Spedale, 2007) and *Dishonorable Passions: Sodomy Laws in America, 1861–2003* (2008).

Noah Feldman is professor of law at Harvard Law School. An expert on church-state issues, he is a former Rhodes Scholar and clerked for Justice David Souter on the U.S. Supreme Court before joining the faculty at NYU Law School. Professor Feldman served as a senior advisor for constitutional law for the Coalition Provisional Authority, Iraq, and is currently a senior adjunct fellow at the Council on Foreign Relations. He is the author of several books, including *After Jihad: America and the Struggle for Islamic Democracy* (2003); *What We Owe Iraq: War and the Ethics of Nation Building* (2004); *Divided by God: America's Church-State Problem—and What We Should Do about It* (2005); and *The Fall and Rise of the Islamic State* (2008).

William E. Forbath holds the Lloyd M. Bentsen Chair in Law and is professor of history at the University of Texas. He is the author of *Law and the Shaping of the American Labor Movement* (1991), *Courting the State: Law and the Making of the Modern American State* (2009), and many articles, book chapters, and essays on legal and constitutional history and theory. His current research concerns the politics of social and economic rights advocacy and jurisprudence in South Africa. Professor Forbath is a member of the editorial boards of *Law and History* and *Law and Social Inquiry: Journal of the American Bar Foundation* and is on the board of directors of the American Society for Legal History and other organizations.

Richard T. Ford is George E. Osborne Professor of Law at Stanford Law School. He is an expert on civil rights, antidiscrimination, and housing law. Before joining the Stanford Law School faculty in 1994, Professor Ford was a Reginald Lewis Fellow at Harvard Law School, a litigation associate with Morrison & Foerster, and a housing policy consultant for the city of Cambridge, Massachusetts. He has also been a commissioner of the Housing Authority of San Francisco. He has written for the *Washington Post, San Francisco Chronicle, Christian Science Monitor*, and *Slate* (www.slate.com), where he is a regular contributor to the *Convictions* legal blog. His books include *Racial Culture: A Critique* (2005) and *The Race Card: How Bluffing about Bias Makes Race Relations Worse* (2008).

Vicki C. Jackson is Carmack Waterhouse Professor of Constitutional Law at Georgetown University Law Center. Upon graduation from law school, Professor Jackson served as a law clerk to Judge Murray Gurfein (U.S. Court of Appeals, Second Circuit), Judge Morris Lasker (U.S. District Court, Southern District of New York), and U.S. Supreme Court Justice Thurgood Marshall. She is coauthor (with Mark Tushnet) of a coursebook on comparative constitutional law and serves as an articles editor for the *International Journal of Constitutional Law*. Her research interests include comparative constitutional law, comparative federalism, and freedom of expression. She served as a deputy assistant attorney general in the Office of Legal Counsel in the U.S. Department of Justice (2000–2001); as a member of the D.C. Bar Board of Governors (1999–2002); as a cochair of the Special Committee on Gender of the D.C. Circuit Task Force on Gender, Race and Ethnic Bias (1992–1995); and as a member of the D.C. Circuit Advisory Committee on Procedures (1992–1998).

Dawn E. Johnsen is professor of law and Ira C. Batman Faculty Fellow at Indiana University School of Law in Bloomington. Professor Johnsen served in the Clinton administration, including as the acting assistant attorney general for the Office of Legal Counsel, where she advised the attorney general, the counsel to the president, and the general counsels of the executive departments. She was the legal director of NARAL Pro-Choice America from 1988 to 1993. She serves on the national board of the American Constitution Society.

Pamela S. Karlan is Kenneth and Harle Montgomery Professor of Public Interest Law at Stanford Law School and codirector of the school's Supreme Court Litigation Clinic. Prior to her teaching career, she clerked for Justice Harry Blackmun and served as assistant counsel at the NAACP Legal Defense Fund, where she specialized in voting rights litigation. From 2003 to 2005, she was a member of the California Fair Political Practice Commission. Professor Karlan is the coauthor of several leading casebooks, including *Constitutional Law* (5th ed., 2005), *The Law of Democracy: Legal Structure of the Political Process* (3rd ed., 2007), and *Civil Rights Actions: Enforcing the Constitution* (2nd ed., 2007), and dozens of scholarly articles. Karlan's résumé includes extensive pro bono litigation in state and federal courts on voting rights, minority rights, and the civil rights of gays and lesbians.

Harold Hongju Koh is dean of Yale Law School and Gerard C. and Bernice Latrobe Smith Professor of International Law. From 1998 to 2001, he served as assistant secretary of state for democracy, human rights, and labor. Before joining Yale, he practiced law at Covington and Burling and at the Office of Legal Counsel at the Department of Justice. Dean Koh is a leading expert on international law and a prominent advocate of human and civil rights. He has argued before the U.S. Supreme Court and testified before the U.S. Congress more than twenty times. He has been awarded ten honorary doctorates and two law school medals and has received more than twenty-five awards for his human rights work. He is the recipient of the 2005 Louis B. Sohn Award from the American Bar Association and the 2003 Wolfgang Friedmann Award from Columbia Law School for his lifetime achievements in international law. He is the author of eight books, including *Transnational Legal Problems* (4th ed., 1994, with Henry Steiner and Detlev Vagts) and *The National Security Constitution* (1990), which won the American Political Science Association's award as the best book on the American presidency.

Larry Kramer is Richard E. Lang Professor of Law and dean of Stanford Law School. He has written and taught in such varied fields as conflict of laws, civil procedure, federalism and its history, and most recently, the role of courts in society. His book *The People Themselves: Popular Constitutionalism and Judicial Review* (2004) sparked renewed interest in the ongoing debate about the relationship between the Supreme Court of the United States and politics. Dean Kramer is a fellow of the American Academy of Arts and Sciences and a member of the American Philosophical Society and the American Law Institute. He has taught at the law schools of New York University, University of Chicago, and University of Michigan. Early in his career, Dean Kramer clerked for Justice William J. Brennan, Jr. of the U.S. Supreme Court and Judge Henry J. Friendly of the U.S. Court of Appeals for the Second Circuit.

Goodwin Liu is professor of law at Boalt Hall Law School and a nationally recognized expert in education law and policy. Professor Liu is codirector of the Chief Justice Warren Institute on Race, Ethnicity and Diversity, a multidisciplinary think tank on civil rights law and policy. Professor Liu clerked for U.S. Supreme Court Justice Ruth Bader Ginsburg and for Judge David S. Tatel of the U.S. Court of Appeals for the D.C. Circuit. He serves on the board of trustees of Stanford University and the board of directors of the American Constitution Society.

William P. Marshall is professor of law at the University of North Carolina in Chapel Hill. Professor Marshall served as deputy White House counsel and deputy assistant to the president of the United States during the Clinton administration, where he worked on issues ranging from freedom of religion to separation of powers. He has published extensively on constitutional law issues and is a nationally recognized First Amendment scholar. He is also a leading expert on federal judicial selection matters and on the interrelationships among the media, law, and politics.

Tracey L. Meares is Walton Hale Hamilton Professor of Law at Yale Law School, a senior research fellow at the Berkeley Center for Criminal Justice, and a senior research fellow at the American Bar Foundation. Prior to joining the faculty at Yale, Meares was the Max Pam Professor of Law and director of the Center for Studies in Criminal Justice at the University of Chicago. In Chicago, Professor Meares worked closely with law enforcement and community groups as part of Project Safe Neighborhoods, a national program to reduce gun violence. She received her B.S. in general engineering from the University of Illinois and her J.D. from the University of Chicago Law School. Upon graduation, Professor Meares clerked for Judge Harlington Wood, Jr., of the U.S. Court of Appeals for the Seventh Circuit, then served as an honors program trial attorney in the Antitrust Division in the U.S. Department of Justice. Her research and teaching interests center on criminal procedure and criminal law policy, with a particular emphasis on empirical investigation of these subjects.

Frank Michelman is Robert Walmsley University Professor at Harvard Law School. He is the author of *Brennan and Democracy* (1999) and numerous articles on property law and theory, constitutional law and theory, local government law, and jurisprudence. He is a member of the board of directors of the U.S. Association of Constitutional Law and of the national advisory board of the American Constitution Society. He is a member of the American Academy of Arts and Sciences, and in 2005, in recognition of his many achievements, he received the Phillips Prize in Jurisprudence from the American Philosophical Society. Professor Michelman has written extensively on comparative constitutional law, with a special interest in the law of South Africa.

Rachel F. Moran is Robert D. and Leslie-Kay Raven Professor of Law at the University of California, Berkeley Law School, and a founding faculty member at the University of California, Irvine School of Law. From 2003 to 2008, she served as director of Berkeley's Institute for the Study of Social Change, and from 1993 to 1996, she was chair of Berkeley's Chicano/Latino Policy Project (now the Center for Latino Policy Research). An expert on civil rights and equality law, she is a member of the American Law Institute and served as president of the Association of American Law Schools from 2008 to 2009. She is the author of *Interracial Intimacy: The Regulation of Race and Romance* (2001); *Educational Policy and the Law* (4th ed., 2002, with Mark Yudof, David Kirp, and Betsy Levin); and *Race Law Stories* (2008, with Devon Carbado).

Robert C. Post is David Boies Professor of Law at Yale Law School. A well-known specialist in First Amendment theory and constitutional jurisprudence, he is the author of *Constitutional Domains: Democracy, Community, Management* (1995) and *Prejudicial Appearances: The Logic of American Antidiscrimination Law* (2001, with K. Anthony Appiah, Judith Butler, Thomas Grey, and Reva Siegel). He edited or coedited *Civil Society and Government* (2002, with Nancy Rosenblum); *Human Rights in Political Transitions: Gettysburg to Bosnia* (1999, with Carla Hesse); *Race and Representation: Affirmative Action* (1996, with Michael Rogin); *Censorship and Silencing: Practices of Cultural Regulation* (1998); and *Law and the Order of Culture* (1990). Professor Post clerked for Chief Judge David L. Bazelon of the U.S. Court of Appeals for the D.C. Circuit and for Justice William J. Brennan, Jr., of the U.S. Supreme Court. He is a former general counsel of the American Association of University Professors. Professor Post has won the Koret Israel Prize and fellowships from the Guggenheim Foundation and the American Council of Learned Societies. He is councilor and librarian of the American Academy of Arts and Sciences and a member of the American Law Institute. He is codirector of Yale's Law and Media Program, a trustee of the National Humanities Center, a member of the executive committee of the American Council of Learned Societies, and a member of the editorial board of *Representations*.

Judith Resnik is Arthur Liman Professor of Law at Yale Law School, where she teaches about federalism, procedure, feminism, and local and global interventions to diminish inequalities and subordination. Her writings include *Migrations and Mobilities: Citizenship, Borders, and Gender* (coedited with Seyla Benhabib, 2009); "Law's Migration: American Exceptionalism, Silent Dialogues, and Federalism's Multiple Ports of Entry" (*Yale Law Journal*, 2006); and "Trial as Error, Jurisdiction as Injury: Transforming the Meaning of Article III" (*Harvard Law Review*, 2000). Professor Resnik has chaired the Sections on Procedure, on Federal Courts, and on Women in Legal Education of the American Association of Law Schools. She is a managerial trustee of the International Association of Women Judges and the founding director of Yale's Arthur Liman Public Interest Program and Fund. In 2001, she was elected a fellow of the American Academy of Arts and Sciences and, in 2002, a member of the American Philosophical Society. In 2008, she received the Fellows of the American Bar Foundation's Outstanding Scholar of the Year Award.

Reva B. Siegel is Nicholas deB. Katzenbach Professor at Yale Law School. Professor Siegel's writing draws on legal history to explore questions of law and inequality and to analyze how courts interact with representative government and popular movements in interpreting the Constitution. Her publications include *Processes of Constitutional Decisionmaking* (with Paul Brest, Sanford Levinson, Jack Balkin, and Akhil Reed Amar, 2006) and recent work on the role of social movement conflict in guiding constitutional change, including: "Equality Talk: Antisubordination and Anticlassification Values in Constitutional Struggles Over Brown" (*Harvard Law Review*, 2004); "Constitutional Culture, Social Movement Conflict and Constitutional Change: The Case of the de facto ERA" (*California Law Review*, 2006); "Dignity and the Politics of Protection: Abortion Restrictions Under Casey/Carhart" (*Yale Law Journal*, 2008), and "Dead or Alive: Originalism as Popular Constitutionalism in Heller" (*Harvard Law Review*, 2008). Professor Siegel is a member of the American Academy of Arts and Sciences, and is active in the American Society for

Legal History and in the American Constitution Society, both in the national organization and as the faculty advisor of Yale's chapter.

Cass R. Sunstein is Felix Frankfurter Professor of Law at Harvard Law School. He clerked for Justice Thurgood Marshall of the U.S. Supreme Court and worked as an attorney-advisor in the Office of the Legal Counsel of the U.S. Department of Justice. Professor Sunstein has testified before congressional committees on many subjects, and he has been involved in constitution-making and law reform activities in several different nations. He is the author of many articles and books, including *After the Rights Revolution: Reconceiving the Regulatory State* (1990), *The Partial Constitution* (1993), *Democracy and the Problem of Free Speech* (1993), *Legal Reasoning and Political Conflict* (1996), *Free Markets and Social Justice* (1997), *One Case at a Time* (1999), *Designing Democracy: What Constitutions Do* (2001), *Why Societies Need Dissent* (2003), *The Second Bill of Rights* (2004), *Radicals in Robes: Why Extreme Right-Wing Courts Are Wrong for America* (2005), *Constitutional Law* (5th ed., 2005, with G. Stone, L. M. Seidman, P. Karlan, and M. Tushnet), *Infotopia: How Many Minds Produce Knowledge* (2006), *Worst-Case Scenarios* (2007), *Republic.com 2.0* (2007), and *Nudge: Improving Decisions about Health, Wealth, and Happiness* (2008, with Richard Thaler).

Mark Tushnet is William Nelson Cromwell Professor of Law at Harvard Law School, a position he assumed in 2006 after teaching at Georgetown University Law Center for twenty-five years. A former fellow of the John Simon Guggenheim Memorial Foundation, the Woodrow Wilson International Center for Scholars, and the Rockefeller Humanities Program, he has authored eighteen books, including the most widely used casebook on constitutional law, a two-volume biography of Thurgood Marshall, *A Court Divided: The Rehnquist Court and the Future of Constitutional Law* (2004), and *Weak Courts, Strong Rights: Judicial Review and Social Welfare Rights* (2007). He is a former president of the Association of American Law Schools and a fellow of the American Academy of Arts and Sciences.

Robin West holds the Frederick J. Haas Chair in Law and Philosophy at Georgetown University Law Center. Professor West has written extensively on gender issues and feminist legal theory, constitutional law and theory, jurisprudence, legal philosophy, and law and literature. Her most recent books are *Marriage, Sexuality, and Gender* (2007) and *Re-imagining Justice: Progressive Interpretations of Formal Equality, Rights, and the Rule of Law* (2003).

Index

Page numbers in *italic* type refer to illustrations.